PATTERNS OF EXPOSITION

B 35348

238
Psychology
Thursday
4:00

Second Edition

PATTERNS OF EXPOSITION

RANDALL E. DECKER

LITTLE, BROWN AND COMPANY

Boston

LIBRARY OF CONGRESS CATALOG CARD NO. 70–186061

SECOND PRINTING

Printed simultaneously in Canada by
Little, Brown & Company (Canada) Limited

PRINTED IN THE UNITED STATES OF AMERICA

TO THE INSTRUCTOR

The second edition of *Patterns of Exposition* departs little in either principles or format from the first and alternate editions. Since the tremendous acceptance of *Patterns of Exposition, Alternate Edition,* we have continued to question instructors who use it or the original edition about their preferences in essay materials and their desires for any basic changes in the books. They have asked little: a third version is frequently requested, but primarily for a continuing change of illustrative selections in order to keep pace, to some extent, with the changing interests of youth. It is important too, we believe, through fresh materials to maintain the same kind of teaching enthusiasm with which the earlier editions have been and are still being used.

The same principles and format have been retained. Twelve of the most highly regarded essays from the other two editions remain in this new one, but thirty-two new selections have been added, several of them anthologized for the first time. Four essays without questions, each employing an effective combination of patterns studied, are grouped in a separate section at the end.

In this edition, as in the others, we have attempted to bring together the best readings to demonstrate expository techniques. We have also tried to make possible their convenient use in whatever ways instructors think best for their own classes. Versatility was one of the many standards used in choosing materials; therefore, only complete essays or free-standing units of larger works have been included. If these, with some inevitable overlap of patterns, are more complicated than excerpts illustrating single principles, they are also more realistic and certainly more useful for other classroom purposes.

Their arrangement here is but one of the many workable orders; the instructor can easily develop another if he so desires. To make such variations convenient, we have nearly always placed inter-essay questions at the ends of sequences, where they can be quickly detected and, if not suitable, easily eliminated or modified.

We have tried to vary the study questions — and undoubtedly have included far more than any one teacher will want — from the purely objective to those calling for some serious self-examination. (A booklet, *A Manual to Accompany Patterns of Exposition, Second Edition,* is available, placing further materials under the instructor's complete control.)

Suggestions for writing assignments to be developed from ideas in the essays are located immediately after each selection. But for classes in which the instructor prefers writing to be done according to the expository pattern under study at the time, regardless of subject matter, topic suggestions are located at the end of each section.

"A Guide to Terms," where matters from *Abstract* to *Unity* are briefly discussed, refers whenever possible to the essays themselves for illustrations. To permit unity and easy access, it is located at the back of the book, but there are continuing cross-references to it in the study questions.

In all respects — in size, content, arrangement, format — we have tried to keep *Patterns of Exposition, Second Edition* uncluttered and easy to use.

The editor would like to express appreciation for the helpful criticism and suggestions provided by his friends and colleagues, especially Robert W. Blackmur, Bill R. Brubaker, M. H. Garfinkel, George Gleason, Elizabeth Green, J. Paxton Hart, Jr., James Mason, Kline A. Nall, and Bonnie Titley. He would also like to thank Jane Aaron, Charles Christensen, and Martha Davis of Little, Brown.

CONTENTS

INTRODUCTION

Exposition is one of the four basic forms of communication, more important to most people than any of the others — narration, description, or argumentation (including persuasion). The novelist and to some extent the sports reporter use narration and description; the lawyer, the salesman, the preacher become skilled in logical argument and persuasion. But these persons are in specialized fields, prepared by specialized training. People in such professions, like the rest of us, are also frequent users of exposition in one way or another.

Exposition means explanation, simply an *exposing* of information or ideas. Its primary function is not to tell a story or relate a happening, although exposition often *uses* narration as one of many techniques. Its primary function is not to create vivid pictures for the reader, although description, too, may at times be a valuable technique of exposition. The primary function of exposition is not to convince or persuade, although, conversely, logical argument and persuasion frequently use exposition as one of their techniques. But the primary function of exposition itself is merely *to explain.*

Even beyond our increasing need for informally written and spoken explanations, we use the processes of written exposition throughout college — in reports, term papers, essay examinations. Most of us use exposition throughout our working lives — in letters, in memoranda, in business and professional reports. Hence there are practical reasons why most college composition courses are devoted primarily to study and practice in exposition. And these, of course, are the reasons this book is devoted to the basic patterns of and other techniques commonly used in expository writing.

There is nothing new about these patterns of exposition; we have been using most of them since we first tried to explain why some types of birds fly south in the winter. But mature writing depends partly on the author's being able to use *deliberately* whichever techniques will do the job best, with the least chance of misunderstanding. We study them to get a clearer view of their functions and possibilities, with the aim of being able to use them more effectively in our own writing.

We examine and practice these techniques separately, realizing they are seldom used separately in practical writing. After all, when we observe and practice for hours a skill involved in tennis or golf, we are not assuming that an entire game will be made up of serving or putting. In writing, we know there is no reason why a process analysis should not be used to assist comparison in some explanations, why illustration might not be valuably aided in certain developments by narration. In good writing, if the patterns do not overlap, it is simply because one alone is sufficient for the purpose.

But besides the study of writing techniques in a college anthology, we have a right to expect real benefit from the reading itself. Reading and thinking about new ideas or experiences is an excellent way to widen horizons, to broaden our interests — and that is an important phase of becoming educated. In general, each set of four essays in this book progresses in complexity and depth. Challenges help our understanding to reach an ever higher level.

The manner of approaching each reading, or the study of it, may be suggested by the instructor. If not, a worthwhile system for the student to give at least a fair trial is this:

1. For the first reading, relax. Read the selection casually, as you would some magazine article, for whatever enjoyment or new ideas you can get without straining. Do not stop to look up new words unless the sentences in which they are used are meaningless until you do. But have a pencil in hand and mark all words you are doubtful about, then go on.

2. When finished with the first reading, put the book down; for a few minutes think over what you have read.

3. Then use the dictionary to help you understand the words you have marked. Do not make the mistake of finding the first or

the shortest definition and trying to memorize it. Instead, look at the various meanings, and for the word's uses as noun, verb, and modifier. *Think* about them. Pronounce the word. Use it in a few sentences. Identify it with similar words you already know. Then see how the author has used it.

4. After you understand all the words, read and think briefly about the assigned questions and remarks following the selection. (The paragraphs in each selection are numbered for easy reference.)

5. Then reread the essay, pausing sometimes to think and to *question,* underlining important ideas, marking sentences or phrases that seem to you especially interesting, misleading, amusing, or well expressed.

6. Then return to the questions at the end. You will probably find that you have already provided most of the answers. If not, give them further thought, referring again to the essay and to "A Guide to Terms" or earlier explanations wherever necessary for thorough understanding.

7. Next, try to *evaluate* the selection. What was the author trying to explain? Did he succeed in explaining? Was his endeavor worthwhile?

Useful as these selections can be, however, they are not intended as models for imitation by students. Each was written, as all expository projects should be, to give a particular audience a particular explanation. The style of some is much too informal for most college writing. Other styles, perhaps from a slower and more sedate age than ours, would be too stately for today. Pure imitation is not the purpose of our study.

But each of the selections does demonstrate one or more of the *patterns* of exposition, which are as useful now as ever. Each can provide, too, some profitable study of other sound principles of writing — principles of effective sentences and paragraphs, mature diction, forceful introductions and closings. The consideration of all these principles, instead of being handled in separate sections, is a continuing study within the basic framework of the expository patterns. The book is designed so that instructors and students can use it in several ways.

PATTERNS OF EXPOSITION

1

Illustrating Ideas by Use of *Example*

examples from own experiences

abstract spacing

The use of examples to illustrate an idea under discussion is the most common, and frequently most efficient, pattern of exposition. It is a method we use almost instinctively; for instance, instead of talking in generalities about the qualities of a good football coach, we cite Coach Rosetti as an example. We may go further and illustrate Rosetti's virtues by a specific account of his handling of a crucial situation in the last Homecoming game. In this way we put our abstract ideas into concrete form — a process that is always an aid to clarity. (As a matter of fact, with the "for instance" in this very paragraph, examples are employed to illustrate the *use* of example.)

Lack of clear illustrations may leave the reader with only a hazy conception of the points the writer has tried to make. Even worse, the reader may try to supply examples from his own knowledge or experience, and these might do the job poorly or even lead him to an impression different from that intended by the author. Since the writer is the one trying to communicate, clarity is primarily his responsibility.

Not only do good examples put into clear, concrete form what otherwise might remain vague and abstract, but the writing also becomes more interesting, with a better chance of holding the reader's attention. With something specific to be visualized, a statement also becomes more convincing — but convincing within certain limitations. If we use the Volkswagen as an example of German workmanship, the reader is probably aware that this car may not be entirely typical. Although isolated examples will not hold up well in logical argument, for ordinary purposes of explanation the Volkswagen example could make its point convincingly enough.

1

As in the selection and use of all materials for composition, of course, the successful writer selects and uses examples cautiously, always keeping in mind the nature of his reader-audience and his own specific purpose for communicating. To be effective, each example must be pertinent, representing the chief qualities of the generality it illustrates. Its function as an example must be either instantly obvious to the reader or fully enough developed so that he learns exactly what it illustrates, and how; Sometimes, however, illustration may be provided best by something other than a real-life example — a fictional anecdote, an analogy, or perhaps a parable that demonstrates the general idea. Here even greater care is needed to be sure these examples are both precise and clear.

Illustration is sometimes used alone as the basic means of development; but it also frequently assists other basic techniques, such as comparison and contrast. In either of its functions, the author may find his purpose best served by one well-developed example, possibly with full background information and descriptive details. But sometimes citing several shorter examples is best, particularly if the author is attempting to show a trend or a prevalence. In more difficult explanations, of course, a careful combination of the two techniques — using both one well-developed example and several shorter examples — may be worth the extra time and effort required.

Whichever method is used, the writer is following at least one sound principle of writing: he is trying to make the general more specific, the abstract more concrete.

JOSEPH WOOD KRUTCH

Joseph Wood Krutch (1893–1970), for many years professor of dramatic literature at Columbia University, was
prominent as an essayist in the diverse fields of dramatic
criticism, philosophy, and natural history. Upon his retirement from Columbia and as drama critic of *The Nation,*
he spent much time in the Arizona desert, where he continued his writing. His best-known books of recent years
are *The Measure of Man* (1954), *The Voice of the Desert*
(1955), *The Great Chain of Life* (1957), *The Forgotten
Peninsula* (1961), *The World of Animals* (1961), *More
Lives Than One* (1962), *Birdsongs in Literature* (1967),
and *The Most Wonderful Animals That Never Were*
(1969).

hypothetical

We Were Not Skeptical Enough

"We Were Not Skeptical Enough" was written for *This I
Believe,* a collection of philosophic observations from
famous people. This necessarily short essay is a convenient
beginning illustration of the use of examples as a basic pattern of exposition.

I was born in what was called "An Age of Unbelief." When I was 1
young I took that description seriously, and I thought that I was
an intellectual because of the number of things I did not believe.

Only very slowly did I come to realize that what was really 2
characteristic of myself and my age was not that we did not believe
anything but that we believed very firmly in a number of things
which are not really so.

We believed, for example, in the exclusive importance of the 3
material, the measurable, and the controllable. We had no doubts
about "what science proves" and we took it for granted that whatever science did not prove was certainly false.

When, for example, "science proved" that man had risen from   4
the lower animals, we believed, as I still do, that this is a fact. But
when science found it difficult to define, or measure, or deal with
the ways in which a man's mind, and character and motives differ
from those of the lower animals, we believed that there was no
important difference between them. The trouble was not that we
were skeptical but that we were not skeptical enough.

We studied man by the methods which had proved fruitful for   5
the study of animals and machines. We learned a great deal about
his reflexes, animal drives, the ways in which he could be conditioned to behave. And then, because our methods did not permit
us to learn anything else about him, we came to the conclusion
that there was nothing else to be learned.

We came to believe, to take the most familiar example, that   6
love was "nothing but" the biological impulses connected with
sex. What is even more important, we came also to believe that
his thinking was "nothing but" his power of rationalization and
that his ideals and values were "nothing but" the results of his
early conditioning. We began to assume that what he believed to
be his free choices were not really anything of the sort; that he
was not the captain of his soul but only what the dialectic of
society or perhaps his infantile fixations had made him. He was,
we tended to believe, not a cause but an effect.

Seldom before in the history of civilization has the world been   7
in so parlous a state and not often before have men seemed to
believe less in a God who would save them. Yet it is at this moment that we have lost faith in man himself as a prime mover
of events.

What I believe in most firmly is *man himself*. And by that I   8
mean something quite specific. I believe that he descended from
the animals but that he has powers which animals share but little,
if at all. I believe that he is something in himself. I believe that
he can will, and choose and prefer.

That means, for example, that society is what he makes it, not   9
that he is what society makes him. It means that he can be permitted to think, not merely conditioned by good or bad propaganda. I believe, therefore, that he can be freed, and that means
a good deal more than given the vote or permitted civil liberties.
The difference between a totalitarian and a democratic society is
the difference between those who believe the individual man

capable of being the captain of his soul and those who believe that he is merely the creature of the society in which he lives.

I believe that we cannot set the world free until we believe that 10 the individual himself is free.

MEANINGS AND VALUES

1. Would you classify this essay as primarily concrete or abstract? Why? (See Guide to Terms: *Concrete/Abstract.*)

2a. Select one abstract statement from this selection (e.g., ". . . he can be freed") and further clarify its meaning by use of a concrete example.
 b. Why do you think the author did not perform this service for us?

3. What kind of irony is expressed in paragraphs 1 and 2? Justify your answer. (Guide: *Irony.*)

4a. It was the author's impression at the time that "not often before have men seemed to believe less in a God who would save them" (par. 7). Does this seem to you a valid observation today? On what do you base your answer?
 b. Do you see any indication in contemporary society that attitudes toward God may now be changing? Explain.

5. Show whatever relation you can between the "false" beliefs discussed by Krutch and the controversial rebellion of modern youth.

6. How might belief that "the individual himself is free" (par. 10) help in setting the world free? Be as specific as possible in your explanation.

EXPOSITORY TECHNIQUES

1a. What generality does the example of paragraph 3 make more specific?
 b. What generality does the example (or examples) of paragraph 4 make more specific?
 c. Show, as briefly as possible, the relation among other examples in paragraphs 3–6 (e.g., are they used in a simple series, perhaps merely to show a "prevalence"?).

2. What is the chief function of paragraph 7?

3a. What is the purpose of the rest of the essay?
 b. Where, if at all, is example used to help explain?

4a. For what types of reader-audience might this author have been more specific in his explanations? (Guide: *Specific/General.*)
 b. Would this service have been beneficial to you? Why, or why not?

DICTION AND VOCABULARY

1. If an intellectual cannot be identified by the number of things he does not believe (par. 1), then how can we identify one?

2. How can we further classify the figure of speech "captain of his soul" (par. 6)? (Guide: *Figures of Speech.*)

3. What does "the dialectic of society" (par. 6) mean?

4a. How would you express the idea that seldom "has the world been in so parlous a state" (par. 7)?
  b. Which way, if either, is better? Why?

5a. The expressions "risen from" and "descended from" the lower animals are both rather common now (both were no doubt regarded as metaphorical at one time). In what respect, if at all, do you consider the usage of one better than the other?
  b. Do you think a writer is justified in using both expressions in the same work (pars. 4 and 8), or does it seem a mere careless lack of consistency? Explain.

SUGGESTIONS FOR WRITING AND DISCUSSION

1. You may wish to pursue further the "rising and descending" aspects of our evolution into human beings (question 5, "Diction and Vocabulary"). If so, there are numerous approaches you could choose from, depending perhaps on your own views of man.

2. Select what you consider to be *one* of the most significant differences between man and even the highest of the "lower animals." Explain this difference and its significance.

3. The author identifies what was characteristic of himself and his age (par. 2). Do the same, but more explicitly, for yourself and your age.

4. What else *is* love but "biological impulses" (par. 6)?

5. Select one important but typical decision that ordinarily seems one of man's "free choices." Show how "free" you think it really is — or how it is more nearly, perhaps, the inevitable result of other factors, themselves uncontrollable.

(NOTE: Suggestions for topics requiring development by use of EXAMPLE are on page 38, at the end of this section.)

JAMES THURBER (1894–1961) was a writer and cartoonist whose essays, short stories, and line drawings have helped enliven and illuminate American life for half a century. After he joined the staff of *The New Yorker* in 1925, most of his writings were first published in that magazine. Some of his collections are in book form: *Is Sex Necessary?* (1929, with E. B. White), *The Owl in the Attic* (1931), *Let Your Mind Alone!* (1937), *The Thurber Carnival* (1945), *The Thurber Album* (1952), and *Thurber Country* (1953). His more recent books are *Alarms and Diversions* (1957), *The Years with Ross* (1959), and *Lanterns and Lances* (1961).

Courtship Through the Ages

"Courtship Through the Ages" was first published in 1939 by *The New Yorker,* and the same year it was included in Thurber's book *My World — and Welcome to It.* Although it would be misleading to call any one selection "typical" of writing as varied as Thurber's, this one is at least representative of the kind of humor that made him famous. It also serves, for us, to illustrate the simplest kind of example usage as a basic technique of development.

Surely nothing in the astonishing scheme of life can have non- 1
plussed Nature so much as the fact that none of the females of any of the species she created really cared very much for the male, as such. For the past ten million years Nature has been busily inventing ways to make the male attractive to the female, but the whole business of courtship, from the marine annelids up to man,

[handwritten margin notes: "Study and underline topic sentence transition devices."]

still lumbers heavily along, like a complicated musical comedy. I have been reading the sad and absorbing story in Volume 6 (Cole to Dama) of the *Encyclopaedia Britannica*. In this volume you can learn all about cricket, cotton, costume designing, crocodiles, crown jewels, and Coleridge, but none of these subjects is so interesting as the Courtship of Animals, which recounts the sorrowful lengths to which all males must go to arouse the interest of a lady.

We all know, I think, that Nature gave man whiskers and a   2 mustache with the quaint idea in mind that these would prove attractive to the female. We all know that, far from attracting her, whiskers and mustaches only made her nervous and gloomy, so that man had to go in for somersaults, tilting with lances, and performing feats of parlor magic to win her attention; he also had to bring her candy, flowers, and the furs of animals. It is common knowledge that in spite of all these "love displays" the male is constantly being turned down, insulted, or thrown out of the house. It is rather comforting, then, to discover that the peacock, for all his gorgeous plumage, does not have a particularly easy time in courtship; none of the males in the world do. The first peahen, it turned out, was only faintly stirred by her suitor's beautiful train. She would often go quietly to sleep while he was whisking it around. The Britannica tells us that the peacock actually had to learn a certain little trick to wake her up and revive her interest: he had to learn to vibrate his quills so as to make a rustling sound. In ancient times man himself, observing the ways of the peacock, probably tried vibrating his whiskers to make a rustling sound; if so, it didn't get him anywhere. He had to go in for something else; so, among other things, he went in for gifts. It is not unlikely that he got this idea from certain flies and birds who were making no headway at all with rustling sounds.

One of the flies of the family Empidae, who had tried everything,   3 finally hit on something pretty special. He contrived to make a glistening transparent balloon which was even larger than himself. Into this he would put sweetmeats and tidbits and he would carry the whole elaborate envelope through the air to the lady of his choice. This amused her for a time, but she finally got bored with it. She demanded silly little colorful presents, something that you couldn't eat but that would look nice around the house. So the male Empis had to go around gathering flower petals and pieces of bright paper to put into his balloon. On a courtship flight a male Empis cuts quite a figure now, but he can hardly be said to be happy. He never knows how soon the female will demand heavier presents, such as Roman coins and gold collar buttons. It seems probable that one day the courtship of the Empidae will fall down, as man's occasionally does, of its own weight.

The bowerbird is another creature that spends so much time   4
courting the female that he never gets any work done. If all the male bowerbirds became nervous wrecks within the next ten or fifteen years, it would not surprise me. The female bowerbird insists that a playground be built for her with a specially constructed bower at the entrance. This bower is much more elaborate than an ordinary nest and is harder to build; it costs a lot more, too. The female will not come to the playground until the male has filled it up with a great many gifts: silvery leaves, red leaves, rose petals, shells, beads, berries, bones, dice, buttons, cigar bands, Christmas seals, and the Lord knows what else. When the female finally condescends to visit the playground, she is in a coy and silly mood and has to be chased in and out of the bower and up and down the playground before she will quit giggling and stand still long enough even to shake hands. The male bird is, of course, pretty well done in before the chase starts, because he has worn himself out hunting for eyeglass lenses and begonia blossoms. I imagine that many a bowerbird, after chasing a female for two or three hours, says the hell with it and goes home to bed. Next day, of course, he telephones someone else and the same trying ritual is gone through with again. A male bowerbird is as exhausted as a night-club habitué before he is out of his twenties.

The male fiddler crab has a somewhat easier time, but it can   5
hardly be said that he is sitting pretty. He has one enormously large and powerful claw, usually brilliantly colored, and you might suppose that all he had to do was reach out and grab some passing cutie. The very earliest fiddler crabs may have tried this, but, if so, they got slapped for their pains. A female fiddler crab will not tolerate any caveman stuff; she never has and she doesn't intend to start now. To attract a female, a fiddler crab has to stand on tiptoe and brandish his claw in the air. If any female in the neighborhood is interested — and you'd be surprised how many are not — she comes over and engages him in light badinage, for which he is not in the mood. As many as a hundred females may pass

the time of day with him and go on about their business. By night-fall of an average courting day, a fiddler crab who has been stand-ing on tiptoe for eight or ten hours waving a heavy claw in the air is in pretty sad shape. As in the case of the males of all species, however, he gets out of bed next morning, dashes some water on his face, and tries again.

The next time you encounter a male web-spinning spider, stop   6
and reflect that he is too busy worrying about his love life to have any desire to bite you. Male web-spinning spiders have a tougher life than any other males in the animal kingdom. This is because the female web-spinning spiders have very poor eyesight. If a male lands on a female's web, she kills him before he has time to lay down his cane and gloves, mistaking him for a fly or a bumblebee who has tumbled into her trap. Before the species figured out what to do about this, millions of males were murdered by ladies they called on. It is the nature of spiders to perform a little dance in front of the female, but before a male spinner could get near enough for the female to see who he was and what he was up to, she would lash out at him with a flat-iron or a pair of garden shears. One night, nobody knows when, a very bright male spinner lay awake worrying about calling on a lady who had been killing suitors right and left. It came to him that this business of dancing as a love display wasn't getting anybody anywhere except the grave. He decided to go in for web-twitching, or strand-vibrat-ing. The next day he tried it on one of the nearsighted girls. In-stead of dropping in on her suddenly, he stayed outside the web and began monkeying with one of its strands. He twitched it up and down and in and out with such a lilting rhythm that the female was charmed. The serenade worked beautifully; the female let him live. The Britannica's spider-watchers, however, report that this system is not always successful. Once in a while, even now, a female will fire three bullets into a suitor or run him through with a kitchen knife. She keeps threatening him from the moment he strikes the first low notes on the outside strings, but usually by the time he has got up to the high notes played around the center of the web, he is going to town and she spares his life.

Even the butterfly, as handsome a fellow as he is, can't always   7
win a mate merely by fluttering around and showing off. Many butterflies have to have scent scales on their wings. Hepialus carries a powder puff in a perfumed pouch. He throws perfume at the ladies when they pass. The male tree cricket, Oecanthus, goes

Hepialus one better by carrying a tiny bottle of wine with him and giving drinks to such doxies as he has designs on. One of the male snails throws darts to entertain the girls. So it goes, through the long list of animals, from the bristle worm and his rudimentary dance steps to man and his gift of diamonds and sapphires. The golden-eye drake raises a jet of water with his feet as he flies over a lake; Hepialus has his powder puff, Oecanthus his wine bottle, man his etchings. It is a bright and melancholy story, the age-old desire of the male for the female, the age-old desire of the female to be amused and entertained. Of all the creatures on earth, the only males who could be figured as putting any irony into their courtship are the grebes and certain other diving birds. Every now and then a courting grebe slips quietly down to the bottom of a lake and then, with a mighty "Whoosh!," pops out suddenly a few feet from his girl friend, splashing water all over her. She seems to be persuaded that this is a purely loving display, but I like to think that the grebe always has a faint hope of drowning her or scaring her to death.

I will close this investigation into the mournful burdens of the male with the *Britannica's* story about a certain Argus pheasant. It appears that the Argus displays himself in front of a female who stands perfectly still without moving a feather. . . . The male Argus the Britannica tells about was confined in a cage with a female of another species, a female who kept moving around, emptying ashtrays and fussing with lampshades all the time the male was showing off his talents. Finally, in disgust, he stalked away and began displaying in front of his water trough. He reminds me of a certain male (Homo sapiens) of my acquaintance who one night after dinner asked his wife to put down her detective magazine so that he could read her a poem of which he was very fond. She sat quietly enough until he was well into the middle of the thing, intoning with great ardor and intensity. Then suddenly there came a sharp, disconcerting *slap!* It turned out that all during the male's display, the female had been intent on a circling mosquito and had finally trapped it between the palms of her hands. The male in this case did not stalk away and display in front of a water trough; he went over to Tim's and had a flock of drinks and recited the poem to the fellas. I am sure they all told bitter stories of their own about how their displays had been interrupted by females. I am also sure that they all ended up singing "Honey, Honey, Bless Your Heart."

MEANINGS AND VALUES

1a. Clarify the meaning of "irony of situation" by using at least one example from this essay. (See Guide to Terms: *Irony*.)
 b. Use at least three examples to illustrate the meaning of "verbal irony."

2. Thurber's writing is sometimes said to have nearly universal appeal — not only because of the humor, but also because of his subjects and his attitude toward them. What appeals would this subject have to various types of people you know?

3a. The author's themes are ordinarily deeper than they may appear to be on the surface, and they are sometimes quite serious. How seriously is he concerned about the mating foolishness of human males? How can you tell?
 b. Explain the relation of this matter of attitude to that of tone in writing. (Guide: *Style/Tone*.)
 c. Describe Thurber's tone in this essay, using no more than two or three descriptive words.

4. How much literal truth, if any, is in the allegation that "none of the females . . . she created really cared very much for the male, as such" (par. 1)?

5. Do you think we are really laughing at the animals themselves when we go to the zoo? If not, what do we laugh at? Explain carefully.

EXPOSITORY TECHNIQUES

1. How does the author remind us with each new example, without making an issue of it, that he is describing people as well as (perhaps even more than) wildlife?

2. List the general ways in which humor is achieved in this selection and illustrate each with a specific example.

3. Briefly explain why some people would classify these examples as personification, whereas others would not. (Guide: *Figures of Speech*.)

4a. Which of the common transitional devices is (or are) used to bridge between paragraphs 2 and 3? (Guide: *Transition*.)
 b. Between 3 and 4?
 c. Between 4 and 5?
 d. How do such matters relate to coherence? (Guide: *Coherence*.)

DICTION AND VOCABULARY

1. Which, if any, of the ways listed in answering question 2 of "Expository Techniques" are matters of diction? Why? (Guide: *Diction.*)

2. If you are not already familiar with the following words as used in this essay, study their meanings as given in the dictionary; nonplussed, lumbers (par. 1); condescends, habitué (4); brandish, badinage (5); doxies (7); intoning, disconcerting (8).

SUGGESTIONS FOR WRITING AND DISCUSSION

1. Explain fully, using specific examples, the real reasons for amusement at a zoo (or, for some people, a barnyard).

2. How do young men today try to impress the girls they are interested in?

3. Examine the possibility that women are interested in male "displays" because such reactions have been "programmed" into them from their earliest childhood.

4. If you are familiar with the aims and methods of the women's liberation movement, how do you think its more radical members would react to Thurber's impressions of courtship?

(NOTE: Suggestions for topics requiring development by use of EXAMPLE are on page 38, at the end of this section.)

LAURENCE J. PETER and RAYMOND HULL

LAURENCE J. PETER was born in Canada in 1919 and received his Ed.D. from Washington State University. With wide experience as a teacher, counselor, school psychologist, prison instructor, consultant, and university professor, he has written more than thirty articles for professional journals as well as the book *Prescriptive Teaching* (1965). He is now associate professor of education, director of the Evelyn Frieden Center for Prescriptive Teaching, and coordinator of programs for emotionally disturbed children at the University of Southern California.

RAYMOND HULL, born in 1919, the son of an English Methodist minister, has lived in British Columbia since 1947. He has had thirty television and stage plays produced and four stage plays published. His articles have been featured in such magazines as *Punch, Maclean's,* and *Esquire.*

The Peter Principle

"The Peter Principle," as it follows, combines the first two chapters of the book by that name, which was published in 1969. It is a clear and orderly illustration of the use of developed examples to give concrete form to an abstract central theme.

When I was a boy I was taught that the men upstairs knew what 1 they were doing. I was told, "Peter, the more you know, the further you go." So I stayed in school until I graduated from college and then went forth into the world clutching firmly these ideas and my new teaching certificate. During the first year of teaching I was upset to find that a number of teachers, school principals, supervisors and superintendents appeared to be unaware of their professional responsibilities and incompetent in executing their duties. For example my principal's main concerns were that all window shades be at the same level, that classrooms should be quiet and that no one step on or near the rose beds. The superintendent's main concerns were that no minority group, no matter how fanatical, should ever be offended and that all official forms be submitted on time. The children's education appeared farthest from the administrator mind.

At first I thought this was a special weakness of the school system in which I taught so I applied for certification in another province. I filled out the special forms, enclosed the required documents and complied willingly with all the red tape. Several weeks later, back came my application and all the documents! 2

No, there was nothing wrong with my credentials; the forms were correctly filled out; an official departmental stamp showed that they had been received in good order. But an accompanying letter said, "The new regulations require that such forms cannot be accepted by the Department of Education unless they have been registered at the Post Office to ensure safe delivery. Will you please remail the forms to the Department, making sure to register them this time?" 3

I began to suspect that the local school system did not have a monopoly on incompetence. 4

As I looked further afield, I saw that every organization contained a number of persons who could not do their jobs. 5

A Universal Phenomenon

Occupational incompetence is everywhere. Have you noticed it? Probably we all have noticed it. 6

We see indecisive politicians posing as resolute statesmen and the "authoritative source" who blames his misinformation on "situational imponderables." Limitless are the public servants who are indolent and insolent; military commanders whose behavioral timidity belies their dreadnaught rhetoric, and governors whose innate servility prevents their actually governing. In our sophistication, we virtually shrug aside the immoral cleric, corrupt judge, incoherent attorney, author who cannot write and English teacher who cannot spell. At universities we see proclamations authored 7 by administrators whose own office communications are hopelessly muddled; and droning lectures from inaudible or incomprehensible instructors.

Seeing incompetence at all levels of every hierarchy — political, legal, educational and industrial — I hypothesized that the cause was some inherent feature of the rules governing the placement of employees. Thus began my serious study of the ways in which employees move upward through a hierarchy, and of what happens to them after promotion. 8

For my scientific data hundreds of case histories were collected. Here are three typical examples. 9

Municipal Government File, Case No. 17. J. S. Minion[1] was a maintenance foreman in the public works department of Excelsior City. He was a favorite of the senior officials at City Hall. They all praised his unfailing affability. 10

"I like Minion," said the superintendent of works. "He has good judgment and is always pleasant and agreeable." 11

This behavior was appropriate for Minion's position: he was not supposed to make policy, so he had no need to disagree with his superiors. 12

The superintendent of works retired and Minion succeeded him. Minion continued to agree with everyone. He passed to his foreman every suggestion that came from above. The resulting conflicts in policy, and the continual changing of plans, soon demoralized the department. Complaints poured in from the Mayor and other officials, from taxpayers and from the maintenance-workers' union. 13

Minion still says "Yes" to everyone, and carries messages briskly back and forth between his superiors and his subordinates. Nominally a superintendent, he actually does the work of a messenger. The maintenance department regularly exceeds its budget, yet fails to fulfill its program of work. In short, Minion, a competent foreman, became an incompetent superintendent. 14

Service Industries File, Case No. 3. E. Tinker was exceptionally zealous and intelligent as an apprentice at G. Reece Auto Repair Inc., and soon rose to journeyman mechanic. In this job he showed 15

---

[1] Some names have been changed, in order to protect the guilty.

outstanding ability in diagnosing obscure faults, and endless patience in correcting them. He was promoted to foreman of the repair shop.

But here his love of things mechanical and his perfectionism became liabilities. He will undertake any job that he thinks looks interesting, no matter how busy the shop may be. "We'll work it in somehow," he says.

He will not let a job go until he is fully satisfied with it.

He meddles constantly. He is seldom to be found at his desk. He is usually up to his elbows in a dismantled motor and while the man who should be doing the work stands watching, other workmen sit around waiting to be assigned new tasks. As a result the shop is always overcrowded with work, always in a muddle, and delivery times are often missed.

Tinker cannot understand that the average customer cares little about perfection — he wants his car back on time! He cannot understand that most of his men are less interested in motors than in their pay checks. So Tinker cannot get on with his customers or with his subordinates. He was a competent mechanic, but is now an incompetent foreman.

Military File, Case No. 8. Consider the case of the late renowned General A. Goodwin. His hearty, informal manner, his racy style of speech, his scorn for petty regulations and his undoubted personal bravery made him the idol of his men. He led them to many well-deserved victories.

When Goodwin was promoted to field marshall he had to deal, not with ordinary soldiers, but with politicians and allied generalissimos.

He would not conform to the necessary protocol. He could not turn his tongue to the conventional courtesies and flatteries. He quarreled with all the dignitaries and took to lying for days at a time, drunk and sulking, in his trailer. The conduct of the war slipped out of his hands into those of his subordinates. He had been promoted to a position that he was incompetent to fill.

AN IMPORTANT CLUE!

In time I saw that all such cases had a common feature. The employee had been promoted from a position of competence to a position of incompetence. I saw that, sooner or later, this could happen to every employee in every hierarchy.

Hypothetical Case File, Case No. 1. Suppose you own a pill-   24
rolling factory, Perfect Pill Incorporated. Your foreman pill roller dies of a perforated ulcer. You need a replacement. You naturally look among your rank-and-file pill rollers.

Miss Oval, Mrs. Cylinder, Mr. Ellipse and Mr. Cube all show   25
various degrees of incompetence. They will naturally be ineligible for promotion. You will choose — other things being equal — your most competent pill roller, Mr. Sphere, and promote him to foreman.

Now suppose Mr. Sphere proves competent as foreman. Later,   26
when your general foreman, Legree, moves up to Works Manager, Sphere will be eligible to take his place.

If, on the other hand, Sphere is an incompetent foreman, he will   27
get no more promotion. He has reached what I call his "level of incompetence." He will stay there till the end of his career.

Some employees, like Ellipse and Cube, reach a level of incom-   28
petence in the lowest grade and are never promoted. Some, like Sphere (assuming he is not a satisfactory foreman), reach it after one promotion.

E. Tinker, the automobile repair-shop foreman, reached his   29
level of incompetence on the third stage of the hierarchy. General Goodwin reached his level of incompetence at the very top of the hierarchy.

So my analysis of hundreds of cases of occupational incompetence   30
led me on to formulate *The Peter Principle:*

In a Hierarchy Every Employee Tends
to Rise to His Level of Incompetence

A NEW SCIENCE!

Having formulated the Principle, I discovered that I had in-   31
advertently founded a new science, hierarchiology, the study of hierarchies.

The term "hierarchy" was originally used to describe the system   32
of church government by priests graded into ranks. The contemporary meaning includes any organization whose members or employees are arranged in order of rank, grade or class.

Hierarchiology, although a relatively recent discipline, appears   33
to have great applicability to the fields of public and private administration.

THIS MEANS YOU!

My Principle is the key to an understanding of all hierarchal   34
systems, and therefore to an understanding of the whole structure
of civilization. A few eccentrics try to avoid getting involved with
hierarchies, but everyone in business, industry, trade-unionism, politics, government, the armed forces, religion and education is so
involved. All of them are controlled by the Peter Principle.

Many of them, to be sure, may win a promotion or two, mov-   35
ing from one level of competence to a higher level of competence.
But competence in that new position qualifies them for still another promotion. For each individual, for *you*, for *me*, the final
promotion is from a level of competence to a level of incompetence.[2]

So, given enough time — and assuming the existence of enough   36
ranks in the hierarchy — each employee rises to, and remains at,
his level of incompetence. Peter's Corollary states:

In time, every post tends to be occupied by an employee who is   37
incompetent to carry out its duties.

WHO TURNS THE WHEELS?

You will rarely find, of course, a system in which *every* em-   38
ployee has reached his level of incompetence. In most instances,
something is being done to further the ostensible purposes for
which the hierarchy exists.

Work is accomplished by those employees who have not yet   39
reached their level of incompetence.

❖   ❖   ❖

A study of a typical hierarchy, the Excelsior City school system,   40
will show how the Peter Principle works within the teaching profession. Study this example and understand how hierarchiology
operates within every establishment.

---

[2] The phenomena of "percussive sublimation" (commonly referred to as "being
kicked upstairs") and of "the lateral arabesque" are not, as the casual observer
might think, exceptions to the Principle. They are only pseudo-promotions. . . .

Let us begin with the rank-and-file classroom teachers. I group 41 them, for this analysis, into three classes: competent, moderately competent and incompetent.

Distribution theory predicts, and experience confirms, that teach- 42 ers will be distributed unevenly in these classes: the majority in the moderately competent class, minorities in the competent and incompetent classes. This graph illustrates the distribution:

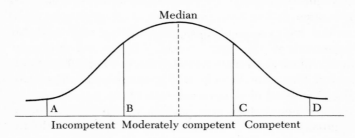

THE CASE OF THE CONFORMIST

An incompetent teacher is ineligible for promotion. Dorothea 43 D. Ditto, for example, had been an extremely conforming student in college. Her assignments were either plagiarisms from textbooks and journals, or transcriptions of the professors' lectures. She always did exactly as she was told, no more, no less. *She was considered to be a competent student.* She graduated with honors from the Excelsior Teachers' College.

When she became a teacher, she taught exactly as she herself 44 had been taught. She followed precisely the textbook, the curriculum guide and the bell schedule.

Her work goes fairly well, except when no rule or precedent is 45 available. For example, when a water pipe burst and flooded the classroom floor, Miss Ditto kept on teaching until the principal rushed in and rescued the class.

"Miss Ditto!" he cried. "In the Name of the Superintendent! 46 There are three inches of water on this floor. Why is your class still here?"

She replied, "I didn't hear the emergency bell signal. I pay 47 attention to those things. You know I do. I'm certain you didn't sound the bell." Flummoxed before the power of her awesome *non sequitur,* the principal invoked a provision of the school code giving him emergency powers in an extraordinary circumstance and led her sopping class from the building.

So, although she never breaks a rule or disobeys an order, she 48 is often in trouble, and will never gain promotion. Competent as a student, *she has reached her level of incompetence as a classroom teacher, and will therefore remain in that position throughout her teaching career.*

The Eligible Majority

Most beginning teachers are moderately competent or competent 49 — see the area from B to D on the graph — and *they will all be eligible for promotion.* Here is one such case.

A Latent Weakness. Mr. N. Beeker had been a competent student, 50 and became a popular science teacher. His lessons and lab periods were inspiring. His students were co-operative and kept the laboratory in order. Mr. Beeker was not good at paper work, but this weakness was offset, in the judgment of his superiors, by his success as a teacher.

Beeker was promoted to head of the science department where 51 he now had to order all science supplies and keep extensive records. *His incompetence is evident!* For three years running he has ordered new Bunsen burners, but no tubing for connecting them. As the old tubing deteriorates, fewer and fewer burners are operable, although new ones accumulate on the shelves.

Beeker is not being considered for further promotion. *His ul-* 52 *timate position is one for which he is incompetent.*

Higher up the Hierarchy. B. Lunt had been a competent student, 53 teacher and department head, and was promoted to assistant principal. In this post he got on well with teachers, students and parents, and was intellectually competent. He gained a further promotion to the rank of principal.

Till now, he had never dealt directly with school-board mem- 54 bers, or with the district superintendent of education. It soon appeared that he lacked the required finesse to work with these high officials. *He kept the superintendent waiting* while he settled a dispute between two children. Taking a class for a teacher who

was ill, *he missed a curriculum revision committee meeting* called
by the assistant superintendent.

He worked so hard at running his school that *he had no energy*   55
for running community organizations. He declined offers to become program chairman of the Parent-Teacher Association, president of the Community Betterment League and consultant to the
Committee for Decency in Literature.

His school lost community support and he fell out of favor with   56
the superintendent. Lunt came to be regarded, by the public and
by his superiors, as an incompetent principal. When the assistant
superintendent's post became vacant, the school board declined to
give it to Lunt. He remains, and will remain till he retires, unhappy
and incompetent as a principal.

The Autocrat. R. Driver, having proved his competence as stu-   57
dent, teacher, department head, assistant principal and principal,
was promoted to assistant superintendent. Previously he had only
to interpret the school board's policy and have it efficiently carried
out in his school. Now, as assistant superintendent, he must participate in the policy discussions of the board, using democratic
procedures.

But Driver dislikes democratic procedures. He insists on his   58
status as an expert. He lectures the board members much as he
used to lecture his students when he was a classroom teacher.
He tries to dominate the board as he dominated his staff when
he was a principal.

The board now considers Driver an incompetent assistant super-   59
intendent. He will receive no further promotion.

Soon Parted. G. Spender was a competent student, English   60
teacher, department head, assistant principal and principal. He
then worked competently for six years as an assistant superintendent
— patriotic, diplomatic, suave and well liked. He was promoted
to superintendent. Here he was obliged to enter the field of school
finance, in which he soon found himself at a loss.

From the start of his teaching career, Spender had never bothered   61
his head about money. His wife handled his pay check, paid all
household accounts and gave him pocket money each week.

Now Spender's incompetence in the area of finance is revealed.   62
He purchased a large number of teaching machines from a fly-by-

night company which went bankrupt without producing any programs to fit the machines. He had every classroom in the city equipped with television, although the only programs available in the area were for secondary schools. Spender has found his level of incompetence.

ANOTHER PROMOTION MECHANISM

The foregoing examples are typical of what are called "line promotions." There is another mode of upward movement: the "staff promotion." The case of Miss T. Totland is typical. 63

Miss Totland, who had been a competent student and an outstanding primary teacher, was promoted to primary supervisor. She now has to teach, not children, but teachers. Yet *she still uses the techniques which worked so well with small children.* 64

Addressing teachers, singly or in groups, she speaks slowly and distinctly. She uses mostly words of one or two syllables. She explains each point several times in different ways, to be sure it is understood. She always wears a bright smile. 65

Teachers dislike what they call her false cheerfulness and her patronizing attitude. Their resentment is so sharp that, instead of trying to carry out her suggestions, they spend much time devising excuses for *not* doing what she recommends. 66

Miss Totland has proved herself incompetent in communicating with primary teachers. She is therefore ineligible for further promotion, *and will remain as primary supervisor, at her level of incompetence.* 67

YOU BE THE JUDGE

You can find similar examples in any hierarchy. Look around you where you work, and pick out the people who have reached their level of incompetence. You will see that in every hierarchy *the cream rises until it sours.* Look in the mirror and ask whether . . . 68

MEANINGS AND VALUES

1a. Has it been your experience that incompetence is really widespread enough to make this selection worthwhile?

b. Support your answer, either way, by examples from your own or your family's experience. (You will not be *proving* anything — merely supporting an observation.)

2. Does it seem feasible to you that our highly successful, complex industrial and educational systems were devised and are run either by incompetent top executives and engineers or by underlings in the hierarchy? Why, or why not?

3. To what extent are people in elective public office subject to the Peter Principle?

4. Clarify the distinction between "line" and "staff" promotions, as referred to in paragraph 63.

5. Specify at least two ways in which an understanding of the Peter Principle might be of value to an individual.

6. Why do people permit themselves to be promoted to levels of incompetence?

EXPOSITORY TECHNIQUES

1. Show how at least two of the standard methods of introduction are used for this exposition. (See Guide to Terms: *Introductions.*)

2a. Where do the authors first give a simple statement of their central theme? (Guide: *Unity.*)

b. How, if at all, is the statement qualified? (Guide: *Qualification.*)

c. Do all portions of the essay serve as "tributaries" into the central theme, thus giving unity to the writing? If not, what are the exceptions?

3a. Several short, undeveloped examples are used in paragraph 1 to show a "prevalence." What is the generality they support?

b. What generality does the list of short examples in paragraph 7 support?

4a. A brief comparison between the examples of paragraph 1 and those of paragraph 7 can be used to show that examples, like words, can achieve differing degrees of specificity. (Guide: *Specific/General.*) Which of the two sets is more general?

b. Is one set then necessarily more, or less, effective than the other? Explain.

5. Paragraphs 2 and 3 comprise a more fully developed example. Which paragraph contains the generalization it supports?

6. All the authors' case file reports, themselves fully developed examples, also *use* example. Analyze any one of these reports for its basic structure, its use of this kind of interior example, and the effectiveness of presentation.

7a. Of the "hundreds of case histories" (par. 9) at the authors' disposal,

why do you think cases 17, 3, and 8 were chosen to use as examples?
b. Were these good choices?

8a. How is the series of developed examples beginning in paragraph 43 organized?
b. How is this organization superior, or inferior, to a less structured, more casual arrangement?
c. Can you think of some other order that would have been as effective? Explain.
d. What advantage is derived from the similar formats and endings of these examples?

DICTION AND VOCABULARY

1. If you are not familiar with the meanings of any of the following words, consult your dictionary: phenomenon (subheading before par. 6); indolent, dreadnaught, innate, servility, incoherent, inaudible (7); hypothesized, inherent (8); succeeded, demoralized (13); protocol (22); inadvertently (31); eccentrics (34); corollary (36); ostensible (38); plagiarisms (43); flummoxed, *non sequitur* (47); latent (50).

SUGGESTIONS FOR WRITING AND DISCUSSION

1. How is it possible, if at all in this complex society, to avoid getting involved with hierarchies (par. 34), other than in occasional dealings with them in the necessary conduct of family affairs? Consider such pertinent matters as methods, penalties, rewards.

2. If one's work is necessarily involved in a hierarchy, what practical methods would you suggest for reaching and remaining on the highest level of *competence*, thereby defying the Peter Principle?

3. From your own knowledge, select an example of incompetence dissimilar to any of those discussed in this essay. Show as well as you can the way in which this person passed his highest level of competence and, if possible, the results of the mistake for himself and others.

4. If you have reasons to doubt the Peter Principle's rather broad claims, show the nature of and justification for your doubts. You should not try to "prove" the principle wrong unless you have at least as much ammunition as the authors do. Remember that they do qualify most of their major generalizations.

(NOTE: Suggestions for topics requiring development by use of EXAMPLE are on page 38, at the end of this section.)

DICK GREGORY, born in St. Louis in 1932, is a popular comedian, nightclub entertainer, recording artist, author, and lecturer at colleges and universities throughout the United States. He won the Missouri mile-run championship in 1951, and while attending Southern Illinois University from 1951 to 1953 and from 1955 to 1956, he was once named the school's outstanding athlete. He served in the United States Army from 1953 to 1955. Gregory's books include the autobiographical *Nigger* (1964), *From the Back of the Bus* (1964), *What's Happening?* (1965), and *No More Lies: The Myths of American History* (1971); and he has recorded an album, *Dick Gregory in Living Black and White*.

The Ghetto Cop

"The Ghetto Cop" (editor's title) is an excerpt from Gregory's book *The Shadow That Scares Me*, published in 1968. Although in this selection Gregory is less dependent on example as a means of primary development than the previous authors have been, his liberal and informal use of varied examples is consistent with his essay's familiar style.

The power structure cannot expect to solve the social problems 1 of the ghetto by the mere physical presence of cops. The violence and strife in the ghetto cannot be contained or suppressed because they do not represent a riot. Five disciplined cops can stop a riot, but the best trained armies in the world cannot contain a legitimate protest.

The attitude of the cop is much more important than his physi- 2
cal presence. If you live in a city whose baseball team has just
won the World Series, or which has been chosen by the Shriners
as the site for their national convention, you will see people take
over the town. They get drunk in the streets, damage property,
and bother passersby. The cop will look the other way because a
big convention is bringing the city millions of dollars. If a cop
can be taught to change his attitude because a convention is bringing a city a lot of money, he had also better be taught not to
mistreat people who are demanding human dignity, which is more
than all the money in the world can buy.

People insist that it is unfair to generalize about the police. The 3
good cop is held up for public inspection and he is supposed to
be the example of law-enforcement officers everywhere. Just as
the one rabbi, priest or minister who goes to Alabama to demonstrate is supposed to represent the whole church. The one beautiful
cop in a neighborhood *will* stand out. He has pride in his job. He
is sensitive to human problems and knows how to talk to the person on the street corner. He has not chosen his job because he
couldn't get hired any place else. He is a cop because he wants to
be; perhaps his father and grandfather before him had devoted
their lives to law enforcement.

The problem cops, and there are many, are those who resented 4
their job when they took it. They are the cops who act like the
judge and the jury when they make an arrest. Their resentment
shows twenty-four hours a day. This situation will never change
until society gives law enforcement a status which is comparable
to the job it is expected to do.

Policemen labor under two basic injustices: inadequate salary 5
and lack of proper training. The cop is the most underpaid man
in American society today. Cops in the large cities should begin
with a minimum salary of ten thousand dollars per year. You must
pay a proper dollar for the job required. More and more potential
teachers are lost to the vocation of education because industry is
able to pay more money. The cop is so important to solving the
social problems which beset the ghetto that America should take
the chance of overpaying him, not underpaying him.

Being an entertainer, I am constantly reminded of the financial 6
injustice which the cop suffers. I have done benefit performances
all over the country for Policemen's Wives, Policemen's Widows,

Policemen's Benevolence Associations, and so on. But I never did a show for the politician's wife or the nightclub owner's wife. They are able to provide for their family in case of emergency, because their earnings are at a higher level than the cop's. If America treated the cop with the respect his job deserves, the family of a cop killed in the line of duty would automatically become the responsibility of government. Some local governments have accepted this responsibility, but such legislation should be enacted across the country in a uniform way.

Imagine yourself a cop in a major urban area. When you put   7
on that uniform in the morning and leave the house, you never know if you will make it back home in the evening. The policeman must live daily with a basic human fright which few other professions share. Yet the cop pays the same price for his haircut that Rockefeller pays. He pays the same amount for the education of his children that the rich executive pays. If a policeman is killed in the line of duty, it is an ethical and moral imperative that society accept the responsibility of scholarships for his children, a home for his family, and other necessary benefits.

Somehow we seem to be able to give foreign aid to countries   8
all over the world, even those countries who openly tell us to "go to hell." We should be able to find the money to give some aid to the cop — proper salary and proper training. Domestic aid to the cop at home is more important than foreign aid to countries abroad. We have a crisis in this country which can destroy us from within. . . . The number one place to begin to solve this problem which calls attention to itself with the haunting chant, "Burn, baby, burn," is through enlightened law enforcement.

There is a psychological factor operating in the injustice to the   9
cop. A man knows when he is being mistreated and it is bound to affect his attitude. This applies to both Negroes and cops. When we finally create an atmosphere in this country where law-enforcement officers are trained and paid in direct proportion to the importance of their job, a new attitude of vocational pride will be evident. If society does not have enough pride in its law-enforcement officers to pay them what they are worth, the cop is more likely to be susceptible to the bribe. If the pay scale is high enough, the cop does not want to risk getting caught taking a bribe for fear of losing his job. He knows he cannot get another job at the same high salary. Honesty and devotion are basic ingredients in vocational pride.

There is also the consideration of security, which is especially   10
important in a dangerous profession. The soldier has security, although often he is not even aware of it. Count up his benefits and
you will find that he has much more security than the cop. And
the soldier's job is easier than the cop's, because the soldier knows
where his enemy is. The enemy even wears a uniform to identify
himself. But the cop doesn't know what his enemy looks like. It
might be that nut the Army rejected! The same man who is too
crazy to go to Vietnam and kill Vietcong is back home in your
neighborhood waiting to assault you. The cop has to deal with
him.

Each new technological advance and the prospect of life in a   11
cybernetic society will place more demands upon the cop. We
will see unions demanding shorter and shorter work weeks. There
will be an increase of leisure time. People will have more time on
their hands, perhaps to be out in the streets. When a man works a
forty-hour week, the cop can count on the foreman watching him
at least eight hours a day!

The prophet Micah insisted that the Lord requires simply that   12
man "do justice." He seems to imply that other problems of human
relationship will be solved when a climate of justice is established.
Justice in America today requires the investment of funds for the
proper training and schooling of law-enforcement officers. The
cop's job is too important for him to be allowed to put on the
uniform without proper training. When I travel to England, it is
frightening to see that the cabdriver in London receives a longer
period of training than the average cop in America. Surely we must
see our cops as more crucial to the total health of society than
England does its cabdrivers. Only through basic research and proper training can just and enlightened law enforcement become
a reality. And this enlightment and sensitivity must come *before*
the cop gets out into the street. Society simply cannot send the
cop out into the street with his nightstick to get on-the-job training
on my head or with my problems, which he has not been trained
to understand. He must become thoroughly aware of my social
problems while he is still in school. All the force in the world
will never totally suppress a legitimate problem. Those who would
deal with social problems must have a basic human understanding.

The cop must be taught the unique problems of ghetto living   13
before he ever goes out on his beat. He must know, for example,
why the man in the ghetto rarely shops at the supermarket. The

supermarket requires him to pay cash. So the man in the ghetto goes to the white local merchant across the street. The prices in that little store are too high already, and the local merchant will try to cheat even more. The ghetto brother knows he is being cheated and it worries him. So when the white merchant turns his back to get the stale day-old loaf of bread, his customer wipes out the cookie rack. It is the customer's way of making up for the cheat. While the merchant is busy putting his thumb on the scale, his pickles disappear.

The cop must understand this injustice. He will see that there is more to the issue than a customer stealing. But if the customer gets caught stealing, the merchant calls a cop. When the ghetto kid gets caught stealing, the merchant grabs him by the ears and holds him until the cops arrive. But what happens when that same kid gets short-changed by the merchant? The kid can't call a cop and get a fair hearing. Cops must be taught to have a responsive and sympathetic ear and listen when that ghetto mother complains that her kids are being shortchanged. Once a cop becomes aware of such practices from the beginning, he can go immediately to the local merchant and say, "We have tremendously explosive social problems in this neighborhood which you could tip off at any moment. Don't shortchange the kids." And if complaints continue to come in, the cop should investigate the basis of the complaint immediately. Such activity would go a long way toward establishing a new image of respect for the cop in the ghetto. And the resentment and frustration which lead to breaking the local merchant's window and looting his store would begin to be alleviated. 14

Understanding ghetto kids presents a special problem for the cop. When a riot breaks out in a high school, the damage is already done and there is little the cop can do besides try to contain the violence. But if the cop had been sensitive to the history of the problem, the riot might have been avoided. For example, two kids have a gun duel in the schoolyard. The incident will very probably be hushed up by the school principal to keep his own record clean downtown. He doesn't want the superintendent of schools questioning his ability to control his pupils. But the seed for further trouble has been sown. A full-scale school riot may erupt which is certainly a more destructive mark on the principal's record. 15

Cops need to learn to work hand in hand with the school. They 16 need to learn to meet ghetto kids on their own level — the "'cause why" level. It is that basic, raw, instinctive level of life which seeks honest and open answers to very basic questions. High school kids know that the cops will be on hand when they throw their dance. 'Cause why is that the only time the cops are around? The cop has the image of only coming around to break up a party.

When cops learn to meet kids on their own level, they will 17 learn the answer to many adolescent mysteries. Like why so many kids choose the street corner or the local hangout instead of the brand-new recreational facilities in the neighborhood. It is a simple fact of Nature. Recreational facilities are geared to a program for boys. But the boys are going to choose to be where the girls are. The girls are at the local hangout. There are certain biological factors which take precedence even over basketball!

When cops learn the conditions of the home environment in the 18 ghetto, they will find out why kids act as they do. How many cops on the beat have actually seen their mother have an affair with their own daddy, let alone another man? Or how many cops have seen their mother take a needle and stick it in her arm and get high? The ghetto kid has seen this. He has looked at his own mother have an affair with a stranger. Of course, she told him it was one of Daddy's friends who came by to talk to her. So they went into the bedroom to talk, closing the door behind them. But Mother never thought that her little seven-year-old kid would peek through the keyhole. After he peeked through the keyhole and saw what he saw, he came back out into the street. He has just seen his mother have an affair with a stranger and the cop is going to tell him to be good? Naturally he will start swinging on the cop because he has to react against something. He can't swing on Momma.

The cop has to go back home with the ghetto kid and find out 19 where he learned that language he uses. Mother and Father would never curse in front of the kid, until they get angry. Then the curse words fly. When you hear these words at age seven, you assume that a dirty word is something to be used as a defensive weapon. So when you walk down the street and a little girl says to you, "You stink," quite naturally you are angry and threatened. It is only natural to turn and say, "Kiss my butt." It is natural because the little seven-year-old has heard Mother and Father use dirty language under the same threatening conditions. The little kid doesn't take a bite out of a good piece of chicken and curse. He smacks his lips and makes funny little grunting noises, just like Momma and Daddy. But when he is threatened, angry, and misused, the little kid curses. His home environment has taught him that response.

Cops must be trained to understand, on the human level, the con-   20
ditions of life and the home environment. It is amazing to see the results of juvenile police who have received private grants to work with kids. They accept the gang leader and work with him. They do not start out resenting him and trying to force him to behave. A loyalty is established between cop and gang, so that the cops often know when and where the big rumble is going to be. By really becoming involved in the life of the gang, and accepting kids on their own level, juvenile cops have been able to contain potentially troublesome situations.

Just and proper training of cops must take into account the tre-   21
mendous responsibility placed upon law-enforcement officers and the great pressures under which they live. Can you imagine a cop running through the streets of New York City, chasing a burglar, and he shoots, missing the culprit and hitting the Russian diplomat coming out of the United Nations Building? That is World War Three! Such is the awesome responsibility placed upon the man with the gun.

Imagine the mental pressure a cop must live under daily in the   22
ordinary line of duty. He sees daily the horror we only read about in the newspapers. We read about a three-year-old girl being sex-ually molested, mutilated, and murdered. The cop sees it for him-self. He walks into an apartment minutes after a man has gone berserk and chopped up his wife and mutilated his kids. Perhaps the cop has little kids of his own waiting for him to come home. What does such a gruesome sight do to a man's mind? How does it affect a man mentally to daily smell and touch dead human beings? It is the cop's job to live in an atmosphere of death — to see dead kids, to hear people moaning, groaning, and crying for help. Society expects the cop to experience such sickening horror and to take it in his stride. He is expected to forget what he has seen and walk back out on the street without holding a grudge. Have we done enough basic research to find out what such an occupational atmo-sphere does to a cop, as a man? Without such basic research, he cannot be adequately trained to deal with the conditions which his job imposes upon him. The cop's daily work is certain to affect him

mentally. One cannot witness daily the horrible reminders of the worst that man can do without developing a low evaluation of humanity. Just and proper training for the cop must take this inevitable reaction into account.

Respect for law and order can never be expected until a climate   23
of justice is created which encompasses both the cop and the man in the ghetto. The cop has to be an authority before he gets into the neighborhood. He must be trained to be an expert in understanding human behavior. He must be skilled in the art of human relationships. He must be a general practitioner trained to doctor social ills. If the cop is not adequately trained, he may be doing the very best he can given the conditions of his job; but his best is still wrong. A man does not become a brain surgeon by receiving on-the-job training in the emergency room of a hospital. The surgeon receives basic knowledge and training in medical school. Then he is ready to operate on a cracked skull and see the raw horror of an exposed brain. He will become a better surgeon with each new operation. But he is trained for his task before he is allowed to perform his very first operation. Basic knowledge and training precede actual practice. And the same thing must happen with law enforcement.

If the man on the street is to respect law and order, the cop must   24
behave like a trained, enlightened authority. A man does not want his authority getting angry, swinging a nightstick, and cursing. Such behavior is like the brain surgeon panicking at the sight of a skull fracture after an automobile accident. If that happens, you might just as well close down the hospital. The patient will die when he sees the look of horror on the surgeon's face. The surgeon is expected to take the crisis in his stride and do his job.

It is the same with the cop. It is easy for the cop to walk down   25
the street when nothing is going on, beating his stick on the lamp-post and waving with a friendly word for everyone sitting on the tenement stoop. But can the cop keep this same air of cool, calm, and authority in the midst of crisis?

Almost every day a cop performs duties as a matter of routine   26
which would scare me to death. A woman giving birth to a baby in the back seat of my car, for example. It doesn't scare the average cop because he has been trained to know what to do when that water bag bursts before the woman gets to the hospital. He recognizes that it is an act of Nature and he knows how to deal with it.

The social revolution in the sore spots of this nation is another   27 act of Nature, a natural response to oppressive conditions. It bears the same marks of pain, violence, and struggle which accompany any birth. From this violent, painful struggle a new America will be born. For the first time, the nation will be christened in the name of freedom, dignity, and justice. During this transitory period of pregnancy, justice demands that the cop be trained to display the same authority and sophistication in the midst of social crisis as he does when a woman gives birth to a baby in the back of his patrol wagon.

It has been said, "Justice belongs to all men, or it belongs to none." Aristotle wrote, "The way to gain good will is to show good will." And the prophet Micah reminds us what the Lord requires for men to live together in peace, love, and harmony, "do justice, love kindness and walk humbly with your God." What better description could there be for a climate in which respect for law and order is guaranteed? To *do* justice means to treat all men with respect and human dignity — Negroes, whites, cops, and all of creation. To love kindness is to consciously seek an atmosphere of human dwelling in which the rights and needs of all men are respected. To walk humbly means to maintain an air of sensitivity which seeks first to understand human expression rather than to thwart or suppress it. Such is the climate of justice. And when that climate is created, respect for law and order — even an increase of genuine love — will follow.

28

MEANINGS AND VALUES

1a. What apparently is the author's attitude toward his subject matter? (See Guide to Terms: *Point of View*.)
  b. How did you determine the preceding answer?
  c. How, if at all, is tone involved in the matter? (Guide: *Style/Tone*.)
2a. Is there any evidence of sentimentality in this essay? (Guide: *Sentimentality*.) If so, is it sufficient to damage the writing's effectiveness?
  b. Explain how this is, or would be, a matter of tone.
3a. What criticism, if any, would an ultra-liberal be apt to make of this essay?
  b. An ultra-conservative?
  c. Judging by "The Ghetto Cop," where would you place Gregory on the liberal-conservative spectrum?
4. How valid and appropriate is the comparison with foreign aid in paragraph 8? Explain.

5. If you see any irony in the comparison of cops and cabdrivers in paragraph 12, what kind is it? Why? (Guide: *Irony.*)

6. Give this essay our three-step critical evaluation. (Guide: *Evaluation.*)

7. If you have read "The Peter Principle," do you think the principle applies to police departments as much as to schools and commercial enterprises? Explain.

EXPOSITORY TECHNIQUES

1a. Cite the paragraphs that use example to achieve concreteness.
 b. Which of these examples, if any, would have benefited by further development?
 c. Which examples, if any, seem poorly chosen for their purposes? How could the choice have been improved?

2. By what methods does the author gain emphasis? (Guide: *Emphasis.*) Provide one example of each method.

3. Consider the following sentences in relation to each other and to the essay's general subject matter: the last sentence in paragraph 4, the first in paragraph 5, and the last in paragraph 8.
 a. Which of these three, if any, seems to you a good statement of the overall central theme? (Guide: *Unity.*)
 b. Do *all* parts of the essay pertain to this statement?
 c. If not, does the writing therefore lack unity — or was your answer to 3a incorrect? Explain.

4a. Which of the author's statements, if they are to be taken literally, should have been more carefully qualified? (Guide: *Qualification.*)
 b. Give your reasons for each.
 c. Indicate how qualification for each could have been achieved with least difficulty.
 d. Which of these generalizations, as used in their own context, do you consider permissible as mere obvious exaggerations (a technique sometimes useful for shock value alone)?
 e. Briefly explain how a writer may jeopardize the effectiveness of his writing (even aside from possible damage to other people) by careless generalizing. Illustrate by using quotations from this essay, if any apply.

5a. What standard techniques are used here for closing. (Guide: *Closings.*)
 b. How effectively?

6a. How does its style help qualify this selection as a familiar essay? (Guide: *Essay; Style/Tone.*)
 b. How, if at all, are its organization and development also involved in the matter?

7a. If you have read "The Peter Principle," point out at least three basic ways in which the writing techniques differ decidedly between it and Gregory's essay.
 b. Is either more effectively written, considering the subject matter with which the authors were working? Explain.

DICTION AND VOCABULARY

1a. Which of the elements of style discussed in your answer to question 7a in "Expository Techniques" are primarily matters of diction? (Guide: *Diction.*) Cite examples.
 b. Which are primarily matters of syntax? (Guide: *Syntax.*) Cite examples.
2a. Gregory consistently uses colloquial and slang terms. (Guide: *Colloquial.*) List or mark these. (Dictionaries will differ as to which are colloquial and which slang, but for our purposes we need not be concerned with the distinction.)
 b. Comment briefly on the appropriateness for this essay of such liberal usage.
3a. What do you think is the usual connotation of the word "cop"? (Guide: *Connotation/Denotation.*)
 b. Do you think Gregory intends this connotation here? Why, or why not?
 c. List the possible alternatives to "cop" and indicate for each whether its choice would have been better or worse.
 d. Be prepared to justify your answers.
4. Consult the dictionary as needed for an understanding of the following words: Shriners (par. 2); potential, beset (5); imperative (7); cybernetic (11); alleviated (14); encompasses (23).

SUGGESTIONS FOR WRITING AND DISCUSSION

1. Consider the statement that "five disciplined cops can stop a riot" (par. 1). If you have had sufficient training or experience to speak with some authority, explain how a relatively small police squad (perhaps five is too small) *can* stop a riot.
2. Compare, with facts if you can, the security of the soldier with that of the policeman (par. 10).
3. What problems other than those of police (par. 11) do you think would multiply or worsen with shorter work weeks? Explain.
4. If you have carefully observed a policeman with special training and the time to work with ghetto children (par. 20), explain how he went about this project and, if possible, how successful and long-lasting were the results.

5. Most British city police (officially designated as *peace* officers) do not carry guns. Weigh objectively and explain the feasibility of such a policy in American cities.

6. Consider the statement that "one cannot witness daily the horrible reminders of the worst that man can do without developing a low evaluation of humanity" (par. 22). If you believe this is even generally true, what kind of advance training could possibly offset that devastating effect? Be objective and as thorough as possible.

Writing Suggestions for Section 1

Illustration by Example

Use one of the following statements or another suggested by them as your central theme. Develop it into a unified composition, using examples from history, current events, or personal experience to illustrate your ideas. Be sure to have your reader-audience clearly in mind, as well as your specific purpose for the communication.

1. Successful businesses keep employees at their highest level of *competence*.
2. Even the "beautiful" cop is still a loser.
3. Laws holding parents responsible for their children's crimes would (or would not) result in serious injustices.
4. You can't always tell a nonconformist just by looking at him.
5. Young people are becoming bored with their "rebellion."
6. Not all women want to be "liberated."
7. One thing is certain about styles: they cannot stay the same.
8. Good sportsmanship is far more than shaking hands with the winner.
9. Religion in the United States is far from dead.
10. Democracy is not always the best form of government.
11. Colonialism has not been entirely bad.
12. Nearly anyone can have a creative hobby.
13. The general quality of television commercials may be improving (or deteriorating).
14. Buying a used automobile (or a _____) is a risky endeavor, even at best.
15. "Some books are to be tasted; others swallowed; and some few to be chewed and digested." (*Francis Bacon*, English scientist-author, 1561–1626.)

2

Analyzing a Subject by *Classification*

People naturally like to sort and classify things. The untidiest urchin, moving into a new dresser of his own, will put his handkerchiefs together, socks and underwear in separate stacks, and perhaps his toads and snails (temporarily) into a drawer of their own. He may classify animals as those with legs, those with wings, and those with neither. As he gets older, he finds that schoolteachers have ways of classifying *him*, not only into a reading group but, periodically, into an "A" or "F" category, or somewhere in between. On errands to the grocery store, he discovers the macaroni in the same department as noodles, the pork chops somewhere near the ham. In reading the local newspaper, he observes that its staff has done some classifying for him, putting most of the comics together and seldom mixing sports stories with the news of bridal showers. Eventually he finds courses neatly classified in the college catalogue, and he knows enough not to look for biology courses under "Social Science." (Examples again — used to illustrate a "prevalence.")

However, our main interest in classification here is its use as a structural pattern for explanatory writing. Many subjects about which either student or graduate may need to write will remain a hodgepodge of facts and opinions unless he can find some system of analyzing the material, dividing the subject into categories, and classifying individual elements into those categories. Here we have the distinction usually made between the rhetorical terms *division* and *classification* — for example, dividing "meat" into pork, beef, mutton, and fowl, then classifying ham and pork chops into the category of "pork." But this distinction is one we need scarcely pause for here; once the need for analysis is recognized, the dividing and classifying become inevitable companions and result in the single scheme of "classification" itself, as we have been discussing it. The original division into parts merely sets up the system which, if well chosen, best serves our purpose.

Obviously, no single system of classification is best for all purposes. Our untidy urchin may at some point classify girls according to athletic prowess, then later by size or shape or hair color. Other people may need entirely different systems of classification: the music instructor classifies girls as sopranos, altos, contraltos; the psychologist, according to their behavioral patterns; the sociologist, according to their ethnic origins.

Whatever the purpose, for the more formal uses of classification ("formal," that is, to the extent of most academic and on-the-job writing), we should be careful to use a logical system that is complete and that follows a consistent principle throughout. It would not be logical to divide Protestantism into the categories of Methodist, Baptist, and Lutheran, because the system would be incomplete and misleading. But in classifying Protestants attending some special conference — a different matter entirely — such a limited system might be both complete and logical. In any case, the writer must be careful that classes do not overlap: to classify the persons at the conference as Methodists, Baptists, Lutherans, and clergy would be illogical, because some are undoubtedly both Lutheran, for instance, and "clergy."

In dividing and classifying we are really using the basic process of outlining. Moreover, if we are dealing with classifiable *ideas*, the resulting pattern *is* our outline, which has been our aim all along — a basic organizational plan.

This process of classification frequently does, in fact, organize much less tangible things than the examples mentioned. We might wish to find some orderly basis for discussing the South's post–Civil War problems. Division might give us three primary categories of information: economic, political, and social. But for a full-scale consideration of these, the major divisions themselves may be subdivided for still more orderly explanation: the economic information may be further divided into agriculture and industry. Now it is possible to isolate and clarify such strictly industrial matters as shortage of investment capital, disrupted transportation systems, and lack of power development.

Any plan like this seems almost absurdly obvious, of course — *after* the planning is done. It appears less obvious, however, to the inexperienced writer who is dealing with a jumble of information he must explain to someone else. This is when he should be aware of the patterns at his disposal, and one of the most useful of these, alone or combined with others, is classification.

HELEN H. NOWLIS was born in Rhode Island in 1913 and educated at Pembroke College of Brown University and at Yale, where she received her Ph.D. in psychology. She then taught in several colleges and served as a research associate at the Institute of Child Welfare of the State University of Iowa before joining the faculty of the University of Rochester as professor of psychology in 1951. At Rochester she has also collaborated in research on the effects of drugs and has served as associate dean and as dean of students. In 1966 and 1967 Nowlis was on leave to serve as director of the NASPA-FDA drug education project. She is presently research consultant on student affairs and professor of psychology at Rochester.

Defining the Problem of Campus Drugs

"Defining the Problem . . ." is the first chapter of Nowlis' book *Drugs on the College Campus* (1969), which had previously been issued as a public document of a drug education project under the Food and Drug Administration. This selection employs a rather common method used in exploring a complex subject: *dividing* it into basic categories (here labeled "problems"), wherein the many smaller, more specific matters are *classified*.

The current use of hallucinogenic drugs by young people is being 1 called the biggest cop-out of all time. A great many people would concur. It could be. But, having said this to the increasing minority of students and young people who are using drugs regularly, who use them occasionally, who do not rule out the possibility that they may try them at some time, or who vigorously defend the right of those who are using drugs to do so, the dialogue is ended. To many educators and others deeply concerned with young people and their personal and social growth and development, the problem is not that simple and the dialogue must continue.

The problem of drugs on the college campus is a problem of   2
ignorance — lack of knowledge about the action of chemical substances on the complex, delicately balanced chemical system that is the living organism, lack of knowledge about the relationship of variations in this system to complex human behavior, lack of knowledge about complex human behavior itself. It is a problem of the tyranny of opinion, attitude, and belief in the absence of knowledge.

It is a problem of *semantics* — of trying to talk, think, and act   3
rationally in an area in which almost every term is entangled in so much myth and emotion and such a variety of implicit assumptions, beliefs, and attitudes that futile argument replaces dialogue and discussion because the participants are neither talking the same language nor proceeding from the same assumptions.

It is a problem of *communication* — among scientists in different   4
disciplines, between scientist and layman, between parents and children, between a generation brought up before automation, television, jet travel, nuclear energy, and the hydrogen bomb, megalopolis, multiuniversity, and the affluent society and a generation which has known no other condition.

It is a problem of *lack of understanding of scientific method and*   5
concepts — lack of understanding that there are no simple relationships between cause and effect, that human behavior has multiple determinants, that there is a difference between correlation and causation, that the design and execution of experiments is open to bias, that a "conclusion" based on an experiment has no meaning except in terms of the design and execution of that experiment, that individuals vary on an almost infinite number of dimensions and that statements about them, even at a biological level, are in terms of averages and probabilities.

It is a problem of *living and learning and growing* in an arena   6
where change is the only constant and where the future is increasingly unpredictable.

It is a problem of *philosophy of social control* in a pluralistic   7
society — of the individual's relationship to societal values and to these values as expressed in law.

It is a problem of *education* and its relationship to current societal   8 values; a problem both of the relationship of the individual to the institution and of the institution to the needs of society.

It is a problem of a *"pill society"* which is increasingly buying the   9 well-advertised proposition that there is a chemical solution for any problem of unpleasantness and discomfort, whether it be physical, psychological, or social (from arthritis to anxiety, from indigestion to tension, from sleeplessness to lack of social and business success) — a society that spends more money on alcohol, tranquilizers, and sleeping pills than it does on education and the Great Society.

It is a problem of *increasing retreat in the face of complex, diffi-*   10 *cult problems* to "blob" thinking, of insisting at the earliest possible moment that everything is all good or all bad and defining good as "not bad" and bad as "not good."

It may be relevant to ask why this society is reacting so violently   11 to the use of the hallucinogens when there are from four to eight million alcoholics in the country, depending on one's definition of alcoholic. Why the uproar over the small minority of students using hallucinogens when self-prescribed use of stimulants and depressants is far more widespread? Why have Americans increased their consumption of cigarettes by nine billion (from 536 billion) during the twelve months ending in June 1967, despite sobering evidence strongly suggesting a relationship between smoking and both cancer and heart disease — and even as they contribute millions to research which will help find a "cure" for these major causes of illness and death? Why does society actively promote the use of alcohol and nicotine while imposing severe legal penalties on the mere possession of other chemical agents? There must be reasons and they should be relevant to the problem at hand.

Why are so many of our most gifted and privileged young people   12 defending the right of their fellow students to use drugs and why are a few of these young people making the use of drugs and the culture that surrounds them a central factor in their lives, at least temporarily? Our first impulse is to say they are sick — but who defines "sick," and how? Our next impulse is to say they are rebelling — against what? Or to say that they are immoral — according to what values? Miserable — why? Searching and exploring — for what?

Why do so many of us think of student drug use exclusively as a   13 medical or legal problem and delegate responsibility for its solution to the physician, the legislator, and the law enforcement officer?

Is such delegation a convenient way to avoid our own responsibilities and to ignore other important social issues? Are health and pathology adequately defined in terms of medical science and practice or do these definitions necessarily involve statements about personal and social values?

Before any of these questions can be explored some terms and concepts must be defined; what we know and, equally important, what we do not know about how chemicals affect the human organism, and what we do and do not know about complex behavior and how it may be affected by chemicals must be surveyed.   14

MEANINGS AND VALUES

1. Do you think that only a minority of students "vigorously defend the right of those who are using drugs to do so" (par. 1)? On what do you base your answer?

2. If you see paradox in the author's first sentence, explain why. (See Guide to Terms: *Paradox.*) If not, why might some people regard it as paradoxical?

3. How important *is* the problem of "knowledge" (par. 2), really, in view of the fact that the use of heroin is increasing rapidly *despite* users' almost certain knowledge of its hazards?

4a. Do you think that we live, learn, and grow in "an arena where change is the only constant" (par. 6) — or is this an exaggeration, perhaps only a neat maneuver with words? Explain.
  b. Is this statement a paradox? Why, or why not?

5a. Illustrate the meaning of "irony" with a quotation from paragraph 9. (Guide: *Irony.*)
  b. What kind is it?

6. Find other examples of irony in paragraph 11. Be prepared to defend your examples.

7. Explain how an understanding of irony and its implications can enhance the meaning and value in reading some expositions, of which this essay may be an example.

EXPOSITORY TECHNIQUES

1. What standard ways of introducing expository writing does this selection employ? (Guide: *Introductions.*)

2a. Explain fully how the apparent *listing* of problems in paragraphs 2–10 can correctly be used to illustrate *division/classification*.

b. As nearly as you can determine, does this classification system fit the standards of logic as proposed in the fifth paragraph of the introductory discussion on classification? Why, or why not?

3a. A much looser and less obvious system of classification determines the basic arrangement of questions in paragraphs 11–13 of the essay. How might we label, roughly, the categories represented?

b. Although these questions are not posed to elicit answers from the reader (at least not at the time of reading), they are not actually rhetorical questions either. (Guide: *Rhetorical Question.*) Why not? What, then, is their purpose?

4a. List or mark at least three clear examples of parallel structure, other than the obvious repetition of "It is a problem of. . . ." (Guide: *Parallel Structure.*)

b. Explain how this essay benefits from such extensive use of parallels.

5a. Cite examples of the periodic sentence in paragraph 1. (Guide: *Emphasis.*)

b. What, if anything, is gained by the use of such sentences?

6a. Is this a formal, informal, or familiar essay? (Guide: *Essay.*)

b. Justify your answer.

DICTION AND VOCABULARY

1. How, if at all, is the problem of "semantics" (par. 3) also one of "connotations"? (Guide: *Connotation/Denotation.*)

2. Consult the dictionary as needed for the meanings of the following words: hallucinogenic, concur (par. 1); implicit (3); megalopolis, affluent (4); determinants, correlation, causation (5); relevant (11); pathology (13).

SUGGESTIONS FOR WRITING AND DISCUSSION

1. In what other areas of human strife does at least a part of the problem seem to be due to semantics (par. 3)? Develop your central theme by the use of examples.

2. Propose and explain some concrete, practical plan of action that could help, in your college or home community, to alleviate just *one* aspect of *one* of the problem categories (pars. 2–10).

3. If you prefer, explain the operation of such a plan already in effect and its apparent degree of success.

4. Is the use of drugs a "cop-out"?

5. Should people have the "right" to use hard drugs if they want to?

(NOTE: Suggestions for topics requiring development by CLASSIFICATION are on page 68, at the end of this section.)

Eric Berne (1910–1970) was a graduate of McGill University's School of Medicine. A psychiatrist, he wrote extensively in that field, lectured at various universities, and served on the psychiatric staff of Mount Sinai Hospital in New York City. He later engaged in private practice and research in California. His books include *Games People Play* (1964), *The Happy Valley* (1968), and *Sex in Human Loving* (1970).

Can People Be Judged by Their Appearance?

"Can People Be Judged by Their Appearance?" was originally published in Berne's *The Mind in Action* (1947) and was later included in a revised edition of his book, *A Layman's Guide to Psychiatry and Psychoanalysis*. This explanation of one theory of basic human types is an example of a scientific subject made readable for nonscientists. Using division and classification as his primary pattern of development, Berne also relies to varying extents on most of the other expository patterns: illustration, comparison and contrast, process analysis, cause and effect, definition, and description.

Everyone knows that a human being, like a chicken, comes from an 1 egg. At a very early stage, the human embryo forms a three-layered tube, the inside layer of which grows into the stomach and lungs, the middle layer into bones, muscles, joints, and blood vessels, and the outside layer into the skin and nervous system.

Usually these three grow about equally, so that the average 2 human being is a fair mixture of brains, muscles, and inward organs. In some eggs, however, one layer grows more than the others, and when the angels have finished putting the child together, he may have more gut than brain, or more brain than muscle. When this happens, the individual's activities will often be mostly with the overgrown layer.

We can thus say that while the average human being is a mixture, some people are mainly "digestion-minded," some "muscle-minded," and some "brain-minded," and correspondingly digestion-bodied, muscle-bodied, or brain-bodied. The digestion-bodied people look thick; the muscle-bodied people look wide; and the brain-bodied people look long. This does not mean the taller a man is the brainier he will be. It means that if a man, even a short man, looks long rather than wide or thick, he will often be more concerned about what goes on in his mind than about what he does or what he eats; but the key factor is slenderness and not height. On the other hand, a man who gives the impression of being thick rather than long or wide will usually be more interested in a good steak than in a good idea or a good long walk. 3

Medical men use Greek words to describe these types of body-build. For the man whose body shape mostly depends on the inside layer of the egg, they use the word *endomorph*. If it depends mostly upon the middle layer, they call him a *mesomorph*. If it depends upon the outside layer, they call him an *ectomorph*. We can see the same roots in our English words "enter," "medium," and "exit," which might just as easily have been spelled "ender," "mesium," and "ectit." 4

Since the inside skin of the human egg, or endoderm, forms the inner organs of the belly, the viscera, the endomorph is usually belly-minded; since the middle skin forms the body tissues, or soma, the mesomorph is usually muscle-minded; and since the outside skin forms the brain, or cerebrum, the ectomorph is usually brain-minded. Translating this into Greek, we have the viscerotonic endomorph, the somatotonic mesomorph, and the cerebrotonic ectomorph. 5

Words are beautiful things to a cerebrotonic, but a viscerotonic knows you cannot eat a menu no matter what language it is printed in, and a somatotonic knows you cannot increase your chest expansion by reading a dictionary. So it is advisable to leave these words and see what kinds of people they actually apply to, remembering again that most individuals are fairly equal mixtures and that what we have to say concerns only the extremes. Up to the present, these types have been thoroughly studied only in the male sex. 6

Viscerotonic Endomorph. If a man is definitely a thick type rather   7
than a broad or long type, he is likely to be round and soft, with
a big chest but a bigger belly. He would rather eat than breathe
comfortably. He is likely to have a wide face, short, thick neck, big
thighs and upper arms, and small hands and feet. He has over-
developed breasts and looks as though he were blown up a little
like a balloon. His skin is soft and smooth, and when he gets bald,
as he does usually quite early, he loses the hair in the middle of his
head first.

The short, jolly, thickset, red-faced politician with a cigar in his   8
mouth, who always looks as though he were about to have a stroke,
is the best example of this type. The reason he often makes a good
politician is that he likes people, banquets, baths, and sleep; he is
easygoing, soothing, and his feelings are easy to understand.

His abdomen is big because he has lots of intestines. He likes to   9
take in things. He likes to take in food, and affection and approval
as well. Going to a banquet with people who like him is his idea
of a fine time. It is important for a psychiatrist to understand the
natures of such men when they come to him for advice.

Somatotonic Mesomorph. If a man is definitely a broad type   10
rather than a thick or long type, he is likely to be rugged and have
lots of muscle. He is apt to have big forearms and legs, and his
chest and belly are well formed and firm, with the chest bigger
than the belly. He would rather breathe than eat. He has a bony
head, big shoulders, and a square jaw. His skin is thick, coarse,
and elastic, and tans easily. If he gets bald, it usually starts on
the front of the head.

Dick Tracy, Li'l Abner, and other men of action belong to this   11
type. Such people make good lifeguards and construction workers.
They like to put out energy. They have lots of muscles and they
like to use them. They go in for adventure, exercise, fighting, and
getting the upper hand. They are bold and unrestrained, and love
to master the people and things around them. If the psychiatrist
knows the things which give such people satisfaction, he is able
to understand why they may be unhappy in certain situations.

Cerebrotonic Ectomorph. The man who is definitely a long type is   12
likely to have thin bones and muscles. His shoulders are apt to sag
and he has a flat belly with a dropped stomach, and long, weak
legs. His neck and fingers are long, and his face is shaped like a

long egg. His skin is thin, dry, and pale, and he rarely gets bald. He looks like an absent-minded professor and often is one.

Though such people are jumpy, they like to keep their energy 13 and don't fancy moving around much. They would rather sit quietly by themselves and keep out of difficulties. Trouble upsets them, and they run away from it. Their friends don't understand them very well. They move jerkily and feel jerkily. The psychiatrist who understands how easily they become anxious is often able to help them get along better in the sociable and aggressive world of endomorphs and mesomorphs.

In the special cases where people definitely belong to one type 14 or another, then, one can tell a good deal about their personalities from their appearance. When the human mind is engaged in one of its struggles with itself or with the world outside, the individual's way of handling the struggle will be partly determined by his type. If he is a viscerotonic he will often want to go to a party where he can eat and drink and be in good company at a time when he might be better off attending to business; the somatotonic will want to go out and do something about it, master the situation, even if what he does is foolish and not properly figured out, while the cerebrotonic will go off by himself and think it over, when perhaps he would be better off doing something about it or seeking good company to try to forget it.

Since these personality characteristics depend on the growth of 15 the layers of the little egg from which the person developed, they are very difficult to change. Nevertheless, it is important for the individual to know about these types, so that he can have at least an inkling of what to expect from those around him, and can make allowances for the different kinds of human nature, and so that he can become aware of and learn to control his own natural tendencies, which may sometimes guide him into making the same mistakes over and over again in handling his difficulties.

MEANINGS AND VALUES

1. Consider men you have known who fit, or nearly fit, into one or another of the three categories of build.
  a. Do they also have the traits described by Berne in paragraphs 8, 9, 11, and 13? Or do you know, perhaps, a "thick" man who hates banquets, a "wide" man who writes poetry, or a "long" man who bullies people?
  b. If so, should we assume that these are learned characteristics? Explain.
2. Illustrate clearly how an understanding of basic types of people can be important to the layman.
3. In view of the fact that so many of a person's characteristics are determined before he is born, what room does the author leave for the possibility of altering or controlling these natural tendencies?
4. If you have read "The Peter Principle" in Section 1, show by use of a clear example how an understanding of Berne's theory might benefit an individual in his personal application of the Peter Principle.

EXPOSITORY TECHNIQUES

1a. Most people, according to the author, are not classifiable in the categories he discusses. Is the classification system then faulty, since it does not include everyone?
  b. Explain the difference, if any, between this system and the faulty classification of Protestants mentioned in the introduction to this section.
2. Study the general organization of this essay.
  a. Which paragraphs give an overall preview of Berne's classification system?
  b. Which paragraphs are devoted to explanations of individual categories?
  c. Where does the author bring the categories together again to show the importance of the whole analysis?
  d. Can you work out another plan that would have presented his material as meaningfully?
3. The author ends each detailed account of type characteristics with a statement of why the psychiatrist needs to know these things (pars. 9, 11, 13). Why is this a valuable technique, even though the essay was not written for psychiatrists?
4. Show the value of the parallel structures in paragraphs 4 and 5. (See Guide to Terms: *Parallel Structure.*)

5. In your opinion, do Berne's occasional attempts at humor — e.g., "the angels" and "cannot eat a menu" — benefit or detract from his explanation? Why?

DICTION AND VOCABULARY

1a. Are the numerous Greek words as bothersome as you expected them to be when you first glanced at the essay? Why, or why not?
  b. Do you think the author expects us really to master them? If not, why did he use them?
2. Aside from the Greek words, you probably found no words with which you were not already familiar. Is this a result of the type of subject matter, the author's concern for his audience, or something else? Explain.

SUGGESTIONS FOR WRITING AND DISCUSSION

1. At the time this essay was written, the types had been "thoroughly studied only in the male sex." Even if the same general traits were characteristic of women, might tradition and social pressures tend to modify the natural tendencies more in women than in men (e.g., women are "not supposed" to go around flexing their muscles or getting into fist fights)? Explain any differences that you would expect.

2. Using examples for illustration, show that basic nature can be changed — or, if you prefer, that such change is very difficult or impossible.

3. Show the practical importance — especially for success in your future career — of understanding people and why they act as they do.

4. Develop the thesis that people of opposite types can sometimes get along more congenially than those of the same type.

(NOTE: Suggestions for topics requiring development by use of CLASSIFI-CATION are on page 68, at the end of this section.)

VANCE PACKARD

VANCE PACKARD, born in Pennsylvania in 1914, spent many years as a newspaper reporter and columnist and as a free-lance contributor to various periodicals. He is a prolific author of books, several of which have been best sellers and are still widely read and quoted. Among them are *The Hidden Persuaders* (1957), *The Status Seekers* (1959), *The Waste Makers* (1960), *The Pyramid Climbers* (1962), and *The Naked Society* (1964).

New Directions of Marriage

"New Directions of Marriage" (editor's title) is a section of Packard's *The Sexual Wilderness*, which was published in 1968. Faced with presenting a tangle of predictions and proposals, the author chose to bring order to his subject matter by an informal but workable system of classification. In one form or another, it is probably the only way order could have been achieved.

Most of the rules regulating marriages and their dissolution were 1
made in eras when the bride and groom could look forward to fewer than half the number of years together that the couples marrying in the next few years can anticipate. For that reason alone, entering into wedlock calls for a new high level of prudence. There is now obviously a greater chance the partners will outgrow each other, lose interest, or become restless. In the past quarter-century, instead of greater prudence, however, we have seen a considerable increase in imprudent embarkations upon marriage.

Wives in the future surely will spend an increasing proportion of 2
their married life as equal partners of the husband free of the

"motherhood-service role," and so will have more options for the outlet of their surplus energy. They can no longer view marriage as a haven where they will be looked after by a husband in return for traditional services rendered.

Instead, more than ever before, women will have not only the opportunity but the expectation to push out for themselves and function as autonomous individuals who happen to have marriage partners. Marriages will apparently continue to be brittle for some time. Families in the immediate future will be expected to be highly mobile, and ever smaller in size.

While, as noted, the traditional economic functions of marriage have shrunk, there are 2 particularly compelling reasons looming why people will be marrying in the coming decade despite the relatively free availability of unmarried sexual partners:

1. The warm, all-embracing companionship that in marriage can endure through the confusion, mobility, and rapid social change of our times.

2. The opportunity to obtain immortality and personal growth for married individuals who perpetuate themselves through reproduction as they help mold personalities of their children and proudly induct them into the larger community.

This opportunity is so profoundly desired by most adult humans who are capable of reproduction that childlessness by choice would seem to be almost as difficult to popularize on any large scale as singleness by choice. Both would probably require intensive, prolonged social conditioning.

The institution of marriage is obviously in need of modifications to fit the modern needs. Author Jerome Weidman made an important point in his book *Your Daughter Iris* when he wrote of today's marriages: "Human beings do not obtain permanent possession of each other when they marry. All they obtain is the right to work at the job of holding on to each other." In pressing for modification of marriage as an institution we should seek above all to assure that the 2 functions of marriage just stated be fulfilled.

A variety of predictions and proposals are being heard today as to how the male-female liaison will or should evolve in the next few decades to meet the changing conditions of modern life. Here, for example, are 8 possible patterns of marriage or near-marriage that are being discussed:

1. *Serial mating.* Sometimes it is called serial monogamy, some-

times serial polygamy, sometimes consecutive polygamy. But the basic idea is pretty much the same for all. It would assume a turnover of partners over the 50-odd years that a man and a woman can expect to live after they first consider marriage. Swedish sociologist Joachim Israel suggested that 4 or 5 marriages might be about par for a lifetime. The mood behind such proposals was summed up by a New York model when she said, "Why lie to yourself? We know we're not going to love one man all our lives." Among others, a psychologist-social worker in California, Virginia Star, has advocated the adoption of renewable marriage contracts. She suggests the contract lapse unless renewed every 5 years.

2. *Unstructured cohabitation.* These are the prolonged affairs 11 without any assumption of permanence or responsibility. Such so-called unstructured liaisons — long popular in the lower classes — have been springing up in many of the larger universities in the off-campus housing. A psychiatrist at the University of California in Berkeley has suggested these liaisons may be the shape of the future. He said, "Stable, open non-marital relationships are pushing the border of what society is going to face in 10 years."[1]

A man's magazine in the mid-1960s presented some unconven- 12 tional views of a woman who had been involved in a national controversy. During the presentation, she was asked, "How many lovers have you had, if you don't mind our asking?"

She responded, "You've got a helluva nerve, but I really don't 13 mind. I've had five, if you count my marriage as an affair . . . five affairs, all of them really wing-dings."

3. *Mutual polygamy.* At a conference of marriage specialists in 14 1966 one expert from a Midwestern university speculated, "If we are moving into a new pattern where we are not claiming that marriage can do all the things that have been assumed, we may be moving into a kind of situation where there will be more than one partner. A compartmentalizing." Each partner in any particular marriage might have several mates, each chosen for a special purpose — for example, economic, recreational, procreational. A more informal variant of this would be "flexible monogamy," which in the view of Phyllis and Eberhard Kronhausen would frankly allow "for variety, friendships, and even sexual experiences with other individuals, if these are desired."[2]

---

[1] "Unstructured Relations," *Newsweek*, July 4, 1966.
[2] Phyllis and Eberhard Kronhausen, *The Sexually Responsive Woman* (New York: Grove Press, 1964), p. 236.

4. *Single-parent marriages by intent.* These, on the Swedish   15
model, would be the females — and occasional males — who yearn
for parenthood without the burdens of wedlock.

5. *Specialists in parenthood.* Anthropologist Margaret Mead, in   16
looking a few decades ahead, suggests the time may come when
pressures to keep the birth rate low will produce a social style "in
which parenthood would be limited to a smaller number of families
whose principal function would be child-rearing; the rest of the
population would be free to function — for the first time in history
— as individuals."[3]

6. *Communal living.* In such a situation, several adult females   17
and several adult males might live together in the same large
dwelling and consider themselves an enlarged communal family,
much as the hippies and other unconventional family groups have
already been doing for some time.

7. *Legalized polygamy for senior citizens.* This is a form of poly-   18
gamy that enables a man to have several wives at the same time.
It has been advanced as a way to ease the demographic problem
created by the fact that after the age of 60 there are increasingly
more females than males in the population. One such proposal was
advanced in the magazine *Geriatrics* by Dr. Victor Kassel, of Salt
Lake City (the Mormon capital). The idea was taken seriously
enough to be debated and unofficially turned down by the National
Council of the Aging. A widow in South Carolina gave one feminine
viewpoint when she said, "I am lonesome — but not that lonesome!"

8. *A variety of liaison patterns functioning in society simultane-*   19
ously. David Mace suggests we are moving toward a 3-layer cake
type of society as far as male-female liaisons are concerned. He
speculated that there may be a coexistence of several patterns. One
pattern, as he sees it, will be that a proportion of the people will
settle for sex freedom. They will not marry, but will drift into
liaisons of long and short terms. There will be no attempt to punish
or suppress such persons. He suggested that the second layer of
this cake would involve somewhat more structuring, with a number
of people choosing to go in and out of marriage and probably
having several marriages in a lifetime, as in the common Hollywood
pattern. Probably in this second layer there will be an attitude of

[3] Margaret Mead, "The Life Cycle and Its Variants: The Division of Roles,"
Daedalus, Summer, 1967.

freedom regarding extramarital sex while the couples are married. He suggested that in the third layer of the cake will be those who accept the concept of exclusive monogamy, preceded in at least some cases by premarital chastity.

Moral standards aside, one complication of most of the 8 possible [20] patterns cited above is that they do not allow sufficiently for the intense desire that most women have for a secure arrangement — or at least women have had this intense desire until very recent times. They have had greater difficulty accepting fluid arrangements, especially after they pass the age of 30, than males.

An even bigger complication is that while most of these arrange- [21] ments might seem attractive in terms of providing the companionship so important to male-female partnerships today, they do not come to terms with the second crucial ingredient of modern marriages: a partnership where there is a sound environment for reaching for immortality through the rearing of children. Thus most should be rejected from serious consideration as socially unfeasible — at least for people interested in having children, and we suspect that those who don't will remain a small minority.

MEANINGS AND VALUES

1. If you have also observed that there has been a "considerable increase in imprudent embarkations upon marriage" (par. 1), what probable reasons can you see for this trend?

2. For what other "compelling reasons" (pars. 4–6), if any, do you think people will still be marrying in the coming decade?

3a. Are most of your acquaintances, consciously or not, really after "immortality and personal growth" (par. 6) when they deliberately have children? Explain.
  b. Does either of these really seem to be a valid reason for such an undertaking today? Explain.

4a. Why has it been more difficult for women than for men to accept "fluid arrangements" after the age of 30 (par. 20)?
  b. Do you have any reason, or reasons, to think this situation is changing? If so, what are they?

5a. Can you determine, from the writing itself, the author's attitude toward his subject matter — e.g., does he favor an abandoning of the one-love-forever concept, which has been the long-standing ideal in most Western cultures?

58

b. What effect, if any, does the attitude have on the success of the essay, on its value as a factual report of the way things are now and the way they are likely to be in the future?

EXPOSITORY TECHNIQUES

1a. Which of the customary methods of introducing an exposition does the author employ? (See Guide to Terms: *Introductions.*)
 b. How effectively?

2a. Show, by providing fresh examples, that the "8 possible patterns" (par. 9) are actually *divisions*, categories into which can be *classified* numerous, more specific proposals for future marriage. (The author has done this for us in some of the categories.)
 b. Is it, then, a completely sound classification system, meeting all the requirements mentioned in the introductory discussion on classification?
 c. If so, be prepared to defend your answer. If not, do you think it is sound enough for the author's purpose? Why, or why not?

3a. The author ordinarily avoids overgeneralizations by a cautious use of qualification. (Guide: *Qualification.*) Cite three examples of his use of this precaution.
 b. Find statements, if any, that would benefit from greater qualification.
 c. If any, why do you think they need it?

DICTION AND VOCABULARY

1a. In this essay Packard often presents his own opinions or impressions — almost inevitable in any summary-analysis, however well rooted in facts — but he never uses the word "I." Cite the ways in which he avoids this usage. (As you know, it is common in student writing — e.g., "I think . . . I am sure . . . I think.")
 b. What are the advantages, if any, in eliminating first-person pronouns?
 c. Where especially, in college writing, are they generally considered entirely inappropriate?

2a. Cite an example of simile. (Guide: *Figures of Speech.*)
 b. Cite two good examples of metaphor. (*Note:* The author's use of "3-layer cake," par. 19, is analogy, a pattern considered in a later section of this book.)

3a. If you were trying to sell the concept of "serial mating" throughout your county, by which of the four possible labels mentioned in paragraph 10 would you call it, in order to minimize opposition? (Guide: *Connotation/Denotation.*)
 b. Explain your choice.

4. Consult the dictionary as needed for full understanding of the following words: options (par. 2); autonomous (3); perpetuate (6); liaison (9, 11); monogamy (10); cohabitation (11).

SUGGESTIONS FOR WRITING AND DISCUSSION

1. Considering longer lives and chaotic times (and the opinions of such people as the New York model), is it already too much to expect that a girl really "in love" with a man now will still love the same man fifty years from now? How about his love for her? Explain.

2. What do you consider the chances for survival of the old 'til-death-do-us-part ideal of marriage, even if we go to a "layer cake type of society"? Why?

3. Packard, for the purposes of his essay, puts "moral standards aside." What effects, if any, can moral standards be expected to have on general public acceptance of changed marital structuring? On what grounds have you formed your opinion?

4. Give your own full explanation of the meaning and implications of "reaching for immortality through the rearing of children."

5. We may often read conflicting "preponderant evidence" that broken homes produce, or do not produce, more than their proportion of juvenile crime and/or future psychological and social problems of the children raised in them. What evidence on this question, either way or both, do you find in your own experience or observation?

6. Does it seem to you that many girls and women expect, or want, marriage to be "a haven where they will be looked after by a husband in return for traditional services rendered"? Analyze your observations in terms of overall society.

7. Do many boys or young men of your acquaintance expect or want to provide such a "haven"? Analyze your observations in terms of overall society.

(NOTE: Suggestions for topics requiring development by use of CLASSIFICATION are on page 68, at the end of this section.)

JAMES A. MICHENER

JAMES A. MICHENER, born in 1907 in New York, received numerous degrees from universities in this country and in Europe. He has taught at Colorado State and at Harvard. In 1947 he was awarded the Pulitzer Prize for *Tales of the South Pacific*, published earlier that year. His other well-known books include *Fires of Spring* (1949), *Return to Paradise* (1951), *The Bridges at Tokori* (1953), *Sayonara* (1954), and *Hawaii* (1959).

The Assumptions of the Middle Class

"The Assumptions of the Middle Class" was first published in *America Against America: The Revolution in Middle-Class Values* (1969). In this writing, unlike the preceding essays using classification, it is the author's personal remembrances and interpretations that are divided into categories for closer study, but in the belief that they are representative of their era and therefore of special significance today.

THE ASSAULT WIDENS

From all sides the barrage continues. Thoughtful blacks in the cities do not want their children educated along the old middle-class lines which produced obedient stenographers and shipping clerks. 1

Young draftees simply cannot accept the simplistic postulates of World Wars I and II: "Congress has declared war. It's our duty to fight." 2

Young ministers, truly wrestling with the problems their congregations bring to them, cannot advise their younger members "to follow in the old paths and everything will work out all right." 3

Particularly, younger college professors gag at indoctrinating 4 their students with a vision of happiness through working for I.B.M. or doing research for the Pentagon. Everywhere I look I find so much rebellion against the values that predominated when I was growing up that I have been forced to reevaluate them.

It seems to me that the assumptions upon which I operated as a young man can best be understood if they are summarized within certain categories. What follows is merely one man's recollection of the forces which formed him. Other men my age will recall other experiences and will identify other forces, but in general most lists would include roughly the same components.

THE PURITAN NOOSE

Within the Christian ethic American society has always inclined toward Puritanism. Any local businessman who wanted to get ahead, any political leader who hoped for long life, has had to pay public homage to Puritan morality, and even the more liberal European Catholic Church, when implanted on our shores, found it expedient to advocate a censorship of, say, films, along ridiculously puritanical lines. I suppose that no single strand of middle-class values has been rejected more totally in recent years than this strangling rope of Puritanism which once bound us so strongly, and against which the young have rebelled with such contempt.

We have lived primarily within a Christian ethic, once largely Protestant, of late increasingly Catholic. Our father figures have been austere men like John Knox, John Calvin, Martin Luther, and Thomas Aquinas. To the perceptive young person today these moral leaders, who used to terrify me with their rectitude, seem slightly ridiculous. One evening, when I tried to introduce the matter of religious ethics to a young group, one girl said, "Please! Today the Pope is just as confused as we are."

THE THREE R's

A cornerstone of middle-class life has been reliance upon education. Through it, immigrants were salvaged and the children of the laboring class set free. A conspicuous feature of American life has been the fact that the upper classes have done precious little in this country for the education of anyone but themselves, whereas the middle and laboring classes have striven consistently for a free, widely dispersed education. I myself, a product of that middle-class faith in education, believe it has been the principal differentiator between America and the rest of the world.

Some years ago in Hawaii a barefooted Japanese cleaning woman demonstrated the middle-class attitude toward education. She told me one day as she was sweeping my apartment that she was worried about her two sons and asked if she might talk with me. I assumed that her boys had gotten themselves mixed up with girls or had stolen a car, but her problems were rather different. "First son, senior Harvard Law School. Top ten. When he graduate he can go into big law firm New York. Or into government? Which one?" I said that since he was a Japanese boy trying to make his way in a Caucasian society it might be wise to establish himself first with his peers, then move into government. She agreed. "Second son, freshman M.I.T. Next year they starting accelerated course advanced calculus" — those were her exact words. "In regular calculus he get only B-minus. Should he try new course?" With wages earned by sweeping apartments, she had sent her sons to two of the best universities in America, five thousand miles from Hawaii.

MAKING IT

A central belief of the middle class in which I grew up was that the son of a ditchdigger could become a college president, whereas the careless son of the top family in town could easily make mistakes from which he would not recover. These twin beliefs were not legendary; each year they were illustrated by specific lives in our community, and are still being illustrated. I have lived in a good many countries in the world, and in no other is social mobility so easily attainable, or so dominant a factor in national life. I realize that I am begging the core question of "Mobility to what?" Young people ridicule the legendary middle-class struggle to achieve upward mobility because they see that a man is often no better off "ahead" than he was when he started. For the moment I shall avoid that challenge.

COMPETENCE

At home, in school, and in church I was reared on the stern belief that in the long run competence set the limits as to what a man could become, and this was drummed into my generation where-ever we turned. If you wanted to play third base in the big leagues you had to learn how to handle ground balls smashed toward the bag. If you shied away from stabbing your hand out at the speeding white bullet, you were not going to be a third baseman. You could be something else, but not that. This was true, we were taught, of all professions. If you wanted to be a lawyer, you went to law school. If you wanted to go into business, you mastered arithmetic and the art of quick decision. The penalty for sliding through life without having mastered any competence was a sentence to medi-ocrity.

By no means did we equate competence with formal education.   12 Horse traders, garage mechanics, and trainmen stood high in our value judgments; and I can still remember the approval with which one of my teachers read that admirable passage from Emerson in which he described how much he admired the farm girl who knew how to subdue a fractious calf by letting the animal suck on her finger as if it were a teat. "I admire people who know how to do things," said Emerson, the high priest of middle-class values, and we shared his enthusiasm. To this day I retain a sense of awe in the presence of anyone who knows how to do something.

Hierarchy

I have always felt that in America our middle-class values were   13 strongly rooted in a sense of hierarchy, and the fact that we have eschewed the trappings of royalty has blinded us, I think, to the other fact that we are the most royalist of peoples. I remember when Arnold Bennett unleashed one of his periodic attacks on the British royal family to the great distress of some Englishmen who were at that moment visiting America. They were outraged that Bennett had dared to speak ill of royalty but were consoled by their New Jersey host, who explained, "Never worry about what your English fools like Arnold Bennett say of your royal family. England may go off the gold standard. She may have a Socialist government. But she will never discard or in any way abuse the royal family, because the people of Iowa would not permit it."

I find this principle of hierarchy, or class consciousness if you   14 prefer, strongly ingrained in American life, and much of the pro-test of the young today has been a legitimate rejection of our country-club pretensions. On the other hand, I do feel that our responsible affection for position and order has been a strong factor in accounting for our stability.

RESPONSIBILITY

At the core of middle-class life has stood the doctrine of responsibility. Not only was a man largely responsible for himself and his family, but groups of families were responsible for their community. If I were asked to specify a major difference between life as it is actually lived in the United States and in Japan or Spain, for example, I would stress the fact that in those other countries there is no public tradition of support for art museums, hospital complexes, universities, and a multitude of other public charities, whereas this sense of responsibility has been strong in America. For tragic and historic reasons, we have not up to now been willing to allow this responsibility to operate in certain areas like race relations or the preservation of our cities, but the tradition for the exercise of such responsibility exists and is available for new creative uses. I would judge this commitment to responsibility to be a major characteristic of American middle-class life.

ACCUMULATION

No one should underestimate the powerful urge felt by the middle class toward accumulation, either of money, or property, or the sillier accouterments of success. I judge this to be one of our strongest motivating factors and one most subject to abuse. The tradition began, I suppose, on the frontier, when it was patently better to have 640 acres of cleared land than a quarter of an acre.

I spoke recently with a man who had just bought a comfortably sized insurance business, and even before he had moved into his new office he was planning for a second, a third, and a fourth office in nearby towns. He explained, "Of course I could make a comfortable living from my new office, but only for a few years. In this business you build volume or the major insurance companies take away your franchise. It's impossible to stay little. You grow big or you perish."

If our middle-class mania for accumulation is subject to abuse, it is also subject to ridicule, and many a father who has spent the years from 22 to 52 in a mad race to accumulate now finds himself powerless to answer his children who ask, "Why did you do it, Pop? What good did you get out of it? What have you to show for the rat race except two cars and three picture windows?" These are terrifying questions to throw at a man in his fifties, for they undermine his hitherto unquestioned faith in accumulating.

OPTIMISM

One of the most appealing of the middle-class virtues has been   19
the tendency toward optimism. There has been reason for this, for in spite of wars, depressions, and other setbacks of considerable dimension, the American middle class has been living in an expanding economy, in which social justice has made conspicuous gains. The middle-class response has been a general euphoria. After all, Kaiser Wilhelm and Adolf Hitler were defeated. Communism was more or less contained, and although a stubborn Democratic party did make frequent incursions to power, the Republican party did return at comforting intervals to run things pretty much as we had grown accustomed to seeing them run. It did not seem preposterous for the middle class to cling to its optimism.

Of course, at its most blatant our optimism took the pathetic   20
form demonstrated by George Babbitt of Zenith City and was properly ridiculed. One of the most disastrous cultural influences ever to hit America was Walt Disney's Mickey Mouse, that idiot optimist who each week marched forth in Technicolor against a battalion of cats, invariably humiliating them with one clever trick after another. I suppose the damage done to the American psyche by this foolish mouse will not be specified for another fifty years, but even now I place much of the blame for Vietnam on the bland attitudes sponsored by our cartoons.

When the original version of this essay was published, I received   21
much criticism for this passage on Mickey Mouse. Some vilified me for having spoken ill of one of our nation's folk heroes. Others rebuked me for having taken seriously what was intended merely as a fairy tale, and one that they revered. And a great many asked, "You didn't mean what you said seriously, did you? Wasn't it all a put-on?" I suppose nothing proves more clearly that I did mean what I said than the seriousness of the criticism that overtook me.

I do indeed believe that the narcotic nonsense of these cartoons —   22 and similar daydreams of American life — dull our sensitiveness to real problems. . . .

MEANINGS AND VALUES

1. What *is* the so-called middle class?

2. Today we repeatedly encounter references to "Puritan morality" (par. 6). Just what is it?

3. Examine more fully the author's opinion that "the upper classes" have done precious little for education (par. 8). Do you agree? Why, or why not?

4. Explain more fully how faith in education may be "the principal differentiator between America and the rest of the world" (par. 8).

5a. Do you suppose the people of Iowa really care much about the British royal family (par. 13)? Justify your viewpoint.
 b. If not, what is the value of this example, if any?

6a. What may be one of the "tragic and historic reasons" referred to in paragraph 15?
 b. In what areas other than race relations and city preservation may they apply?

7a. What abuses have resulted from our urge to accumulate (par. 16)?
 b. Among your acquaintances, do you think any sizable proportion of middle-aged men really had an "unquestioned" faith in accumulating until shaken up by the younger generation? Explain.

8. The author implies that the Republican Party has always been the "middle-class" party. Can you recall from your study of history whether this observation is entirely accurate? Explain.

9. Consider carefully the statement (par. 20) that Mickey Mouse was one of the most disastrous cultural influences ever to hit America.
 a. To what extent, if at all, does it function as paradox? Explain. (See Guide to Terms: *Paradox.*)
 b. To what extent does it function as irony of situation? Explain. (Guide: *Irony.*)

10a. Describe what seems to be the author's attitude toward his subject.
 b. How, if at all, does this attitude affect the essay's tone? (Guide: *Style/Tone.*)
 c. His reactions to the deaths of the old assumptions vary considerably. What quality does this variation subtly impart to his tone?

11a. Where would you place this essay on an objective-subjective continuum? (Guide: *Objective/Subjective Writing.*)
 b. If you have read the Nowlis and/or Packard essays, how do the three (or two) compare in this respect?

c. Which degree of objectivity would be preferable for most college term papers?

EXPOSITORY TECHNIQUES

1a. Do the author's "categories" meet all the requirements for a sound system of classification? Explain any exceptions.
  b. Is the system clearly presented, the categories properly differentiated? Explain any exceptions.

2a. Undergraduates are usually discouraged from using subheadings in their college writing, as they may tend to produce choppiness and poor coherence. (Guide: *Coherence.*) Would Michener's essay have been better, or worse, without them?
  b. Explain the reasons for your answer, noting any basic differences between his writing and most college papers.

3a. Are the four examples the author selected for his introduction well chosen for the purpose? Why, or why not?
  b. Is the example of the cleaning woman (par. 9) worth the rather extensive development given it? Justify your answer.
  c. All the categories are illustrated by examples with the exception of "Making It" (par. 10). Would it too have been improved by the use of examples? Why, or why not?
  d. Do you think the rather trivial Emerson example (par. 12) is a good one for its purpose? Why, or why not?

4a. Which, if any, of Michener's statements would have benefited from greater qualification? (Guide: *Qualification.*)
  b. Why?
  c. How might you have done the qualifying?

DICTION AND VOCABULARY

1a. List or mark five figures of speech in this essay. (Guide: *Figures of Speech.*)
  b. Note the specific kind of each, and comment on its effectiveness.
  c. How is the use of such figurative language a matter of style? (Guide: *Style/Tone.*) Use comparison with nonfigurative examples, if necessary, in order to explain how style is affected.

2. Use the dictionary as needed to become familiar with the following words and their meanings: postulates (par. 2); components (5); homage, expedient (6); ethic (6, 7); perceptive, rectitude (7); peers (9); fractious (12); eschewed (13); hierarchy (13, 14); accouterments, patently (16); euphoria, contained, incursions (19); blatant, psyche (20); vilified, revered (21).

SUGGESTIONS FOR WRITING AND DISCUSSION

Explore the meaning and implications (from your generation's and/or your own standpoint) of any one of the following quotations. Then devise your own statement of central theme, modifying or negating as you prefer, and develop it as a thoughtful oral or written composition, as assigned.

1. ". . . a vision of happiness through working for I.B.M. or doing research for the Pentagon" (par. 4).
2. ". . . the strangling rope of Puritanism . . ." (par. 6).
3. ". . . a sentence to mediocrity" (par. 11).
4. ". . . we are the most royalist of peoples" (par. 13).
5. ". . . legitimate rejection of our country-club pretenses" (par. 14).
6. ". . . responsible affection for position and order . . . a strong factor in accounting for our stability" (par. 14).
7. ". . . commitment to responsibility . . ." (par. 15).
8. ". . . the sillier accouterments of success" (par. 16).
9. ". . . blame for Vietnam on the bland attitude sponsored by our cartoons" (par. 20).

WRITING SUGGESTIONS FOR SECTION 2

Classification

Use division and classification (into at least three categories) as your basic method of analyzing one of the following subjects from one point of view. Narrow the topic as necessary to enable you to do a thorough job.

1. College students.	12. Methods of studying for exams.
2. College teachers.	13. Attitudes toward life.
3. Athletes.	14. Lies.
4. Coaches.	15. Selling techniques.
5. Salespeople.	16. Tastes in clothes.
6. Hunters (or fishermen).	17. Television programs.
7. Parents.	18. Sailing vessels.
8. Marijuana users.	19. Horses (or other animals).
9. Policemen.	20. Love.
10. Summer (or part-time) jobs.	21. Immorality.
11. Motivations for study.	22. Contemporary music.

3

Explaining by Means of *Comparison* and *Contrast*

One of the first expository methods we used as children was *comparison,* noticing similarities of objects, qualities, and actions, or *contrast,* noticing their differences. We compared the color of the new puppies with that of their mother, contrasted our father's height with our own. Then the process became more complicated, and we employ it frequently in college essay examinations or term papers when we compare or contrast forms of government, reproductive systems of animals, or ethical philosophies of man. Later, in the business or professional worlds, we may prepare important reports based on comparison and contrast — between kinds of equipment for purchase, the personnel policies of different departments, or precedents in legal matters. Nearly everyone uses the process, though he may not be aware of this, many times a day — in choosing a head of lettuce, in deciding what to wear to school, in selecting a house or a friend or a religion.

In the more formal scholastic and professional uses of comparison and contrast, however, an ordered plan is needed to avoid having a mere list of characteristics or a frustrating jumble of similarities and differences. If the author wants to avoid communication blocks that will prevent his "getting through" to his reader, he will observe a few basic principles of selection and development. These principles apply mostly to comparisons between two subjects only; if three or more are to be considered, the usual method is to compare or contrast them in pairs.

A *logical* comparison or contrast can be made only between subjects of the same general type. (Analogy, a special form of comparison used for another purpose, is discussed in the next section.) For example, contrasting a pine and a maple could be useful or meaningful, but little would be gained, except exercise in sentence construction, by contrasting the pine and the pansy.

Of course, logical but informal comparisons that are merely incidental to the basic structure, and hence follow no special pattern, may be made in any writing. But once committed to a formal full-scale analysis by comparison or contrast, the careful writer ordinarily gives the subjects similar treatment. Points used for one should also be used for the other, and usually in the same order. All pertinent points should be explored — pertinent, that is, to the purpose of the comparison.

The purpose and the complexity of materials will usually indicate their arrangement and use. Sometimes the purpose is merely to point out *what* the likenesses and differences are, sometimes it is to show the *superiority* of one thing over another — or possibly to convince the reader of the superiority, as this is also a technique of argumentation. The purpose may be to explain the *unfamiliar* (wedding customs in Ethiopia) by comparing to the *familiar* (wedding customs in Kansas). Or it may be to explain or emphasize some other type of *central idea,* as in most of the essays in this section.

One of the two basic methods of comparison is to present all the information on the two subjects, one at a time, and to summarize by combining their most important similarities and differences. This method may be desirable if there are few points to compare, or if the individual points are less important than the overall picture they present. Therefore, this procedure might be a satisfactory means of showing the relative difficulty of two college courses, or comparing two viewpoints concerning an automobile accident. (Of course, as in all other matters of expository arrangement, the last subject discussed is in the most emphatic position.)

However, if there are several points of comparison to be considered, or if the points are of individual importance, alternation of the material would be a better arrangement. Hence, in a detailed comparison of Oak Valley and Elm Hill hospitals, we might compare their sizes, locations, surgical facilities, staffs, and so on, always in the same order. To tell all about Oak Valley and then all about Elm Hill would create a serious communication block, requiring the reader constantly to call on his memory of what was cited earlier, or to turn back to the first group of facts again and again in order to make the meaningful comparisons that the author should have made for him.

Often the subject matter or the purpose itself will suggest a more casual treatment, or some combination or variation of the two basic methods. We might present the complete information on the first subject, then summarize it point by point within the complete information on the second. In other circumstances (as in "The Spider and the Wasp" in Section 5), it may be desirable simply to set up the thesis of likeness or difference, and then to explain a *process* that demonstrates this thesis. And, although expository comparisons and contrasts are frequently handled together, it is sometimes best to present all similarities first, then all differences — or vice versa, depending on the emphasis desired.

In any basic use of "comparison" (conveniently, the term is most often used in a general sense to cover both comparison and contrast), the important thing is to have a plan that is selected to suit the purpose and materials and thoughtfully worked out in advance.

W. H. AUDEN

W. H. AUDEN was born in York, England, in 1907 and studied at Oxford University. After he had already earned a wide reputation as a writer of both poetry and prose, Auden emigrated to the United States in 1939 and later became an American citizen. He taught at the University of Michigan, at Smith College, and from 1956 to 1961 at Oxford as professor of poetry. A member of the Academy of Arts and Letters, Auden has also received many other honors and awards, including the Pulitzer Prize in 1948 and the National Medal for Literature in 1967. Among his many books are *Poems* (1930), his first; *For the Time Being* (1944); *Shield of Achilles* (1956); and *About the House* (1965).

The Almighty Dollar

"The Almighty Dollar" is a short essay from Auden's book, *The Dyer's Hand and Other Essays,* published in 1963. It is a clear example of development by use of contrast. Auden has liberally used abstract generalities without including examples, a fact perhaps best explained by the nature of the reader-audience he must have had in mind: perceptive readers, no doubt, imaginative enough to supply accurate examples for themselves and thus comprehend his ideas clearly.

Political and technological developments are rapidly obliterating   1
all cultural differences and it is possible that, in a not remote future, it will be impossible to distinguish human beings living on one area of the earth's surface from those living on any other, but our different pasts have not yet been completely erased and cul-

tural differences are still perceptible. The most striking difference between an American and a European is the difference in their attitudes towards money. Every European knows, as a matter of historical fact, that, in Europe, wealth could only be acquired at the expense of other human beings, either by conquering them or by exploiting their labor in factories. Further, even after the Industrial Revolution began, the number of persons who could rise from poverty to wealth was small; the vast majority took it for granted that they would not be much richer nor poorer than their fathers. In consequence, no European associates wealth with personal merit or poverty with personal failure.

To a European, money means power, the freedom to do as he 2 likes, which also means that, consciously or unconsciously, he says: "I want to have as much money as possible myself and others to have as little money as possible."

In the United States, wealth was also acquired by stealing, but 3 the real exploited victim was not a human being but poor Mother Earth and her creatures who were ruthlessly plundered. It is true that the Indians were expropriated or exterminated, but this was not, as it had always been in Europe, a matter of the conquerer seizing the wealth of the conquered, for the Indian had never realized the potential riches of his country. It is also true that, in the Southern states, men lived on the labor of slaves, but slave labor did not make them fortunes; what made slavery in the South all the more inexcusable was that, in addition to being morally wicked, it didn't even pay off handsomely.

Thanks to the natural resources of the country, every American, 4 until quite recently, could reasonably look forward to making more money than his father, so that, if he made less, the fault must be his; he was either lazy or inefficient. What an American values, therefore, is not the possession of money as such, but his power to make it as a proof of his manhood; once he has proved himself by making it, it has served its function and can be lost or given away. In no society in history have rich men given away so large a part of their fortunes. A poor American feels guilty at being poor, but less guilty than an American *rentier*[1] who had inherited wealth but is doing nothing to increase it; what can the latter do but take to drink and psychoanalysis?

---

[1] A French word meaning "a person of property or of independent means." [Ed.]

In the Fifth Circle on the Mount of Purgatory,[2] I do not think 5 that many Americans will be found among the Avaricious; but I suspect that the Prodigals may be almost an American colony. The great vice of Americans is not materialism but a lack of respect for matter.

MEANINGS AND VALUES

1. Drawing on your knowledge of American economic history, comment on the accuracy of Auden's statement that the "real exploited victim was not a human being" (par. 3).

2. Do you agree that every American can no longer "reasonably look forward to making more money than his father"? Explain.

3. Relative to other benefits of making money, how important to Americans you know is the making of money as a proof of "manhood"? Will your answer differ according to the financial status of the people you know?

4. Which of Auden's statements would you, as a student or young employee, have felt obliged to qualify if you had been writing this essay? Why? (See Guide to Terms: *Qualification*.)

5. Americans are widely accused (even by themselves) of having a disgustingly materialistic society. What specific evidence can you find, if any, that would support Auden's final statement?

6. If you have read Michener's essay in the preceding section, how do you think Auden would answer the questions directed at "Pop" (par. 18)? Why?

EXPOSITORY TECHNIQUES

1. Which sentence indicates that the author will use contrast, not comparison, as his means of development? Explain.

2. He disposes of the European attitude toward money in the first two paragraphs, then discusses the American attitude without interruption.

 a. Would it have been better to use a point-by-point contrast? Why, or why not?

 b. Demonstrate that the points of contrast are, or are not, arranged in

---

[2] An allusion to Dante's *Divine Comedy*, Part Two, "The Purgatorio," in which dead sinners were punished on various ledges ("circles" around the mountain) during their wait for Paradise (at the mountain top). On the fifth ledge were the Hoarders and the Wasters. [Ed.]

the same order in the two sections. What is the advantage of the author's arrangement?

c. Which is given greater emphasis by its position, the European or the American attitude? (Guide: *Emphasis.*) Under what conditions would the opposite arrangement have been more desirable?

3a. Which of the author's sentences most clearly states his central theme?

b. Are all parts of the essay relevant to this theme? (Guide: *Unity.*)

4a. How long is the introduction to this essay?

b. Is it long enough? (Guide: *Introductions.*)

5a. Ordinarily, when contrast or comparison is used, the two contrasted (or compared) units are brought together again in the closing. Explain why you do, or do not, find the closing effective as it is. (Guide: *Closings.*)

b. How, if at all, does it suggest the type of reader-audience Auden probably had in mind?

c. Is it therefore entirely spoiled for other types? Justify your answer.

DICTION AND VOCABULARY

1. Is the use of a foreign word (*rentier*) justified in this context? Why, or why not?

2. Study the author's uses of the following words, consulting the dictionary as needed: ruthlessly, expropriated (par. 3); avaricious, prodigals, materialism (5).

SUGGESTIONS FOR WRITING AND DISCUSSION

1. Select any one of Auden's statements in paragraphs 3 and 4 (or paragraphs 1 and 2, if you have spent much time in Europe), qualify it as you think best, and use it as your central theme. Presupposing a less perceptive audience than did Auden, illustrate your generalization fully by use of examples.

2. Show what effect the increasing industrialization of Europe has had, or will be likely to have, on the Europeans' attitude toward money.

3. If applicable, develop a classification system to explain what you consider the various American attitudes toward making and/or using money.

4. Select one modern way of becoming wealthy (one not depending on exploitation of natural resources) and explain how this may be accomplished even by a person with little capital or special talent, but with abundant desire and energy.

(NOTE: Suggestions for topics requiring development by use of COMPARISON and CONTRAST are on page 93, at the end of this section.)

RUSSELL BAKER, born in Virginia in 1925, is a graduate of Johns Hopkins University and a veteran of World War II. He has spent his career as a newspaperman and columnist on the staffs of the *Baltimore Sun* and the *New York Times*. He lives in Washington. Baker's books are *An American in Washington* (1961), *No Cause for Panic* (1964), and *All Things Considered* (1965).

Hairesy

"Hairesy" was written in 1969 for Baker's "Observer" column in the *New York Times*. This controversial subject, in itself seemingly unimportant and even by then considered trite by many, is used in comparison with historical events long past to suggest a possibly greater social significance than is commonly attributed to it.

Official opposition to the wearing of long hair is not peculiar to our electronic-petroleum society. Alexander the Great, believing that the beard afforded too convenient a handle to the enemy in close combat, ordered his entire army to shave. 1

St. Paul subsequently elevated the argument from the level of military convenience to a question of virtue with his declaration that "Long hair is a shame unto a man," and this philosophical objection is probably the case most frequently made by parents today when trying to persuade their sons to get a haircut. 2

At the end of the eleventh century, the Pope decreed that persons who wore the hair long should be excommunicated while living and not prayed for when dead. In this, he was zealously supported by clerical authorities throughout Europe. 3

In "Extraordinary Popular Delusions and the Madness of Crowds," written by Charles Mackay and published in 1841, we are told that St. Wulstan, Bishop of Worcester, became positively enraged upon sighting a man with long hair.

"He declared against the practice as one highly immoral, criminal and beastly," Mackay writes, suggesting that the bishop had a good deal more in common with twentieth century father figures than one might have supposed, considering that 900 years divide the reverend gentleman and liberated modern man.

Indeed, St. Wulstan seems to have been the prototype for our contemporary police magistrates who are fond of sentencing the young to haircuts for minor infractions of the municipal code.

St. Wulstan, according to Mackay, "continually carried a small knife in his pocket, and whenever anybody offending in this respect knelt before him to receive his blessing, he would whip it out slily, and cut off a handful, and then, throwing it in his face, tell him to cut off the rest, or he would go to Hell."

Our own barberpole magistrates have had little effect in saving the mass of American youth from post-mortem damnation. Fashion is a more compelling force than fear of fire in a remote future. St. Wulstan and his colleagues found it just as hard to withstand in the Middle Ages as parents do today.

Henry I of England appears to have been an exceedingly difficult obstacle to the forces of salvation. He affected long ringlets down the back and shoulders, a style that would now be described as ultra-hippie, and naturally, being a king, carried the court with him despite the harangues of the Archbishop of Canterbury.

A chronicler of the period reports that men, "forgetting their birth, transformed themselves, by the length of their haires [*sic*], into the semblance of womankind," and that when they became bald "they knit about their heads certain rolls and braidings of false hair."

It is curious to see this ancient quarrel between church and fashion being re-enacted in a century distinguished for its indifference to, if not disbelief in, Godliness. Many half-baked sociological conclusions may be leaped at.

Is it too far-fetched, for example, to suggest that the medieval church and the twentieth-century advocates of close barbering — the corporations, government, the military, the police and their magistrates, parents generally — represent similar historical forces?

The medieval church represented an old political order that had 13 worked well for centuries, but which was beginning to break under the new challenge of nationalism. The state, though still an undeveloped and only half-formed idea, was beginning to assert itself against supremacy of the church, and the growth of kingly power could not have left the bishops unaffected.

Perhaps the state — having been perfected in our time into the 14 superstate, in which the individual must yield whenever his individuality conflicts with "the good of society" — has reached the level at which the church stood when the kings began to challenge it.

If so, it is an institution on the defensive. Its officers are not, of 15 course, bishops, but corporation executives, generals, politicians, judges and parents. Can it be that they sense the challenge to the state, as the church once sensed the state's challenge to its own supremacy, in the aggression of their subjects against minor edicts?

But why should hair, such a trivial matter, be the issue on which 16 institutions choose to fight? Perhaps because it is such an utterly trivial matter. The great institution's power is measured at its peak in terms of its ability to invoke compliance in small things, and when its writ no longer runs to the trivial it may sense, quite correctly, that its power is waning.

St. Wulstan applied the shears himself when he had the chance. 17 So do our magistrates. Still the church waned, and the state grew, and the state may also wane. Nine hundred years is a long time, and scissors have never yet stopped history.

MEANINGS AND VALUES

1. Precisely what, in the author's view, is threatening the present "state," much as the state threatened the medieval church?

2a. Who decides what issue the institutions will fight about (par. 16)?
 b. How is such a "decision" reached?

3a. Illustrate the meaning of "irony of situation" by use of paragraph 11, or some part of it. (See Guide to Terms: *Irony*.)
 b. By the use of paragraph 16, or some part of it.

4a. Explain how scissors have become a symbol by the end of this essay. What is symbolized? (Guide: *Symbolism*.)
 b. What kind of symbol is it?

5a. Explain how long hair itself may have been regarded as a symbol in recent years.

b. What kind of symbol?

6a. How reasonable do you consider the author's "half-baked sociological conclusion" (pars. 11–12)?

b. Even if it seems highly logical, why is he entirely correct (metaphorically, of course) to call it "half-baked"?

EXPOSITORY TECHNIQUES

1a. List or mark the comparisons that help build the author's major one.

b. Is their development complete enough to achieve their purpose? If not, explain.

2a. Show the ways in which the author qualifies his major comparison. (Guide: *Qualification*.)

b. What advantages, if any, are gained by this careful qualifying?

3. What additional pattern of exposition could the first half of this selection be used to illustrate? Show how.

4a. What seems to have determined the order of presentation of the historical figures?

b. Why do you think the author chose to develop St. Wulstan more fully than the others?

c. Was this a successful choice? Why, or why not?

5a. Show how the transition into the case of St. Wulstan (who died in 1095 A.D.) was smoothly provided for in paragraph 3. (Guide: *Transition*.)

b. What transitional device, if any, helps to bridge paragraphs 1 and 2? Paragraphs 5 and 6? Paragraphs 7 and 8?

c. Aside from meanings imparted, what useful function does paragraph 11 serve? Explain.

6. Is this essay a better example of concrete or of abstract writing? Why? (Guide: *Concrete/Abstract*.)

7. The central theme of the essay appears very slowly, a practice often dangerous to unity in expository writing. (Guide: *Unity*.)

a. What is the theme?

b. Where did you first recognize its *full* meaning?

c. How much, if any, does this writing suffer because of the delay? Explain.

DICTION AND VOCABULARY

1a. The "state" that began to challenge the medieval church was government, the nationalistic, independent authority of kings. What is the present "state," as the word is used in paragraph 15? How do you know?

 b. What has your generation more commonly called it?

 c. What is the disadvantage, if any, to using such a word as "state" loosely or with shifted meanings within the same writing?

2a. Cite an example of verbal irony in paragraph 8, and justify your selection. (Guide: *Irony.*)

 b. In paragraph 9.

3. Why are the references to Alexander, the Pope, and the saints not "allusions" in the rhetorical sense? (Guide: *Allusion.*)

4. This author's style is noteworthy in part because of his fresh and sometimes colorful selection of words and their arrangement. (Guide: *Diction; Syntax.*)

 a. Cite two examples of word choice and/or combinations (e.g., "barber-pole magistrates") that you think are classifiable as colorful diction.

 b. Cite two complete sentences that demonstrate fresh or colorful syntax.

 c. How, if at all, do these elements of style also help to create a special tone in the writing? (Guide: *Style/Tone.*)

5a. How appropriate is the coined word used as a title?

 b. Would it have been less appropriate, or more so, in a more formal piece? Explain.

6. Study the author's uses of the following words, consulting your dictionary as needed: excommunicated, zealously (par. 3); prototype, infractions (6); post-mortem (8); harangues (9); chronicler (10); nationalism (13); edicts (15); invoke, compliance, writ (16); waning (16, 17).

SUGGESTIONS FOR WRITING AND DISCUSSION

1. How compelling a force is fashion in your generation?

2. For what reasons, other than mere fashion, do today's young men wear their hair long, since it must be less convenient and comfortable than, say, the ill-favored crew cut?

3. Explain the relation, if any in your view, between long hair and the "good of society" (par. 14).

4. Explain, if you prefer, the relation between long hair and "Godliness" (par. 11).

5. Consider your answer to question 5a of "Meanings and Values." What other symbols do you see in the youthful customs of today? Explain how they are symbolic.

(NOTE: Suggestions for topics requiring development by use of COMPARISON and CONTRAST are on page 93, at the end of this section.)

VINE DELORIA, JR., a Standing Rock Sioux born in 1924, is the son of an Episcopalian minister and educator. He attended prep school in the east, joined the Marines, and went on to seminary studies at Iowa State University. (He is no longer a practicing minister.) Deloria is a crusader for the American Indian and an admirer of Black Panthers Carl Foreman and Roy Innes. He is presently at work on his second book on "the idea of tribalism."

Tribalization of the White Man

"Tribalization of the White Man" (editor's title) is an excerpt from Deloria's book *Custer Died for Your Sins*, published in 1969. In this piece the comparison itself is the central theme, and there can be little doubt as to the pattern needed to develop the exposition. The manner in which the development is achieved, however, is worth our attention.

In the corporate structure, formal and informal, Indian tribalism 1 has its greatest parallels and it is through this means that Indians believe that modern society and Indian tribes will finally reach a cultural truce. The corporation forms the closest attempt of the white man to socialize his individualism and become a tribal man. And certainly when one thinks back to what has been written over the last decade about corporate existence, one can see the startling parallels.

The devasting books of Vance Packard and William H. White 2 outlined in detail how the corporation impinges upon individual man in his private life and reorients him toward non-individual goals. In the 1950's no existence was hated by the undergraduate

as much as that of the organization man. The early beatnik and his
a career was nipped in the bud rather than let it develop in the insidious ways of corporate existence.
descendant, the hippie, both abhorred the organization man. Many

But in the corporation, man was offered a tribal existence of 3
security and ease. The corporation provided everything a man might
need if he were to maintain an affluent life over and above that of
non-corporate man and befitting a person of vast educational
achievement. The higher the degree, the more privileges bestowed
upon corporate man. With untold fringe benefits covering all conceivable circumstances which might arise, organization man dwelt
in an economic tribe to which he needed only give his allegiance
and daylight hours. In return he had social and economic security
rarely equalled since the days of feudalism.

Post-war developments of the corporation created the phenom- 4
enon of the merger. As corporations were piled together to form
conglomerates, it became possible for a man to work for a great
many corporations which were enclosed within one monstrous holding corporation so diversified that it rarely knew how far its tentacles
extended.

The corporation became comparable to the great Indian coali- 5
tions such as the Iroquois and the Creek confederacies which
stretched for thousands of square miles and in which a member
was entirely safe and at home. And like the Indian tribes, success
was measured against those outside the corporations, by prestige
and honors. Where eagle feathers measured an Indian's successes,
thickness of carpets measured executive success. Where a war chief
might be given his choice of the loot of a war, the annual bonus
and stock option became a regular means of rewarding the successful executive, home fresh from the competitive wars.

In short, corporate life since the last world war has structured 6
itself along the lines taken a couple of centuries earlier by Indian
tribes as they developed their customs and traditions of social
existence. Totems have been replaced by trade marks, powwows
by conventions, and beads by gray flannels. War songs have been
replaced by advertising slogans. As in the tribe, so in the corporation
the "chief" reigns supreme.

The life of the rugged individualist, beloved hero of Republican 7
hymns, has now disappeared. The little family grocery or drug store,
such as spawned the two chief contestants of the 1968 Presidential

campaign, has now become the outpost, the frontier settlement, of the corporate conglomerate giant. Small businesses have all but vanished over the past two decades as the "chain" has driven them out of existence. Opportunity now exists within the corporate giant as a member of the tribe. The individual seeks fame only in bringing home the honors for his company.

Classifying the corporation as the tribe takes a little reorientation for most Americans because they are so quick to judge by outward appearances. Rarely do they meditate on how something really operates. Instead they want to believe that because something is shiny and appears new, it is new.   8

But in understanding the corporation as a form of tribalism, a number of new paths of understanding are made possible. The life of organization man is not simply one of allegiance to a cold unfeeling machine. Rather it becomes a path by which he can fulfill himself within certain limits. But going outside of the limits is taboo. It negates the existence by which organization man has defined himself and allowed himself to be defined. Just as a Cherokee or Sioux would have never done anything to eliminate himself from the tribe and accepted the limits by which the tribe governed itself, so the organization man must remain within the limits of his corporate existence.   9

The primary purpose of the tribe, then and now, was to ensure as beneficial a life as possible for members of the tribe. The hunting grounds of the tribe had to be defended at all costs. Outside of that, individual freedom ran rampant. Certainly the CDC proposed by CORE, which will cover all aspects of social existence, purports to do the same.   10

It would appear then that we are witnessing the gradual tribalization of the white man as his economic tribes become more and more oriented toward social services for their members. What is now needed is the frank admittance by the white man that he is tribalizing and the acknowledgment that his tribalism will gradually replace government as we now know it, submerging the differentiated society into a number of related economic social units.   11

When executives can admit what they are doing, then it will be possible to form programs around those left out of corporate existence — the poor — and organize them as tribes also, completing the circuit from Pilgrimish individualism to corporate tribalism.   12

Preliminary treaty-making — price fixing — has been declared wrong because it infringed upon non-corporate victims. The government decreed that until these victims became sufficiently strong to embark on corporate warfare, it would protect them. Government thus stands as arbitrator between corporate and non-corporate man, a role previously occupied by the Onondagas in the Iroquois League.

MEANINGS AND VALUES

1. It would be easy to think of numerous examples of "formal" corporate structures, but what are "informal" ones (par. 1)? Supply examples as necessary in order to clarify.

2a. What irony, if any, do you see in the author's theme? (See Guide to Terms: *Irony*.)

b. If it is true that "in the corporate structure Indian tribalism has its greatest parallels" (par. 1), do you see anything ironic in some of the symbols of the antiestablishment hippie culture? If so, explain. (Guide: *Symbolism*.)

3. How, if at all, might we regard the hippie movement itself as a new (though still unstructured) form of tribalism? List any parallels that seem significant.

4. Use the three-point system of evaluation to judge the success of this selection. (Guide: *Evaluation*.)

5. If you have read the Baker essay preceding this one, does Baker's tentative concept of a "waning state" (pars. 16–17) seem more or less feasible than Deloria's contention in paragraph 11 — or are the two basically compatible? (Keep in mind Baker's rather broad application of the word "state.")

EXPOSITORY TECHNIQUES

1 - 4 paragraphs.

1a. The author supports his general comparison with many minor ones, some only implied. List or mark all comparisons. *5 - 7 implicit comp.*

b. Can you determine any pattern in their order of presentation? If so, what is it? *8 main theme*

c. How well do the comparisons substantiate the theme?

2a. Which of the comparisons, if any, are also examples? Of what?

b. Which are themselves illustrated by examples?

3. If this essay has good coherence, what specific factors apparently help to achieve it? (Guide: *Coherence*.) If not, explain why.

states theme in first sentence.

4a. Where, if at all, does the author reach a full declaration of his theme's significance?
  b. Does it seem sufficiently prepared for, to impress the logical reader? Why, or why not?

5a. If you find in this essay any tendency toward overgeneralization, specify where. (Guide: *Qualification.*)
  b. Explain why you think each overgeneralization might be improved by further qualification.

DICTION AND VOCABULARY

1a. Cite five figures of speech that you consider particularly effective. (Guide: *Figures of Speech.*)
  b. Indicate the kind of each.

2a. Which of the author's figures of speech (listed above or not) would you also classify as clichés? Why? (Guide: *Cliché.*)
  b. What is the danger of writing in clichés?
  c. How much, if at all, do these damage the overall effectiveness of this essay?

3. The author indicates (par. 9) that the organization man defines himself within the corporate structure. Explain in your own way the meaning of "defines" in this sense.

4. Use the dictionary as necessary to understand the meanings of the following words: impinges, abhorred, insidious (par. 2); affluent (3); phenomenon, merger (4); conglomerates (4, 7); coalitions (5); purports (10).

SUGGESTIONS FOR WRITING AND DISCUSSION

1. If you have had experience with a corporation, first-hand or vicariously through a friend or relative, support, modify, or negate one of the following statements:
  a. In the corporation, man finds "security and ease" (par. 3).
  b. There "the individual seeks fame only in bringing home the honors for his company" (par. 7).
  c. "The life of organization man is not simply one of allegiance to a cold unfeeling machine" (par. 9).

2. Do you believe that there are no longer ample possibilities for being a "rugged individualist" (par. 7)? Supply as many examples as necessary to support your thesis.

3. What are the penalties when an organization (tribal) man eliminates himself from the tribe (par. 9)? Be specific.

4. Name other ways, outside the corporate structure, that modern man can "define" himself satisfactorily, and select one of these for more detailed explanation. Use examples liberally.

5. Explore the idea that tribalism will replace government as we now know it (par. 11). Briefly explain, if you can, how such a system might be able to provide necessary governmental functions.

6. What do you think is the possibility that the hippie movement may become (or has become) another element in the widening tribalization foreseen by the author? (Further develop, if you like, your answer to question 3 of "Meanings and Values.")

(NOTE: Suggestions for topics requiring development by use of COMPARISON and CONTRAST are on page 93, at the end of this section.)

BRUCE CATTON, born in Michigan in 1899, is a Civil War specialist whose early career included reporting for various newspapers. He was the recipient of both the Pulitzer Prize for historical work and the National Book Award in 1954. He has served as director of information for the United States Department of Commerce and has written many books, including *Mr. Lincoln's Army* (1951), *Glory Road* (1952), *A Stillness at Appomattox* (1953), *The Hallowed Ground* (1956), *America Goes to War* (1958), *The Coming Fury* (1961), *Terrible Swift Sword* (1963), and *Never Call Retreat* (1966). Since 1954 Catton has been editor of *American Heritage.*

Grant and Lee: A Study in Contrasts

"Grant and Lee: A Study in Contrasts" was written as a chapter of *The American Story*, a collection of essays by noted historians. In this study, as in most of his other writing, Catton does more than recount the facts of history: he shows the significance within them. It is a carefully constructed essay, using contrast and comparison as the entire framework for his explanation.

When Ulysses S. Grant and Robert E. Lee met in the parlor of a modest house at Appomattox Court House, Virginia, on April 9, 1865, to work out the terms for the surrender of Lee's Army of Northern Virginia, a great chapter in American life came to a close, and a great new chapter began.

These men were bringing the Civil War to its virtual finish. To be sure, other armies had yet to surrender, and for a few days the fugitive Confederate government would struggle desperately and vainly, trying to find some way to go on living now that its chief

From *The American Story*, edited by Earl Schenk Miers. Copyright © 1956 by Broadcast Music, Inc. Reprinted by permission.

support was gone. But in effect it was all over when Grant and Lee signed the papers. And the little room where they wrote out the terms was the scene of one of the poignant, dramatic contrasts in American history.

They were two strong men, these oddly different generals, and   3
they represented the strengths of two conflicting currents that, through them, had come into final collision.

Back of Robert E. Lee was the notion that the old aristocratic   4
concept might somehow survive and be dominant in American life.

Lee was tidewater Virginia, and in his background were family,   5
culture, and tradition . . . the age of chivalry transplanted to a New World which was making its own legends and its own myths. He embodied a way of life that had come down through the age of knighthood and the English country squire. America was a land that was beginning all over again, dedicated to nothing much more complicated than the rather hazy belief that all men had equal rights and should have an equal chance in the world. In such a land Lee stood for the feeling that it was somehow of advantage to human society to have a pronounced inequality in the social structure. There should be a leisure class, backed by ownership of land; in turn, society itself should be keyed to the land as the chief source of wealth and influence. It would bring forth (according to this ideal) a class of men with a strong sense of obligation to the community; men who lived not to gain advantage for themselves, but to meet the solemn obligations which had been laid on them by the very fact that they were privileged. From them the country would get its leadership; to them it could look for the higher values — of thought, of conduct, of personal deportment — to give it strength and virtue.

Lee embodied the noblest elements of this aristocratic ideal.   6
Through him, the landed nobility justified itself. For four years, the Southern states had fought a desperate war to uphold the ideals for which Lee stood. In the end, it almost seemed as if the Confederacy fought for Lee; as if he himself was the Confederacy . . . the best thing that the way of life for which the Confederacy stood could ever have to offer. He had passed into legend before Appomattox. Thousands of tired, underfed, poorly clothed Confederate soldiers, long since past the simple enthusiasm of the early days of the struggle, somehow considered Lee the symbol of everything for which they had been willing to die. But they could not quite put this feeling into words. If the Lost Cause, sanctified by so much

heroism and so many deaths, had a living justification, its justification was General Lee.

Grant, the son of a tanner on the Western frontier, was everything Lee was not. He had come up the hard way and embodied nothing in particular except the eternal toughness and sinewy fiber of the men who grew up beyond the mountains. He was one of a body of men who owed reverence and obeisance to no one, who were self-reliant to a fault, who cared hardly anything for the past but who had a sharp eye for the future.   7

These frontier men were the precise opposites of the tidewater aristocrats. Back of them, in the great surge that had taken people over the Alleghenies and into the opening Western country, there was a deep, implicit dissatisfaction with a past that had settled into grooves. They stood for democracy, not from any reasoned conclusion about the proper ordering of human society, but simply because they had grown up in the middle of democracy and knew how it worked. Their society might have privileges, but they would be privileges each man had won for himself. Forms and patterns meant nothing. No man was born to anything, except perhaps to a chance to show how far he could rise. Life was competition.   8

Yet along with this feeling had come a deep sense of belonging to a national community. The Westerner who developed a farm, opened a shop, or set up in business as a trader, could hope to prosper only as his own community prospered — and his community ran from the Atlantic to the Pacific and from Canada down to Mexico. If the land was settled, with towns and highways and accessible markets, he could better himself. He saw his fate in terms of the nation's own destiny. As its horizons expanded, so did his. He had, in other words, an acute dollars-and-cents stake in the continued growth and development of his country.   9

And that, perhaps, is where the contrast between Grant and Lee becomes most striking. The Virginia aristocrat, inevitably, saw himself in relation to his own region. He lived in a static society which could endure almost anything except change. Instinctively, his first loyalty would go to the locality in which that society existed. He would fight to the limit of endurance to defend it, because in defending it he was defending everything that gave his own life its deepest meaning.   10

The Westerner, on the other hand, would fight with an equal tenacity for the broader concept of society. He fought so because everything he lived by was tied to growth, expansion, and a con-   11 stantly widening horizon. What he lived by would survive or fall with the nation itself. He could not possibly stand by unmoved in the face of an attempt to destroy the Union. He would combat it with everything he had, because he could only see it as an effort to cut the ground out from under his feet.

So Grant and Lee were in complete contrast, representing two 12 diametrically opposed elements in American life. Grant was the modern man emerging; beyond him, ready to come on the stage, was the great age of steel and machinery, of crowded cities and a restless, burgeoning vitality. Lee might have ridden down from the old age of chivalry, lance in hand, silken banner fluttering over his head. Each man was the perfect champion of his cause, drawing both his strengths and his weaknesses from the people he led.

Yet it was not all contrast, after all. Different as they were — in 13 background, in personality, in underlying aspiration — these two great soldiers had much in common. Under everything else, they were marvelous fighters. Furthermore, their fighting qualities were really very much alike.

Each man had, to begin with, the great virtue of utter tenacity 14 and fidelity. Grant fought his way down the Mississippi Valley in spite of acute personal discouragement and profound military handicaps. Lee hung on in the trenches at Petersburg after hope itself had died. In each man there was an indomitable quality . . . the born fighter's refusal to give up as long as he can still remain on his feet and lift his two fists.

Daring and resourcefulness they had, too; the ability to think 15 faster and move faster than the enemy. These were the qualities which gave Lee the dazzling campaigns of Second Manassas and Chancellorsville and won Vicksburg for Grant.

Lastly, and perhaps greatest of all, there was the ability, at the 16 end, to turn quickly from war to peace once the fighting was over. Out of the way these two men behaved at Appomattox came the possibility of a peace of reconciliation. It was a possibility not wholly realized, in the years to come, but which did, in the end, help the two sections to become one nation again . . . after a war whose bitterness might have seemed to make such a reunion wholly impossible. No part of either man's life became him more than the part he played in their brief meeting in the McLean house at Appomattox. Their behavior there put all succeeding generations of Americans in their debt. Two great Americans, Grant and Lee —

very different, yet under everything very much alike. Their encounter at Appomattox was one of the great moments of American history.

MEANINGS AND VALUES

1a. Clarify the assertions that through Lee "the landed nobility justified itself" and that "if the Lost Cause . . . had a living justification," it was General Lee (par. 6).

 b. Why are these assertions pertinent to the central theme?

2a. Does it seem reasonable that "thousands of tired, underfed, poorly clothed Confederate soldiers" had been willing to fight for the aristocratic system in which they would never have had even a chance to be aristocrats? Why, or why not?

 b. Can you think of more likely reasons why they were willing to fight?

3. Under any circumstances today might such a social structure as the South's be best for a country? Explain.

4a. What countries of the world have recently been so torn by internal war and bitterness that reunion has seemed, or still seems, impossible?

 b. Do you see any basic differences between the trouble in those countries and that in America at the time of the Civil War?

5a. The author calls Lee a symbol (par. 6). Was Grant also a symbol? If so, of what?

 b. How would you classify this kind of symbolism? (See Guide to Terms: *Symbol.*)

EXPOSITORY TECHNIQUES

1. Make an informal list of paragraph numbers from 3 to 16, and note by each whether the paragraph is devoted primarily to Lee, to Grant, or to direct comparison or contrast of the two. This chart will show you Catton's basic pattern of development. (Notice, for instance, how the broad information of paragraphs 4–6 and 7–9 seems almost to "funnel" down through the narrower summaries in 10 and 11 and into paragraph 12, where the converging elements meet and the contrast is made specific.)

2. What new technique of development is started in paragraph 13?

3a. What is gained, or lost, by the use of a single sentence for paragraph 3?

 b. For paragraph 4?

4a. How many paragraphs does the introduction comprise?

 b. How successfully does it fulfill the three basic requirements of a good introduction? (Guide: *Introductions.*)

5. Show how Catton has constructed the beginning of each paragraph so that there is a smooth transition from the one preceding it. (Guide: *Transition.*)

6. The author's conclusion is really only the explanation of one of his integral points — and this method, if not carefully planned, runs the risk of ending too abruptly and leaving the reader unsatisfied. How has Catton avoided this hazard? (Guide: *Closings.*)

7a. What seems to be the author's attitude toward Grant and Lee?
 b. Show how his tone reflects this attitude. (Guide: *Style/Tone.*)

DICTION AND VOCABULARY

1. Why would a use of colloquialisms have been inconsistent with the tone of this writing?

2a. List or mark all metaphors in paragraphs 1, 3, 5, 7–11, 16. (Guide: *Figures of Speech.*)
 b. Comment on their general effectiveness.

3. If you are not already familiar with the following words, study their meanings as given in the dictionary and as used in this essay: virtual, poignant (par. 2); concept (4); sinewy, obeisance (7); implicit (8); tenacity (11); diametrically, burgeoning (12); aspiration (13); fidelity, profound, indomitable (14); succeeding (16).

4. Explain how the word "poignant" aptly describes this contrast of two men (par. 2).

SUGGESTIONS FOR WRITING AND DISCUSSION

1. Find, by minor research, an account of some incident in the life of Grant or Lee which can be used, in suitable essay form, to illustrate one of Catton's points.

2. Select some other dramatic moment in history and show its long-range significance.

3. Select some important moment in your own life and show its long-range significance.

4. Explain how someone you know symbolizes a philosophy or way of life.

WRITING SUGGESTIONS FOR SECTION 3

~~Comparison and Contrast~~

also analogy

Base your central theme on one of the following, and develop your composition primarily by use of comparison and/or contrast. Use examples liberally for clarity and concreteness, chosen always with your purpose and reader-audience in mind.

Home life + dorm life

Public vs. private schools

1. The working conditions of two jobs.
2. Two kinds of home life.
3. The sea at two different times.
4. Two ways to quit smoking.
5. Two modes of travel.
6. The innate qualifications needed for success in two careers.
7. The natural temperaments of two acquaintances.
8. Two types of protesters.
9. Two styles in protest demonstrations.
10. Two restaurants.
11. Two poets.
12. Two policemen.
13. The teaching techniques of two instructors or former teachers.
14. Two methods of parental handling of teenage problems.
15. Two family attitudes toward the practice of religion.
16. Two "moods" of the same town at different times.
17. The personalities (or atmospheres) of two cities or towns of similar size.
18. Two acquaintances who exemplify different ways of serving humanity.
19. Two acquaintances who seem to symbolize different philosophies of life.
20. Two different attitudes toward the same thing or activity: one "practical," the other romantic or aesthetic.
21. The beliefs and practices of two religions or denominations concerning *one* aspect of religion.

22. Two courses on the same subject: one in high school and one in college.

23. The differing styles of two players of some sport or game.

24. *One* aspect of city life and of life on a farm, in a small town, or in a suburb.

25. *One* aspect of military life and of civilian life.

26. The hazards of frontier life and those of today.

4

Using *Analogy* as an Expository Device

Analogy is a special form of comparison that is used for a specific purpose: to explain something abstract or difficult to understand by showing its similarity to something concrete or easy to understand. A much less commonly used technique than logical comparison (and contrast), analogy is, nonetheless, a highly efficient means of explaining some difficult concepts or of giving added force to the explanations.

Logical comparison is made between two members of the same general class, usually assuming the same kind of interest in the subject matter of both. But in analogy we are really concerned only with the subject matter of one, using a second just to help explain the first. The two subjects, quite incomparable in most respects, are never of the same general class; if they are, we then have logical comparison, not analogy.

If the analogy is to be effective, the writer should be able to assume that his reader is familiar enough with the easier subject, or can quickly be made so, that it really helps explain the more difficult one. A common example is the explanation of the human circulatory system, which we may have trouble comprehending, by comparing the heart and arteries with a pump forcing water through the pipes of a plumbing system. This analogy has been carried further to liken the effect of cholesterol deposits on the inner walls of the arteries to mineral deposits that accumulate inside water pipes and eventually close them entirely. Although there is little logical similarity between a steel pipe and a human artery, the *analogical* similarity would be apparent to most readers — but the analogy might cause even greater confusion for any who did not know about pumps.

Distinguishing between analogy and metaphor is sometimes difficult. The difference is basically in their purpose: the function of a metaphor is merely *to describe*, to create a brief, vivid image for the reader; the function of analogy is primarily one of exposition, *to explain*, rather than to describe. In this sense, however, the function of a metaphor is actually *to suggest* an analogy: instead of showing the similarities of the heart and the pump, a metaphor might simply refer to "that faithful pump inside my chest," implying enough of a comparison to serve its purpose as description. (We can see here why some people refer to analogy as "extended" metaphor.) The analogist, when trying to explain the wide selection of college subjects and the need for balance in a course of study, could use the easily understood principle of a cafeteria, which serves Jell-O and lemon meringue pie, as well as meat and potatoes. If his purpose had been only to create an image, to describe, he might have referred simply to the bewildering variety in "the cafeteria of college courses" — and that would have been a metaphor. (For another example of analogy, see the explanation of *Unity*, in Guide to Terms.)

As useful as analogy can be in exposition, however, it is a risky technique to use in logical argument. It should never be offered anywhere as *proof*. The two subjects of any analogy, although similar in one or more useful ways, are basically too unlike to form any kind of dependable evidence.

LOREN C. EISELEY

LOREN C. EISELEY, born in Nebraska in 1907, is Benjamin Franklin Professor of Anthropology and the History of Science at the University of Pennsylvania, where he also served as Provost from 1959 to 1961. He is a Guggenheim Foundation Fellow and has been in charge of anthropological expeditions for various universities and for the Smithsonian Institution. Eiseley is also a respected naturalist and conservationist; he has served on many public service boards and commissions and has been awarded many honorary degrees and medals. Widely published in both scholarly and popular magazines, Eiseley has also written several books, including *The Immense Journey* (1957), *Darwin's Century* (1959), *The Firmament of Time* (1960), *The Mind as Nature* and *Francis Bacon and the Modern Dilemma* (1962), *The Unexpected Universe* (1969), and *The Night Country* (1971).

The World Eaters

"The World Eaters," as used here, is the first portion of a chapter by that title in Eiseley's book *The Invisible Pyramid*, published in 1970. It is somewhat representative of Eiseley's famous literary style, which is poetic, faintly wistful, and suggestive of the beautiful but often stark or unfathomable mysteries of which he so frequently writes. The simple analogy established in this excerpt, which appears early in Eiseley's book, is referred to frequently in his subsequent chapters, and terms such as "spore bearers," significant only in relation to the analogy, are used throughout as synonyms for "mankind."

It came to me in the night, in the midst of a bad dream, that perhaps man, like the blight descending on a fruit, is by nature a para- 1

Reprinted by permission of Charles Scribner's Sons from *The Invisible Pyramid*, pages 53–54, by Loren C. Eiseley. Copyright © 1970 by Loren Eiseley.

site, a spore bearer, a world eater. The slime molds are the only creatures on the planet that share the ways of man from his individual pioneer phase to his final immersion in great cities. Under the microscope one can see the mold amoebas streaming to their meeting places, and no one would call them human. Nevertheless, magnified many thousand times and observed from the air, their habits would appear close to our own. This is because, when their microscopic frontier is gone, as it quickly is, the single amoeboid frontiersmen swarm into concentrated aggregations. At the last they thrust up overtoppling spore palaces, like city skyscrapers. The rupture of these vesicles may disseminate the living spores as far away proportionately as man's journey to the moon.

It is conceivable that in principle man's motor throughways resemble the slime trails along which are drawn the gathering mucors that erect the spore palaces, that man's cities are only the ephemeral moment of his spawning — that he must descend upon the orchard of far worlds or die. Human beings are a strange variant in nature and a very recent one. Perhaps man has evolved as a creature whose centrifugal tendencies are intended to drive it as a blight is lifted and driven outward across the night. 2

I do not believe . . . that this necessity is written in the genes of men, but it would be foolish not to consider the possibility, for man as an interplanetary spore bearer may be only at the first moment of maturation. After all, *Mucoroides* and its relatives must once have performed their act of dissemination for the very first time. In man, even if the feat is cultural, it is still possible that some incalculable and ancient urge lies hidden beneath the seeming rationality of institutionalized science. For example, a young space engineer once passionately exclaimed to me, "We must give all we have. . . ." It was as though he were hypnotically compelled by that obscure chemical, acrasin, that draws the slime molds to their destiny. And is it not true also that observers like myself are occasionally bitterly castigated for daring to examine the motivation of our efforts toward space? In the intellectual climate of today one should strive to remember the words that Herman Melville accorded his proud, fate-confronting Captain Ahab, "All my means are sane, my motive and my object mad." 3

The cycles of parasites are often diabolically ingenious. It is to the unwilling host that their ends appear mad. Has earth hosted a new disease — that of the world eaters? Then inevitably the spores must fly. Short-lived as they are, they must fly. Somewhere far out- 4 ward in the dark, instinct may intuitively inform them, lies the garden of the worlds. We must consider the possibility that we do not know the real nature of our kind. Perhaps *Homo sapiens*, the wise, is himself only a mechanism in a parasitic cycle, an instrument for the transference, ultimately, of a more invulnerable and heartless version of himself.

Or, again, the dark may bring him wisdom.   5

I stand in doubt as my forebears must once have done at the edge   6
of the shrinking forest. I am a man of the rocket century; my knowl-
edge, such as it is, concerns our past, our dubious present, and our possible future. I doubt our motives, but I grant us the benefit of the doubt and, like Arthur Clarke, call it, for want of a better term, "childhood's end." I also know, as did Plato, that one who has spent his life in the shadow of great wars may, like a captive, blink and be momentarily blinded when released into the light.

MEANINGS AND VALUES

1a. Explain more fully, and in your own words, the author's reference to man's cities as "only the ephemeral moment of his spawning" (par. 2).
  b. How does this contradict the more common view of our "advanced" civilization?
2. In what sense might it be that we would "die" unless we could descend on the "orchard of far worlds" (par. 2)?
3. Why do you suppose the author considered the rather innocent sounding declaration of the space engineer (par. 3) to be significant enough to warrant using as an example?
4. On what grounds are observers like Eiseley occasionally "castigated" for questioning the motivations of our space efforts (par. 3)?
5. Is there any reason to assume that an "ultimate" version of man would be more "heartless" than the present one (par. 4)? Why, or why not?
6. If you have read the Catton essay in Section 3, which of the two generals more nearly represented forces and attitudes that were fore-runners of today's space explorations? Explain.

EXPOSITORY TECHNIQUES

1a. After reading Eiseley's first sentence, we naturally make several assumptions (perhaps unconsciously) about this essay. Based on impressions from this sentence, how would you describe the probable tone of the coming writing? (See Guide to Terms: *Style/Tone*.)

    b. Would you assume that the writing will be mainly objective or subjective? (Guide: *Objective/Subjective*.)

    c. What will the central theme probably be? (Guide: *Unity*.)

    d. What will be the basic pattern of development?

    e. In which, if any, of these respects is the development itself not consistent with the introductory sentence?

2a. On what basis, if at all, can the choice of this analogy (to help explain an abstract concept) be justified, inasmuch as most readers probably know little about *Mucoroides?*

    b. Why is this not a logical comparison?

    c. The author sees three similarities between spore bearers and man. Where does he first compactly and clearly state them.

3a. List or mark each instance of qualification in this selection. (Guide: *Qualification*.)

    b. Has the author overdone his qualifying? Why, or why not?

4. Which, if any, of the common means of achieving emphasis has the author employed? (Guide: *Emphasis*.)

5. Why do you, or do you not, consider the quotation from Captain Ahab fitting and worthwhile (par. 3)?

DICTION AND VOCABULARY

1a. In what sense could man's eruption into space be "cultural" (par. 3)?

    b. What is the implication of the word combination, "seeming rationality" (par. 3)?

    c. Why does the author preface "science" (par. 3) with "institutionalized"?

2a. How, if at all, is the author justified in using terms so scientific that even the educated reader may very well never have heard of them — e.g., mucors, *Mucoroides*, acrasin?

    b. Did they bother you — that is, did they create a serious barrier between you and the author's ideas? Why, or why not?

3. Judging by the diction of this writing, what types of reader-audience do you think the author was writing for? Or, if you prefer, what types of readers did he *not* expect to appeal to? Why?

4. If the meanings of any of the following words are not clear, consult your dictionary: immersion, amoebas, aggregations, ~~vesicles~~ (par. 1); disseminate (1, 2); ephemeral, variant, centrifugal (2); maturation, castigated (3); diabolically (4).

SUGGESTIONS FOR WRITING AND DISCUSSION

1. Explain fully the theory of human beings as a "strange variant in nature" (par. 2).

2. If Eiseley's bad dream or some aspect of it should be true, what, if anything, ought we to be doing about it? Or, if you prefer, what is the likelihood that man is only an instrument of transference to a different kind of being?

3. What influences in outer space could conceivably bring about ultimate dramatic changes in man's genetic make-up?

4. If anything in your religious tenets, or your former ones, is opposed to interplanetary probing, explain it and the reasons for it.

5. Why, really, do we spend so much money and effort to reach the moon and to explore it?

(NOTE: Suggestions for topics requiring development by use of ANALOGY are on page 123, at the end of this section.)

A. DELAFIELD SMITH

A. DELAFIELD SMITH, a native New Yorker born in 1893, was graduated from Princeton University and Harvard Law School, receiving his LL.B. degree in 1916. With the exception of a year in the American Expeditionary Forces during World War I, Smith practiced law in New York City until 1937. Since that time his career has been devoted primarily to duties as attorney for the United States Social Security Board and as assistant general counsel of the Federal Security Agency and of the Department of Health, Education and Welfare. A prolific writer, his work has been published most often in professional journals.

Law as the Means to Freedom

"Law as the Means to Freedom" is from Smith's book *The Right to Live* (1955). His theme is simple and no doubt instantly clear to some readers; but others have always thought of law as a necessary evil, a *restriction* of freedom designed solely for security, and for these readers the author needs to provide some clear explanation of his thesis. He has chosen to use the analogy of game-playing, leaving it general enough, however, so that each reader can mentally supply whatever game he knows best, be it football, dominoes, or something in between.

We need to see what the true meaning and function of law is, not 1 in terms of authority, which is so commonly mistaken for law, but in terms of the rule of law in the ideal sense as a guide and challenge to the human will.

The best example of how law, in the ideal sense, works, how it 2 evokes the sense of freedom and stimulates the individual is the

From *The Right to Live*, by A. Delafield Smith. Reprinted by permission of the publisher, University of North Carolina Press.

survey of a game. Have you ever asked yourself why the participation in a game is so excellent a medium for self-expression and character development? This question is often superficially answered in terms of the rein given to the competitive instincts of the individual and his "zest" for conquest. But have you ever considered that here, in a game, and perhaps here alone, we human beings really do act almost completely under the aegis of law? That, rather than competition, is the real source of the game's restorative value for the human spirit. Analyze the process step by step and you must be convinced that this is the truth.

Your first step upon entering a game is the assumption of a distinct personality. You become clothed in a personality defined by the rules of the game. You assume a legal or game personality. You may describe yourself as a first baseman, as a right guard, or as a dealer. But however you describe yourself you will see that what you have described is a legal status — one of the focal points in a legal pattern with rights and obligations suitable to the position. These rights and duties are defined by the rules under whose empery you have thus put both yourself and all others with whom you have dealings. Your status, your rights, your obligations, all are secure, for the rules of the game are almost sure to be followed. The game indeed is defined by its rules. These are purely abstract. They are wholly free of will and dictation. They are pure rules of action composed usually in some physical setting which they serve to interpret and fashion till it becomes an arena of human action, just as, for example, the rules of the highway, in relation to the highway pattern itself, provide individuals with an arena on which they can operate successfully. Now the rules of the game have many functions. They, in fact, define the very goals that the players seek. One wins only in the context of the rules of the game. They determine inexorably the consequences of the player's action, every play that he makes. He acts solely in relation to the rules. Their empery is accepted like a fact or a circumstance. Finally, they challenge and stimulate him for he uses the rules to win. The game is otherwise unmanaged. An umpire or a referee is but an interpreter of the rules. He *can* be wrong. Such is the conception. This, then, may furnish an introduction to the real function of law in society.

Law gave birth to the concept of freedom. True it is that you can have no security in a siuation in which every person and everything around you acts capriciously, unpredictably, or, in other words, lawlessly; but the point I wish to make is that while you would have no security in such an environment, it is more significant that you would have no freedom in such an environment. The reason you could not be free in such a situation is that you could not get anywhere you wanted to go or successfully do anything you wanted to do. You could make no plan in the expectation of carrying it out. You cannot possibly carry out any aim or goal of your own unless you have some basis for calculating what results may follow from any given act or activity of your own. Unless you can determine in advance what are the prospects and limitations of a given course of behavior, you cannot act intelligently. Whatever intelligence you may have will do you no good. You cannot adjust your own step to anyone else's step nor can you relate your conduct to any series of events or occurrences outside yourself except to the extent that they follow a pattern that you can learn about in advance of your action.

The only way to promote freedom is to devise a set of rules and   5 thus construct a pattern which the various members of that society can follow. Each can then determine his own acts in the light of his knowledge of the rules. On this basis each can predict his field of action in advance and what results are likely to ensue from his acts; and so he gains freedom to plan and to carry out his plans. The more you attempt to administer society, however, the less free it becomes. There is opportunity for freedom of choice only in acting subject to the rules, and then only if the rules are freed of any element of will or dictation. If these rules are just rules that tell you what method or act will yield what results, like the rules of a game, you can then freely determine your own play. You can use the rules to win the game. The more abstract and objective the rule, the freer is the individual in the choice of his alternatives. The rules must be so written as to cover every possible eventuality of choice and action.

MEANINGS AND VALUES

1. How, if at all, could the theme of this essay be regarded as a paradox? (See Guide to Terms: *Paradox.*)

2a. Clarify the author's statement (par. 3) that the rules of a game "are purely abstract." (Guide: *Concrete/Abstract.*)

  b. In paragraph 5 he makes the point that laws, too, should be abstract and "objective." Show how these two conditions are entirely consistent with each other. (Guide: *Objective/Subjective.*)

3. Why do you think Smith considers the lack of security resulting from lawlessness to be less significant than the parallel lack of freedom (par. 4)?

4. The author says that you can use laws to "win the game" (par. 5). Explain what this means to you.

5. Do you find any contradiction between the essay's last sentence and the statement that "the more you attempt to administer society, the less free it becomes" (par. 5)? Show either their consistency or lack of it.

EXPOSITORY TECHNIQUES

1a. List or mark all the specific points of similarity between Smith's analogy and the concepts it analogizes.

  b. What, if anything, does the extent of this list suggest about the choice of analogy? Explain.

2a. What are the important differences between the analogy and what it helps to explain?

  b. How, if at all, do these differences prevent Smith's process from being classifiable as a logical comparison?

3. Explain why this comparison cannot properly be called a metaphor or simile. (Guide: *Figures of Speech.*)

4. How is smooth transition achieved between paragraphs 1 and 2? Between 2 and 3? Between 3 and 4? (Guide: *Transition.*)

5. In this short writing the author uses many abstract generalizations, rarely making any effort to give them concrete form.

  a. What does this fact suggest about the nature of the reader-audience he was writing for?

  b. Why would this method be unsatisfactory for a different type of audience? Be specific.

  c. Choose three of Smith's abstract statements and show how they could be made concrete for a different type of reader.

DICTION AND VOCABULARY

1. If you are not sure of the meanings of any of the following words, use the dictionary: evokes, aegis (par. 2); empery, inexorably (3); capriciously (4); ensue (5).

SUGGESTIONS FOR WRITING AND DISCUSSION

1. Choose one game with which you are most familiar and use it to demonstrate the "restorative value for the human spirit" because of the players' acting "under the aegis of law" (par. 2).

2. Using examples, show specifically, in terms of Smith's theories, why the laws of dictatorships cannot produce the kind of freedom described.

3. Select one of the following apparent restraints of freedom and, by using examples and by referring to Smith's analogy, explain concretely how the "restraint" actually contributes to freedom.
   a. Required attendance at school.
   b. A category of traffic laws.
   c. Requirement of emission-control devices on automobiles.
   d. Pet-control ordinances.
   e. Construction codes.
   f. Zoning restrictions.
   g. "Open housing" laws.
   h. Restrictions on use of city parks for protest demonstrations.
   i. Restrictions on use of state parks for rock festivals.

4. Use one of the following abstract statements of Smith's as your central theme and provide examples to develop it clearly for some specified audience.
   a. "However you describe yourself [in a game] . . . what you have described is a legal status — one of the focal points in a legal pattern with rights and obligations suitable to the position" (par. 3).
   b. "These [rules of a game] are purely abstract. They are wholly free of will and dictation" (par. 3).
   c. "You cannot possibly carry out any aim or goal of your own unless you have some basis for calculating what results may follow from any given act or activity of your own" (par. 4).
   d. "The more you attempt to administer society . . . the less free it becomes" (par. 5).
   e. "The more abstract and objective the rule, the freer is the individual in the choice of his alternatives" (par. 5).

(NOTE: Suggestions for topics requiring development by use of ANALOGY are on page 123, at the end of this section.)

MARTIN LUTHER KING, JR.

MARTIN LUTHER KING, JR. (1929–1968) was a Baptist clergyman, the president of the Southern Christian Leadership Conference, and a respected leader in the nationwide movement toward equal rights for Negroes. He was born in Atlanta, Georgia, and earned degrees from Morehouse College (A.B., 1948), Crozer Theological Seminary (B.D., 1951), Boston University (Ph.D., 1955), and Chicago Theological Seminary (D.D., 1957). He held honorary degrees from numerous other colleges and universities and was awarded the Nobel Peace Prize in 1964. Some of his books are *Why We Can't Wait* (1964), *Stride Toward Freedom* (1958), and *Strength to Love* (1963). King was assassinated April 4, 1968, in Memphis, Tennessee.

The World House

"The World House" is from King's book *Where Do We Go from Here: Chaos or Community?*, published in 1967. His theme, the absolute necessity for international understanding and cooperation throughout the world, is recognized by most people today but ignored by them as much as possible, perhaps because it seems to present such insoluble problems. We can assume, therefore, that King uses analogy more for emphasis than for primary explanation. It serves his purpose well.

Some years ago a famous novelist died. Among his papers was 1 found a list of suggested plots for future stories, the most prominently underscored being this one: "A widely separated family inherits a house in which they have to live together." This is the great new problem of mankind. We have inherited a large house, a great "world house" in which we have to live together — black and white, Easterner and Westerner, Gentile and Jew, Catholic and Protestant, Moslem and Hindu — a family unduly separated in ideas, culture and interest, who, because we can never again live apart, must learn somehow to live with each other in peace.

However deeply American Negroes are caught in the struggle to   2
be at last at home in our homeland of the United States, we cannot ignore the larger world house in which we are also dwellers. Equality with whites will not solve the problems of either whites or Negroes if it means equality in a world society stricken by poverty and in a universe doomed to extinction by war.

All inhabitants of the globe are now neighbors. This world-wide   3
neighborhood has been brought into being largely as a result of the modern scientific and technological revolutions. The world of today is vastly different from the world of just one hundred years ago. A century ago Thomas Edison had not yet invented the incandescent lamp to bring light to many dark places of the earth. The Wright brothers had not yet invented that fascinating mechanical bird that would spread its gigantic wings across the skies and soon dwarf distance and place time in the service of man. Einstein had not yet challenged an axiom and the theory of relatively had not yet been posited.

Human beings, searching a century ago as now for better under-   4
standing, had no television, no radios, no telephones and no motion pictures through which to communicate. Medical science had not yet discovered the wonder drugs to end many dread plagues and diseases. One hundred years ago military men had not yet developed the terrifying weapons of warfare that we know today — not the bomber, an airborne fortress raining down death; nor napalm, that burner of all things and flesh in its path. A century ago there were no skyscraping buildings to kiss the stars and no gargantuan bridges to span the waters. Science had not yet peered into the unfathomable ranges of interstellar space, nor had it penetrated oceanic depths. All these new inventions, these new ideas, these sometimes fascinating and sometimes frightening developments came later. Most of them have come within the past sixty years, sometimes with agonizing slowness, more characteristically with bewildering speed, but always with enormous significance for our future.

The years ahead will see a continuation of the same dramatic   5 developments. Physical science will carve new highways through the stratosphere. In a few years astronauts and cosmonauts will probably walk comfortably across the uncertain pathways of the moon. In two or three years it will be possible, because of the new supersonic jets, to fly from New York to London in two and one-half hours. In the years ahead medical science will greatly prolong the lives of men by finding a cure for cancer and deadly heart ailments. Automation and cybernation will make it possible for working people to have undreamed-of amounts of leisure time. All this is a dazzling picture of the furniture, the workshop, the spacious rooms, the new decorations and the architectural pattern of the large world house in which we are living.

Along with the scientific and technological revolution, we have   6
also witnessed a world-wide freedom revolution over the last few decades. The present upsurge of the Negro people of the United States grows out of a deep and passionate determination to make freedom and equality a reality "here" and "now.' In one sense the civil rights movement in the United States is a special American phenomenon which must be understood in the light of American history and dealt with in terms of the American situation. But on another and more important level, what is happening in the United States today is a significant part of a world development.

We live in a day, said the philosopher Alfred North Whitehead,   7
"when civilization is shifting its basic outlook; a major turning point in history where the pre-suppositions on which society is structured are being analyzed, sharply challenged, and profoundly changed." What we are seeing now is a freedom explosion, the realization of "an idea whose time has come," to use Victor Hugo's phrase. The deep rumbling of discontent that we hear today is the thunder of disinherited masses, rising from dungeons of oppression to the bright hills of freedom. In one majestic chorus the rising masses are singing, in the words of our freedom song, "Ain't gonna let nobody turn us around." All over the world like a fever, freedom is spreading in the widest liberation movement in history. The great masses of people are determined to end the exploitation of their races and lands. They are awake and moving toward their goal like a tidal wave. You can hear them rumbling in every village street, on the docks, in the houses, among the students, in the churches and at political meetings. For several centuries the direction of history flowed from the nations and societies of Western Europe out into

the rest of the world in "conquests" of various sorts. That period, the era of colonialism, is at an end. East is moving West. The earth is being redistributed. Yes, we are "shifting our basic outlooks."

These developments should not surprise any student of history. Oppressed people cannot remain oppressed forever. The yearning for freedom eventually manifests itself. The Bible tells the thrilling story of how Moses stood in Pharaoh's court centuries ago and cried, "Let my people go." This was an opening chapter in a continuing story. The present struggle in the United States is a later chapter in the same story. Something within has reminded the Negro of his birthright of freedom, and something without has reminded him that it can be gained. Consciously or unconsciously, he has been caught up by the spirit of the times, and with his black brothers of Africa and his brown and yellow brothers in Asia, South America and the Caribbean, the United States Negro is moving with a sense of great urgency toward the promised land of racial justice.

Nothing could be more tragic than for men to live in these revolutionary times and fail to achieve the new attitudes and the new mental outlooks that the new situation demands. In Washington Irving's familiar story of Rip Van Winkle, the one thing that we usually remember is that Rip slept twenty years. There is another important point, however, that is almost always overlooked. It was the sign on the inn in the little town on the Hudson from which Rip departed and scaled the mountain for his long sleep. When he went up, the sign had a picture of King George III of England. When he came down, twenty years later, the sign had a picture of George Washington. As he looked at the picture of the first President of the United States, Rip was confused, flustered and lost. He knew not who Washington was. The most striking thing about this story is not that Rip slept twenty years, but that he slept through a revolution that would alter the course of human history.

One of the great liabilities of history is that all too many people fail to remain awake through great periods of social change. Every society has its protectors of the status quo and its fraternities of the indifferent who are notorious for sleeping through revolutions. But today our very survival depends on our ability to stay awake, to adjust to new ideas, to remain vigilant and to face the challenge of change. The large house in which we live demands that we transform this world-wide neighborhood into a world-wide brotherhood.

Together we must learn to live as brothers or together we will be forced to perish as fools.

We must work passionately and indefatigably to bridge the gulf 11 between our scientific progress and our moral progress. One of the great problems of mankind is that we suffer from a poverty of the spirit which stands in glaring contrast to our scientific and technological abundance. The richer we have become materially, the poorer we have become morally and spiritually.

Every man lives in two realms, the internal and the external. The 12 internal is that realm of spiritual ends expressed in art, literature, morals and religion. The external is that complex of devices, techniques, mechanisms and instrumentalities by means of which we live. Our problem today is that we have allowed the internal to become lost in the external. We have allowed the means by which we live to outdistance the ends for which we live. So much of modern life can be summarized in that suggestive phrase of Thoreau: "Improved means to an unimproved end." This is the serious predicament, the deep and haunting problem, confronting modern man. Enlarged material powers spell enlarged peril if there is not proportionate growth of the soul. When the external of man's nature subjugates the internal, dark storm clouds begin to form.

Western civilization is particularly vulnerable at this moment, for 13 our material abundance has brought us neither peace of mind nor serenity of spirit. An Asian writer has portrayed our dilemma in candid terms:

> You call your thousand material devices "labor-saving machinery," yet you are forever "busy." With the multiplying of your machinery you grow increasingly fatigued, anxious, nervous, dissatisfied. Whatever you have, you want more; and wherever you are you want to go somewhere else . . . your devices are neither time-saving nor soul-saving machinery. They are so many sharp spurs which urge you on to invent more machinery and to do more business.[1]

This tells us something about our civilization that cannot be cast aside as a prejudiced charge by an Eastern thinker who is jealous of Western prosperity. We cannot escape the indictment.

This does not mean that we must turn back the clock of scientific 14 progress. No one can overlook the wonders that science has wrought

[1] Abraham Mitrie Rihbany, *Wise Men from the East and from the West*, Houghton Mifflin, 1922.

for our lives. The automobile will not abdicate in favor of the horse and buggy, or the train in favor of the stagecoach, or the tractor in favor of the hand plow, or the scientific method in favor of ignorance and superstition. But our moral and spiritual "lag" must be redeemed. When scientific power outruns moral power, we end up with guided missiles and misguided men. When we foolishly minimize the internal of our lives and maximize the external, we sign the warrant for our own day of doom.

Our hope for creative living in this world house that we have inherited lies in our ability to re-establish the moral ends of our lives in personal character and social justice. Without this spiritual and moral reawakening we shall destroy ourselves in the misuse of our own instruments.   15

MEANINGS AND VALUES

1a. What are the "pre-suppositions" on which society has been structured (par. 7)?
  b. What were the "various sorts" of "conquests" which came out of Western Europe (par. 7)?

2. Does it seem to you that the author overgeneralizes in his apparent assumption (pars. 7, 8) that all the world's "rumbling of discontent" is directed toward Western "oppression" of those who are not white? Explain.

3. List at least five of the intervening "chapters" (between the first and the present chapters) of the "continuing story" discussed in paragraph 8.

4. How do you explain the author's reference to "an unimproved end" (par. 12), in view of the many billions of dollars Americans have deliberately taxed themselves during recent years, in order to aid underdeveloped countries all over the world?

5a. Judging from what you see and read, do you agree with Rihbany (par. 13) that Americans are "increasingly fatigued, anxious, nervous, dissatisfied"?
  b. Illustrate the meaning of "irony" by using this quotation. (See Guide to Terms: *Irony*.)

6. If you have read "The Almighty Dollar" (Section 3), show the relation between Auden's central idea and the last sentence of the Rihbany quotation (par. 13).

7. Use the three-point system of evaluation to measure the success of "The World House." (Guide: *Evaluation*.)

EXPOSITORY TECHNIQUES

1a. Is King's primary analogy well chosen for the job it has to do? Explain.
  b. In what sense does the analogy also serve as a "frame" for the essay?
  c. Could it have been used effectively to greater extent in explaining the world situation? Justify your answer.
  d. Does the author's use of the metaphor, "neighborhood" (pars. 3, 10), seem consistent with his analogy of a "house"? Explain.

2. Show precisely how the story of Rip Van Winkle also qualifies as an analogy.

3. Cite the paragraphs where illustration by example is an important means of clarification.

4. Of what value, if any, is King's frequent use of direct quotations?

5. What is gained by the author's consistent use of "we" instead of "you" in his various charges, when obviously some of them do not apply to himself?

6. King wrote (as he spoke) to communicate with all kinds of people, including the semiliterate. This fact no doubt accounts for his use of the uncomplicated analogy to give added force, if not added clarity, to his remarks. List the other ways that the nature of his reader-audience apparently influenced this writing. Illustrate with examples from the essay.

7a. Which of the standard techniques for introducing exposition does the author use in the first paragraph? (Guide: *Introductions.*)
  b. How effective is this introduction?

8a. Which of the standard techniques for closing exposition does the author use in the last paragraph? (Guide: *Closings.*)
  b. How effective is this closing?

DICTION AND VOCABULARY

1. King makes liberal use of figures of speech in this essay. (Guide: *Figures of Speech.*)
  a. Within a small part of paragraph 4, you can find three different kinds. What are they?
  b. List or mark the most effective figure of speech in each of the following paragraphs, and identify the type of each: 5, 7, 8, 11–13.

2a. Although King was a well-educated and articulate man, there are few words in any of his public writings (or addresses) that necessitate use of a dictionary. How do you account for this fact?

b. However, if you are not sure of the following, consult your dictionary: cybernation (par. 5); manifests (8); subjugates (12); vulnerable, indictment (13).

SUGGESTIONS FOR WRITING AND DISCUSSION

1. Explain how "spiritual ends" (par. 12) may be expressed in art, using examples to clarify your explanation.

2. Select any one of Rihbany's sentences (par. 13) to be your central theme, and change the "you" to "we" and the "your" to "our." Develop by use of examples and/or by use of comparison and contrast.

3. Projecting King's primary analogy, show the diversity of the "family" by developing a classification system to encompass all the "relatives" trying to live together in the world house. Give examples of countries or peoples that fit into each of the "relative" categories.

4. Projecting King's primary analogy, explain a practical idea for handling the domineering "relative" who is peaceful only as long as he can impose his preferences on others.

5. Explore the possible ways in which an ordinary citizen, having little talent or time, could still help "family" relationships in the new world house. From your findings compose a specific statement of theme and base your writing or discussion on it.

(NOTE: Suggestions for topics requiring development by use of ANALOGY are on page 123, at the end of this section.)

ALDO LEOPOLD

ALDO LEOPOLD (1887–1948) was born in Iowa and began his career in forestry and conservation when in 1909 he joined the United States Forest Service in Arizona and New Mexico. He later became chief of operations for this district, and he and his colleagues developed most of the basic policy of forest management and helped form the National Forest policies. Leopold left forestry in 1928 to engage in wildlife management, conducting technical surveys of wildlife populations and serving as game consultant for several states. In 1933 the University of Wisconsin created a chair of game management for Leopold. He died fighting a grass fire in Wisconsin.

The Land Pyramid

"The Land Pyramid" is from Leopold's *Sand County Almanac*, which was first published in 1948 and has been regarded with new respect in recent years, as attention to ecology has become more widespread. Leopold's subject is considerably more complex, and therefore more difficult to explain coherently, than were the others of this section. To achieve his purpose, the author employs several of the patterns of exposition, but he relies chiefly on analogy.

An ethic to supplement and guide the economic relation to land 1 presupposes the existence of some mental image of land as a biotic mechanism. We can be ethical only in relation to something we can see, feel, understand, love, or otherwise have faith in.

The image commonly employed in conservation education is "the 2 balance of nature." For reasons too lengthy to detail here, this figure of speech fails to describe accurately what little we know about the land mechanism. A much truer image is the one employed in ecology: the biotic pyramid. I shall first sketch the pyramid as a symbol of land, and later develop some of its implications in terms of land-use.

Plants absorb energy from the sun. This energy flows through   3
a circuit called the biota, which may be represented by a pyramid consisting of layers. The bottom layer is the soil. A plant layer rests on the soil, an insect layer on the plants, a bird and rodent layer on the insects, and so on up through various animal groups to the apex layer, which consists of the larger carnivores.

The species of a layer are alike not in where they came from,   4
or in what they look like, but rather in what they eat. Each successive layer depends on those below it for food and often for other services, and each in turn furnishes food and services to those above. Proceeding upward, each successive layer decreases in numerical abundance. Thus, for every carnivore there are hundreds of his prey, thousands of their prey, millions of insects, uncountable plants. The pyramidal form of the system reflects this numerical progression from apex to base. Man shares an intermediate layer with the bears, raccoons, and squirrels which eat both meat and vegetables.

The lines of dependency for food and other services are called   5
food chains. Thus soil-oak-deer-Indian is a chain that has now been largely converted to soil-corn-cow-farmer. Each species, including ourselves, is a link in many chains. The deer eats a hundred plants other than oak, and the cow a hundred plants other than corn. Both, then, are links in a hundred chains. The pyramid is a tangle of chains so complex as to seem disorderly, yet the stability of the system proves it to be a highly organized structure. Its functioning depends on the co-operation and competition of its diverse parts.

In the beginning, the pyramid of life was low and squat; the   6
food chains short and simple. Evolution has added layer after layer, link after link. Man is one of thousands of accretions to the height and complexity of the pyramid. Science has given us many doubts, but it has given us at least one certainty: the trend of evolution is to elaborate and diversify the biota.

Land, then, is not merely soil; it is a fountain of energy flow-   7
ing through a circuit of soils, plants, and animals. Food chains are the living channels which conduct energy upward; death and decay

return it to the soil. The circuit is not closed; some energy is dissipated in decay, some is added by absorption from the air, some is stored in soils, peats, and long-lived forests; but it is a sustained circuit, like a slowly augmented revolving fund of life. There is always a net loss by downhill wash, but this is normally small and offset by the decay of rocks. It is deposited in the ocean and, in the course of geological time, raised to form new lands and new pyramids.

The velocity and character of the upward flow of energy depend on the complex structure of the plant and animal community, much as the upward flow of sap in a tree depends on its complex cellular organization. Without this complexity, normal circulation would presumably not occur. Structure means the characteristic numbers, as well as the characteristic kinds and functions, of the component species. This interdependence between the complex structure of the land and its smooth functioning as an energy unit is one of its basic attributes. 8

When a change occurs in one part of the circuit, many other parts must adjust themselves to it. Change does not necessarily obstruct or divert the flow of energy; evolution is a long series of self-induced changes, the net result of which has been to elaborate the flow mechanism and to lengthen the circuit. Evolutionary changes, however, are usually slow and local. Man's invention of tools has enabled him to make changes of unprecedented violence, rapidity, and scope. 9

One change is in the composition of floras and faunas. The larger predators are lopped off the apex of the pyramid; food chains, for the first time in history, become shorter rather than longer. Domesticated species from other lands are substituted for wild ones, and wild ones are moved to new habitats. In this world-wide pooling of faunas and floras, some species get out of bounds as pests and diseases, others are extinguished. Such effects are seldom intended or foreseen; they represent unpredicted and often untraceable readjustments in the structure. Agricultural science is largely a race between the emergence of new pests and the emergence of new techniques for their control. 10

Another change touches the flow of energy through plants and animals and its return to the soil. Fertility is the ability of soil to receive, store, and release energy. Agriculture, by overdrafts on the soil, or by too radical a substitution of domestic for native species 11 in the superstructure, may derange the channels of flow or deplete storage. Soils depleted of their storage, or of the organic matter which anchors it, wash away faster than they form. This is erosion.

Waters, like soil, are part of the energy circuit. Industry, by pol- 12 luting waters or obstructing them with dams, may exclude the plants and animals necessary to keep energy in circulation.

Transportation brings about another basic change: the plants or 13 animals grown in one region are now consumed and returned to the soil in another. Transportation taps the energy stored in rocks, and in the air, and uses it elsewhere; thus we fertilize the garden with nitrogen gleaned by the guano birds from the fishes of seas on the other side of the Equator. Thus the formerly localized and self-contained circuits are pooled on a world-wide scale.

The process of altering the pyramid for human occupation re- 14 leases stored energy, and this often gives rise, during the pioneer-ing period, to a deceptive exuberance of plant and animal life, both wild and tame. These releases of biotic capital tend to be-cloud or postpone the penalties of violence.

❊   ❊   ❊

This thumbnail sketch of land as an energy circuit conveys three 15 basic ideas:

1. That land is not merely soil.
2. That the native plants and animals kept the energy circuit open; others may or may not.
3. That man-made changes are of a different order than evo-lutionary changes, and have effects more comprehensive than is intended or foreseen.

These ideas, collectively, raise two basic issues: Can the land 16 adjust itself to the new order? Can the desired alterations be ac-complished with less violence?

Biotas seem to differ in their capacity to sustain violent con- 17 version. Western Europe, for example, carries a far different pyra-mid than Caesar found there. Some large animals are lost; swampy forests have become meadows or plowland; many new plants and animals are introduced, some of which escape as pests; the re-maining natives are greatly changed in distribution and abundance. Yet the soil is still there and, with the help of imported nutrients, still fertile; the waters flow normally; the new structure seems to function and to persist. There is no visible stoppage or derangement of the circuit.

Western Europe, then, has a resistant biota. Its inner processes   18
are tough, elastic, resistant to strain. No matter how violent the
alterations, the pyramid, so far, has developed some new *modus
vivendi* which preserves its habitability for man, and for most of
the other natives.

Japan seems to present another instance of radical conversion   19
without disorganization.

Most other civilized regions, and some as yet barely touched   20
by civilization, display various stages of disorganization, varying
from initial symptoms to advanced wastage. In Asia Minor and
North Africa diagnosis is confused by climatic changes, which may
have been either the cause or the effect of advanced wastage. In
the United States the degree of disorganization varies locally; it
is worst in the Southwest, the Ozarks, and parts of the South, and
least in New England and the Northwest. Better land-uses may
still arrest it in the less advanced regions. In parts of Mexico,
South America, South Africa, and Australia a violent and accelerating wastage is in progress, but I cannot assess the prospects.

This almost world-wide display of disorganization in the land   21
seems to be similar to disease in an animal, except that it never
culminates in complete disorganization or death. The land recovers,
but at some reduced level of complexity, and with a reduced
carrying capacity for people, plants, and animals. Many biotas
currently regarded as "lands of opportunity" are in fact already
subsisting on exploitative agriculture, i.e. they have already exceeded their sustained carrying capacity. Most of South America
is overpopulated in this sense.

In arid regions we attempt to offset the process of wastage   22
by reclamation, but it is only too evident that the prospective
longevity of reclamation projects is often short. In our own West,
the best of them may not last a century.

The combined evidence of history and ecology seems to support   23
one general deduction: the less violent the man-made changes,
the greater the probability of successful readjustment in the pyramid. Violence, in turn, varies with human population density; a
dense population requires a more violent conversion. In this respect,
North America has a better chance for permanence than Europe,
if she can contrive to limit her density.

This deduction runs counter to our current philosophy, which   24
assumes that because a small increase in density enriched human
life, that an indefinite increase will enrich it indefinitely. Ecology
knows of no density relationship that holds for indefinitely wide
limits. All gains from density are subject to a law of diminishing
returns.

Whatever may be the equation for men and land, it is improb-   25
able that we as yet know all its terms. Recent discoveries in mineral
and vitamin nutrition reveal unsuspected dependencies in the up-
circuit: incredibly minute quantities of certain substances determine the value of soils to plants, of plants to animals. What of
the down-circuit? What of the vanishing species, the preservation
of which we now regard as an esthetic luxury? They helped build
the soil; in what unsuspected ways may they be essential to its
maintenance? Professor Weaver proposes that we use prairie flowers
to re-flocculate the wasting soils of the dust bowl; who knows for
what purpose cranes and condors, otters and grizzlies may some day
be used?

MEANINGS AND VALUES

1a. With a first casual reading, the various analogical comparisons Leopold uses may seem confusing and even conflicting. If you can now
   see the relation of these parts to the overall analogy, compose one
   direct analogical summary of the land process as a pyramid, relating
   the following to it: "layers," "links" and "chains," "circuits."

 b. Explain why, complicated as it seems, this analogy is a "much truer
   image" than the more common "balance of nature" analogy (par. 2).

2a. If it is "only too evident" to you that the prospective longevity of
   reclamation projects is often short (par. 22), what is your "evidence"?

 b. If not, what do you think might prevent long-range success of such
   projects as desert irrigation?

3a. Is this essay more accurately classified as objective or subjective?
   Why? (See Guide to Terms: *Objective/Subjective.*)

 b. Where, if at all, is the author guilty of sentimentality (an easy matter, it seems, for writers on ecology)? (Guide: *Sentimentality.*)

 c. To what extent, if at all, is sentimentality a matter of objectivity?

4. How may ecological analyses by someone like Leopold perform some
   functions better than the contributions of many modern ecologists?

5. Now that you have carefully read "The Land Pyramid," are you

better prepared to "see, feel, understand, love, or otherwise have faith in" the land, thus providing a better basis for a land "ethic" (par. 1)? Why?

6. Measure the overall success of this essay by applying the three-point evaluation system. (Guide: *Evaluation*.)

EXPOSITORY TECHNIQUES

1a. Explain precisely why Leopold's use of the "biotic pyramid" is analogy rather than logical comparison.
 b. To what extent, if at all, could it be offered as proof of the complex interdependence of soil, plants, and animals?
2. Suggest a specific way, or ways, in which Leopold's analogy could have been made clearer.
3a. Assuming the same complexity of the land process as did Leopold, supply another analogy by which to explain it, showing roughly how it would work.
 b. What limitations, if any, do you see in your analogy?
4a. Suggest patterns other than analogy which might have been used more extensively to explain the land process.
 b. If any of these seem especially promising, explain briefly how it would be used.
 c. If you were the author, would you still come back to analogy of some kind? Why, or why not?
5a. Select two of the author's paragraphs to demonstrate clearly how the abstract may be made concrete by the use of examples. (Guide: *Concrete/Abstract*.)
 b. Cite at least one paragraph that would have benefited in the same way by use of examples. Be prepared to justify your answer.
6. What structural function is served by the summary in paragraph 15?
7a. Which of the standard expository closing techniques are used for this essay? (Guide: *Closings*.)
 b. How effectively?

DICTION AND VOCABULARY

1. Could the analogy's clarity have ben improved by earlier definition of some words — e.g., "land," "circuit" — for the writer's intended usage? If so, give specific examples and show the advantage to be gained.
2a. What is the meaning of the Latin term in paragraph 18?
 b. What does its use suggest about the reader-audience the author apparently had in mind?

c. Would its use tend to "turn off" another type of reader — or would it even matter? Why, or why not?

d. Is anything in its use really inconsistent with the tone of the rest of the writing? Explain.

3. Study the uses of the following words, consulting your dictionary as necessary for the meanings: ethic (par. 1); biotic (1 and others); carnivores (3); diverse (5); accretions (6); dissipated, augmented (7); attributes (8); habitats (10); derangement (17); exploitative (21); longevity (22); esthetic (25).

SUGGESTIONS FOR WRITING AND DISCUSSION

1. Show, by using examples liberally, the range and extent of ecological violence made possible by the invention of tools (par. 9). What is a logical remedy — should we stop inventions, outlaw some tools already invented, or what?

2. If you have had experience or training in agricultural science, use one developed example and several briefer ones to explain or support the last sentence of paragraph 10.

3. If you have sufficient knowledge on the subject, fully develop a specific example of the generalization in paragraph 12.

4. If you are familiar with some part of the United States seriously affected by biotic "disorganization" (par. 20), explain its causes and/or show what attempts have been made, successfully or not, to arrest the deterioration.

5. Do you think that science can indefinitely continue to provide substitutes for disrupted energy circuits, e.g., fertilizers for depleted soil? Why, or why not?

6. Analyze the prospective longevity (par. 22) of some extensive reclamation project with which you are familiar (e.g., reforestation, an irrigation project, the restoration of a strip-mined area). What are its chances for permanent success? Why?

Writing Suggestions for Section 4

Analogy

(In any normal situation, of course, the analogy is chosen to help explain a theme-idea that already exists — such as those in the first group below. But for classroom training, which even at best is bound to be somewhat artificial, it is sometimes permissible to work from the other direction, to develop a theme that fits some preselected analogy-symbol. Your instructor will indicate which of the groups he prefers you to use.)

1. State a central theme about one of the following general topics or a suitable one of your own, and develop it into a composition by use of an analogy of your own choosing.

   a. A well-organized school system or business establishment.

   b. Starting a new kind of business or other enterprise.

   c. The long-range value of programs for underprivileged children.

   d. The complexity of narcotics control.

   e. The need for cooperation between management and labor.

   f. Today's intense competition for success.

   g. Women's liberation in a "man's world."

   h. The results of ignorance.

   i. The dangers of propaganda.

2. Select an analogy-symbol from the following list and fashion a worthwhile theme that it can illustrate. Develop your composition as instructed.

   a. A freeway at commuting time.

   b. Building a road through a wilderness.

   c. Building a bridge across a river.

   d. A merry-go-round.

   e. A wedding.

   f. A car-wash.

   g. Flood-destruction of a levee.

   h. The tending of a young orchard.

   i. An animal predator stalking prey.

   j. A medical clinic.

   k. A juggling act.

   l. An oasis.

   m. The game of baseball.

   n. A spider's web.

o. A kaleidoscope.

p. A fine clock.

3. Use one of the following suggestions on which to build a complete statement of the central theme for your writing. Develop your composition as instructed.

a. A college education as a savings account.

b. A good book as a long hike.

c. A freshman at registration (or orientation) as a mouse in a maze.

d. The church as a giant oak standing alone.

e. "Playing the field" as a smorgasbord.

f. The college curriculum as a smorgasbord.

g. Racial prejudice as a malignant growth.

h. A selling technique as that of catching a fish.

i. A military unit as a machine.

j. College as a mountain to be climbed.

k. Success as a magnet.

5

Explaining through *Process Analysis*

Process analysis explains how the steps of an operation lead to its completion. Although in one narrow sense it may be considered a kind of narration, process analysis has an important difference in purpose, and hence in approach. Other narration is mostly concerned with the story itself, or with a general concept illustrated by it, but process tells of methods that end in specified results. We might narrate a story about a rifle — its purchase, its role in colorful episodes, perhaps its eventual retirement from active service. (We could, for other purposes, *define* "rifle," or *classify* the types of rifles, no doubt *compare* and *contrast* these types and *illustrate* by examples.) But to show how a rifle works, or how it is manufactured, or how it should be cared for — this is process, and it sometimes becomes the basic pattern of an exposition.

Most writers are especially concerned with two kinds of process, both of them apparent in the preceding example of rifles: the directional, which explains how to *do* something (how to shoot a gun or how to clean it); and the informational, which explains how something is or was *done* (how guns are manufactured). The directional process can vary from the instructions on a shampoo bottle to a detailed plan showing how to make the United Nations more effective. The informational process, on the other hand, might explain the steps of a wide variety of operations or actions or mental processes, with no how-to-do-it purpose at all — how someone went about choosing a college or how the planet Earth was formed. Informational process analysis has been seen in earlier selections: Peter and Hull explained how the Peter Principle works; Leopold explains how food chains conduct energy.

125

Most process analyses are explained in simple, chronological steps. Indeed, the exact order is sometimes of greatest importance, as in a recipe. But occasionally there are problems in organization. The step-by-step format may need to be interrupted for descriptions, definitions, or other explanatory asides. And, still more of a problem, some processes defy a strict chronological treatment, because several things occur simultaneously. To explain the operating process of a gasoline engine, for example, the writer would be unable to convey at once everything that happens at the same time. Some way must be found to present the material in *general* stages, organized as subdivisions, so that the reader can see the step-by-step process through the confusion of interacting relationships.

Another difficulty in explaining by process analysis is estimating what knowledge the reader may already have. Presuming too little background may quickly result in his boredom or even irritability, with a resulting communication block; presuming too much will almost certainly lose him through bewilderment. Like a chain dependent on its weakest link for its strength, the entire process analysis can fail because of just one unclear point that makes the rest unintelligible.

ERNEST HEMINGWAY

ERNEST HEMINGWAY (1899–1961), an American best known as a novelist and short-story writer, began his writing career as a cub reporter on the *Kansas City Star*. During World War I he was wounded while serving with the Italian infantry as an ambulance driver. After the war he did some writing in the United States and for several years in Europe, supporting himself as a foreign correspondent for the *Toronto Star*. Among Hemingway's many famous novels are *The Sun Also Rises* (1926), *A Farewell to Arms* (1929), *For Whom the Bell Tolls* (1940), *Across the River and Into the Trees* (1950), and *The Old Man and the Sea* (1952). The latter won the 1953 Pulitzer Prize in fiction and was instrumental in winning Hemingway the Nobel Prize for Literature in 1954. The Nobel Prize committee praised his "forceful and style-making mastery of the art of modern narration."

The Bull Fight as Symbolism

"The Bull Fight as Symbolism" (editor's title) is from Hemingway's book *By-Line* (1967), a collection of his articles and dispatches of four decades. This piece was written early in Hemingway's career as a writer, and his later famous prose style was only beginning to develop. But the selection gives us an example of simple, step-by-step analysis of uncomplicated process.

Bull fighting is not a sport. It is a tragedy, and it symbolizes the struggle between man and the beasts. There are usually six bulls to a fight. A fight is called a corrida de toros. Fighting bulls are bred like race horses, some of the oldest breeding establishments being several hundred years old. A good bull is worth about $2,000.

Reprinted by permission of Charles Scribner's Sons from *By-Line: Ernest Hemingway,* pages 96–98, edited by William White. Copyright © 1967 by Mary Hemingway.

They are bred for speed, strength and viciousness. In other words a good fighting bull is an absolutely incorrigible bad bull.

Bull fighting is an exceedingly dangerous occupation. In sixteen fights I saw there were only two in which there was no one badly hurt. On the other hand it is very remunerative. A popular espada gets $5,000 for his afternoon's work. An unpopular espada though may not get $500. Both run the same risks. It is a good deal like Grand Opera for the really great matadors except they run the chance of being killed every time they cannot hit high C. 2

No one at any time in the fight can approach the bull at any time except directly from the front. That is where the danger comes. There are also all sorts of complicated passes that must be done with the cape, each requiring as much technique as a champion billiard player. And underneath it all is the necessity for playing the old tragedy in the absolutely custom bound, law-laid-down way. It must all be done gracefully, seemingly effortlessly and always with dignity. The worst criticism the Spaniards ever make of a bull fighter is that his work is "vulgar." 3

The three absolute acts of the tragedy are first the entry of the bull when the picadors receive the shock of his attacks and attempt to protect their horses with their lances. Then the horses go out and the second act is the planting of the banderillos. This is one of the most interesting and difficult parts but among the easiest for a new bull fight fan to appreciate in technique. The banderillos are three-foot, gaily colored darts with a small fish hook prong in the end. The man who is going to plant them walks out into the arena alone with the bull. He lifts the banderillos at arm's length and points them toward the bull. Then he calls "Toro! Toro!" The bull charges and the banderillero rises to his toes, bends in a curve forward and just as the bull is about to hit him drops the darts into the bull's hump just back of his horns. 4

They must go in evenly, one on each side. They must not be shoved, or thrown or stuck in from the side. This is the first time the bull has been completely baffled, there is the prick of the darts that he cannot escape and there are no horses for him to charge into. But he charges the man again and again and each time he gets a pair of the long banderillos that hang from his hump by their tiny barbs and flop like porcupine quills. 5

Last is the death of the bull, which is in the hands of the matador 6 who has had charge of the bull since his first attack. Each matador has two bulls in the afternoon. The death of the bull is most formal and can only be brought about in one way, directly from the front by the matador who must receive the bull in full charge and kill him with a sword thrust between the shoulders just back of the neck and between the horns. Before killing the bull he must first do a series of passes with the muleta, a piece of red cloth he carries about the size of a large napkin. With the muleta the torero must show his complete mastery of the bull, must make the bull miss him again and again by inches, before he is allowed to kill him. It is in this phase that most of the fatal accidents occur.

The word "toreador" is obsolete Spanish and is never used. The torero is usually called an espada or swordsman. He must be proficient in all three acts of the fight. In the first he uses the cape and does veronicas and protects the picadors by taking the bull out and away from them when they are spilled to the ground. In the second act he plants the banderillos. In the third act he masters the bull with the muleta and kills him.   7

Few toreros excel in all three departments. Some, like young Chicuelo, are unapproachable in their cape work. Others like the late Joselito are wonderful banderilleros. Only a few are great killers. Most of the greatest killers are gypsies.   8

MEANINGS AND VALUES

1. Show precisely how Hemingway's use of "symbolizes" (par. 1) fits our own meaning of the term, or that it does not. (See Guide to Terms: *Symbolism.*)

2a. How would you describe the tone of this writing? (Guide: *Style/ Tone.*)

b. How, if at all, is such tone presumably related to the author's personal attitude toward his subject?

3. Evaluate this selection by use of the three-point system. (Guide: *Evaluation.*)

EXPOSITORY TECHNIQUES

1. In what important respect is a process of this sort more readily analyzed and clearly explained than are many others?

2. Should the author's beginning reference to symbolism have been

picked up later, perhaps woven through the process explanation itself? Why, or why not?

3. This essay shows the beginning of Hemingway's later characteristic syntax style. (Guide: *Syntax*.) What distinctiveness of syntax do you find, especially in sentence structures? Use examples to illustrate.

DICTION AND VOCABULARY

1. Is the author's use of Spanish terms excessive? Why, or why not?
2. Does he clarify the meanings of Spanish words sufficiently for a reader who understands neither Spanish nor bull fighting? Support your answer with examples.

SUGGESTIONS FOR WRITING AND DISCUSSION

1. Why do you think the conduct of such an event as a bull fight is so closely prescribed by rules? What counterparts, in this respect, do you see in our own sports?
2. Is bull fighting more brutal and barbaric (a common accusation in the United States) than any of our own sports? Be specific, and use developed examples to support your theme.
3. Select one sport popular in the United States, and show the symbolism inherent in it. If possible, also show the effect of this symbolism on the sport's popularity.
4. Why do you think people *really* go to such events as a bull fight?
5. Is bull fighting likely to be legalized in the United States? Do you think it should be?

(NOTE: Suggestions for topics requiring development by PROCESS ANALYSIS are on page 156, at the end of this section.)

ALEXANDER PETRUNKEVITCH

ALEXANDER PETRUNKEVITCH (1875–1964) was a Russian-born zoologist who taught at several leading American universities and received honors from others. He was one of the world's foremost authorities on spiders, and his first important book, published in 1911, was *Index Catalogue of Spiders of North, Central, and South America.* He later achieved distinction for his writings on zoological subjects as well as for his translations of English poetry into Russian and Russian poetry into English. Two of his other books are *Choice and Responsibility* (1947) and *Principles of Classification* (1952).

The Spider and the Wasp

"The Spider and the Wasp" was first published in the August 1952 issue of *Scientific American.* This essay should be particularly interesting to students of composition because it demonstrates not only exposition of natural process but also semiscientific writing that has been made understandable, perhaps even fascinating, for completely nonscientific readers. It is also a good illustration of the successful interweaving of several expository techniques.

In the feeding and safeguarding of their progeny insects and spiders   1
exhibit some interesting analogies to reasoning and some crass examples of blind instinct. The case I propose to describe here is that of the tarantula spiders and their archenemy, the digger wasps of the genus Pepsis. It is a classic example of what looks like intelligence pitted against instinct — a strange situation in which the victim, though fully able to defend itself, submits unwittingly to its destruction.

Most tarantulas live in the tropics, but several species occur in the   2
temperate zone and a few are common in the southern U.S. Some
varieties are large and have powerful fangs with which they can
inflict a deep wound. These formidable looking spiders do not,
however, attack man; you can hold one in your hand, if you are
gentle, without being bitten. Their bite is dangerous only to insects
and small mammals such as mice; for man it is no worse than a
hornet's sting.

Tarantulas customarily live in deep cylindrical burrows, from   3
which they emerge at dusk and into which they retire at dawn. Mature males wander about 'after dark in search of females and occasionally stray into houses. After mating, the male dies in a few
weeks, but a female lives much longer and can mate several years in
succession. In a Paris museum is a tropical specimen which is said
to have been living in captivity for 25 years.

A fertilized female tarantula lays from 200 to 400 eggs at a time;   4
thus it is possible for a single tarantula to produce several thousand
young. She takes no care of them beyond weaving a cocoon of silk
to enclose the eggs. After they hatch, the young walk away, find
convenient places in which to dig their burrows and spend the rest
of their lives in solitude. The eyesight of tarantulas is poor, being
limited to a sensing of change in the intensity of light and to the
perception of moving objects. They apparently have little or no
sense of hearing, for a hungry tarantula will pay no attention to a
loudly chirping cricket placed in its cage unless the insect happens
to touch one of its legs.

But all spiders, and especially hairy ones, have an extremely deli-   5
cate sense of touch. Laboratory experiments prove that tarantulas
can distinguish three types of touch: pressure against the body wall,
stroking of the body hair, and riffling of certain very fine hairs on
the legs called trichobothria. Pressure against the body, by the finger
or the end of a pencil, causes the tarantula to move off slowly for a
short distance. The touch excites no defensive response unless the
approach is from above where the spider can see the motion, in
which case it rises on its hind legs, lifts its front legs, opens it fangs
and holds this threatening posture as long as the object continues to
move.

The entire body of a tarantula, especially its legs, is thickly   6
clothed with hair. Some of it is short and wooly, some long and stiff.
Touching this body hair produces one of two distinct reactions.

When the spider is hungry, it responds with an immediate and swift attack. At the touch of a cricket's antennae the tarantula seizes the insect so swiftly that a motion picture taken at the rate of 64 frames per second shows only the result and not the process of capture. But when the spider is not hungry, the stimulation of its hairs merely causes it to shake the touched limb. An insect can walk under its hairy belly unharmed.

The trichobothria, very fine hairs growing from dislike membranes on the legs, are sensitive only to air movement. A light breeze makes them vibrate slowly, without disturbing the common hair. When one blows gently on the trichobothria, the tarantula reacts with a quick jerk of its four front legs. If the front and hind legs are stimulated at the same time, the spider makes a sudden jump. This reaction is quite independent of the state of its appetite.   7

These three tactile responses — to pressure on the body wall, to moving of the common hair, and to flexing of the trichobothria — are so different from one another that there is no possibility of confusing them. They serve the tarantula adequately for most of its needs and enable it to avoid most annoyances and dangers. But they fail the spider completely when it meets its deadly enemy, the digger wasp Pepsis.   8

These solitary wasps are beautiful and formidable creatures. Most species are either a deep shiny blue all over, or deep blue with rusty wings. The largest have a wing span of about four inches. They live on nectar. When excited, they give off a pungent odor — a warning that they are ready to attack. The sting is much worse than that of a bee or common wasp, and the pain and swelling last longer. In the adult stage the wasp lives only a few months. The female produces but a few eggs, one at a time at intervals of two or three days. For each egg the mother must provide one adult tarantula, alive but paralyzed. The mother wasp attaches the egg to the paralyzed spider's abdomen. Upon hatching from the egg, the larva is many hundreds of times smaller than its living but helpless victim. It eats no other food and drinks no water. By the time it has finished its single Gargantuan meal and become ready for wasphood, nothing remains of the tarantula but its indigestible chitinous skeleton.   9

The mother wasp goes tarantula-hunting when the egg in her ovary is almost ready to be laid. Flying low over the ground late on a sunny afternoon, the wasp looks for its victim or for the mouth of a tarantula burrow, a round hole edged by a bit of silk. The sex of   10 the spider makes no difference, but the mother is highly discriminating as to species. Each species of Pepsis requires a certain species of tarantula, and the wasp will not attack the wrong species. In a cage with a tarantula which is not its normal prey, the wasp avoids the spider and is usually killed by it in the night.

Yet when a wasp finds the correct species, it is the other way 11 about. To identify the species the wasp apparently must explore the spider with her antennae. The tarantula shows an amazing tolerance to this exploration. The wasp crawls under it and walks over it without evoking any hostile response. The molestation is so great and so persistent that the tarantula often rises on all eight legs, as if it were on stilts. It may stand this way for several minutes. Meanwhile the wasp, having satisfied itself that the victim is of the right species, moves off a few inches to dig the spider's grave. Working vigorously with legs and jaws, it excavates a hole 8 to 10 inches deep with a diameter slightly larger than the spider's girth. Now and again the wasp pops out of the hole to make sure that the spider is still there.

When the grave is finished, the wasp returns to the tarantula to 12 complete her ghastly enterprise. First she feels it all over once more with her antennae. Then her behavior becomes more aggresive. She bends her abdomen, protruding her sting, and searches for the soft membrane at the point where the spider's legs join its body — the only spot where she can penetrate the horny skeleton. From time to time, as the exasperated spider slowly shifts ground, the wasp turns on her back and slides along with the aid of her wings, trying to get under the tarantula for a shot at the vital spot. During all this maneuvering, which can last for several minutes, the tarantula makes no move to save itself. Finally the wasp corners it against some obstruction and grasps one of its legs in her powerful jaws. Now at last the harassed spider tries a desperate but vain defense. The two contestants roll over and over on the ground. It is a terrifying sight and the outcome is always the same. The wasp finally manages to thrust her sting into the soft spot and holds it there for a few seconds while she pumps in the poison. Almost immediately the tarantula falls paralyzed on its back. Its legs stop twitching; its heart stops beating. Yet it is not dead, as is shown by the fact that if taken from the wasp it can be restored to some sensitivity by being kept in a moist chamber for several months.

After paralyzing the tarantula, the wasp cleans herself by drag- 13 ging her body along the ground and rubbing her feet, sucks the drop of blood oozing from the wound in the spider's abdomen, then grabs a leg of the flabby, helpless animal in her jaws and drags it down to the bottom of the grave. She stays there for many minutes, sometimes for several hours, and what she does all that time in the dark we do not know. Eventually she lays her egg and attaches it to the side of the spider's abdomen with a sticky secretion. Then she emerges, fills the grave with soil carried bit by bit in her jaws, and finally tramples the ground all around to hide any trace of the grave from prowlers. Then she flies away, leaving her descendant safely started in life.

In all this the behavior of the wasp evidently is qualitatively dif- 14
ferent from that of the spider. The wasp acts like an intelligent ani-
mal. This is not to say that instinct plays no part or that she reasons as man does. But her actions are to the point; they are not automatic and can be modified to fit the situation. We do not know for certain how she identifies the tarantula — probably it is by some olfactory or chemo-tactile sense — but she does it purposefully and does not blindly tackle a wrong species.

On the other hand, the tarantula's behavior shows only confusion. 15
Evidently the wasp's pawing gives it no pleasure, for it tries to move away. That the wasp is not simulating sexual stimulation is certain because male and female tarantulas react in the same way to its advances. That the spider is not anesthetized by some odorless secre-
tion is easily shown by blowing lightly at the tarantula and making it jump suddenly. What, then, makes the tarantula behave as stupidly as it does?

No clear, simple answer is available. Possibly the stimulation by 16
the wasp's antennae is masked by a heavier pressure on the spider's body, so that it reacts as when prodded by a pencil. But the explana-
tion may be much more complex. Initiative in attack is not in the nature of tarantulas; most species fight only when cornered so that escape is impossible. Their inherited patterns of behavior apparently prompt them to avoid problems rather than attack them. For exam-
ple, spiders always weave their webs in three dimensions, and when a spider finds that there is insufficient space to attach certain threads in the third dimension, it leaves the place and seeks another, instead of finishing the web in a single plane. This urge to escape seems to arise under all circumstances, in all phases of life, and to take the place of reasoning. For a spider to change the pattern of its web is as impossible as for an inexperienced man to build a bridge across a chasm obstructing his way.

In a way the instinctive urge to escape is not only easier but often   17
more efficient than reasoning. The tarantula does exactly what is
most efficient in all cases except in an encounter with a ruthless and
determined attacker dependent for the existence of her own species
on killing as many tarantulas as she can lay eggs. Perhaps in this
case the spider follows its usual pattern of trying to escape, instead
of seizing and killing the wasp, because it is not aware of its danger.
In any case, the survival of the tarantula species as a whole is pro-
tected by the fact that the spider is much more fertile than the wasp.

MEANINGS AND VALUES

1. Briefly summarize the "qualitative" differences between the behavior
    of the tarantula and that of the wasp.

2. What is the likelihood that some humans also have inherited patterns
    of behavior that "prompt them to avoid problems rather than attack
    them" (par. 16)? Use concrete examples, if possible, to support your
    view.

3. What parallels to the tarantula-wasp relationship can you find in the
    history of nations? Be explicit and explain.

4a. Describe the type, or types, of readers for whom you think *Scientific
    American* is meant to appeal. (Do not jump to conclusions: if not
    familiar with the magazine, you may have to browse through a few
    issues.)

  b. If you had been the editor, why would you have selected (or not
    selected) this piece to publish?

EXPOSITORY TECHNIQUES

1a. Where does the author state his central theme?
  b. Is this a desirable location? Why, or why not?

2a. What is the primary function of the process analysis in relation to
    the central theme?
  b. How successfully does it accomplish its purpose?

3. In paragraph 9 the author goes from pure description of the wasp
    into the narrative account that involves both wasp and spider. How
    does he arrange the content itself to provide smooth and natural
    transition, hence ensuring coherence? (See Guide to Terms: *Transi-
    tion* and *Coherence.*)

4. The author also usually arranges his subject materials to help achieve
    effective *inter*paragraph transitions so that one gets an echo of the

last part of one paragraph when reading the topic sentence of the next. List or mark the uses of this transitional device.

5. Effective coherence also depends to a great extent on smooth sentence-to-sentence transitions. The time sequence is often the most difficult of these to write so that "then . . . then . . . then" is avoided. List or mark the eight introductory devices showing time relationship in paragraph 12, and notice their variety.

6a. How many paragraphs constitute the closing?
 b. What function do they serve in addition to concluding the selection?

7. This essay utilizes, to varying extents, the expository patterns of cause and effect, definition, induction, and description. It can also be used to illustrate three patterns we have already studied.
 a. What are the patterns?
 b. Explain their use in this essay.

DICTION AND VOCABULARY

1. Do such informal expressions as "pops out of the hole" (par. 11), "for a shot at the vital spot," and "pumps in the poison" (12) help or hinder the essay's success? Why?

2. Consider such expressions as "beautiful and formidable creatures" (par. 9), "terrifying sight" (12), and "ghastly enterprise" (13).
 a. Are these expressions objective or subjective? (Guide: *Objective/ Subjective.*) Explain why.
 b. Why would they be, or not be, suitable in a scientific report?
 c. What useful purpose, if any, do they serve here?

3a. What do your answers to questions 1 and 2 indicate about the author's tone? (Guide: *Style/Tone.*)
 b. How would you describe his tone?
 c. Explain why it is, or is not, suitable to his subject matter and to his audience.

4. Any specialist writing on a technical subject for a lay audience (as much of *Scientific American*'s audience is) has a problem with professional terminology. Consider this author's use of "trichobothria" (par. 5), "chitinous" (9), "olfactory," and "chemo-tactile" (14).
 a. Does there seem to be an excessive use of technical language?
 b. Do you think these words could have been avoided without weakening scientific exactness? If so, how?
 c. Does their use create a communication block for the lay reader, or does the author succeed in avoiding this fault?
 d. Why has he bothered to define "trichobothria" — even repeating his definition — but not the others?

5. The use of "Gargantuan" (par. 9) is an allusion. (Guide: *Figures of Speech.*) Explain the source to which the author alludes and the word's meaning in this essay.

6. Consult the dictionary as needed for a full understanding of the following words, especially as used in this essay: progeny, archenemy, classic (par. 1); formidable (2); perception (4); riffling (5); dislike (7); tactile (8); pungent, chitinous (9); discriminating (10); evoking, molestation (11); harassed (12); secretion (13); qualitatively, olfactory, chemo-tactile (14); ruthless (17).

SUGGESTIONS FOR WRITING AND DISCUSSION

1. Use the tarantula-wasp relationship as the basis of an analogy to explain the relationship between two persons that you know.

2. Use analogy as suggested above to explain the historical relationship between two specific countries.

3. Using patterns of illustration and comparison, distinguish between intellectual and instinctive human behavior.

4. Compare or contrast man's motives for killing with those of animals. Some use of classification might also be helpful in this assignment.

(NOTE: Suggestions for topics requiring development by PROCESS ANALYSIS are on page 156, at the end of this section.)

JESSICA MITFORD was born in England in 1917, a sister of the novelist and biographer, Nancy Mitford. She is married to an American lawyer and lives in California. Her books are her autobiography, *Daughters and Rebels* (1960); the famous best seller, *The American Way of Death* (1963); and *The Trial of Dr. Spock* (1969).

To Dispel Fears of Live Burial

"To Dispel Fears of Live Burial" (editor's title) is a portion of *The American Way of Death*, a book described in the *New York Times* as a "savagely witty and well-documented exposé." The "savagely witty" style, evident in this selection, does not obscure the fact of its being a tightly organized, step-by-step process analysis.

Embalming is indeed a most extraordinary procedure, and one must wonder at the docility of Americans who each year pay hundreds of millions of dollars for its perpetuation, blissfully ignorant of what it is all about, what is done, how it is done. Not one in ten thousand has any idea of what actually takes place. Books on the subject are extremely hard to come by. They are not to be found in most libraries or bookshops. 1

In an era when huge television audiences watch surgical operations in the comfort of their living rooms, when, thanks to the animated cartoon, the geography of the digestive system has become familiar territory even to the nursery school set, in a land where the satisfaction of curiosity about almost all matters is a national pastime, the secrecy surrounding embalming can, surely, hardly be attributed to the inherent gruesomeness of the subject. 2

Custom in this regard has within this century suffered a complete reversal. In the early days of American embalming, when it was performed in the home of the deceased, it was almost mandatory for some relative to stay by the embalmer's side and witness the procedure. Today, family members who might wish to be in attendance would certainly be dissuaded by the funeral director. All others, except apprentices, are excluded by law from the preparation room.

A close look at what does actually take place may explain in large   3 measure the undertaker's intractable reticence concerning a procedure that has become his major *raison d'être*. Is it possible he fears that public information about embalming might lead patrons to wonder if they really want this service? If the funeral men are loath to discuss the subject outside the trade, the reader may, understandably, be equally loath to go on reading at this point. For those who have the stomach for it, let us part the formaldehyde curtain. . . .

The body is first laid out in the undertaker's morgue — or rather,   4 Mr. Jones is reposing in the preparation room — to be readied to bid the world farewell.

The preparation room in any of the better funeral establishments   5 has the tiled and sterile look of a surgery, and indeed the embalmer–restorative artist who does his chores there is beginning to adopt the term "dermasurgeon" (appropriately corrupted by some mortician-writers as "demisurgeon") to describe his calling. His equipment, consisting of scalpels, scissors, augers, forceps, clamps, needles, pumps, tubes, bowls and basins, is crudely imitative of the surgeon's as is his technique, acquired in a nine- or twelve-month post-high-school course in an embalming school. He is supplied by an advanced chemical industry with a bewildering array of fluids, sprays, pastes, oils, powders, creams, to fix or soften tissue, shrink or distend it as needed, dry it here, restore the moisture there. There are cosmetics, waxes and paints to fill and cover features, even plaster of Paris to replace entire limbs. There are ingenious aids to prop and stabilize the cadaver: a Vari-Pose Head Rest, the Edwards Arm and Hand Positioner, the Repose Block (to support the shoulders during the embalming), and the Throop Foot Positioner, which resembles an old-fashioned stocks.

Mr. John H. Eckels, president of the Eckels College of Mortuary   6 Science, thus describes the first part of the embalming procedure:

"In the hands of a skilled practitioner, this work may be done in a comparatively short time and without mutilating the body other than by slight incision — so slight that it scarcely would cause serious inconvenience if made upon a living person. It is necessary to remove the blood, and doing this not only helps in the disinfecting, but removes the principal cause of disfigurements due to discoloration."

Another textbook discusses the all-important time element: "The earlier this is done, the better, for every hour that elapses between death and embalming will add to the problems and complications encountered. . . ." Just how soon should one get going on the embalming? The author tells us, "On the basis of such scanty information made available to this profession through its rudimentary and haphazard system of technical research, we must conclude that the best results are to be obtained if the subject is embalmed before life is completely extinct — that is, before cellular death has occurred. In the average case, this would mean within an hour after somatic death." For those who feel that there is something a little rudimentary, not to say haphazard, about this advice, a comforting thought is offered by another writer. Speaking of fears entertained in early days of premature burial, he points out, "One of the effects of embalming by chemical injection, however, has been to dispel fears of live burial." How true; once the blood is removed, chances of live burial are indeed remote.

To return to Mr. Jones, the blood is drained out through the veins and replaced by embalming fluid pumped in through the arteries. As noted in *The Principles and Practices of Embalming,* "every operator has a favorite injection and drainage point — a fact which becomes a handicap only if he fails or refuses to forsake his favorites when conditions demand it." Typical favorites are the carotid artery, femoral artery, jugular vein, subclavian vein. There are various choices of embalming fluid. If Flextone is used, it will produce a "mild, flexible rigidity. The skin retains a velvety softness, the tissues are rubbery and pliable. Ideal for women and children." It may be blended with B. and G. Products Company's Lyf-Lyk tint, which is guaranteed to reproduce "nature's own skin texture . . . the velvety appearance of living tissue." Suntone comes in three separate tints: Suntan; Special Cosmetic Tint, a pink shade "especially indicated for young female subjects"; and Regular Cosmetic Tint, moderately pink.

About three to six gallons of a dyed and perfumed solution of   9
formaldehyde, glycerin, borax, phenol, alcohol and water is soon
circulating through Mr. Jones, whose mouth has been sewn together with a "needle directed upward between the upper lip and
gum and brought out through the left nostril," with the corners
raised slightly "for a more pleasant expression," If he should be
bucktoothed, his teeth are cleaned with Bon Ami and coated with
colorless nail polish. His eyes, meanwhile, are closed with flesh-
tinted eye caps and eye cement.

The next step is to have at Mr. Jones with a thing called a trocar.   10
This is a long, hollow needle attached to a tube. It is jabbed into the
abdomen, poked around the entrails and chest cavity, the contents
of which are pumped out and replaced with "cavity fluid." This
done, and the hole in the abdomen sewn up, Mr. Jones's face is
heavily creamed (to protect the skin from burns which may be
caused by leakage of the chemicals), and he is covered with a sheet
and left unmolested for a while. But not for long — there is more,
much more, in store for him. He has been embalmed, but not yet
restored, and the best time to start the restorative work is eight to
ten hours after embalming, when the tissues have become firm and
dry.

The object of all this attention to the corpse, it must be remem-   11
bered, is to make it presentable for viewing in an attitude of healthy
repose. "Our customs require the presentation of our dead in the
semblence of normality . . . unmarred by the ravages of illness,
disease or mutilation," says Mr. J. Sheridan Mayer in his *Restorative
Art*. This is rather a large order since few people die in the full
bloom of health, unravaged by illness and unmarked by some dis-
figurement. The funeral industry is equal to the challenge: "In
some cases the gruesome appearance of a mutilated or disease-ridden
subject may be quite discouraging. The task of restoration may seem
impossible and shake the confidence of the embalmer. This is the
time for intestinal fortitude and determination. Once the formative
work is begun and affected tissues are cleaned or removed, all doubts
of success vanish. It is surprising and gratifying to discover the
results which may be obtained."

The embalmer, having allowed an appropriate interval to elapse,   12
returns to the attack, but now he brings into play the skill and equipment of sculptor and cosmetician. Is a hand missing? Casting one in
plaster of Paris is a simple matter. "For replacement purposes, only
a cast of the back of the hand is necessary; this is within the ability

of the average operator and is quite adequate." If a lip or two, a nose or an ear should be missing, the embalmer has at hand a variety of restorative waxes with which to model replacements. Pores and skin texture are simulated by stippling with a little brush, and over this cosmetics are laid on. Head off? Decapitation cases are rather routinely handled. Ragged edges are trimmed, and head joined to torso with a series of splints, wires and sutures. It is a good idea to have a little something at the neck — a scarf or high collar — when time for viewing comes. Swollen mouth? Cut out tissue as needed from inside the lips. If too much is removed, the surface contour can easily be restored by padding with cotton. Swollen necks and cheeks are reduced by removing tissue through vertical incisions made down each side of the neck. "When the deceased is casketed, the pillow will hide the suture incisions . . . as an extra precaution against leakage, the suture may be painted with liquid sealer."

The opposite condition is more likely to present itself — that of 13 emaciation. His hypodermic syringe now loaded with massage cream, the embalmer seeks out and fills the hollowed and sunken areas by injection. In this procedure the backs of the hands and fingers and the under-chin area should not be neglected.

Positioning the lips is a problem that recurrently challenges the 14 ingenuity of the embalmer. Closed too tightly, they tend to give a stern, even disapproving expression. Ideally, embalmers feel, the lips should give the impression of being ever so slightly parted, the upper lip protruding slightly for a more youthful appearance. This takes some engineering, however, as the lips tend to drift apart. Lip drift can sometimes be remedied by pushing one or two straight pins through the inner margin of the lower lip and then inserting them between the two front upper teeth. If Mr. Jones happens to have no teeth, the pins can just as easily be anchored in his Armstrong Face Former and Denture Replacer. Another method to maintain lip closure is to dislocate the lower jaw, which is then held in its new position by a wire run through holes which have been drilled through the upper and lower jaws at the midline. As the French are fond of saying, *il faut souffrir pour être belle.*[1]

If Mr. Jones has died of jaundice, the embalming fluid will very 15 likely turn him green. Does this deter the embalmer? Not if he has intestinal fortitude. Masking pastes and cosmetics are heavily laid

[1] You have to suffer if you want to be beautiful.

on, burial garments and casket interiors are color-correlated with particular care, and Jones is displayed beneath rose-colored lights. Friends will say, "How *well* he looks." Death by carbon monoxide, on the other hand, can be rather a good thing from the embalmer's viewpoint: "One advantage is the fact that this type of discoloration is an exaggerated form of a natural pink coloration." This is nice because the healthy glow is already present and needs but little attention.

The patching and filling completed, Mr. Jones is now shaved, 16 washed and dressed. Cream-based cosmetic, available in pink, flesh, suntan, brunette and blond, is applied to his hands and face, his hair is shampooed and combed (and, in the case of Mrs. Jones, set), his hands manicured. For the horny-handed son of toil special care must be taken; cream should be applied to remove ingrained grime, and the nails cleaned. "If he were not in the habit of having them manicured in life, trimming and shaping is advised for better appearance — never questioned by kin."

Jones is now ready for casketing (this is the present participle of 17 the verb "to casket"). In this operation his right shoulder should be depressed slightly "to turn the body a bit to the right and soften the appearance of lying flat on the back." Positioning the hands is a matter of importance, and special rubber positioning blocks may be used. The hands should be cupped slightly for a more lifelike, relaxed appearance. Proper placement of the body requires a delicate sense of balance. It should lie as high as possible in the casket, yet not so high that the lid, when lowered, will hit the nose. On the other hand, we are cautioned, placing the body too low "creates the impression that the body is in a box."

Jones is next wheeled into the appointed slumber room where a 18 few last touches may be added — his favorite pipe placed in his hand or, if he was a great reader, a book propped into position. (In the case of little Master Jones a Teddy bear may be clutched.) Here he will hold open house for a few days, visiting hours 10 A.M. to 9 P.M.

MEANINGS AND VALUES

1a. What is the author's tone? (See Guide to Terms: *Style/Tone*.)
  b. Try to analyze the effect this tone had, at first reading, on your impressions of the subject matter itself.

c. Form a specific comparison between this effect of tone and the effect of "tone of voice" in spoken language.

2. Why was it formerly "almost mandatory" for some relative to witness the embalming procedure (par. 2)?

3a. Do you believe that public information about this procedure would cost mortuaries much embalming business (par. 3)? Why, or why not?

b. Why *do* people subject their dead to such a process?

4. Use the three-part system of evaluation to judge the success of this process analysis. (Guide: *Evaluation.*)

EXPOSITORY TECHNIQUES

1a. What is the central theme? (Guide: *Unity.*)

b. Which parts of the writing, if any, do not contribute to the theme, thus damaging unity?

c. What other elements of the writing contribute to, or damage, good unity?

2a. Beginning with paragraph 4, list or mark the transitional devices that help to bridge between paragraphs. (Guide: *Transition.*)

b. Briefly explain how coherence is aided by such interparagraph transitions.

3. In this selection, far more than in most, emphasis can best be studied in connection with style. In fact, the two are almost indistinguishable here, and few, if any, of the other methods of achieving emphasis are used at all. (Guide: *Emphasis; Style/Tone.*) Consider each of the following stylistic qualities (some may overlap; others are included in diction) and illustrate, by examples, how each does create emphasis.

a. Number and selection of details — e.g., the equipment and "aids" of paragraph 5.

b. Understatement — e.g., the "chances of live burial," paragraph 7.

c. Special use of quotations — e.g., ". . . that the body is in a box," paragraph 17.

d. Sarcasm and/or other forms of irony (Guide: *Irony*) — e.g., "How *well* he looks," paragraph 15.

DICTION AND VOCABULARY

1. Much of the essay's unique style (with resulting emphasis) is also classifiable as qualities of diction. Use examples to illustrate the following. (Some may be identical to those of the preceding answer. but they need not be.)

   a. Choice of common, low-key words to achieve sarcasm through understatement — e.g., "This is nice . . . ," paragraph 15.
   b. Terms of violence — e.g., "returns to the attack," paragraph 12.
   c. Terms of the living — e.g., "will hold open house," paragraph 18.
   d. The continuing use of "Mr. Jones."

2a. Illustrate the meaning of "connotation" with examples of quotations from morticians. (Guide: *Connotation/Denotation.*)
   b. Are these also examples of "euphemism"?
   c. Show how the author uses these facts to her own advantage — i.e., again, to achieve emphasis.

3a. Comment briefly on the quality and appropriateness of the metaphor that ends the introduction. (Guide: *Figures of Speech.*)
   b. Is this, in any sense, also an allusion? Why, or why not?

4. Use the dictionary as needed to understand the meanings of the following words: docility, perpetuation (par. 1); inherent, mandatory (2); intractable, reticence, *raison d'être* (3); ingenious (5); rudimentary, cellular, somatic (7); carotid artery, femoral artery, subclavian vein (8); semblance (11); simulated, stippling, sutures (12); emaciation (13); dispel (7, title).

SUGGESTIONS FOR WRITING AND DISCUSSION

1. What evidence can you find that "the satisfaction of curiosity about almost all matters is a national pastime" (par. 2)? Is this a good thing or not? Why?

2. Burial customs differ widely from country to country, sometimes from area to area in this country. If you can, describe one of the more distinctive customs and, if possible, show its sources — e.g., nature of the climate, "old country" tradition.

3. What do you foresee as near- and far-future trends or radical changes in American burial practices? Why?

4. You may wish to develop further your answers to question 3 of "Meanings and Values": the rationale of a large majority of people who do use this mortuary "service" for their departed relatives.

5. If you like, explain your personal preferences and the reasons for them.

(NOTE: Suggestions for topics requiring development by PROCESS ANALYSIS are on page 156, at the end of this section.)

NORMAN MAILER

NORMAN MAILER was born in New Jersey in 1923, served in the United States Army during World War II, and was cofounder and columnist of *The Village Voice*. He is a prolific contributor of magazine articles and author of books on many subjects. They include *The Naked and the Dead* (1948), *Barbary Shore* (1951), *The Deer Park* (1955), *The White Negro* (1958), *Advertisements for Myself* (1959), *Deaths for the Ladies and Other Disasters* (poetry, 1962), *The Presidential Papers* (1963), *An American Dream* (1965), *Cannibals and Christians* (1966), *Why Are We in Viet Nam?* (1967), *Miami and the Siege of Chicago* (1968), and *The Prisoner of Sex* (1971). *The Armies of the Night*, published in 1968, won the National Book Award and merited Mailer's selection as cowinner of the Pulitzer Prize.

The Psychology of Astronauts

"The Psychology of Astronauts" is a selection from the chapter by that title in *Of a Fire on the Moon*, published in 1970. It offers a good illustration of Mailer's reporting style and also exemplifies a far more subtle type of process analysis than any we have yet considered. Here the unstated "process" is that of magazine writers determined to get a human interest story from public figures who, although compelled to be amiable, are still unwilling to bare their "human" selves for public inspection.

Since the astronauts were being guarded against infection, they 1 were seen next behind the protection of a glass wall in the visitors' room at the Lunar Receiving Laboratory. An entire building had been constructed to quarantine them on their return, a species of hospital dormitory, galley and laboratory for the moon rocks. Since

From *Of a Fire on the Moon*, by Norman Mailer. Copyright © 1969, 1970 by Norman Mailer. Reprinted by permission of Little, Brown and Company.

for twenty-one days after their return they would not be able to be in the same room with their families, or with the NASA technicians and officials who would debrief them, a chamber like the visitors' room in a prison had been built with a plate-glass partition hermetically sealed from floor to ceiling running down the middle. Dialogue through the glass wall proceeded through microphones.

Now, for the rest of the day, the astronauts would receive the 2 other media layers here: TV, radio, wire service, magazines, etc. Now the magazine writers could sit within a few feet of their subjects, and yet — as if suggesting some undiscovered metaphysical properties of glass — they were obliged at the same time to feel a considerable distance away. Perhaps the full lighting on the astronauts and the relative gloom on the writers' side of the enclosure may have suggested the separation of stage and audience, but probably the effect was due most to the fact that laying-on of hands through that glass, so certainly shatterproof, could never occur, and so there was a dislocation of the sense of space. The astronauts were near enough to sit for a portrait, but — through the glass — they were as far away as history.

There was a new intimacy to the questions however. The set- 3 ting was of aid, and besides, the magazine writers were in need of more. One of them took up immediately on the question which had bothered Aquarius,[1] but the approach was practical now. How indeed would the astronauts spend their time if they found they could not get off the moon? Would they pray, would they leave messages for their family, or would they send back information on the moon? Such were the alternatives seen by the questioner.

Aldrin had the happy look of a linebacker who is standing right 4 in the center of a hole in the line as the runner tries to come through. "I'd probably spend it working on the availability of the ascent engine."

That brought a laugh, and there would be others to follow, but 5 the twenty or so magazine writers had the leisure to ask their questions out of a small group, and so there was not the itch of the newspaperman to look for a quick lead and therefore ask brutal or leading or tendentious questions. Indeed there was no need to ask any question whatever just so that the journalist and his newspaper could be identified as present at the conference. (Such identi-

[1] The author. [Ed.]

fications give smaller newspapers and their reporters a cumulative status over the years with public relations men.) No, here the magazine writers could take their time, they could pursue a question, even keep after the astronaut. Covertly, the mood of a hunt was on. Since they would have more time to write their pieces, by severer standards would they be judged. So they had to make the astronauts come to life whether the astronauts wished to exhibit themselves or not.

Will you take personal mementos? Armstrong was asked.   6

"If I had a choice, I guess I'd take more fuel." he said with a   7
smile for the frustration this might cause the questioner.

The magazine writers kept pushing for personal admission, dis-   8
closure of emotion, admission of unruly fear — the astronauts looked to give replies as proper and well-insulated as the plate glass which separated them. So Armstrong replied to a question about his intuition by making a short disclaimer, which concluded, "Interpret the problem properly, then attack it." Logical positivism all the way was what he would purvey. Don't make predictions without properly weighted and adequate inventories of knowledge. Surely he trusted his intuitions, the questioner persisted. "It has never been a strong suit," said Armstrong in a mild and honest voice. Obviously, the natural aim of technology was to make intuition obsolescent, and Armstrong was a shining knight of technology. But, in fact, he had to be lying. A man who had never had strong intuitions would never have known enough about the sensation to disclaim its presence in himself.

Would he at least recognize that his endeavor was equal in mag-   9
nitude to Columbus' adventure?

He disclaimed large reactions, large ideas. "Our concern has   10
been directed mainly to doing the job." He virtually said, "If not me, another." If they would insist on making him a hero, he would be a hero on terms he alone would make clear. There had been only one Columbus — there were ten astronauts at least who could do the job, and hundreds of men to back them up. He was the representative of a collective will.

Sitting in his drab gray-green suit, a suit as close to no color as   11
possible, his shirt pale blue, his tie nondescript dark gray-blue, a blue-green wall behind him (perhaps to hint at empyreans of sky) his neck seemed subtly separated from his collar, as if — no matter how neatly he was dressed — his clothes felt like a tent to him, like

a canvas drop out of which his head protruded through the hole of his collar. They were popping baseballs at him, he was dodging.

"Will you keep a piece of the moon for yourself?" asked a questioner. It was a beautiful question. If he admitted desire, one 12 could ask if the Armstrong house would sleep on nights of full moon when the piece of rock bayed silently to its distant mistress, and emanations wandered down the stairs. But Armstrong said stiffly, "At this time, no plans have been made" . . . (Would he ever have the desire to steal a rock, Aquarius asked silently.) "No," Armstrong went on, "that's not a prerogative we have available to us." He could of course have said, "We can't do it," but in trouble he always talked computerese. The use of "we" was discouraged. "A joint exercise has demonstrated" became the substitution. "Other choices" became "peripheral secondary objectives." "Doing our best" was "obtaining maximum advantage possible." "Confidence" became "very high confidence level." "Ability to move" was a "mobility study." "Turn off" was "disable"; "turn on" became "enable." It was as if the more natural forms of English had not been built for the computer: Latin maybe, but not simple Anglo-Saxon. That was too primitive a language — only the general sense could be conveyed by the words: the precise intent was obliged to be defined by the tone of the voice. Computerese preferred to phase out such options. The message had to be locked into a form which could be transmitted by pulse or by lack of pulse, one binary digit at a time, one bit, one bug to be installed in each box. You could not break through computerese.

Through it all, Collins would smile, turn his sensitive presence 13 as eyes to the questioners, ears to the answer. His smile would flicker at the plastic obsidian impenetrability of computerese. "Darn it all," his smile would seem to say to the magazine writers, "if I had to learn how to translate this stuff, I'm sure you fellows can do as well!" Once again, Collins was being asked few questions.

They turned after a while to Aldrin and began to draw some 14 flecks of a true-blooded response. He was, of course, equally impenetrable in the beginning, but after a time he may have made the mistake of essaying a joke. Asked of his reactions to visiting the moon, he proceeded to build a wall of verbal brick, then abruptly with that clumsy odd sobriety, almost engaging, with which he was forever showing his willingness to serve, Aldrin made a remark about having been a boy scout. "I attained the rank of tenderfoot," he said. He gave a discomfited smile. "I hope I don't have a tender foot after walking around the moon." It was so bad a joke that one had to assume it was full of interior reference for him, perhaps some natural male anxiety at the thought of evil moon rays passing into one's private parts. A glum expression sat next to gloom — the damnedest things can happen to a good man.

Then they queried Aldrin on personal mementos. Would he be taking any along? 15

Well, yes, he admitted reluctantly, he would be taking a little family jewelry along. He stopped, he looked mulish. It was obvious he didn't want to go on. The primitive value of the objects, their power, their retention of charms, their position in the possible hierarchy of the amulets would be vitiated by describing them. On the other hand, a high quotient of availability-for-miscellaneous-unprogrammed-situations (known in the old days as charity, spontaneity, or generosity of spirit) also ranked high in good astronaut qualifications. So Aldrin gave answers even if he didn't want to. 16

Well, he admitted, the family jewelry were . . . *rings.* He had two heavy gold rings on two fingers. Yes, he nodded distrustfully, looking for a moment like a chow forced to obey a command he cannot enjoy, yes, on the flight, he would probably still be wearing them. 17

What else in the way of family jewelry? 18

But now Aldrin had had enough. "Personal category," he grunted. 19

A Viennese or German correspondent asked in a heavy accent of Armstrong, "Have you had any der-reams?" 20

Dreams. Armstrong smiled. He couldn't say he did. The smile was as quick to protect him as the quick tail flick of a long-suffering cow standing among horseflies in a summer meadow's heat, yes, smile-and-flick went Armstrong, "I guess after twenty hours in a simulator, I guess I sometimes have dreams of computers." 21

Yet as the questions went on, the game was turning. The German might have asked his question about dreams with the happy anticipation that any material provided would offer a feast — the symbols of the dream were pot roast after all and gravied potatoes to the intellectual maw of a nice German head, but the answer, frustrating as nearly all the answers had been, now succeeded in working up a counterpressure. Slowly, unmistakably, the intellectuals and writers on the dark side of the glass were becoming a little weary of the astronauts. Collins' implacable cheerful cool, Aldrin's doughty monk's cloth of squaredom, Armstrong's near-to- 22 facetious smile began to pique their respect. The questions began to have a new tone, an edge, the subtlest quivering suggestion that intellectual contempt was finally a weapon not to be ignored. Were these astronauts not much more than brain-programmed dolts? The contempt was a true pressure. For give an athlete brains, give an aviator brains, give an engineer a small concealed existence as presumptive poet, and whatever is not finished in the work of their ego, whatever is soft in their vanity, will then be exercised by the contempt of an intellectual. The writers were pushing Armstrong now.

Why, why ultimately, they were asking, is it so important to go   23
to the moon? Man to man, they were asking, brain to brain, their leverage derived from the additional position of asking as writer to small-town boy: why is it important?

Armstrong tried to be general. He made a speech in fair com-   24
puterese about the nation's resources, and the fact that NASA's efforts were now tapped into this root. Well, then, asked a dry voice, are we going to the moon only for economic reasons, only to get out of an expensive hole? No, said Armstrong.

Do you see any philosophical reason why we might be going?   25
the voice went on, as if to imply: are you aware there is philosophy to existence as well?

Armstrong had now been maneuvered to the point where there   26
was no alternative to offer but a credo, or claim that he was spiritually neuter. That would have violated too much in him. Yes, he blurted now, as if, damn them and damn their skills, they had wanted everything else of him this day, they had had everything else of him, including his full cooperation, now damn them good, they could have his philosophy too if they could comprehend it. "I think we're going," he said, and paused, static burning in the yaws of his pause. "I think we're going to the moon because it's in the nature of the human being to face challenges." He looked a little defiant, as if probably they might not know, some critical number of them might never know what he was talking about, "It's by the nature of his *deep inner soul*." The last three words came out as if they had seared his throat by their extortion. How his privacy had been invaded this day. "Yes," he nodded, as if noting what he had had to give up to writers, "we're required to do these things just as salmon swim upstream."

MEANINGS AND VALUES

1a. Specify the sentences in which the author first establishes, indirectly, what "process" he is sharing with us?
 b. A short time later he tells us again, this time more specifically defining the aim of the process. Where does he do this?

2a. Where was the turning point between failure and success in the process itself?
 b. Exactly what brought it about, as the author sees it?
 c. Does it seem to you that this would really have been a strong enough force to break the barrier? Explain.

3a. Identify the subtle symbolism of the glass partition. (See Guide to Terms: *Symbolism*.)
 b. Would it have been better if somehow it had been labeled "symbol," so we would not miss its significance? Explain.

4a. How clearly, if at all, do the three astronauts emerge as distinguishable personalities?
 b. Summarize, as well as you can, the characterizations.
 c. Why were the men so reluctant to let their real selves show through?

5. What, if anything, is the author saying subtly about Armstrong — an undermeaning, so to speak — in the last paragraph? Justify your answer carefully.

6. In such a highly subjective writing as this, the author's attitude toward his subject is almost certain to show in his tone. (Guide: *Style/Tone*.) Analyze Mailer's attitude toward this press conference and toward each of the astronauts.

7. Any worthwhile author, experienced in studying and analyzing human nature, should have insights to share that might easily be missed by the less observant. Cite at least three such penetrating insights in this selection.

8. What subtle irony, if any, do you see in the fact that the reporters won? (Guide: *Irony*.)

9. If you have read "The World Eaters" (Section 4), what might Eiseley have suggested as our real reason for going to the moon?

10. If you have read the Petrunkevitch selection, do you see any parallels in the processes explained in the two writings? If so, explain, noting carefully any basic differences as well.

EXPOSITORY TECHNIQUES

1. Other than merely to get the subject started, what is the basic function of paragraphs 1 and 2?

2a. Is the real nature of this process established early enough for maximum value?

b. Would it have been better if the author had been more explicit, perhaps even using the term "process"? Why, or why not?

3. Paragraph 5 makes good use of one of the patterns of exposition previously studied. Which one?

4. A basic and important job of any writer is his selection of details to be included, and Mailer obviously reported only a small part of what he saw and heard at this press conference. Cite several representative examples from the writing that illustrate his degree of skill in selection.

DICTION AND VOCABULARY

1. Carefully analyze the quality of diction in this essay, and try to determine the contributing causes of it. (Guide: *Diction;* and others as needed.) Report your findings concisely, in summary form, using examples only to illustrate.

2a. Early in paragraph 13 you will find an example of sarcasm. (Guide: *Irony.*) What is it?

b. How is it a matter of diction as well?

c. What does its tone indicate about the author's attitude toward Collins?

3. List or mark at least five sentences or portions of sentences that you think exhibit a high quality of syntax. (Guide: *Syntax.*) What, precisely, do you admire about them?

4. Cite two similes and two metaphors that seem particularly effective. (Guide: *Figures of Speech.*) For each of them, tell why.

5a. Some readers may feel that Mailer uses too many difficult words. What do you think?

b. To what extent does a sound answer to the above depend on the reader-audience he was expecting?

c. What kind of reader-audience do you think Mailer expected; or, if you prefer, what type of reader does he *not* expect?

6. Mailer is widely admired (and sometimes made fun of) for his distinctive style. Show how, if at all, it is really "style" we have considered in the first five questions. (Guide: *Style/Tone.*)

7. If you are not certain of the meanings of any of the following words, use a dictionary: debrief (par. 1); metaphysical (2); tendentious, cumulative, covertly (5); logical positivism, purvey, obsolescent (8); disclaimer (8, 10); virtually (10); nondescript, empyreans (11); emanations, prerogative, peripheral, binary (12); obsidian (13); essaying, sobriety, engaging, discomfited (14); amulets, vitiated (16); maw, implacable, doughty, facetious, pique, dolts, presumptive (22); credo, neuter, yaws, extortion (26).

SUGGESTIONS FOR WRITING AND DISCUSSION

1. Why must we assume (or is it unnecessary to assume) that the "natural aim of technology [is] to make intuition obsolescent" (par. 8)?

2. Why would a person who had never had strong intuitions not know "enough about the sensation to disclaim its presence in himself" (par. 8)?

3. Compare and/or contrast, in all ways possible, the significant aspects of the daring of Columbus and that of the first astronauts.

4. Show how the dreams of astronauts might be especially significant to psychologists and psychiatrists.

5. Do you think that it is really "in the nature of the human being to face challenges" (par. 26)? (Consider, for instance, the reverse possibility that it is as basic to human nature to "play it safe.")

6. Discuss other examples of the fairly common conflict (however low-keyed) between the "thinkers" and the "doers" of the world.

7. What is an "intellectual"?

8. Why do we make the stupendous sacrifices necessary for moon flights and explorations? Are they worth it?

Writing Suggestions for Section 5

Process Analysis

1. From one of the following topics develop a central theme into an *informational* process analysis showing:

    a. How you selected a college.

    b. How you selected your future career or major field of study.

    c. How your family selected a home.

    d. How a potential riot was stopped.

    e. How religious faith is achieved.

    f. How gasoline is made.

    g. How the air in _____ becomes polluted.

    h. How lightning kills.

    i. How foreign policy is made.

    j. How political campaigns are financed.

    k. How _____ Church was rebuilt.

    l. How fruit blossoms are pollinated.

2. Select a specific reader-audience and write a *directional* process analysis on one of the following topics. (Although none of the four illustrative essays is of this type, it is widely used in certain kinds of textbooks and for various utilitarian, how-to-do-it purposes. Few of these, however, achieve any noteworthy literary value.) Show:

    a. How to *do* any of the processes suggested by topics 1a–e. (This treatment will require a different viewpoint, completely objective, and may require a different organization.)

    b. How to overcome shyness.

    c. How to overcome stage fright.

    d. How to make the best use of study time.

    e. How to write a college composition.

    f. How to sell an ugly house.

    g. How to prepare a livestock or any other entry for a fair.

    h. How to start a club (or some other kind of recurring activity).

    i. How to reduce the number of highway accidents in an area.

    j. How to survive a tornado (or other natural disaster).

    k. How to select a car.

    l. How to develop moral (or physical) courage.

6

Analyzing *Cause* and *Effect* Relationships

Unlike process analysis, which merely tells *how*, causal analysis seeks to explain *why*. The two may be combined, but they need not be — many people have driven a car successfully after being told how to do it, never knowing or caring why the thing moved when the key was turned and a pedal or two manipulated.

Some causes and effects are not very complicated; at least the need for their explanation requires only a simple statement. A car may sit in the garage for a while because its owner has no money for a license tag, and sometimes this is explanation enough. But frequently a much more thorough analysis is required, and this may even become the basic pattern of an exposition.

To explain fully the causes of a war or depression or election results the writer must seek not only *immediate* causes (the ones he encounters first) but also *ultimate* causes (the basic, underlying factors that help to explain the more apparent ones.) The business or professional man, as well as the student, often has pressing need for this type of analysis. How else could he fully understand or report on a failing sales campaign, diminishing church membership, a local increase of traffic accidents, or teenage use of hard drugs? The immediate cause of a disastrous warehouse fire could be faulty electrical wiring, but this might be attributed in turn to the company's unwise economy measures, which might be traced even further to undue pressures on the management to show large profits. The written analysis might logically stop at any point, of course, depending entirely on its purpose and the reader-audience for which it is intended.

Similarly, both the immediate and ultimate *effects* of an action or situation may, or may not, need to be fully explored. If a 5 per cent pay raise is granted, what will be the immediate effect on the cost of production, leading to what ultimate effects on prices and, in some cases, on the whole economy of a business, a town, or perhaps the entire nation?

In earlier selections of this book we have seen several examples of causal analysis. In Section 1, for instance, Peter and Hull are concerned with the ultimate causes of incompetence in public life, and Gregory is to some extent concerned with both immediate and ultimate causes of police-ghetto strife.

Causal analysis is one of the chief techniques of reasoning; and if the method is used at all, the reader must always have confidence in its thoroughness and logic. Some faults in causal reasoning are these:

1. Never mistake the fact that something happens with or after another occurrence as evidence of a causal relationship — for example, that a black cat crossing the road caused the flat tire a few minute later, or that a course in English composition caused a student's nervous breakdown that same semester.

2. Consider all possibly relevant factors before attributing causes. Perhaps studying English did result in a nervous breakdown, but the cause may also have been ill health, trouble at home, or the anguish of a love affair. (The composition course, by providing an "emotional" outlet, may even have helped *postpone* the breakdown!)

3. Support the analysis by more than mere assertions: offer evidence. It would not often be enough to *tell* why Shakespeare's wise Othello believed the villainous Iago — the dramatist's lines should be used as evidence, possibly supported by the opinions of at least one literary scholar. If explaining that capital punishment deters crime, do not expect the reader to take your word for it — give before-and-after statistics or the testimony of reliable authorities.

4. Be careful not to omit any links in the chain of causes or effects unless you are certain that the readers for whom the writing is intended will automatically make the right connections themselves — and this is frequently a dangerous assumption. To unwisely omit one or more of the links might leave the reader with only a vague, or even erroneous, impression of the causal connection, possibly

invalidating all that follows and thus making the entire writing ineffective.

5. Be honest and objective. The writer (or thinker) who brings his old prejudices to the task of causal analysis, or who fails to see the probability of *multiple* causes or effects, is almost certain to distort his analysis or to make it so superficial, so thin, as to be almost worthless.

Ordinarily the method of causal analysis is either to work logically from the immediate cause (or effect) down toward the most basic, or to start with the basic and work up toward the immediate. But after he has at least analyzed the subject in his mind and decided what his purpose requires in the paragraph or entire composition, the writer will usually find that a satisfactory pattern suggests itself.

RALPH WALDO EMERSON (1803–1882), essayist, poet, and philosopher, was born in Boston and prepared for a career in the ministry at Harvard College. A few years after he became pastor of a church in Boston, however, his increasing doubts about orthodox religion prompted him to seek other means of personal fulfillment, and writing became his career. Among his best-known prose works are the essays "Nature," first published anonymously in 1836; "The American Scholar," first delivered as an address at Harvard College in 1837; "Self-Reliance" and "The Over-Soul" (1841), "Experience" (1844), and "The Poet" (1850).

War's Place in Human Progress

"War's Place in Human Progress" (editor's title) is excerpted from Emerson's "War." Readers may find the selection surprisingly contemporary in some respects, if perhaps disheartening in its optimism, inasmuch as it was written a whole century and several devastating wars ago. It illustrates a simple and direct pattern of cause/effect analysis, used by Emerson as a means of building to the optimistic theme itself.

It has been a favorite study of modern philosophy to indicate the steps of human progress, to watch the rising of a thought in one man's mind, the communication of it to a few, to a small minority, its expansion and general reception, until it publishes itself to the world by destroying the existing laws and institutions, and the generation of new. Looked at in this general and historical way, many things wear a very different face from that they show near by, and one at a time — and, particularly, war. War, which to sane men at the present day begins to look like an epidemic insanity, breaking out here and there like the cholera or influenza, infecting men's

1

brains instead of their bowels — when seen in the remote past, in the infancy of society, appears a part of the connexion of events, and, in its place, necessary.

As far as history has preserved to us the slow unfoldings of any 2 savage tribe, it is not easy to see how war could be avoided by such wild, passionate, needy, ungoverned, strong-bodied creatures. For in the infancy of society, when a thin population and improvidence make the supply of food and of shelter insufficient and very precarious, and when hunger, thirst, ague and frozen limbs universally take precedence of the wants of the mind and the heart, the necessities of the strong will certainly be satisfied at the cost of the weak, at whatever peril of future revenge. It is plain, too, that in the first dawnings of the religious sentiment, *that* blends itself with their passions and is oil to the fire. Not only every tribe has war-gods, religious festivals in victory, but *religious wars.*

The student of history acquiesces the more readily in this copious 3 bloodshed of the early annals, bloodshed in God's name too, when he learns that it is a temporary and preparatory state, and does actively forward the culture of man. War educates the senses, calls into action the will, perfects the physical constitution, brings men into such swift and close collision in critical moments that man measures man. On its own scale, on the virtues it loves, it endures no counterfeit, but shakes the whole society until every atom falls into the place its specific gravity assigns it. It presently finds the value of good sense and of foresight, and Ulysses takes rank next to Achilles. The leaders, picked men of a courage and vigor tried and augmented in fifty battles, are emulous to distinguish themselves above each other by new merits, as clemency, hospitality, splendor of living. The people imitate the chiefs. The strong tribe, in which war has become an art, attack and conquer their neighbors, and teach them their arts and virtues. New territory, augmented numbers and extended interests call out new virtues and abilities, and the tribe makes long strides. And, finally, when much progress has been made, all its secrets of wisdom and art are disseminated by its invasions. Plutarch, in his essay "On the Fortune of Alexander," considers the invasion and conquest of the East by Alexander as one of the most bright and pleasing pages in history; and it must be owned he gives sound reason for his opinion. It had the effect of uniting into one great interest the divided commonwealths of Greece, and infusing a new and more enlarged public spirit into the councils of their statesmen. It carried the arts and language and philosophy of the Greeks into the sluggish and barbarous nations of Persia, Assyria and India. It introduced the arts of husbandry among tribes of hunters and shepherds. It weaned the Scythians and Persians from some cruel and licentious practices to a more civil way of life. It introduced the sacredness of marriage among them. It built seventy cities, and sowed the Greek customs and humane laws over Asia, and united hostile nations under one code. It brought different families of the human race together — to blows at first, but afterwards to truce, to trade and to intermarriage. It would be very easy to show analogous benefits that have resulted from military movements of later ages.

Considerations of this kind lead us to a true view of the nature and office of war. We see it is the subject of all history; that it has been the principal employment of the most conspicuous men; that it is at this moment the delight of half the world, of almost all young and ignorant persons; that it is exhibited to us continually in the dumb show of brute nature, where war between tribes, and between individuals of the same tribe, perpetually rages. The microscope reveals miniature butchery in atomies and infinitely small biters that swim and fight in an illuminated drop of water; and the little globe is but a too faithful miniature of the large.

What does all this war, beginning from the lowest races and reaching up to man, signify? Is it not manifest that it covers a great and beneficent principle, which nature had deeply at heart? What is that principle? — It is self-help. Nature implants with life the instinct of self-help, perpetual struggle to be, to resist opposition, to attain to freedom, to attain to a mastery and the security of a permanent, self-defended being; and to each creature these objects are made so dear that it risks its life continually in the struggle for these ends.

But whilst this principle, necessarily, is inwrought into the fabric of every creature, yet it is but *one* instinct; and though a primary one, or we may say the very first, yet the appearance of the other instincts immediately modifies and controls this; turns its energies into harmless, useful and high courses, showing thereby what was its ultimate design; and finally, takes out its fangs. The instinct of self-help is very early unfolded in the coarse and merely brute form of war, only in the childhood and imbecility of the other instincts, and remains in that form only until their development. It is the ignorant and childish part of mankind that is the fighting part. . . .

The scandal which we feel in such facts certainly shows that we 7
have got on a little. All history is the decline of war, though the slow
decline. All that society has yet gained is mitigation: the doctrine
of the right of war still remains.

For ages (for ideas work in ages, and animate vast societies of 8
men) the human race has gone on under the tyranny — shall I so
call it? — of this first brutish form of their effort to be men; that is,
for ages they have shared so much of the nature of the lower animals, the tiger and the shark, and the savages of the water-drop.
They have nearly exhausted all the good and all the evil of this
form: they have held as fast to this degradation as their worst
enemy could desire; but all things have an end, and so has this.
The eternal germination of the better has unfolded new powers,
new instincts, which were really concealed under this rough and
base rind. The sublime question has startled one and another happy
soul in different quarters of the globe — Cannot love be, as well as
hate? Would not love answer the same end, or even a better? Cannot peace be, as well as war?

This thought is no man's invention, neither St. Pierre's nor Rous- 9
seau's, but the rising of the general tide in the human soul — and
rising highest, and first made visible, in the most simple and pure
souls, who have therefore announced it to us beforehand; but
presently we all see it. It has now become so distinct as to be a
social thought: societies can be formed on it. It is expounded,
illustrated, defined, with different degrees of clearness; and its
actualization, or the measures it should inspire, predicted according
to the light of each seer.

The idea itself is the epoch; the fact that it has become so distinct 10
to any small number of persons as to become a subject of prayer and
hope, of concert and discussion — *that* is the commanding fact. This
having come, much more will follow. Revolutions go not backward.
The star once risen, though only one man in the hemisphere has yet
seen its upper limb in the horizon, will mount and mount, until it
becomes visible to other men, to multitudes, and climbs the zenith
of all eyes. And so it is not a great matter how long men refuse to
believe the advent of peace; war is on its last legs; and a universal
peace is as sure as is the prevalence of civilization over barbarism,
of liberal governments over feudal forms. The question for us is
only *How soon?*

MEANINGS AND VALUES

1a. Is it still true that we can expect the "necessities of the strong" (in view of "hunger, thirst, ague and [or] frozen limbs") to be satisfied at the cost of the weak (par. 2)? Justify your answer.
  b. To what extent, if at all, may the war making or war threatening of even modern super-powers be due to these same "necessities"?
2. Has "religious sentiment" been the cause of war more recently than the days of tribal warfare (par. 2)? If so, give examples.
3a. In listing the effects of warfare (par. 3), Emerson uses the present tense (e.g., "educates the senses"). Do you think he meant that these effects were still true at the time he wrote?
  b. Which, if any, of them are still the results of war? Explain.
4. Carefully consider the statement that war "is the subject of all history" (par. 4). Does this seem true to you, either directly or indirectly? Why, or why not?
5a. List other specific ways in which the energies of the instinct of self-help may be turned into "harmless, useful, and high courses" (par. 6).
  b. Show how each could help to replace the urge for self-help through fighting.
6. The author says, in paragraph 9, that societies can be formed on the concept of love and peace. Now, a century later, have any such societies been formed? If so, what are they?
7. Should we conclude that Emerson was wrong, or at least over-optimistic, because his ideal of love and peace surplanting war has still not come to pass? Why, or why not?

EXPOSITORY TECHNIQUES

1a. Which pattern of exposition is used in a sort of mini-version in the first sentence?
  b. The overall introduction, however, exemplifies one of the standard methods of opening an exposition. What is it? (See Guide to Terms: *Introductions.*)
2. All of paragraph 3 is given to the effects of early wars, and these apparently are meant as ultimate effects. What, as nearly as we can tell, were the immediate effects? Why does Emerson not also enumerate those?
3a. About halfway through paragraph 3 is an abrupt change. What is the author doing then and until the end of the paragraph?
  b. What is gained by this procedure?

4a. Although the word "cause" is not used to identify it, in paragraph 5 we reach what is, in Emerson's opinion, the ultimate cause of war. What is it?

 b. Soon afterward, in paragraph 6, he briefly gives us a new set of effects. These are the effects of what?

5. What is the chief function of paragraphs 9 and 10, in relation to the cause/effect analysis?

DICTION AND VOCABULARY

1a. Identify the sources and original uses of the two allusions in paragraph 3.

 b. What is the figurative meaning of the two as Emerson employs them?

2. How can an "idea" be an "epoch," as the author claims in paragraph 10? Explain the overall significance of his statement.

3. Why would it be unfair of us to condemn Emerson's seemingly blatant use of a cliché at the end of paragraph 10?

4. Use the dictionary as necessary to understand the following words and their meanings: improvidence, ague (par. 2); acquiesces, copious, annals, augmented, emulous, disseminated, licentious, analogous (3); atomies (4); mitigation (7); animate, degradation (8); expounded, seer (9); limb, advent (10).

SUGGESTIONS FOR WRITING AND DISCUSSION

1. Explain the meaning and present-day significance of Emerson's observation that all society "has yet gained is mitigation: the doctrine of the right of war still remains" (par. 7).

2. How, if at all, can the people of a threatened country make significant love contact with the people of a dictator nation in which freedom of contact with foreigners is rigidly controlled?

3. Propose one practical idea, consistent with love and peace, by which a tribe or modern nation might satisfy the self-help instincts listed in paragraph 5. Carefully consider and explain both the merits and the hazards of your plan.

4. When, if at all, should a free and peace-loving nation go to the rescue, with force, of a weaker country whose freedom and peace are threatened by stronger forces?

5. Develop more fully, if you like, your answer to question 7 of "Meanings and Values." Do not ignore the catastrophic proportions of wars during the intervening century and the fact that the world is still in constant danger of another.

(NOTE: Suggestions for topics requiring development by analysis of CAUSE and EFFECT are on page 190, at the end of this section.)

LYNN WHITE, JR.

LYNN WHITE, JR., born in California in 1907, was educated at Stanford and Harvard. He has received many
honors and fellowships in his field of history, primarily of
the Renaissance. White served for fifteen years as professor at and president of Mills College, and he has also
taught at Stanford and at the University of California, Los
Angeles, where he has been a professor since 1958. His
many published works include *Medieval Technology and
Social Change* (1962), *The Transformation of the Roman
World* (1966), *Machina ex Deo: Essays in the Dynamism
of Western Culture* (1968).

The Ecologic Crisis and Christian Arrogance

"The Ecologic Crisis and Christian Arrogance" is a portion
of White's "The Historical Roots of Our Ecologic Crisis,"
published originally in *Science* magazine (March 1967)
and later in *The Environmental Handbook*. Here the
historian-author probes deeply into our Western culture
for an explanation of what he sees as one of the primary
causes of the potential environmental disaster.

Since both *science* and *technology* are blessed words in our con- 1
temporary vocabulary, some may be happy at the notions, first, that,
viewed historically, modern science is an extrapolation of natural
theology and, second, that modern technology is at least partly to
be explained as an occidental, voluntarist realization of the Christian
dogma of man's transcendence of, and rightful mastery over, nature.
But, as we now recognize, somewhat over a century ago science
and technology — hitherto quite separate activities — joined to give
mankind powers which, to judge by many of the ecologic effects,

From *Science*, Vol. 155 (March 10, 1967), pages 1203–1207. Copyright 1967 by
the American Association for the Advancement of Science. Reprinted by permission of the author and the publisher.

are out of control. If so, Christianity bears a huge burden of guilt.

I personally doubt that disastrous ecologic backlash can be 2 avoided simply by applying to our problems more science and more technology. Our science and technology have grown out of Christian attitudes toward man's relation to nature which are almost universally held not only by Christians and neo-Christians but also by those who fondly regard themselves as post-Christians. Despite Copernicus, all the cosmos rotates around our little globe. Despite Darwin, we are *not*, in our hearts, part of the natural process. We are superior to nature, contemptuous of it, willing to use it for our slightest whim. The newly elected governor of California, like myself a churchman, but less troubled than I, spoke for the Christian tradition when he said (as is alleged), "when you've seen one redwood tree, you've seen them all." To a Christian a tree can be no more than a physical fact. The whole concept of the sacred grove is alien to Christianity and to the ethos of the West. For nearly two millennia Christian missionaries have been chopping down sacred groves, which are idolatrous because they assume spirit in nature.

What we do about ecology depends on our ideas of the man- 3 nature relationship. More science and more technology are not going to get us out of the present ecologic crisis until we find a new religion, or rethink our old one. The beatniks, who are the basic revolutionaries of our time, show a sound instinct in their affinity for Zen Buddhism, which conceives of the man-nature relationship as very nearly the mirror image of the Christian view. Zen, however, is as deeply conditioned by Asian history as Christianity is by the experience of the West, and I am dubious of its viability among us.

Possibly we should ponder the greatest radical in Christian his- 4 tory since Christ: Saint Francis of Assisi. The prime miracle of Saint Francis is the fact that he did not end at the stake, as many of his left-wing followers did. He was so clearly heretical that a general of the Franciscan Order, Saint Bonaventura, a great and perceptive Christian, tried to suppress the early accounts of Franciscanism. The key to an understanding of Francis is his belief in the virtue of humility — not merely for the individual but for man as a species. Francis tried to depose man from his monarchy over creation and set up a democracy of all God's creatures. With him the ant is no longer simply a homily for the lazy, flames a sign of the thrust of the soul toward union with God; now they are Brother Ant and

Sister Fire, praising the Creator in their own ways as Brother Man
does in his.

Later commentators have said that Francis preached to the birds   5
as a rebuke to men who would not listen. The records do not read
so: he urged the little birds to praise God, and in spiritual ecstasy
they flapped their wings and chirped rejoicing. Legends of saints,
especially the Irish saints, had long told of their dealings with
animals but always, I believe, to show their human dominance over
creatures. With Francis it is different. The land around Gubbio in
the Apennines was being ravaged by a fierce wolf. Saint Francis,
says the legend, talked to the wolf and persuaded him of the error
of his ways. The wolf repented, died in the odor of sanctity, and was
buried in consecrated ground.

What Sir Steven Ruciman calls "the Franciscan doctrine of the   6
animal soul" was quickly stamped out. Quite possibly it was in part
inspired, consciously or unconsciously, by the belief in reincarnation held by the Cathar heretics who at that time teemed in Italy
and southern France, and who presumably had got it originally from
India. It is significant that at just the same moment, about 1200,
traces of metempsychosis are found also in western Judaism, in the
Provençal *Cabbala*. But Francis held neither to transmigration of
souls nor to pantheism. His view of nature and of man rested on a
unique sort of pan-psychism of all things animate and inanimate,
designed for the glorification of their transcendent Creator, who, in
the ultimate gesture of cosmic humility, assumed flesh, lay helpless
in a manger, and hung dying on a scaffold.

I am not suggesting that many contemporary Americans who are   7
concerned about our ecologic crisis will be either able or willing to
counsel with wolves or exhort birds. However, the present increasing disruption of the global environment is the product of a dynamic
technology and science which were originating in the Western
medieval world against which Saint Francis was rebelling in so
original a way. Their growth cannot be understood historically apart
from distinctive attitudes toward nature which are deeply grounded
in Christian dogma. The fact that most people do not think of these
attitudes as Christian is irrelevant. No new set of basic values has
been accepted in our society to displace those of Christianity. Hence
we shall continue to have a worsening ecologic crisis until we reject
the Christian axiom that nature has no reason for existence save to
serve man.

The greatest spiritual revolutionary in Western history, Saint Francis, proposed what he thought was an alternative Christian view of nature and man's relation to it: he tried to substitute the idea of the equality of all creatures, including man, for the idea of man's limitless rule of creation. He failed. Both our present science and our present technology are so tinctured with orthodox Christian arrogance toward nature that no solution for our ecologic crisis can be expected from them alone. Since the roots of our trouble are so largely religious, the remedy must also be essentially religious, whether we call it that or not. We must rethink and refeel our nature and destiny. The profoundly religious, but heretical, sense of the primitive Franciscans for the spiritual autonomy of all parts of nature may point a direction. I propose Francis as a patron saint for ecologists.

MEANINGS AND VALUES

1. Early in the essay the author identifies himself as a Christian. How does this fact contribute to the overall effectiveness of the essay?
2. Illustrate the meaning of the following by specific examples from this writing. (See Guide to Terms: *Irony.*)
    a. Irony of situation.
    b. Verbal irony.
    c. Sarcasm.
3a. Show how such usage of irony helps to establish the tone of this essay. (Guide: *Style/Tone.*)
    b. What may we surmise from the tone about the author's attitude toward his subject? (Guide: *Point of View.*)
    c. How does it help to classify the writing as objective or subjective? (Guide: *Objective/Subjective.*)
4a. How, if at all, is the last sentence of paragraph 2 symbolic? (Guide: *Symbolism.*)
    b. What examples of symbolism, if any, do you find in paragraph 4?
5. Explain more fully the "mirror image" metaphor in paragraph 3. (It is not essential to be very familiar with either Zen Buddhism or Christianity in order to do this.)
6. Evaluate this essay. (Guide: *Evaluation.*)
7. If you have read Leopold's "The Land Pyramid," what relation, if any, can you see between White's central theme and any of Leopold's major points?

EXPOSITORY TECHNIQUES

1. The author pushes aside at once, or ignores, the immediate causes of threatened ecologic disaster and arrives at the ultimate cause he intends to discuss.
   a. Where does he first state this ultimate cause?
   b. Name five immediate causes that he ignores entirely.
   c. Why do you suppose he feels justified in doing this?
   d. Do you agree? Why, or why not?
2a. Where is the central theme first clearly stated.
   b. What effect, if any, does this placement and clarity have on the essay's unity (Guide: *Unity.*)
3a. The author sometimes uses a sharp contrast as tributary to his main theme. Cite as many such uses as possible.
   b. What specific effects are gained by any, or all, of these contrasts?
4a. What standard techniques are used in the introduction? (Guide: *Introductions.*)
   b. Do these combine to make an appropriate and effective beginning? Why, or why not?

DICTION AND VOCABULARY

1. The author often chooses words whose connotations help to emphasize his ideas. Two of these in the first paragraph are "blessed" and "notions." (Guide: *Connotation/Denotation.*)
   a. What connotation does each of these have for you?
   b. Show how these connotations, subtle as they may be, are used to the writer's advantage.
   c. Cite two other examples of words with useful connotations.
2. Which of the four words cited in answering question 1 can, as used in the essay, also illustrate sarcasm? Why? (Guide: *Irony.*)
3. Although perhaps more difficult to isolate and discuss, another important element of White's style is his appropriate, often fresh syntax. (Guide: *Syntax.*) Cite three examples of this which appeal to you and explain why.
4. Familiarize yourself with the following words and their meanings, consulting your dictionary as necessary: extrapolation, voluntarist, dogma (par. 1); ethos, millennia (2); affinity, viability (3); heretical, homily (4); reincarnation, heretics, metempsychosis, transmigration, pantheism, panpsychism (6); exhort, irrelevant, axiom (7); tinctured, arrogance, autonomy (8).

5a. If the author's use of difficult words seems excessive to you, choose any four of them, restudy their meanings, and suggest easier words that would have done the author's job as precisely. (Guide: *Diction.*)

 b. What do your findings suggest about this aspect of the author's diction?

 c. Should a college student expect exemption from such words? Why, or why not?

SUGGESTIONS FOR WRITING AND DISCUSSION

1. Explain, with liberal use of examples, how the joining of science and technology gave mankind such tremendous powers (par. 1).

2. If you see symbolic meaning in the last sentence of paragraph 2, expand on its meaning in whatever direction it seems to require. (Guide: *Symbolism.*)

3. Discuss the importance of symbolism in Christianity, using as many examples as possible.

4. If the beatniks generally had an affinity for Zen Buddhism (par. 3), what spiritual direction, if any, has been the earmark of their heirs, the hippies? Avoid overgeneralization and explore all possibilities.

5. If you have studied the Bible or Christian tradition to some extent, explain if possible the real source, or sources, of Christianity's so-called arrogance toward nature (par. 8).

6. Much of Christianity is, of course, based solidly on Judaism. If you are familiar with Jewish religion, culture, or tradition, to what extent may Christian "arrogance toward nature" be explained by Jewish influences?

7. If you see any connection between White's theme and Americans' relations with the native Indians, explain what it is and show its significance, if any. (Be especially careful not to overgeneralize.)

8. If you have read Leopold's "The Land Pyramid," develop any point of relationship between its theme and White's.

(NOTE: Suggestions for topics requiring development by analysis of CAUSE and EFFECT are on page 190, at the end of this section.)

LAWRENCE CASLER, born in 1932, is professor of psychology at the State University of Genesco, New York. He received his Ph.D. in social psychology from Columbia University in 1962. Casler has published articles on the developmental psychology of infants, the social psychology of marriage, nudism, hypnosis, and ESP.

This Thing Called Love Is Pathological

"This Thing Called Love Is Pathological," of which the following selection is a greater part, was first published in the December 1969 issue of *Psychology Today*. In his search for ultimate causes and effects of romantic love, Casler is far from romantic and may even draw sparks from some of his readers. (But personal agreement has never been requisite for objective analysis of another's views and methods.)

Men have died from time to time and worms have eaten them, but not for love.
— Act IV, Scene 1, *As You Like It*

Magazines, movies and television teach us the joys of love. Advertisers insist that we must look good and smell good in order to escape loveless solitude. Artists, philosophers and hippies urge their varying versions of Love; and most psychotherapists hold that the ability to love is a sign — sometimes *the* sign — of mental health.

To suggest that this emphasis on lovingness is misplaced is to risk being accused of arrested development, coldness, low self-image, or

Abridged from *Psychology Today* Magazine, December 1969. A section of the characteristics of love was deleted. Copyright © Communications/Research/Machines, Inc. Reprinted by permission.

some unmentionable deficiency. Still, the expanding frontiers of psychology require a reconsideration of love at this time.

We shall be concerned, chiefly, with what is generally called "romantic" love. But many of these observations may be applicable to other varieties as well.   3

Love, like other emotions, has causes . . . and consequences. Temporarily setting aside an inquiry into why, or whether, love makes the world go 'round, makes life worth living, and conquers all, let us consider the somewhat more manageable question of causality. Love between man and woman has many determinants, but instinct is not one of them. Anthropologists have described entire societies in which love is absent, and there are many individuals in our society who have never loved. To argue that such societies and individuals are "sick" or "the exception that proves the rule" (whatever *that* means) is sheer arrogance. Love, when it exists, is a learned emotion. Explanations for its current prevalence must be sought elsewhere than in the genes.   4

Most individuals in our society, beset by parent-bred, competition-bred insecurity, need acceptance, confirmation, justification. Part of this need is inescapable. Life requires continual decision-making: white vs. red wine, honesty vs. dishonesty, etc. In the presence of uncertainty, most of us need to know that we are making the right decisions, so we seek external validation. We are, therefore, absurdly pleased when we meet someone who shares our penchant for Palestrina or peanut butter. Should we find one person whose choices in many different matters coincide with our own, we will value this buttress of our self-esteem. This attachment to a source of self-validation constitutes one important basis for love.   5

While the relationship between loving and being loved is an intimate one, this is not to say that love is automatically reciprocated. Indeed, it may lead to feelings of revulsion if the individual's self-image is already irretrievably low: "Anyone who says he loves *me* must be either a fool or a fraud." Still a person is relatively likely to love someone who loves him. Indirect support for this generalization comes from a number of experiments in which persons are falsely informed that they are liked (or disliked) by other members of their group. This misinformation is enough to elicit congruent feelings in most of the deceived subjects. A similar kind of feedback often operates in the elaborate American game of dating. The young woman, for any of several reasons, may pretend to like her   6 escort more than is actually the case. The man, hungry for precisely this kind of response, responds favorably and in kind. And the woman, gratified by this expression of affection, now feels the fondness she had formerly feigned. Falling in love may be regarded, in cases such as these, as a snowball with a hollow core.

Nevertheless, we do not fall in love with everyone who shows 7 acceptance of us. Other needs clamor for satisfaction. And the more needs that one person satisfies, the more likely are we to love that person. One of the foremost needs is called, very loosely, sex. Our love is elicited not simply by the ego-booster, but by the ego-booster with sex appeal.

The mores of our society discourage us from seeking sexual grati- 8 fication from anyone with whom we do not have a preexisting relationship. As a result, the more ego-boosting a relationship is, the greater the tendency will be for the booster to serve — actually or potentially — as a sex-satisfier. But it is also true that a person who gives one sexual pleasure tends to boost one's ego. Once again, the snowball effect is obvious.

Society emphasizes, furthermore, the necessity for love to precede 9 sex. Although many disregard this restriction, others remain frightened or disturbed by the idea of a purely sexual relationship. The only way for many sexually aroused individuals to avoid frustration or anxiety is to fall in love — as quickly as possible. More declarations of love have probably been uttered in parked cars than in any other location. Some of these surely are nothing more than seduction ploys, but it is likely that self-seduction is involved in many cases.

For most of us, the internal and external pressures are so great 10 that we can no longer "choose" to love or not love. Loving becomes inevitable, like dying or getting married. We are so thoroughly brainwashed that we come to pity or scorn the person who is not in love. (Of course, the pity or scorn may be self-directed, but not for long: anyone who does not have the inner resources to stand alone can usually impose himself upon somebody else who is equally incapacitated.)

Our society, besides being love-oriented, is marriage-oriented. 11 From early childhood on, we hear countless statements beginning, "When (not *if*) you get married. . . ." And, just as love is regarded as a prerequisite for sex, it is regarded as a prerequisite for marriage. Consequently, the insecurity and the fear of social punishment that force most of us into marriage provide additional powerful motives for falling in love. (The current value of marriage as a social institution, while open to question, is beyond the scope of this essay.)

To summarize, the *causes* of love are the needs for security, sexual 12 satisfaction, and social conformity. Thus viewed, love loses its uniqueness. Hatred, too, in societies that are as aggression-oriented as ours is love-oriented, may reflect these same needs. To state that love is a superior emotion is to express a current cultural bias. Nothing is good or bad but culture makes it so. . . .

Let us turn now to a consideration of the *consequences* of love. 13 First, being in love makes it easier to have guilt-free sex, to marry, and to view oneself as a normal, healthy citizen of the Western world. Love also tends to alter certain psychological processes. According to a charming quotation that I've been able to trace back no further than its utterance in an old movie called *Mr. Skeffington,* "A woman is beautiful only when she is loved." The statement, however, is not quite accurate. A woman (likewise a man, a worm, a grain of sand) may become beautiful when the perceiver has been primed with LSD, hypnosis, or anything else that can induce hallucinations. In short, love may create the error of over-evaluation. The doting lover is doomed either to painful disillusion or to the permanent delusion that so closely resembles psychosis.

Some may argue that I am speaking of immature infatuation, 14 rather than real love. Mature love, they may insist, is a broadening, deepening experience. This postulation of the salutary effects of love is so pervasive that we must examine its validity. First, there is the matter of evidence. Subjective reports are notoriously unreliable, and experimental studies are nonexistent. The claim that love promotes maturity is unpersuasive without some indication that the individual would not have matured just as readily in the absence of love. Indeed, to the extent that love fosters dependency, it may be viewed as a deterrent to maturity.

I am not asserting that the effects of love always border on the 15 pathological. I *am* saying that the person who seeks love in order to obtain security will become, like the alcoholic, increasingly dependent on this source of illusory well-being. The secure person who seeks love would probably not trap himself in this way. But would the secure person seek love at all?

One inference to be drawn from the material here is that the non- 16 loving person in our society is likely to be in a state of either very good or very poor mental health. The latter possibility requires no extended explanation. One of the standard stigmata of emotional disturbance is the inability to love. Most schools of psychotherapy aim specifically at the development of this ability. Some therapies go so far as to designate the therapist himself as a proper recipient of the patient's newly released love impulses (perhaps on the assumption that if the patient can love his therapist, he can love anybody).

The other part of the statement — that a love-free person can be 17 in excellent mental health — may seem less acceptable. But if the need for a love relationship is based largely on insecurity, conformity to social pressures, and sexual frustration, then the person who is secure, independent, and has a satisfying sex life will not need to love. He will, rather, be a person who does not find his own company boring — a person whose inner resources are such that other persons, although they provide pleasure and stimulation, are not absolutely necessary. We have long been enjoined to love others as we love ourselves. But perhaps we seek love relationships with others only because we do not love ourselves sufficiently.

What would a healthy love-free person be like? One might assume 18 that coldness would be among his most salient characteristics. But a cold person is simply one who does not give us the warmth we want or need. The attribution of coldness says more about the person doing the attributing than it does about the person being characterized. Absence of warmth is responded to negatively only by those insecure persons who interpret it as rejection. (Similarly, a nymphomaniac has been defined as a woman whose sex drive is stronger than that of the person who is calling her a nymphomaniac.)

Would the love-free person be egotistical? Perhaps, but only if 19 that term is relieved of its ugly connotations. To be self-centered does not mean to disregard the worth of other people. It does imply that other people are reacted to within a frame of reference that is centered on the self. There is nothing reprehensible about this. In fact, most psychologists would probably accept the position that we are *all* self-centered. No matter how other-directed our actions may appear, they are functions of *our* perception of the world, based, in turn, on *our* previous experiences. Since every act is a "self-ish" one, evaluative criteria should be applied only to the effects of selfishness, rather than to selfishness, *per se*.

This essay has not been anti-love, but pro-people. I view society's 20 emphasis on love as both an effect and a cause of the insecurity, dependency, and frightened conformity that may be the death of us all. To love a person means, all too often, to use that person. And exploitation, even if mutual, is incompatible with human growth. Finally, like a crutch, love may impede the exercise of our own potential for growth, and thus tend to perpetuate itself.

Perhaps the goal of social reformers should be not love, but   21
respect — for others and, most of all, for self.

MEANINGS AND VALUES

1. If the author's ideas of romantic love and its causes are even partially correct, to what other "varieties" of love might they also apply (par. 3)?
2a. The author states that most individuals are beset by insecurity (par. 5). How is this insecurity "parent-bred"?
 b. How is it "competition-bred"?
3. Is anyone you know so "secure" that he has no need for love at all (par. 15)? Briefly provide some support for your answer.
4. Clarify the author's concept of "self-seduction" (par. 9).
5. In paragraph 18, is the author saying that there is no such being as a "cold" person, except in the view of the person wanting to relate to him? Clarify.
6. How convincingly does the author demonstrate that "love, as it exists, is a learned emotion" (par. 4)? Justify your answer objectively.
7a. The author states that his essay has not been "anti-love" (par. 20). Do you agree? Why, or why not?
 b. Has reading it in any way affected your own attitude toward love? Explain.
8. If you have read Packard's "New Directions of Marriage," show whatever significant relationship you find between his ideas and Casler's statement (par. 11) that "insecurity and the fear of social punishment . . . force most of us into marriage."
9a. If you have read Krutch's "We Were Not Skeptical Enough," how do you think he would have reacted to Casler's assertion (par. 12) that "nothing is good or bad but culture makes it so"?
 b. To what extent, if at all, would he have found Casler guilty of the same "mistakes" he was guilty of himself when younger?

EXPOSITORY TECHNIQUES

1a. Which, if any, of the author's causes do you consider immediate and which ultimate? Why?
 b. Which of the consequences would you so classify in each category? Why?

2a. Cite the specific devices by which this author keeps us oriented to his step-by-step development — no doubt to prevent any sense of disorder, with resulting frustration and loss of attention.

   b. Explain how unity is served by this attention to orderliness. (See Guide to Terms: *Unity.*)

   c. How is coherence served? (Guide: *Coherence.*)

3. Which of the common introductory techniques does the author employ? (Guide: *Introductions.*)

4a. Which of the methods for closing are used? (Guide: *Closings.*)

   b. Suggest one other way this writing might have been concluded.

5. Would greater use of qualification have improved the effectiveness of this writing? (Guide: *Qualification.*) If so, cite instances and show how the qualifying could be achieved.

DICTION AND VOCABULARY

1a. Cite three clichés in paragraph 4. (Guide: *Clichés.*)

   b. Is their use careless or intentional? Why?

2. Is the "snowball" (pars. 6, 8) used as a figure of speech, as analogy, or as a sort of hybrid? Why? (Guide: *Figures of Speech.*)

3a. What is your dictionary's denotative meaning of "egotistical" (par. 19)?

   b. Does this differ appreciably from the usual connotation of the word? If so, how?

   c. Is it apt to be "relieved of its ugly connotations"?

4. Use the dictionary as necessary in order to understand the meanings of the following words, especially as Casler uses them: pathological (title and par. 15); psychotherapists (1); causality, determinants, anthropologists (4); validation, penchant, Palestrina (5); reciprocated, irretrievably, elicit, congruent, feigned (6); mores (8); ploys (9); prerequisite (11); psychosis (13); postulation, salutary (14); stigmata (16); enjoined (17); salient, attribution, nymphomaniac (18); reprehensible, *per se* (19); impede, perpetuate (20).

SUGGESTIONS FOR WRITING AND DISCUSSION

1. In raising our own children, how can we be certain to prevent "parent-bred" insecurity (par. 5)?

2. Are our society's old mores against "having sex" without a preexisting relationship (par. 8) among those mores the younger generation is rebelling against? Are they included, perhaps, in the "Puritan noose" to which Michener refers in his essay in Section 2?

3. If you agree that pressures on most people are so great that loving becomes inevitable (par. 10), provide specific, concrete examples (for the author's pure abstractions) of how this pressure system works.

4. Compose an answer, as you see it, to the author's question (par. 15), ". . . would the secure person seek love at all?"

5. Carefully consider the definition composed by an Americans psychiatrist, Harry Stack Sullivan: "When the satisfaction or security of another person becomes as significant to one as is one's own, then a state of love exists. So far as I know, under no other circumstances is a state of l⸻ ⸻pular usage." Show the rela-⸻ n this view of love and that

⸻ ⸻othing is good or bad but ⸻ ⸻ its weaknesses. Use clear

⸻ ⸻evelopment by analysis of ⸻ t the end of this section.)

Thursday 31 —
Friday
Monday
tuesday
wednesday
thursday
Friday
Monday
Tues

ARTHUR SCHLESINGER, JR.

ARTHUR SCHLESINGER, JR., born in Ohio in 1917, son of a prominent American historian, has been since 1966 professor of humanities at the City University of New York. He was educated at Harvard, where he later became professor of history. From 1961 to 1964 he served as special assistant to Presidents Kennedy and Johnson. Schlesinger has long been a prolific and popular essayist and commentator on political and social issues. He received the Pulitzer Prize for History in 1945. Among his books are a three-volume history of the New Deal era, *The Age of Roosevelt* (1957, 1959, and 1960), *The Politics of Hope* (1962), *A Thousand Days: John F. Kennedy in the White House* (1965), and *The Bitter Heritage: Vietnam and American Democracy* (1966).

The Crisis of American Masculinity

"The Crisis of American Masculinity," first published in *Esquire* in 1958, is a thoughtful and thorough analysis of a subject that the author considers a serious problem. In this well-balanced and solidly constructed writing, Schlesinger examines, but is not satisfied with, immediate causes. He then probes deeper, and it is in his examination of ultimate causes that the essay becomes a worthwhile contribution.

What has happened to the American male? For a long time, he 1 seemed utterly confident in his manhood, sure of his masculine role in society, easy and definite in his sense of sexual identity. The frontiersmen of James Fenimore Cooper, for example, never had any concern about masculinity; they were men, and it did not occur to them to think twice about it. Even well into the twentieth century, the heroes of Dreiser, of Fitzgerald, of Hemingway remain men. But one begins to detect a new theme emerging in some of these authors, especially in Hemingway: the theme of the male hero increasingly preoccupied with proving his virility to himself. And by mid-century, the male role had plainly lost its rugged clarity of outline. Today men are more and more conscious of maleness not as a fact but as a problem. The ways by which American men affirm their masculinity are uncertain and obscure. There are multiplying signs, indeed, that something has gone badly wrong with the American male's conception of himself.

On the most superficial level, the roles of male and female are   2
increasingly merged in the American household. The American man is found as never before as a substitute for wife and mother — changing diapers, washing dishes, cooking meals and performing a whole series of what once were considered female duties. The American woman meanwhile takes over more and more of the big decisions, controlling them indirectly when she cannot do so directly. Outside the home, one sees a similar blurring of function. While men design dresses and brew up cosmetics, women become doctors, lawyers, bank cashiers and executives. "Women now fill many 'masculine' roles," writes the psychologist, Dr. Bruno Bettelheim, "and expect their husbands to assume many of the tasks once reserved for their own sex." They seem an expanding, aggressive force, seizing new domains like a conquering army, while men, more and more on the defensive, are hardly able to hold their own and gratefully accept assignments from their new rulers. A recent book bears the stark and melancholy title *The Decline of the American Male.*

Some of this evidence, it should be quickly said, has been pushed   3
too far. The willingness of a man to help his wife around the house may as well be evidence of confidence in masculinity as the opposite; such a man obviously does not have to cling to masculine symbols in order to keep demonstrating his maleness to himself. But there is more impressive evidence than the helpful husband that this is an age of sexual ambiguity. It appears no accident, for example, that the changing of sex — the Christine Jorgensen phenomenon — so fascinates our newspaper editors and readers; or that homosexuality, that incarnation of sexual ambiguity, should be enjoying a cultural boom new in our history. Such developments surely

express a deeper tension about the problem of sexual identity. . . .

Psychoanalysis backs up the theatre and the movies in emphasiz-   4
ing the obsession of the American male with his manhood. "Every
psychoanalyst knows," writes one of them, "how many emotional
difficulties are due to those fears and insecurities of neurotic men
who are unconsciously doubting their masculinity." "In our civilization," Dr. Theodor Reik says, "men are afraid that they will not be
men enough." Reik adds significantly: "And women are afraid that
they might be considered only women." Why is it that women
worry, not over whether they can fill the feminine role, but whether
filling that role is enough, while men worry whether they can fill the
masculine role at all? How to account for this rising tide of male
anxiety? What has unmanned the American man?

There is currently a fashionable answer to this question. Male   5
anxiety, many observers have declared, is simply the result of female aggression: what has unmanned the American man is the
American woman. The present male confusion and desperation, it is
contended, are the inevitable consequence of the threatened femini-
zation of American society. The victory of women is the culmination
of a long process of masculine retreat, beginning when Puritanism
made men feel guilty about sex and the frontier gave women the
added value of scarcity. Fleeing from the reality of femininity,
the American man, while denying the American woman juridical
equality, transformed her into an ideal of remote and transcendent
purity with overriding authority over the family, the home, the
school and culture. This habit of obeisance left the male psychologically disarmed and vulnerable when the goddess stepped off the
pedestal and demanded in addition equal economic, political and
legal rights. In the last part of the nineteenth century, women won
their battle for equality. They gained the right of entry into one
occupation after another previously reserved for males. Today they
hold the key positions of personal power in our society and use this
power relentlessly to consolidate their mastery. As mothers, they
undermine masculinity through the use of love as a technique of
reward and punishment. As teachers, they prepare male children for
their role of submission in an increasingly feminine world. As wives,
they complete the work of subjugation. . . .

Or so a standard indictment runs; and no doubt there is some-   6
thing in it. American women have unquestionably gained through
the years a place in our society which American men have not been

psychologically prepared to accept. Whether because of Puritanism or frontier, there has been something inmature in the traditional American male attitude toward women — a sense of alarm at times amounting to panic. Almost none of the classic American novels, for example, presents the theme of mature and passionate love. Our nineteenth-century novelists saw women either as unassailable virgins or abandoned temptresses — never simply as women. One looks in vain through *Moby Dick* and *The Adventures of Huckleberry Finn*, through Cooper and Poe and Whitman, for an adult portrayal of relations between men and women. "Where," Leslie Fiedler has asked, "is the American *Madame Bovary, Anna Karenina, Wuthering Heights,* or *Vanity Fair?*"

Yet the implication of the argument that the American man has   7
been unmanned by the emancipation of the American woman is that the American man was incapable of growing up. For the nineteenth-century sense of masculinity was based on the psychological idealization and the legal subjection of women; masculinity so spuriously derived could never — and should never — have endured. The male had to learn to live at some point with the free and equal female. Current attempts to blame "the decline of the American male" on the aggressiveness of the American female amount to a confession that, under conditions of free competition, the female was bound to win. Simple observation refutes this supposition. In a world of equal rights, some women rise; so too do some men; and no pat generalization is possible about the sexual future of society. Women have gained power in certain ways; in others, they have made little progress. . . . Those amiable prophets of an impending American matriarchy (all men, by the way) are too pessimistic.

Something more fundamental is involved in the unmanning of   8
American men than simply the onward rush of American women. Why is the American man so unsure today about his masculine identity? The basic answer to this is surely because he is so unsure about his identity in general. Nothing is harder in the whole human condition than to achieve a full sense of identity — than to know who you are, where you are going, and what you mean to live and die for. From the most primitive myths to the most contemporary novels — from Oedipus making the horrified discovery that he had married his mother, to Leopold Bloom and Stephen Dedalus searching their souls in Joyce's Dublin and the haunted characters of Kafka trying to make desperate sense out of an incomprehensible

universe — the search for identity has been the most compelling human problem. That search has always been ridden with trouble and terror. And it can be plausibly argued that the conditions of modern life make the quest for identity more difficult than it has ever been before.

The pre-democratic world was characteristically a world of status   9
in which people were provided with ready-made identities. But modern western society — free, equalitarian, democratic — has swept away all the old niches in which people for so many centuries found safe refuge. Only a few people at any time in human history have enjoyed the challenge of "making" themselves; most have fled from the unendurable burden of freedom into the womblike security of the group. The new age of social mobility may be fine for those strong enough to discover and develop their own roles. But for the timid and the frightened, who constitute the majority in any age, the great vacant spaces of equalitarian society can become a nightmare filled with nameless horrors. Thus mass democracy, in the very act of offering the individual new freedom and opportunity, offers new moral authority to the group and thereby sets off a new assault on individual identity. Over a century ago Alexis de Tocqueville, the perceptive Frenchman who ruminated on the contradictions of equality as he toured the United States in the Eighteen Thirties, pointed to the "tyranny of the majority" as a central problem of democracy. John Stuart Mill, lamenting the decline of individualism in Great Britain, wrote: "That so few now dare to be eccentric marks the chief danger of the time." How much greater that danger seems a century later!

For our own time has aggravated the assault on identity by add-   10
ing economic and technological pressures to the political and social pressures of the nineteenth century. Modern science has brought about the growing centralization of the economy. We work and think and live and even dream in larger and larger units. William H. Whyte, Jr., has described the rise of "the organization man," working by day in immense business concerns, sleeping by night in immense suburban developments, deriving his fantasy life from mass-produced entertainments, spending his existence, not as an individual, but as a member of a group and coming in the end to feel guilty and lost when he deviates from his fellows. Adjustment rather than achievement becomes the social ideal. Men no longer fulfill an inner sense of what they *must* be; indeed, with the cult of the group, that inner sense itself begins to evaporate. Identity con-

sists, not of self-realization, but of smooth absorption into the group. Nor is this just a matter of passive acquiescence. The group is aggressive, imperialistic, even vengeful, forever developing new weapons with which to overwhelm and crush the recalcitrant individual. Not content with disciplining the conscious mind, the group today is even experimenting with means of violating the subconscious. The subliminal invasion represents the climax of the assault on individual identity.

It may seem a long way from the loss of the sense of self to the 11 question of masculinity. But if people do not know *who* they are, it is hardly surprising that they are no longer sure what sex they are. Nigel Dennis's exuberant novel, *Cards of Identity*, consists of a series of brilliant variations on the quest for identity in contemporary life. It reaches one of its climaxes in the tale of a person who was brought up by enlightened parents to believe that there was no such thing as pure male or female — everyone had elements of both — and who accepted this proposition so rigorously that he (she) could not decide what his (her) own sex was. "In what identity do you intend to face the future?" someone asks. "It seems that nowadays," comes the plaintive reply, "one must choose between being a woman who behaves like a man, and a man who behaves like a woman. In short, I must choose to be one in order to behave like the other." If most of us have not yet quite reached that condition of sexual chaos, yet the loss of a sense of identity is obviously a fundamental step in the decay of masculinity. And the gratification with which some American males contemplate their own decline should not obscure the fact that women, for all their recent legal and economic triumphs, are suffering from a loss of identity too. It is not accidental that the authors of one recent book described modern woman as the "lost sex."

If this is true, then the key to the recovery of masculinity does 12 not lie in any wistful hope of humiliating the aggressive female and restoring the old masculine supremacy. Masculine supremacy, like white supremacy, was the neurosis of an immature society. It is good for men as well as for women that women have been set free. In any case, the process is irreversible, that particular genie can never be put back into the bottle. The key to the recovery of masculinity lies rather in the problem of identity. When a person begins to find out *who* he is, he is likely to find out rather soon what sex he is.

For men to become men again, in short, their task is to recover 13 a sense of individual spontaneity. And to do this a man must visualize himself as an individual apart from the group, whatever it is, which defines his values and commands his loyalty. There is no reason to suppose that the group is always wrong: to oppose the group automatically is nearly as conformist as to surrender to it automatically. But there is every necessity to recognize that the group is one thing and the individual — oneself — is another. One of the most sinister of present-day doctrines is that of *togetherness*. The recovery of identity means, first of all, a new belief in apartness. It means a determination to resist the overpowering conspiracy of blandness, which seeks to conceal all tension and conflict in American life under a blanket of locker-room affability. And the rebirth of spontaneity depends, at bottom, on changes of attitude *within* people — changes which can perhaps be described, without undue solemnity, as moral changes. These changes will no doubt come about in as many ways as there are individuals involved. . . .

The achievement of identity, the conquest of a sense of self —   14 these will do infinitely more to restore American masculinity than all the hormones in the test tubes of our scientists. "Whoso would be a *man*," said Emerson, "must be a nonconformist" and, if it is the present writer who adds the italics, nonetheless one feels that no injustice is done to Emerson's intention. How can masculinity, femininity, or anything else survive in a homogenized society, which seeks steadily and benignly to eradicate all differences between the individuals who compose it? If we want to have *men* again in our theatres and our films and our novels — not to speak of in our classrooms, our business offices and our homes — we must first have a society which encourages each of its members to have a distinct identity.

MEANINGS AND VALUES

1. What are some of the "uncertain and obscure" ways "by which American men affirm their masculinity" (par. 1)?

2. Do you agree that the merging of male and female roles in the American household is "on the most superficial level" (par. 2)? Explain.

3. Consider the author's abstract generalization that "nothing is harder in the whole human condition than to achieve a full sense of identity" (par. 8).

a. Attempt to clarify this statement by specific, concrete references to experiences of your own or those of acquaintances, not necessarily of your own generation.

b. The author says (par. 11) that "the loss of this sense of identity is obviously a fundamental step in the decay of masculinity." If after contemplation this fact does seem "obvious" to you, clarify for the benefit of others. If not, show where your doubt begins.

4. Show how women's loss of identity may be responsible for their being the "lost sex" (par. 11).

5a. Show precisely *how* the "group" might be considered "aggressive, imperialistic, even vengeful" with the "recalcitrant individual" (par. 10).

b. To what extent do you agree with these charges? Explain.

6a. Do you agree that the "homogenized society" seeks "steadily and benignly to eradicate all differences" (par. 14)?

b. If so, show precisely how this is accomplished.

c. Does the author's use of the word "benignly" contradict the quotation in question 5 — or is he discussing two separate influences? Explain.

7. In what specific respects might your generation especially be charged with the further merging of male and female roles?

8. If you have read the Krutch essay in Section 1, explain how the central themes of these two essays are related.

9. If you have read the Mailer selection in Section 5, you may recall his assertion that the "natural aim of technology [is] to make intuition obsolescent."

a. What, if anything, does this threatened "intuition" have to do with a person's "identity"?

b. Show by use of specific examples what other effects technology itself can have on an individual's self-identity.

EXPOSITORY TECHNIQUES

1. A study of the basic structure of this essay can be rewarding for the serious student of composition.

a. Which paragraphs does the author use to set up the problem and, by inductive reasoning (a technique to be studied more thoroughly in Section 8), to show its significance?

b. Next he examines *immediate* causes and finds them lacking. Which paragraphs does he devote to them?

c. In which paragraphs does he probe into the ultimate causes? With what words does he signal the beginning of this, the most important aspect of his discussion?

2a. Identify at least two places where the author states his own central theme.
  b. Are all his materials relevant enough to this theme to provide good unity? (See Guide to Terms: *Unity.*) Justify your answer.
3. Although the author uses many examples throughout his writing, he leaves some important generalizations unsupported by illustration of any kind. What are these? Defend, if you can, this apparent neglect.
4a. What standard techniques are used in paragraph 14 to close this essay? (Guide: *Closings.*)
  b. How effectively are they used?

DICTION AND VOCABULARY

1a. Select five of Schlesinger's best figures of speech and identify by kind. (Guide: *Figures of Speech.*)
  b. Comment on their originality and effectiveness.
2. Consult your dictionary as needed for the meanings of the following words: ambiguity, incarnation (par. 3); culmination, juridical, transcendent, obeisance, subjugation (5); spuriously (7); compelling (8); equalitarian, ruminated (9); acquiescence, recalcitrant, subliminal (10); rigorously, plaintive (11); benignly, eradicate (14).
3. It may seem that Schlesinger's writing contains a relatively large number of difficult words. There are two criteria for the justifiability of such usage: reader-audience and need.
  a. How may the nature of Schlesinger's reader-audience be used for such justification? Would your answer have been different if this essay had been written for a daily newspaper? If so, how?
  b. From question 2 above, select five of the words you were least familiar with and show, if you can, how the author's exact shade of meaning could, or could not, have been conveyed economically by more ordinary language. (The use of almost any word can be justified if needed to convey economically the precise shade of meaning intended. But writing, for whatever audience, is weakened by the use of big or unusual words just for the words' sake — or to show off the author's vocabulary.)
  c. Form a conclusion about this aspect of Schlesinger's diction. (Guide: *Diction.*)

SUGGESTIONS FOR WRITING AND DISCUSSION

1. Use one of the following statements by Schlesinger (or a modification of it) as your own central theme on which to develop a full-fledged composition or discussion.

a. ". . . the search for identity has [always] been the most compelling human problem" (par. 8).

b. "The group is aggressive, imperialistic, even vengeful, forever developing new weapons with which to overwhelm and crush the recalcitrant individual" (par. 10).

c. ". . . women, for all their recent legal and economic triumphs, are suffering from a loss of identity too" (par. 11).

d. ". . . to oppose the group automatically is nearly as conformist as to surrender to it automatically" (par. 13).

2. How practical do you consider the hippie and dropout kind of "nonconformity" as a means of achieving individuality and personal identity? Why?

3. Select one practical means by which the "organization man" can recover a "sense of spontaneity," can become an "individual apart from the group" while still earning his living within it. Develop this plan fully, show the difficulties and rewards, and explain just *how* it would be a means of liberation. (Refer, if you like, to Deloria's "Tribalization of the White Man" in Section 3.)

4. Judge Samuel S. Leibowitz (New York criminal lawyer, judge, and longtime student of juvenile crime) blames increasing juvenile delinquency on decreasing respect for authority, stemming directly from lack of respect for the father at home. His unconditional "solution" to the problem: "Put father back at the head of the family." Based on your own experiences, observations, and study, develop a composition showing the assumptions on which this theory is apparently based, its merits, and its limitations.

Writing Suggestions for Section 6

Analysis of Cause and Effect

Analyze the immediate and ultimate causes and/or effects of one of the following subjects, or another suggested by them. (Be careful that your analysis does not develop into a mere listing of superficial "reasons.")

1. The shortage of summer jobs for students.
2. The ethnic makeup of a neighborhood.
3. Some *minor* discovery or invention.
4. The popularity of some modern singer or other celebrity admired especially by young people.
5. The popularity of some fad of clothing or hair style.
6. The widespread fascination for antique cars (or guns, furniture, dishes, etc.).
7. The widespread enjoyment of fishing or hunting.
8. Student cheating.
9. Failure of the "perfect" vacation.
10. One man's decision to be a conscientious objector.
11. Too much pressure (on you or an acquaintance) for good school grades.
12. Your being a member of some minority ethnic or religious group.
13. Your association, as an outsider, with members of such a group.
14. The decision of some close acquaintance to enter the religious life.
15. Some unreasonable fear or anxiety that afflicts you or someone you know well.
16. Your need to conform.
17. Your tendency toward individualism. *or away from*

make sure you specify it is immediatly cause. or ultimate cause.

7

Using *Definition* to Help Explain

Few writing faults can cause a more serious communication block between writer and reader than using key terms that can have various meanings or shades of meaning. Such terms, to be useful rather than detrimental, must be adequately defined.

Of the two basic types of definition, only one is our special concern as a pattern of exposition. But the other, the simpler form, is often useful to clarify meanings of concrete or noncontroversial terms. This simple process is similar to that used most in dictionaries: either providing a synonym (for example, cinema: a motion picture), or placing the word in a class and then showing how it differs from others of the same class (for example, metheglin: an alcoholic liquor made of fermented honey — here the general class is "liquor," and the differences between metheglin and other liquors are that it is "alcoholic" and "made of fermented honey").

More pertinent to our study of structural patterns, however, is *extended* definition, a technique that may be vitally important when using an abstract term. Packard and Michener (Section 2) carefully define most of their terms as they develop classification systems, and Leopold (Section 4) must define "biota" and "biotic pyramid" in order to gain full benefit from his analogy.

Even with abstract terms that are less scientific than Leopold's, such as "liberal" or "conservative," "loyalty" or "freedom," most readers are too limited by their own experiences and opinions (and no two sets are identical) for the writer to expect understanding of the exact sense in which he uses the terms. He has a right, of course, to use such abstract words any way he chooses — as long as his

191

readers know what that way is. The importance of making this meaning clear becomes crucial when the term is used as a key element of the overall explanation. And sometimes the term being defined is even more than a key element: it may be the subject itself. For instance, to define "The Peter Principle" (Section 1) was really the primary purpose of the writing, even though the authors use examples almost exclusively as a *means* of defining.

Extended definition, unlike the simple, dictionary type, follows no set and formal pattern. Often the reader is not even aware of the process. Because it is an integral part of the overall subject, extended definition is written in the same tone as the rest of the exposition, usually with an attempt to interest the reader, as well as to inform him.

There are some expository techniques peculiar to definition alone. The purpose may be served by giving the background of the term. Or the definition may be clarified by negation, sometimes called "exclusion" or "differentiation," by showing what is *not* meant by the term. Still another way is to enumerate the characteristics of what is defined, sometimes isolating an essential one for special treatment.

To demonstrate the possibilities in these patterns, we can use the term "juvenile delinquency," which might need defining in some contexts since it certainly means different things to different people. (Where do we draw the line, for instance, between "boyish pranks" and delinquency, or between delinquent and nondelinquent experimentation with sex or marijuana?) We might show how attitudes toward juvenile crime have changed: "youthful high spirits" was the label for some of our grandfathers' activities that would be called "delinquency" today. Or we could use negation, eliminating any classes of juvenile wrongdoing not considered delinquency in the current discussion. Or we could simply list characteristics of the juvenile delinquent or isolate one of these — disrespect for authority or lack of consideration for other people — as a universal.

But perhaps the most dependable techniques for defining are the basic expository patterns already studied. The writer could illustrate his meaning of "juvenile delinquency" by giving *examples* from his own experience, from newspaper accounts, or from other sources. (Every one of the introductions to the ten sections of this book, each a definition, relies greatly on illustration by example, as does the Peter/Hull selection.) He could analyze the subject by *classification* of types or degrees of delinquency. He could use the process of *comparison* and *contrast,* perhaps between delinquent and non-delinquent youths. Showing the *causes* and *effects* of juvenile crime could help explain his attitude toward it, and hence its meaning for him. He might choose to use *analogy,* perhaps comparing the child to a young tree growing grotesque because of poor care and attention. Or a step-by-step analysis of the *process* by which a child becomes delinquent might, in some cases, help explain the intended meaning.

Few extended definitions would use all these methods, but the extent of their use must always depend on three factors: (1) the term itself, since some are more elusive and subject to misunderstanding than others; (2) the function the term is to serve in the writing, since it would be foolish to devote several pages to defining a term that serves only a casual or unimportant purpose; and (3) the prospective reader-audience, since the writer wants to avoid insulting the intelligence or background of his readers, yet wants to go far enough to be sure of their understanding.

But this, of course, is a basic challenge in any good writing — analyzing the prospective reader and writing for the best effect on *him.*

ALBERT SCHWEITZER

ALBERT SCHWEITZER (1875–1965), a few months before
his death, celebrated his ninetieth birthday near Lam-
barene, Gabon (in Equatorial Africa), at the sprawling
hospital complex he had founded and where he had spent
most of his last fifty-three years. Dr. Schweitzer, an Alsa-
tian, became eminent early in his life as a teacher and
scholar (with doctoral degrees in both philosophy and
theology), noted musician, and expert in organ construction. At the age of thirty, having decided to devote the rest
of his life to service in Africa, he began his medical education. Dr. Schweitzer received many international awards,
including the Nobel Peace Prize for 1952.

Reverence for Life

"Reverence for Life" is excerpted from Schweitzer's book
by that title, which was published in Germany in 1966
and, translated by Reginald H. Fuller, in the United States
in 1969. In this selection the author defines his key term —
a matter of vital importance since the term might otherwise be open to diverse connotations and interpretations.

Explore everything around you, penetrate to the furthest limits of   1
human knowledge, and always you will come up against something
inexplicable in the end. It is called life. It is a mystery so inexplicable
that the knowledge of the educated and the ignorant is purely relative when contemplating it.

But what is the difference between the scientist who observes in   2
his microscope the most minute and unexpected signs of life; and
the old farmer who by contrast can barely read or write, who stands

in springtime in his garden and contemplates the buds opening on the branches of his trees? Both are confronted with the riddle of life. One may be able to describe life in greater detail, but for both it remains equally inscrutable. All knowledge is, in the final analysis, the knowledge of life. All realization is amazement at this riddle of life — a reverence for life in its infinite and yet ever-fresh manifestations. How amazing this coming into being, living, and dying! How fantastic that in other existences something comes into being, passes away again, comes into being once more, and so forth from eternity to eternity! How can it be? We can do all things, and we can do nothing. For in all our wisdom we cannot create life. What we create is dead.

Life means strength, will, arising from the abyss, dissolving into the abyss again. Life is feeling, experience, suffering. If you study life deeply, looking with perceptive eyes into the vast animated chaos of this creation, its profundity will seize you suddenly with dizziness. In everything you recognize yourself. The tiny beetle that lies dead in your path — it was a living creature, struggling for existence like yourself, rejoicing in the sun like you, knowing fear and pain like you. And now it is no more than decaying matter — which is what you will be sooner or later, too. . . .

What is this recognition, this knowledge within the reach of the most scientific and the most childlike? It is reverence for life, reverence for the unfathomable mystery we confront in our universe, an existence different in its outward appearance and yet inwardly of the same character as our own, terribly similar, awesomely related. The strangeness between us and other creatures is here removed.

Reverence for the infinity of life means removal of the alienation, restoration of empathy, compassion, sympathy. And so the final result of knowledge is the same as that required of us by the commandment of love. Heart and reason agree together when we desire and dare to be men who seek to fathom the depths of the universe.

Reason discovers the bridge between love for God and love for men — love for all creatures, reverence for all being, compassion with all life, however dissimilar to our own.

I cannot but have reverence for all that is called life. I cannot avoid compassion for everything that is called life. That is the beginning and foundation of morality. Once a man has experienced it and continues to do so — and he who has once experienced it will continue to do so — he is ethical. He carries his morality within him and can never lose it, for it continues to develop within him. He who has never experienced this has only a set of superficial principles. These theories have no root in him, they do not belong to him, and they fall off him. The worst is that the whole of our generation had only such a set of superficial principles. Then the time came to put the ethical code to the test, and it evaporated. For centuries the human race had been educated with only a set of superficial principles. We were brutal, ignorant, and heartless without being aware of it. We had no scale of values, for we had no reverence for life.

It is our duty to share and maintain life. Reverence concerning 8 all life is the greatest commandment in its most elementary form. Or expressed in negative terms: "Thou shalt not kill." We take this prohibition so lightly, thoughtlessly plucking a flower, thoughtlessly stepping on a poor insect, thoughtlessly, in terrible blindness because everything takes its revenge, disregarding the suffering and lives of our fellow men, sacrificing them to trivial earthly goals.

Much talk is heard in our times about building a new human race. 9 How are we to build a new humanity? Only by leading men toward a true, inalienable ethic of our own, which is capable of further development. But this goal cannot be reached unless countless individuals will transform themselves from blind men into seeing ones and begin to spell out the great commandment which is: Reverence for Life. Existence depends more on reverence for life than the law and the prophets. Reverence for life comprises the whole ethic of love in its deepest and highest sense. It is the source of constant renewal for the individual and for mankind.

MEANINGS AND VALUES

1. Demonstrate, by using two seemingly unlikely examples, that "all knowledge is [or is not], in the final analysis, the knowledge of life" (par. 2).

2. What is meant by the reference to "other existences" in paragraph 2? (Can the author, a Christian, be referring to reincarnations?)

3a. Consider the statement that "we can do all things, and we can do nothing" (par. 2). Can this qualify as paradox? As irony? (See Guide to Terms: *Paradox; Irony.*)

 b. If the latter, what kind? Justify your answers.

4. Explain more fully the meaning of the last sentence of paragraph 5.
5. The author says, "Then the time came to put the ethical code to the test, and it evaporated" (par. 7). To what "test" do you think he was referring? Why?
6. Clarify how, in Schweitzer's view, "thoughtlessly stepping on a poor insect . . . takes its revenge" (par. 8).
7. Do you think that the author is trying to make a case against killing at all? Why, or why not?
8. What other possible meanings, or shades of meaning, might the key phrase "reverence for life" seem to have, without a thorough defining?
9a. If you have read the White selection in Section 6, what striking parallels do you see between the two authors' theories?
  b. Each goes further than the other in at least one important respect. What are they?
  c. Which of the two is more convincing? Why?

EXPOSITORY TECHNIQUES

1a. Do you consider this essay primarily abstract or concrete? Why? (Guide: *Abstract/Concrete.*)
  b. Would the definition have been much improved by more of either the concrete or the abstract? Why, or why not?
  c. Why do you suppose the author selected the beetle (par. 3), a flower, and an insect (par. 8) to serve his purposes? (Remember that a good writer always *selects:* details seldom "just happen" to best advantage.)
2a. Cite two examples of parallel structure in this essay. (Guide: *Parallel Structure.*)
  b. What advantage, if any, is gained by their use?
3a. How does the author achieve emphasis on the points he wants stressed? (Guide: *Emphasis.*)
  b. Cite at least one example of each method used.
4a. The author obviously feels strongly about this subject, which makes it difficult, no doubt, to avoid sentimentality or melodrama. Do you think that he did avoid it?
  b. If not, precisely where not?
  c. To what extent, if at all, does or would sentimentality damage the credibility of his message?

DICTION AND VOCABULARY

1a. Why would it be difficult to determine much, from your reading of this selection, about the quality of Schweitzer's diction and syntax? (Guide: *Diction; Syntax.*)

b. Use examples to illustrate the elements of these that we *can* appraise with some certainty.

2. Consult the dictionary as necessary for the meanings of the following words: inexplicable (par. 1); inscrutable, manifestations (2); abyss, perceptive, profundity (3); unfathomable (4); alienation, empathy, (5); superficial (7); comprises (9).

SUGGESTIONS FOR WRITING AND DISCUSSION

1. The author says that "in all our wisdom we cannot create life" (par. 2). Do you believe this? Why, or why not?

2. If you fully understand and agree with the following statement, use it as your central theme on which to develop your oral or written composition: "All realization is amazement at this riddle of life . . ." (par. 2).

3. If you have ever studied life deeply and been seized by "its profundity" (par. 3), relate this experience and analyze its significance in your life.

4. If you agree that reverence for life is "the beginning and foundation of morality" (par. 7), explain this relation more concretely than did Schweitzer.

5. If you understand Schweitzer's meaning, concretely explain the "set of superficial principles" with which the human race had been educated for centuries (par. 7).

6. Show clearly the practical connection, if you see one, between reverence for insect life and respect for human life. If you do not, show how Schweitzer's idea (par. 8) is more a romantic notion than a practical fact.

7. If you have read the Leopold essay in Section 4, you may have noticed that his theme is quite different from Schweitzer's, even though the subject matter itself is similar. Relate the two themes in a kind of third viewpoint, bridging the ideas of the two pioneer conservationists.

(NOTE: Suggestions for topics requiring development by use of DEFINITION are on page 221, at the end of this section.)

RALPH NADER, born in Connecticut in 1934, is a lawyer, author, lecturer, and "consumer defender" of wide renown and respect. He served with the United States Army, was graduated magna cum laude from Princeton in 1955, received his law degree at Harvard in 1958, and was admitted to the Connecticut and Massachusetts bars and to Supreme Court practice in Hartford. A recipient of a Nieman Fellows award, Nader has lectured on history and government at the University of Hartford and at Princeton. His book *Unsafe at Any Speed* was published in 1965, and he has written numerous articles and essays for periodicals.

We Need a New Kind of Patriotism

"We Need a New Kind of Patriotism," written for *Life*, illustrates the use of definition to analyze a common term which, far too often, is disastrous to logical dialogue because of its widely varying interpretations. (Of course, preliminary agreement on terminology, or at least the recognition of the need for one, can often be invaluable when people honestly try to understand each other's motives.) This definition is also ideal for our purposes because of the many varied techniques Nader employs to extend it.

At a recent meeting of the national PTA, the idealism and commitment of many young people to environmental and civil rights causes were being discussed. A middle-aged woman, who was listening closely, stood up and asked: "But what can we do to make young people today patriotic?" 1

In a very direct way, she illuminated the tensions contained in the idea of patriotism. These tensions, which peak at moments of public contempt or respect for patriotic symbols such as the flag, have in 2

From *Life* Magazine, July 9, 1971. Reprinted by permission of the author.

the past few years divided the generations and pitted children against parents. Highly charged exchanges take place between those who believe that patriotism is automatically possessed by those in authority and those who assert that patriotism is not a pattern imposed but a condition earned by the quality of an individual's, or a people's, behavior. The struggle over symbols, epithets and generalities impedes a clearer understanding of the meaning and value of patriotism. It is time to talk of patriotism, not as an abstraction steeped in nostalgia, but as behavior that can be judged by the standard of "liberty and justice for all."

Patriotism can be a great asset for any organized society, but it can also be a tool manipulated by unscrupulous or cowardly leaders and elites. The development of a sense of patriotism was a strong unifying force during our Revolution and its insecure aftermath. Defined then and now as "love of country," patriotism was an extremely important motivating force with which to confront foreign threats to the young nation. It was no happenstance that *The Star Spangled Banner* was composed during the War of 1812 when the Redcoats were not only coming but already here. For a weak frontier country beset by the competitions and aggressions of European powers in the New World, the martial virtues were those of sheer survival. America produced patriots who never moved beyond the borders of their country. They were literally defenders of their home.

As the United States moved into the 20th century and became a world power, far-flung alliances and wars fought thousands of miles away stretched the boundaries of patriotism. "Making the world safe for democracy" was the grandiose way Woodrow Wilson put it. At other times and places (such as Latin America) it became distorted into "jingoism." World War II was the last war that all Americans fought with conviction. Thereafter, when "bombs bursting in air" would be atomic bombs, world war became a suicidal risk. Wars that could be so final and swift lost their glamour even for the most militaristically minded. When we became the most powerful nation on earth, the old insecurity that made patriotism into a conditioned reflex of "my country right or wrong" should have given way to a thinking process; as expressed by Carl Schurz: "Our country . . . when right, to be kept right. When wrong, to be put right." It was not until the Indochina war that we began the search for a new kind of patriotism.

If we are to find true and concrete meaning in patriotism, I suggest   5
these starting points. First, in order that a free and just consensus be
formed, patriotism must once again be rooted in the individual's
own conscience and beliefs. Love is conceived by the giver (citizens) when merited by the receiver (the governmental authorities).
If "consent of the governed" is to have any meaning, the abstract
ideal of country has to be separated from those who direct it; otherwise the government cannot be evaluated by its citizens. The
authorities in the State Department, the Pentagon, or the White
House are not infallible; they have been and often are wrong, vain,
misleading, shortsighted or authoritarian. When they are, leaders
like these are shortchanging, not representing, America. To identify
America with them is to abandon hope and settle for tragedy.
Americans who consider themselves patriotic in the traditional sense
do not usually hesitate to heap criticism in domestic matters over
what they believe is oppressive or wasteful or unresponsive government handling of their rights and dignity. They should be just as
vigilant in weighing similar government action which harnesses
domestic resources for foreign involvements. Citizenship has an
obligation to cleanse patriotism of the misdeeds done in its name
abroad.

The flag, as the Pledge of Allegiance makes clear, takes its mean-   6
ing from that "for which it stands"; it should not and cannot stand
for shame, injustice and tyranny. It must not be used as a bandanna
or a fig leaf by those unworthy of this country's leadership.

Second, patriotism begins at home. Love of country in fact is   7
inseparable from citizen action to make the country more lovable.
This means working to end poverty, discrimination, corruption,
greed and other conditions that weaken the promise and potential
of America.

Third, if it is unpatriotic to tear down the flag (which is a symbol   8
of the country), why isn't it more unpatriotic to desecrate the country itself — to pollute, despoil and ravage the air, land and water?
Such environmental degradation makes the "pursuit of happiness"
ragged indeed. Why isn't it unpatriotic to engage in the colossal
waste that characterizes so many defense contracts? Why isn't it
unpatriotic to draw our country into a mistaken war and then keep
extending the involvement, with untold casualties to soldiers and
innocents, while not telling Americans the truth? Why isn't the
deplorable treatment of returning veterans by government and

industry evaluated by the same standards as is their dispatch to war? Why isn't the systematic contravention of the U.S. Constitution and the Declaration of Independence in our treatment of minority groups, the poor, the young, the old and other disadvantaged or helpless people crassly unpatriotic? Isn't all such behavior contradicting the innate worth and the dignity of the individual in America? Is it not time to end the tragic twisting of patriotism whereby those who work to expose and correct deep injustices, and who take intolerable risks while doing it, are accused of running down America by the very forces doing just that? Our country and its ideals are something for us to uphold as individuals and together, not something to drape, as a deceptive cloak, around activities that mar or destroy these ideals.

Fourth, there is no reason why patriotism has to be so heavily associated, in the minds of the young as well as adults, with military exploits, jets and missiles. Citizenship must include the duty to advance our ideals actively into practice for a better community, country and world, if peace is to prevail over war. And this obligation stems not just from a secular concern for humanity but from a belief in the brotherhood of man — "I am my brother's keeper" — that is common to all major religions. It is the classic confrontation — barbarism *vs.* the holy ones. If patriotism has no room for deliberation, for acknowledging an individual's sense of justice and his religious principles, it will continue to close minds, stifle the dissent that has made us strong, and deter the participation of Americans who challenge in order to correct, and who question in order to answer. We need only to recall recent history in other countries where patriotism was converted into an epidemic of collective madness and destruction. A patriotism manipulated by the government asks only for a servile nod from its subjects. A new patriotism requires a thinking assent from its citizens. If patriotism is to have any "manifest destiny," it is in building a world where all mankind is our bond in peace.

MEANINGS AND VALUES

1. Use the term "patriotism" to illustrate why dictionary definitions are sometimes inadequate for proper usage.
2a. Specifically, why are epithets and generalities dangerous (par. 2)?
 b. Cite two examples of these regarding patriotism.

c. In what other areas besides patriotism do epithets and generalities frequently cause trouble?

3. In the author's reference to "highly charged exchanges" (par. 2), do you consider the contrast valid and fair in all respects? Why, or why not?

4. What are the "martial virtues" (par. 3)?

5. Explain more clearly the significance of the "classic confrontation" (par. 9).

6a. Cite two examples of "collective madness" mentioned near the end of the essay.
 b. Show precisely how so-called patriotism fostered this madness.

7. Do you think the author means to condone flag desecration by those who disagree with official policies? Why, or why not?

8a. Is this primarily objective or subjective writing? (See Guide to Terms: *Objective/Subjective*.) How can you tell?
 b. Would the essay have been more effective with greater emphasis on one or the other? Explain.

9. If you have read Smith's essay in Section 4, how, if at all, do some of the more radical attitudes toward patriotism affect other peoples' freedom?

EXPOSITORY TECHNIQUES

1. What are the merits of the author's choice of incident and quotation with which to introduce his subject?

2a. Which of the basic patterns of exposition is used extensively beginning with the second paragraph?
 b. Why, if at all, does it seem inevitable that this technique would have to be used at some point of development?

3a. Where is the simple dictionary definition of "patriotism" given?
 b. Is it useful in this extended definition? Why, or why not?

4a. Which of the special techniques of definition is used in paragraphs 3 and 4?
 b. Why is it particularly important to this definition?

5. What other defining techniques, including regular "patterns," do you find used throughout the rest of the definition? Be specific, citing paragraph numbers.

6. How suitable to these materials is the itemizing by "first," "second," etc.? Why?

7a. How effective do you consider the use of the long series of questions in paragraph 8? Why?
 b. Are these rhetorical questions? (Guide: *Rhetorical Question*.)

8. What methods of achieving emphasis are used in this selection? Cite specific examples. (Guide: *Emphasis*.)

9. Is further qualification needed for any of the author's generalities? (Guide: *Qualification*.) If so, which? (Consider the possibly undesirable implications of statements and questions such as the first sentence of paragraph 8, where it may sound as if the author thinks that one must automatically be a country desecrator if he opposes flag burning or that flag burners do not sometimes degrade the environment.)

10. Which of the regular techniques of closing are used here? (Guide: *Closings*.)

DICTION AND VOCABULARY

1a. Is the author's use of the word "symbol" (pars. 2, 8) apparently consistent with our own meaning of the word? (Guide: *Symbolism*.)
  b. What other patriotic symbols can you think of?

2. Consider the author's uses of "generalities" (par. 2), "abstract" (2, 5), and "concrete" (5). (Guide: *Specific/General; Concrete/Abstract*.) Does he use the terms in the same way that we know them? Explain any differences.

3a. List or mark the metaphors and similes in paragraphs 5, 6, and 8, and note which each is.
  b. Comment briefly on their freshness and effectiveness.

4a. What words, if any, can you find that seem particularly useful or damaging because of their strong connotations?
  b. If there are any, show why.

5. Consult your dictionary as necessary to be sure of the following words: epithets, impedes, steeped (par. 2); martial (3); grandiose, jingoism (4); consensus, infallible (5); desecrate, degradation, contravention, crassly (8); secular, servile, manifest (9).

SUGGESTIONS FOR WRITING AND DISCUSSION

1. Compare and/or contrast the type of dissent Nader himself is best known for with that of political extremists.

2. Analyze, as objectively as possible, the potential *effects* of such demonstrations as flag burning and marching under the flag of an enemy. (Consider the effects on such areas as the conference table and battlefield, as well as the possibility of altering attitudes toward war.)

3. If you see any modern equivalent to the Redcoats of 1812 (par. 3), explain the likeness and tell whether you would choose to wait until they are "already here" before counterattacking.

4. Eliminating the parenthetic portions of Nader's sentence, to what extent does your impression of "love" coincide with his (par. 5)?

5. Several presidents, of both political parties, claimed to be telling the truth, as nearly as possible, about the war in Southeast Asia (par. 8). Do you think, then, that the author is justified in flatly stating that they did not? Support your answer.

6. Explain more thoroughly the "deplorable treatment" of returning veterans (par. 8) — or, if you consider this an unsupportable generality, show why.

7. What contravention of the Constitution and Declaration of Independence (par. 8) has caused mistreatment of the "young" and/or the "old" — or, if you prefer, how is this an unsupportable generality?

8. The author says that all major religions have a common belief that "I am my brother's keeper" (par. 8). If you know of any exceptions, explain fully.

(NOTE: Suggestions for topics requiring development by use of DEFINITION are on page 221, at the end of this section.)

Time magazine essays are sometimes the result of group effort by members of the staff and are therefore printed without a by-line. The following selection is one of these.

On Courage in the Lunar Age

"On Courage in the Lunar Age" was a *Time* essay in July 1969. Unlike the selection by Schweitzer, whose job was to define his own composite term needed as a label for personal views, this essay is concerned with updating the meaning of an old word that is "redefined by each generation." It therefore seems important to consider all aspects, or at least representative aspects, both past and present.

"Courage leads starward, fear toward death," wrote Seneca. Man 1 needs courage simply to live in spite of knowing that he must die. He needs it to live richly — to take risks and thereby define himself. There are many kinds of courage, moral and physical, but all involve a struggle against heavy odds. In that sense, the astronauts' courage is new and not easily classified.

Obviously it takes brave men to climb into that capsule and 2 undergo the immense risks that lie between the earth and the moon and the earth again. Yet, to thoughtful skeptics, the superorganized voyage of Apollo 11 suggests that lone, individual courage belongs to the past. The astronauts often seem to be interchangeable parts of a vast mechanism. They are buffered by a thousand protective devices, encased in layers of metal and wires and transistors, their very heartbeats monitored for deviation. Most of their decisions are made by computers. Hundreds of ships, planes, doctors and technicians stand by to rescue them from error. All this is strikingly different from the lonely struggles of the ancient mariners and American pioneers, the early Polar explorers like Scott and Peary, the early aviators like the Wright brothers and Lindbergh. To many of today's young, who view courage in moral terms as a battle against impersonal organization, the astronauts do not seem particularly heroic precisely because they epitomize the organization man.

Fear Is Worse than Death

Courage, like morality, is redefined by each generation. "The monsters of this sea are everywhere," reported a Phoenician explorer several centuries before Christ, "and keep swimming around the slow-moving ships." The monsters were whales, the sea the Bay of Biscay. In succeeding generations men would skim over that water as if it were a pool, and the heroism of the early sailors on their scary voyage would resemble that of fearful children in the dark. What the explorer does by courage, the settler does by habit. What the father does by taking a deep breath, the son will do with a yawn. If Neil Armstrong and Edwin Aldrin succeed in leaving their footsteps on the moon, the steps may soon become a path — and the path a highway.

Still, there is more to valor than merely being first. For the Stoics, courage was every man's key to the province of the divine. From the Jewish defenders of Masada to the early Christian martyrs to the passive resisters Gandhi and Martin Luther King, the going was the goal — to be afraid was worse than death itself.

For lesser men, courage has often been a means to lesser ends. "Who gets wealth that puts not from the shore?" asked Poet Samuel Daniel in England's expansive 16th century. "Danger hath honor; great designs their fame / Glory doth follow, courage goes before." Daniel's poem was the mercantile ethic frozen in meter. In that spirit, the conquistadors braved terra incognita to bleed Montezuma of his gold; the slave traders kidnaped tribesmen from Africa. In that spirit empires were created — and the conflicts of colonialism that still haunt the world. The motives for these enterprises were not necessarily ignoble. Few men takes risks for gain alone if glory does not follow, and most see in their glory a benefit to all mankind.

Whether used for good or ill, courage has never been in large supply in any society. Today's troubled feeling that it used to be far more common stems from the relatively recent Western belief that individualism equals virtue. The notion is contrary to the older (and Eastern) conviction that virtue lies in seeking balance with the community on earth and with the universe beyond. Especially in America, where individual courage once tamed the wilderness, pessimists now see an antlike mass society. There is no West to be wild in; the only terra incognita is under water. The plains are paved, farms are corporations, and, with too many of the young, dreams of adventure have been replaced by the haze of pot. Even in war, the brave man is not often truly alone with death. The team supports him, the group succors him. In the Philippine night, during World War II, Admiral Mitscher ordered an entire fleet to turn on its lights. The lives of 100,000 men were risked to let some 200 pilots see their way home. In Viet Nam, 50 planes suspended their air war for eight hours to try to rescue Major Jim Kasler, a popular ace who had gone down over North Viet Nam.

Yet a national character is like a genetic one; it may die in the   7
grandfather only to reappear in the face of a child. Seemingly, whenever America has been in crisis, courage has been reasserted. The quality has both old and new dimensions in the technological age. Man's restless probes into the unknown have not exhausted his chances of danger and courage; they have merely spurred him to probe further. The more he knows, the bigger his frontier, from the atom to space. In a day of committee decisions and anonymous heroes, he has changed his style — but not much else.

Despite the moon shot's vast supportive forces, the astronauts   8
themselves are essentially loners. Before they take off, they have no guarantees of success, let alone survival. Airborne, they can be aided only so far. After that, like the very earliest adventurers, they are on their own. Out in space, the future confronts the past. If they are stranded, no Navy will light their way home, no friendly tribes will take them in.

GRACE UNDER PRESSURE

Sometimes it seems as if the astronauts have been chosen by   9
some secret P.R.[1] quotient to project a wholesome, understated

[1] I.e., public relations. [Ed.]

image. Bravery yes, but no heroics; little eccentricities yes, but no flamboyance. Their press conferences are small Seas of Tranquillity. But, as with all other professional risk takers, the very absence of excitement suggests the presence of courage. In most valorous men there must be a diminution of the imaginative faculty. "Neither the sun nor death can be looked at steadily," wrote La Rochefoucauld. The talk of "fuel margins" and EVAs is, in part, a way of giving the eyes a rest. Moreover, each astronaut has the kind of test-pilot fatalism that calms — and deadens — the nerves. They need it. In the past, there were more imagined terrors to be dispelled. Today, the known dangers of failure, mechanical and human, are more numerous and harder to dismiss. The astronauts knew that if, on landing, the lunar module tilted more than 35°, they would be marooned on the moon. Each could remember that, with the best life insurance science could provide, three colleagues burned to death in a spaceship.

It is unimportant to dwell on why the astronauts have taken their 10 risk. Undoubtedly, glory has something to do with it. So does sheer ego, plus the simpler notions of patriotism and unwillingness to let the team down. What is important is that individual valor can be preserved in a collective age. Hemingway once defined courage as "grace under pressure." In their balloon-shaped, ungainly suits, the Apollo 11 astronauts have demonstrated that man, despite his murderous and chaotic past, can still achieve a state of grace.

MEANINGS AND VALUES

1. What is meant by the statement that out in space "the future confronts the past" (par. 8)?

2. Why does it seem likely (or unlikely) that "in most valorous men there must be a diminution of the imaginative faculty" (par. 9)?

3a. Would you classify this writing as primarily concrete or abstract? (See Guide to Terms: *Concrete/Abstract.*)
  b. Illustrate your reasons by citing passages from the essay.
  c. Would clarity and general effectiveness have been improved by the use of more abstraction or concreteness? Explain.

4a. What is the author's attitude toward his subject?
  b. In what way, if at all, is the matter of tone involved? (Guide: *Style/ Tone.*)

c. Is the tone entirely appropriate for the best treatment of the subject? Why, or why not?

5a. What does the author mean when he says man needs to take risks in order to "define himself" (par. 1)?

b. If you have read the Mailer selection in Section 5, show the relation, if any, between these risks and Armstrong's "challenges."

6a. The author implies (par. 6) that the older, Eastern idea of virtue is related somehow to a different view of courage from ours. Explain this implied relation, whether or not you agree with it.

b. What signs of change do you see in regard to the traditional Western faith in the virtue of individualism, as opposed to a love of "balance" (par. 6)?

c. If you have read the White and/or Schweitzer essays in this book, show how their central themes pertain directly to this difference in concept.

EXPOSITORY TECHNIQUES

1a. What standard introductory methods have been used for this essay? (Guide: *Introductions.*)

b. Suggest two other techniques that might have been used effectively. Be specific.

2a. Which, if any, of the basic patterns of exposition are used in developing this extended definition? Cite paragraphs to support your answer.

b. What other techniques are used? Use specific examples for illustration, consulting the introductory comments on definition as necessary.

3. Why do you think the author disposed of the negative attitudes toward modern courage before considering the more positive aspects?

4a. What standard methods of closing are used? (Guide: *Closings.*)

b. How effective do you consider the closing?

c. Suggest, if you can, one other specific method that might have been as effective.

DICTION AND VOCABULARY

1a. Select five of the author's best figures of speech and identify the kind of each. (Guide: *Figures of Speech.*)

b. Comment briefly on the freshness and effectiveness of each.

2a. Who was Seneca (par. 1)?

b. Who, or what, was Masada (par. 4)?

c. Who was La Rochefoucauld (par. 9)?

d. Are they used here as figurative allusions? Why, or why not? (Guide: *Figures of Speech.*)

3. The author occasionally uses "courage," "bravery," and "valor," or their related forms, interchangeably (pars. 2, 4, 6, 9, 10), and your dictionary may confirm the fact that, in denotation, they are synonyms. (Guide: *Connotation/Denotation*.) If your personal *connotations* of the three words differ in any way, explain the difference.

4. Use the dictionary as necessary to understand the meanings of the following words: skeptics, buffered, monitored, deviation, epitomize (par. 2); conquistadors, ignoble (5); terra incognita (5, 6); succors (6); flamboyance, diminution, fatalism, dispelled (9).

SUGGESTIONS FOR WRITING AND DISCUSSION

1. Select one of the following quotations and convert it any way you like into a clear statement of your central theme. Develop your composition or discussion around this statement, using whatever patterns of exposition will make your treatment most lucid and thorough.
   a. "Courage, like morality, is redefined by each generation" (par. 3).
   b. ". . . the going was the goal — to be afraid was worse than death itself" (par. 4).
   c. "Few men take risks for gain alone if glory does not follow . . ." (par. 5).
   d. ". . . dreams of adventure have been replaced by the haze of pot" (par. 6).
   e. ". . . the brave man is not often alone with death" (par. 6).
   f. "Sometimes it seems as if the astronauts have been chosen by some secret P.R. quotient to project a wholesome, understated image" (par. 9). (If you have read the Mailer essay in Section 5, you may wish to use it for reference or to show a relationship of ideas.)
   g. ". . . the kind of test-pilot fatalism that calms — and deadens — the nerves" (par. 9).

(NOTE: Suggestions for topics requiring development by use of DEFINITION are on page 221, at the end of this section.)

CLAUDE BROWN, a playwright and versatile author, was
born in New York in 1937 and attended Howard University from 1961 to 1965. Some of his plays were performed
by the American Afro-Negro Theater Guild in New York.
Brown's autobiographical book, *Manchild in the Promised
Land* (1965), was well received by readers and critics
alike; his articles and essays have been published in
numerous periodicals.

The Language of Soul

"The Language of Soul" was originally published in
Esquire in April 1968. "Soul," Brown's key term, is extremely fluid and elusive, and he has extensively illustrated
and explained in order to make its definition fully understood and appreciated.

Perhaps the most soulful word in the world is "nigger." Despite   1
its very definite fundamental meaning (the Negro man), and disregarding the deprecatory connotation of the term, "nigger" has
a multiplicity of nuances when used by soul people. Dictionaries
define the term as being synonymous with Negro, and they generally point out that it is regarded as a vulgar expression. Nevertheless, to those of chitlins-and-neck-bones background the word
nigger is neither a synonym for Negro nor an obscene expression.

"Nigger" has virtually as many shades of meaning in Colored   2
English as the demonstrative pronoun "that", prior to application to
a noun. To some Americans of African ancestry (I avoid using the
term Negro whenever feasible, for fear of offending the Brothers
X, a pressure group to be reckoned with), nigger seems preferable

to Negro and has a unique kind of sentiment attached to it. This is exemplified in the frequent — and perhaps even excessive — usage of the term to denote either fondness or hostility.

It is probable that numerous transitional niggers and even established exsoul brothers can — with pangs of nostalgia — reflect upon a day in the lollipop epoch of lives when an adorable lady named Mama bemoaned her spouse's fastidiousness with the strictly secular utterance: "Lord, how can one nigger be so hard to please?" Others are likely to recall a time when that drastically lovable colored woman, who was forever wiping our noses and darning our clothing, bellowed in a moment of exasperation: "Nigger, you gonna be the death o' me." And some of the brethren who have had the precarious fortune to be raised up, wised up, thrown up or simply left alone to get up as best they could, on one of the nation's South Streets or Lenox Avenues, might remember having affectionately referred to a best friend as "My nigger."

The vast majority of "back-door Americans" are apt to agree with Webster — a nigger is simply a Negro or black man. But the really profound contemporary thinkers of this distinguished ethnic group — Dick Gregory, Redd Foxx, Moms Mabley, Slappy White, etc — are likely to differ with Mr. Webster and define nigger as "something else" — a soulful "something else." The major difference between the nigger and the Negro, who have many traits in common, is that the nigger is the more soulful.

Certain foods, customs and artistic expressions are associated almost solely with the nigger: collard greens, neck bones, hog maws, black-eyed peas, pigs' feet, etc. A nigger has no desire to conceal or disavow any of these favorite dishes or restrain other behavioral practices such as bobbing his head, patting his feet to funky jazz, and shouting and jumping in church. This is not to be construed that all niggers eat chitlins and shout in church, nor that only niggers eat the aforementioned dishes and exhibit this type of behavior. It is to say, however, that the soulful usage of the term nigger implies all of the foregoing and considerably more.

The Language of Soul — or, as it might also be called, Spoken Soul or Colored English — is simply an honest vocal portrayal of black America. The roots of it are more than three hundred years old.

Before the Civil War there were numerous restrictions placed on the speech of slaves. The newly arrived Africans had the prob-

lem of learning to speak a new language, but also there were in-
hibitions placed on the topics of the slaves' conversation by slave
masters and overseers. The slaves made up songs to inform one
another of, say, the underground railroads' activity. When they
sang *Steal Away* they were planning to steal away to the North,
not to heaven. Slaves who dared to speak of rebellion or even
freedom usually were severely punished. Consequently, Negro slaves
were compelled to create a semi-clandestine vernacular in the way
that the criminal underworld has historically created words to
confound law-enforcement agents. It is said that numerous Negro
spirituals were inspired by the hardships of slavery, and that what
later became songs were initially moanings and coded cotton-field
lyrics. To hear these songs sung today by a talented soul brother
or sister or by a group is to be reminded of an historical spiritual
bond that cannot be satisfactorily described by the mere spoken
word.

The American Negro, for virtually all of his history, has con-   8
stituted a vastly disproportionate number of the country's illiterates.
Illiteracy has a way of showing itself in all attempts at vocal expression by the uneducated. With the aid of colloquialisms, malapropisms, battered and fractured grammar, and a considerable
amount of creativity, Colored English, the sound of soul, evolved.

The progress has been cyclical. Often terms that have been dis-   9
carded from the soul people's vocabulary for one reason or another
are reaccepted years later, but usually with completely different
meaning. In the Thirties and Forties "stuff" was used to mean
vagina. In the middle Fifties it was revived and used to refer to
heroin. Why certain expressions are thus reactivated is practically
an indeterminable question. But it is not difficult to see why certain terms are dropped from the soul language. Whenever a soul
term becomes popular with whites it is common practice for the
soul folks to relinquish it. The reasoning is that "if white people
can use it, it isn't hip enough for me." To many soul brothers there
is just no such creature as a genuinely hip white person. And there
is nothing more detrimental to anything hip than to have it fall
into the square hands of the hopelessly unhip.

White Americans wrecked the expression "something else." It   10
was bad enough that they couldn't say "sump'n else," but they
weren't even able to get out "somethin' else." They had to go
around saying *something else* with perfect or nearly perfect enunci-

ation. The white folks invariably fail to perceive the soul sound in soulful terms. They get hung up in diction and grammar, and when they vocalize the expression it's no longer a soulful thing. In fact, it can be asserted that spoken soul is more of a sound than a language. It generally possesses a pronounced lyrical quality which is frequently incompatible to any music other than that ceaseless and relentlessly driving rhythm that flows from poignantly spent lives. Spoken soul has a way of coming out metered without the intention of the speaker to invoke it. There are specific phonetic traits. To the soulless ear the vast majority of these sounds are dismissed as incorrect usage of the English language and, not infrequently, as speech impediments. To those so blessed as to have had bestowed upon them at birth the lifetime gift of soul, these are the most communicative and meaningful sounds ever to fall upon human ears: the familiar "mah" instead of "my," "gonna" for "going to," "yo" for "your." "Ain't" is pronounced "ain' "; "bread" and "bed," "bray-ud" and "bay-ud"; "baby" is never "bay-bee" but "bay-buh"; Sammy Davis Jr. is not "Sammee" but a kind of "Sam-eh"; the same goes for "Eddeh" Jefferson. No matter how many "man's" you put into your talk, it isn't soulful unless the word has the proper plaintive, nasal "maee-yun."

Spoken soul is distinguished from slang primarily by the fact that the former lends itself easily to conventional English, and the latter is diametrically opposed to adaptations within the realm of conventional English. Police (pronounced pō'lice) is a soul term, whereas "The Man" is merely slang for the same thing. Negroes seldom adopt slang terms from the white world and when they do the terms are usually given a different meaning. Such was the case with the term "bag." White racketeers used it in the Thirties to refer to the graft that was paid to the police. For the past five years soul people have used it when referring to a person's vocation, hobby, fancy, etc. And once the appropriate term is given the treatment (soul vocalization) it becomes soulful.

However, borrowings from spoken soul by white men's slang — particularly teen-age slang — are plentiful. Perhaps because soul is probably the most graphic language of modern times, everybody who is excluded from Soulville wants to usurp it, ignoring the formidable fettering to the soul folks that has brought the language about. Consider "uptight," "strung-out," "cop," "boss," "kill 'em," all now widely used outside Soulville. Soul people never question the origin of a slang term; they either dig it and make it a part of their vocabulary or don't and forget it. The expression "uptight," which meant being in financial straits, appeared on the soul scene in the general vicinity of 1953. Junkies were very fond of the word and used it literally to describe what was a perpetual condition with them. The word was pictorial and pointed; therefore it caught on quickly in Soulville across the country. In the early Sixties when "uptight" was on the move, a younger generation of soul people in the black urban communities along the Eastern Seaboard regenerated it with a new meaning: "everything is cool, under control, going my way." At present the term has the former meaning for the older generation and the latter construction for those under thirty years of age.

It is difficult to ascertain if the term "strung-out" was coined   13
by junkies or just applied to them and accepted without protest. Like the term "uptight" in its initial interpretation, "strung-out" aptly described the constant plight of the junkie. "Strung-out" had a connotation of hopeless finality about it. "Uptight" implied a temporary situation and lacked the overwhelming despair of "strung-out."

The term "cop," (meaning "to get"), is an abbreviation of the   14
word "copulation." "Cop," as originally used by soulful teen-agers in the early Fifties, was deciphered to mean sexual coition, nothing more. By 1955 "cop" was being uttered throughout national Soulville as a synonym for the verb "to get," especially in reference to illegal purchases, drugs, pot, hot goods, pistols, etc. ("Man, where can I cop now?") But by 1955 the meaning was all-encompassing. Anything that could be obtained could be "copped."

The word "boss," denoting something extraordinarily good or   15
great, was a redefined term that had been popular in Soulville during the Forties and Fifties as a complimentary remark from one soul brother to another. Later it was replaced by several terms such as "groovy," "tough," "beautiful" and, most recently, "out of sight." This last expression is an outgrowth of the former term "way out," the meaning of which was equivocal. "Way out" had an ad hoc hickish ring to it which made it intolerably unsoulful and consequently it was soon replaced by "out of sight," which is also likely to experience a relatively brief period of popular usage. "Out of sight" is better than "way out," but it has some of the same negative, childish taint of its predecessor.

The expression, "kill 'em," has neither a violent nor a malicious 16 interpretation. It means "good luck," "give 'em hell," or "I'm pulling for you," and originated in Harlem from six to nine years ago.

There are certain classic soul terms which, no matter how often 17 borrowed, remain in the canon and are reactivated every so often, just as standard jazz tunes are continuously experiencing renaissances. Among the classical expressions are: "solid," "cool," "jive" (generally as a noun), "stuff," "thing," "swing" (or "swinging"), "pimp," "dirt," "freak," "heat," "larceny," "busted," "okee doke," "piece," "sheet" (a jail record), "squat," "square," "stash," "lay," "sting," "mire," "gone," "smooth," "joint," "blow," "play," "shot," and there are many more.

Soul language can be heard in practically all communities 18 throughout the country, but for pure, undiluted spoken soul one must go to Soul Street. There are several. Soul is located at Seventh and "T" in Washington, D.C., on One Two Five Street in New York City; on Springfield Avenue in Newark; on South Street in Philadelphia; on Tremont Street in Boston; on Forty-seventh Street in Chicago, on Fillmore in San Francisco, and dozens of similar locations in dozens of other cities.

As increasingly more Negroes desert Soulville for honorary mem- 19 bership in the Establishment clique, they experience a metamorphosis, the repercussions of which have a marked influence on the young and impressionable citizens of Soulville. The expatriates of Soulville are often greatly admired by the youth of Soulville, who emulate the behavior of such expatriates as Nancy Wilson, Ella Fitzgerald, Eartha Kitt, Lena Horne, Diahann Carroll, Billy Daniels, or Leslie Uggams. The result — more often than not — is a trend away from spoken soul among the young soul folks. This abandonment of the soul language is facilitated by the fact that more Negro youngsters than ever are acquiring college educations (which, incidentally, is not the best treatment for the continued good health and growth of soul); integration and television, too, are contributing significantly to the gradual demise of spoken soul.

Perhaps colleges in America should commence to teach a course 20 in spoken soul. It could be entitled the Vocal History of Black America, or simply Spoken Soul. Undoubtedly there would be no difficulty finding teachers. There are literally thousands of these experts throughout the country whose talents lie idle while they await the call to duty.

Meanwhile the picture looks dark for soul. The two extremities in   21
the Negro spectrum — the conservative and the militant — are both
trying diligently to relinquish and repudiate whatever vestige they
may still possess of soul. The semi-Negro — the soul brother intent
on gaining admission to the Establishment even on an honorary
basis — is anxiously embracing and assuming conventional English. The other extremity, the Ultra-Blacks, are frantically adopting
everything from a Western version of Islam that would shock the
Caliph right out of his snugly fitting shintiyan to anything that
vaguely hints of that big, beautiful, bountiful black bitch lying in
the arms of the Indian and Atlantic Oceans and crowned by the
majestic Mediterranean Sea. Whatever the Ultra-Black is after, it's
anything but soulful.

MEANINGS AND VALUES

1a. Describe what seems to be the author's attitude toward his subject
    in general.
 b. What is his attitude toward the "Ultra-Black"? How can you tell?
 c. What is it toward the "semi-Negro"? How can you tell?
 d. Where do you suppose he would class himself from one soul "ex-
    tremity" to the other? Why?

2a. Show the relation between Brown's attitude toward his subject in
    general and the general tone of the writing. (See Guide to Terms:
    Style/Tone.)
 b. Describe his tone when he refers to the "Ultra-Black."
 c. Does tone help or hinder the effectiveness of the writing? If either,
    explain the reason for your answer and cite any important exceptions.

3. How do you account for the fact that soul expressions spread so
   easily through the much larger white youth subculture?

4. What value do you see, if any, in reading about a highly colloquial
   "language" used by only a portion of a minority people — a language,
   at that, which even the author regards as dying?

EXPOSITORY TECHNIQUES

1a. What are the hazards of using, without preliminaries or explanation,
    a developed example as an introduction? (Guide: *Introductions.*)
 b. How well, if at all, has Brown avoided these hazards?
 c. Show where, and how, the author achieves smooth transition into the
    basic definition, in this case also the central theme.

2. The introductory example itself is, of course, an extended definition. What methods are used in its development?

3a. Where else, if at all, are extended definitions used to develop the larger one?

b. Cite two examples of the simpler, nonextended type of definition.

4a. Does the author handle the extensive use of examples well, or does he allow them to move in and take over the essay (perhaps really using a framework of definition merely for the purpose of the examples, rather than vice versa)? Be specific in justifying your answer.

b. How is this a matter of unity? (Guide: *Unity.*)

c. Does this essay have desirable unity?

5. Several other techniques are used in the major definition. Cite any uses you can find of the following methods:

a. Giving historical background.

b. Showing by negation.

c. Enumerating characteristics.

d. Comparing and/or contrasting.

e. Analyzing causes and/or effects.

6. Demonstrate, by use of at least two well-chosen paragraphs, how the author makes his abstract statements concrete. (Guide: *Concrete/ Abstract.*)

DICTION AND VOCABULARY

1. Demonstrate, by using examples (other than "nigger") from this essay, the importance of connotation in differentiating soul language from standard English. (Guide: *Connotation/Denotation.*)

2. Undoubtedly, spoken soul includes more earthy expressions than any examples used. Is the author justified in ignoring these? Why, or why not?

3a. Select two sentences from this essay in which you think the syntax is notably either good or bad, and analyze them to determine why. (Guide: *Syntax.*)

b. Comment briefly on the quality of syntax in general.

4a. You may notice an unusually large proportion of difficult, or at least multisyllable, words in this selection. How, if at all, does this fact hurt, or help, the overall effectiveness?

b. If you find any words whose same precise function could have been served by simpler words, list or mark them and supply the substitutions.

c. Would such changes improve the style? (Guide: *Style/Tone.*) The readability for an average educated reader? Explain.

5. Use the dictionary as necessary to become familiar with the following words and their meanings: deprecatory, nuances (par. 1); feasible

(2); nostalgia, fastidiousness, secular, precarious (3); profound (4); maws, funky, construed (5); clandestine, vernacular (7); malapropisms (8); cyclical (9); poignantly, phonetic, impediments, plaintive (10); diametrically (11); graphic, formidable, fettering, regenerated (12); ascertain (13); coition (14); equivocal, ad hoc (15); canon, renaissances (17); clique, metamorphosis, repercussions, expatriates, facilitated, demise (19); repudiate, vestige, caliph, shintiyan (21).

SUGGESTIONS FOR WRITING AND DISCUSSION

1. Show why many soul brothers are correct, or incorrect, in their belief that there is "no such creature as a genuinely hip white person" (par. 9).

2. Objectively present the reasons for *and* against the offering of college courses in "Spoken Soul" (par. 20).

3. If you can do so with some degree of authority, explain what the "Ultra-Black" *is* after (par. 21).

4. You may wish to expand your answer to question 3 of "Meanings and Values." For example, explain the irony that at the very time when large numbers of young Negroes are deserting soul, the usage of soul-derived expressions has become widespread among white youths.

5. Explain how one can tell genuine soul music from the imitation and from other similar types of music.

6. Describe some other "spiritual bond" or bonds (par. 7), not necessarily pertaining to race, that are sometimes formed by hardship or tragedy.

Writing Suggestions for Section 7

Definition

Develop a composition for a specified purpose and audience, using whatever expository patterns will help convey a clear understanding of your meaning of one of the following terms:

1. Soul music.
2. "Establishment."
3. Conscience.
4. Religion.
5. Bigotry.
6. War "atrocity."
7. Evolution.
8. Rationalization.
9. Empathy.
10. Altruism.
11. Hypocrisy.

12. Humor.
13. Sophistication.
14. Naiveté.
15. Cowardice.
16. Wisdom.
17. Integrity.
18. Morality.
19. Sin.
20. Social poise.
21. Intellectual (the person).
22. Conservationist.

Sports

8

Reasoning by Use of *Induction* and *Deduction*

Induction and deduction, important as they are in argumentation, may also be useful methods of exposition. They are often used simply to explain a stand or conclusion, without any effort or need to win converts.

Induction is the process by which we accumulate evidence until, at some point, we can make the "inductive leap" and thus reach a useful *generalization*. The science laboratory employs this technique; hundreds of tests and experiments and analyses may be required before the scientist will generalize, for instance, that polio is caused by a certain virus. It is also the primary technique of the prosecuting attorney who presents pieces of inductive evidence, asking the jury to make the inductive leap and conclude that the accused did indeed kill the victim. On a more personal level, of course, we all learned to use induction at a very early age. We may have disliked the taste of orange juice, winter squash, and carrots, and we were not too young to make a generalization: orange-colored food tastes bad.

Whereas induction is the method of reaching a potentially useful generalization (for example, Professor Kalowski always gives an "F" to students who cut his class three times), *deduction* is the method of *using* such a generality, now accepted as a fact (for example, if we cut this class again today, we will get an "F"). Working from a generalization already formulated — by ourselves, by someone else, or by tradition — we may deduce that a specific thing or circumstance that fits into that generality will act the same. Hence, if convinced that orange-colored food tastes bad, we will be reluctant to try pumpkin pie.

222

A personnel manager may have discovered over the years that electronics majors from Central College are invariably well trained in their field. His induction may have been based on the evidence of observations, records, and the opinions of fellow Rotary members; and, perhaps without realizing it, he has made the usable generalization about the training of Central College electronics majors. Later, when he has an application from Tom Ortega, a graduate of Central College, his *de*ductive process will probably work as follows: Central College turns out well-trained electronics majors; Ortega was trained at Central; therefore, Ortega must be well trained. Here he has used a generalization to apply to a specific case.

Put in this simplified form (which, in writing, it seldom is),* the deductive process is also called a "syllogism" — with the beginning generality known as the "major premise" and the specific that fits into the generality known as the "minor premise." For example:

Major premise — Orange-colored food is not fit to eat.
Minor premise — Pumpkin pie is orange-colored.
Conclusion — Pumpkin pie is not fit to eat.

Frequently, however, the validity of one or both of the premises may be questionable, and here is one of the functions of *in*duction: to give needed support — with evidence such as opinions of experts, statistics, and results of experiments or surveys — to the *de*ductive syllogism, whether stated or implied. Deductive reasoning, in whatever form presented, is only as sound as both its premises. The child's conviction that orange-colored food is not fit to eat was not necessarily true; therefore his conclusion about pumpkin pie is not very trustworthy. The other conclusions, that we will automatically get an "F" by cutting Kalowski's class and that Ortega is well trained in electronics, can be only as reliable as the original generalizations that were used as deductive premises. If the gen-

---

* Neither induction nor deduction is confined even to a particular order of presentation. If we use specific evidence to *reach* a generalization, it is induction regardless of which part is stated first in a written or spoken account. (Very likely, both the prosecutor's opening remarks and Dr. Salk's written reports presented their generalizations and then the inductive evidence by which they had been reached.) But if we use a generality in which to *place* a specific, it is still deduction, however stated. (Hence, the reasoning of the personnel manager might be: "Ortega must be well trained because he was educated at C.C., and there's where they really know how to do it.")

eralizations themselves were based on flimsy or insufficient evidence, any future deduction using them is likely to be erroneous.

These two faults are common in induction: (1) the use of *flimsy* evidence — mere opinion, hearsay, or analogy, none of which can support a valid generalization — instead of verified facts or opinions of reliable authorities; and (2) the use of *too little* evidence, leading to a premature inductive leap.

The amount of evidence needed in any situation depends, of course, on purpose and audience. The success of two Central College graduates might be enough to convince some careless personnel director that all Central electronics graduates would be good employees, but two laboratory tests would not have convinced Dr. Salk, or any of his colleagues, that he had learned anything worthwhile about the polio virus. The authors of the Declaration of Independence, in explaining to a wide variety of readers and listeners why they considered the king tyrannical, listed twenty-eight despotic acts of his government, each of which was a verifiable fact, a matter of public record.

Induction and deduction are highly logical processes, and any trace of weakness can seriously undermine an exposition that depends on their reasonableness. (Such weakness can, of course, be even more disastrous in argument.) Although no induction or deduction ever reaches absolute, 100 per cent certainty, we should try to get from these methods as high a degree of *probability* as possible. (We can never positively prove, for instance, that the sun will rise in the east tomorrow, but thousands of years of inductive observation and theorizing make the fact extremely probable — and certainly sound enough for any working generalization.)

The student using induction and deduction in compositions, essay examinations, or term papers — showing that Stephen Crane was a naturalistic writer, or that the Peace Corps has improved our image abroad — should always assume that he will have a skeptical audience that wants to know the logical basis for *all* generalizations and conclusions.

BENJAMIN FRANKLIN (1706–1790) was born in Boston, but lived most of his life in Philadelphia. His versatility as statesman and diplomat, author, scientist, and inventor is well known, both in this country and abroad, and his biography is a rags-to-riches classic. Many people of his time agreed with the noted French economist, Robert Jacques Turgot, who stated, "He snatched the lightning from the skies and the sceptre from tyrants." Franklin's interest in an astonishing variety of fields remained acute until his death at eighty-four. To quote from the *Encyclopaedia Britannica:* "Of all the founding fathers of the United States, Franklin, were there such a thing as reincarnation, would adapt himself most readily to the complexities of the latter half of the 20th century."

On the Choice of a Mistress

"On the Choice of a Mistress" (editor's title) has had a unique history under many titles, but its existence was not even known to the public until many years after Franklin's death. Three versions of it were found in 1850 among the papers of his then deceased grandson, William Temple Franklin. Thereafter it passed through a variety of ownerships and was occasionally printed, but furtively and in limited supply — once under the title "A Philosopher in Undress." Although the piece had enjoyed a sort of locker-room fame for some time, not until 1926 was it published in a widely read biography, written by Phillips Russell, who called Benjamin Franklin "the first civilized American."

My dear Friend,[1]   June 25. 1745

I know of no Medicine fit to diminish the violent natural Inclinations you mention; and if I did, I think I should not communi-

1

From *The Papers of Benjamin Franklin,* Vol. 3, edited by Leonard W. Labaree, 1961. Reprinted by permission of the publisher, Yale University Press.
[1] The addressee is unknown; the letter may in fact be an essay in the form of a letter.

cate it to you. Marriage is the proper Remedy. It is the most natural State of Man, and therefore the State in which you are most likely to find solid Happiness. Your Reasons against entring into it at present, appear to me not well-founded. The circumstantial Advantages you have in View by postponing it, are not only uncertain, but they are small in comparison with that of the Thing itself, the being *married and settled*. It is the Man and Woman united that make the compleat human Being. Separate, she wants his Force of Body and Strength of Reason; he, her Softness, Sensibility and acute Discernment. Together they are more likely to succeed in the World. A single Man has not nearly the Value he would have in that State of Union. He is an incomplete Animal. He resembles the odd Half of a Pair of Scissars. If you get a prudent healthy Wife, your industry in your Profession, with her good Œconomy, will be a Fortune sufficient.

But if you will not take this Counsel, and persist in thinking a Commerce with the Sex inevitable, then I repeat my former Advice, that in all your Amours you should *prefer old Women to young ones*. You call this a Paradox, and demand my Reasons. They are these:

1. Because as they have more Knowledge of the World and their Minds are better stor'd with Observations, their Conversation is more improving and more lastingly agreable.

2. Because when Women cease to be handsome, they study to be good. To maintain their Influence over Men, they supply the Diminution of Beauty by an Augmentation of Utility. They learn to do a 1000 Services small and great, and are the most tender and useful of all Friends when you are sick. Thus they continue amiable. And hence there is hardly such a thing to be found as an old Woman who is not a good Woman.

3. Because there is no hazard of Children, which irregularly produc'd may be attended with much Inconvenience.

4. Because thro' more Experience, they are more prudent and discreet in conducting an Intrigue to prevent Suspicion. The Commerce with them is therefore safer with regard to your Reputation. And with regard to theirs, if the Affair should happen to be known, considerate People might be rather inclin'd to excuse an old Woman who would kindly take care of a young Man, form his Manners

by her good Counsels, and prevent his ruining his Health and Fortune among mercenary Prostitutes.

5. Because in every Animal that walks upright, the Deficiency   7 of the Fluids that fill the Muscles appears first in the highest Part: The Face first grows lank and wrinkled; then the Neck; then the Breast and Arms; the lower Parts continuing to the last as plump as ever: So that covering all above with a Basket, and regarding only what is below the Girdle, it is impossible of two Women to know an old from a young one. And as in the dark all Cats are grey, the Pleasure of corporal Enjoyment with an old Woman is at least equal, and frequently superior, every Knack being by Practice capable of Improvement.

6. Because the Sin is less. The debauching a Virgin may be her   8 Ruin, and make her for Life unhappy.

7. Because the Compunction is less. The having made a young   9 Girl *miserable* may give you frequent bitter Reflections; none of which can attend the making an old Woman *happy*.

8[thly and Lastly] They are *so grateful!!*   10

Thus much for my Paradox. But still I advise you to marry directly;   11 being sincerely Your affectionate Friend.

MEANINGS AND VALUES

1. The author refers to his thesis as a paradox. Explain how it does, or does not, fit our own definition of paradox. (See Guide to Terms: *Paradox.*)

2. What is to be gained and/or lost by learning that great men, past or present, are not always perfect models of propriety (contrary, of course, to what we are sometimes led to believe as small children)?

3. How seriously do you think Franklin meant this to be taken? Why?

4a. Why do you suppose Franklin's grandson, having changed his mind at least once about publication, kept the letter's existence a secret from the public until his death?

  b. Would you do the same today, in similar circumstances? Why, or why not? (Refer, if you like, to Michener's "Assumptions of the Middle Class," Section 2.)

EXPOSITORY TECHNIQUES

1. Is the reasoning of this piece inductive or deductive? Explain your reasons carefully, as though to a person who was not aware of any difference between the two.

2. Is the numbering of parts in exposition such as this a good technique, or not? Why?

3. If this, as many believe, was really not a letter at all, but an essay intended for public readership, what is gained by framing it in the form of a letter?

DICTION AND VOCABULARY

1. Writing styles change with the years and centuries. Identify the elements of diction and syntax in this writing which you think distinguish it from the style of modern authors. Use examples from the essay to clarify. (Guide: *Diction; Syntax.*)

2. What kind of figure of speech, if any, is the reference to "Scissars" in paragraph 1? (Guide: *Figures of Speech.*)

3. The words "commerce" (pars. 2, 6) and "want" (par. 1) are used here with somewhat different meanings than are common today. What do they mean in this writing?

4. Use your dictionary as necessary to be sure of the meanings of the following words: discernment (par. 1); amours (2); diminution, augmentation, amiable (4); corporal (7); debauching (8); compunction (9).

SUGGESTIONS FOR WRITING AND DISCUSSION

1. Develop your answer to question 2 of "Meanings and Values" into a full-scale composition or discussion, using examples for illustration. State your purpose clearly, show effects, and avoid a mere cataloging of sins and foibles.

2. If you have experienced or seriously observed the women's liberation movement, use its viewpoint to comment on one or more of Franklin's "Reasons" or on his argument for marrying. (You might assume this

essay to have been published in a modern advice column, perhaps in *Playboy* or *Esquire*.)

3. If you have read Michener's essay in Section 2, what effect do you think the "Puritan Noose" had on middle-class Franklin, who was much closer to it in time than we are (and by geography than many of us)? Or, if it seems more feasible, what does this reading suggest about the "Noose" in colonial America itself?

(NOTE: Suggestions for topics requiring development by INDUCTION and DEDUCTION are on page 250, at the end of this section.)

JOHN F. KENNEDY

JOHN F. KENNEDY (1917–1963), the youngest man and first Roman Catholic ever elected to the presidency of the United States, took office in Washington on January 20, 1961. Born and educated in Massachusetts, he served with the United States Navy during World War II and received the Purple Heart for injuries sustained when his PT boat was rammed and sunk in the Pacific. He served six years in the United States House of Representatives and eight years in the Senate before his presidential candidacy. President Kennedy was assassinated in Dallas, Texas, on November 22, 1963.

The Memory of a Nation

"The Memory of a Nation" (editor's title) was written as the foreword to *The American Heritage New Illustrated History of the United States,* published the year of the President's death. Although not as noteworthy for drama of content and prose as many of his public addresses, the selection does exemplify Kennedy's clear and forceful style, and it illustrates one of the simplest uses of induction in exposition: a central theme supported directly by the evidence from which it was formed.

There is little that is more important for an American citizen to know than the history and traditions of his country. Without such knowledge, he stands uncertain and defenseless before the world, knowing neither where he has come from nor where he is going. With such knowledge, he is no longer alone but draws a strength far greater than his own from the cumulative experience of the past and a cumulative vision of the future. 1

Knowledge of our history is, first of all, a pleasure for its own   2
sake. The American past is a record of stirring achievement in the
face of stubborn difficulty. It is a record filled with figures larger
than life, with high drama and hard decision, with valor and with
tragedy, with incidents both poignant and picturesque, and with
the excitement and hope involved in the conquest of a wilderness
and the settlement of a continent. For the true historian — and for
the true student of history — history is an end in itself. It fulfills a
deep human need for understanding and the satisfaction it provides
requires no further justification.

Yet, though no further justification is required for the study of   3
history, it would not be correct to say that history serves no further
use than the satisfaction of the historian. History, after all, is the
memory of a nation. Just as memory enables the individual to learn,
to choose goals and stick to them, to avoid making the same mistake
twice — in short, to grow — so history is the means by which a nation establishes its sense of identity and purpose. The future arises
out of the past, and a country's history is a statement of the values
and hopes which, having forged what has gone before, will now
forecast what is to come.

As a means of knowledge, history becomes a means of judgment.   4
It offers an understanding of both the variety and unity of a nation
whose credo is *E Pluribus Unum* — out of many, one. It reminds us
of the diverse abundance of our people, coming from all races and
all parts of the world, of our fields and mountain ranges, deserts and
great rivers, our green farmlands and the thousand voices of our
cities. No revolution in communication or transportation can destroy
the fact that this continent is, as Walt Whitman said, "a nation
of nations." Yet it also reminds us that, in spite of the diversity of
ethnic origin, of geographic locale, of occupation, of social status,
of religious creed, of political commitment, Americans are united by
an ancient and encompassing faith in progress, justice, and freedom.

Our history thus tests our policy: Our past judges our present.   5
Of all the disciplines, the study of the folly and achievements of
man is best calculated to foster the critical sense of what is permanent and meaningful amid the mass of superficial and transient
questions which make up the day-to-day clamor. The history of our
nation tells us that every action taken *against* the freedoms of conscience and expression, *against* equality before the law and equality
of opportunity, *against* the ordinary men and women of the country

is an action taken *against* the American tradition. And it tells us that every action taken *for* a larger freedom and a more equal and spacious society is one more step toward the realization of what Herbert Croly once called "the promise of American life."

A knowledge of history is more than a means of judgment: It is also a means of sympathy — a means of relating our own experience with the experience of other peoples and lands struggling for national fulfillment. We may sometimes forget, for example, that the United States began as an underdeveloped nation which seized its independence by carrying out a successful revolution against a colonial empire. We may forget that, in the first years of the new republic, George Washington laid down the principle of no "permanent alliances" and enjoined the United States to a course of neutralism in the face of the great-power conflicts then dividing the civilized world. We may forget that, in the first stages of our economic development, our national growth was stimulated to a considerable degree by "foreign aid" — that is, investment from abroad — and by public investment and direction on the part of our state and local as well as our national government. We may forget that our own process of economic change was often accompanied by the issue of wildcat paper money, by the repudiation of bonds, by disorder, fraud, and violence. If we recall the facts of our own past, we may better understand the problems and predicaments of contemporary "new nations" laboring for national development in circumstances far less favorable than our own — and we will, in consequence, become less liable to the national self-righteousness which is both unworthy of our own traditions and a bane of international relations.

A knowledge of history is, in addition, a means of strength. "In times of change and danger," John Dos Passos wrote just before World War II, "when there is a quicksand of fear under men's reasoning, a sense of continuity with generations gone before can stretch like a life line across the scary present." Dos Passos called his book *The Ground We Stand On* — and the title concisely defines the role of the past in preparing us for the crisis of the present and the challenge of the future. When Americans fight for individual liberty, they have Thomas Jefferson and James Madison beside them; when they strive for social justice, they strive alongside Andrew Jackson and Franklin Roosevelt; when they work for peace and a world community, they work with Woodrow Wilson; when they fight and die in wars to make men free, they fight and die with Abraham Lincoln. Historic continuity with the past, as Justice Oliver Wendell Holmes said, "is not a duty; it is only a necessity."

A knowledge of history is, above all, a means of responsibility — of responsibility to the past and of responsibility to the future . . . of responsibility to those who came before us and struggled and sacrificed to pass on to us our precious inheritance of freedom . . . and of responsibility to those who will come after us and to whom we must pass on that inheritance with what new strength and substance it is within our power to add. "Fellow citizens," Abraham Lincoln said, "we cannot escape history. . . . The fiery trial through which we pass will light us down, in honor or dishonor, to the latest generation." American history is not something dead and over. It is always alive, always growing, always unfinished — and every American today has his own contribution to make to the great fabric of tradition and hope which binds all Americans, dead and living and yet to be born, in a common faith and a common destiny.

8

MEANINGS AND VALUES

1. In what respects are the circumstances of contemporary new nations "far less favorable" than were our own (par. 6)? Supply specific examples.

2. How has our "national self-righteousness" sometimes been a "bane of international relations" (par. 6)?

3a. What "fiery trials" since the obvious one of Lincoln's day has America passed through which may "light us down . . . to the latest generation" (par. 8)?

  b. Are we passing through any such trials now? If so, explain their probable significance for future generations.

4a. What evidence do we have, if any, of Americans' widespread interest in their historic past?

  b. Are the reasons for this interest suggested by remarks in "The Memory of a Nation"? Explain.

  c. Can you think of ways in which such interest could be employed more usefully than it is? If so, how?

5. If you have read "Hairesy" (Section 3), what historical fact would Baker think worth our noting in relation to modern trends?

EXPOSITORY TECHNIQUES

1a. Where does Kennedy first state his central theme?
  b. Show how this theme is also the main generalization, the *result* of inductive reasoning previously performed.
  c. What dictated the actual placement of this generalization?

2a. The author presents five units of his inductive process. Briefly identify the five, using convenient labels provided by the author in the sentences introducing each.
  b. The first inductive unit is different in kind from the other four. Explain the difference.
  c. Comment on the effectiveness of the author's inductive support for his central theme.

3. Examples used to illustrate these five subthemes are few and not very specific. (See Guide to Terms: *Specific/General.*)
  a. Is this a shortcoming, or can it be explained in the author's purpose for writing and the needs of the essay? If so, how?
  b. Demonstrate by examples selected from this essay the fact that there are *degrees* of specificity between the extremes of "general" and "specific."

4. List or mark transitional devices used by the author to move smoothly from one paragraph to another. (Guide: *Transition.*)

5a. Identify the analogy used in paragraph 3 and comment on its effectiveness.
  b. Why is this more aptly classified as analogy than as metaphor?

6. One characteristic of much of Kennedy's writing (including his speeches) is his frequent use of parallel structures and word groupings, a matter primarily of syntax. (Guide: *Parallel Structure.*)
  a. In which paragraphs do we find a pronounced use of this technique?
  b. The use of such parallels contributes to emphasis and also to the famous Kennedy style. (Guide: *Style/Tone.*) Try to analyze this effect and comment on the reason for it.

DICTION AND VOCABULARY

1. Consistently in his varied writings, an important element of Kennedy's style is his use of figurative language and his careful choice of forceful and precisely "right" words.
  a. In this selection find six figures of speech that contribute to its stylistic effectiveness and identify the kind of each.
  b. From this selection supply six examples of words or word combinations that seem especially well chosen for the job they do. Are these

words the kind that could come only from an advanced education and large vocabulary? If not, what makes them effective?

2. Use a dictionary if you are not completely familiar with the following words: poignant (par. 2); ethnic, encompassing (4); foster, transient (5); repudiation, bane (6).

SUGGESTIONS FOR WRITING AND DISCUSSION

1. What, if anything, fulfills your "deep human need for understanding" (par. 2)? Explain how this is, or why it is not, accomplished.

2. Describe an effective teaching technique of a history teacher you have had, or do a comparative study of two history teachers' techniques.

3. If you were a history instructor, what new or unusual techniques would you bring to your teaching?

4. If you have studied the problems the United States has with one Communist country, explain what you think should be *one* facet of future United States policy toward that country, and the reasons for it. (Do not argue — merely explain.)

5. Some young people today blame their indifference and weak sense of responsibility on the constant threat of annihilation via the hydrogen bomb. To what extent does this threat *actually* affect your own attitude toward planning and working for the future? Explain fully.

6. Do you closely follow the developments of world affairs, as reported in newspapers and news magazines? Explain why, or why not.

7. In his inaugural address, President Kennedy said that, despite the burdens of the long struggle ahead, he did not believe any of us would exchange places with any other people or any other generation. Would you make such an exchange, if possible — for instance, to a "safer," more serene period of history? Explain why, or why not.

8. President Kennedy's assassination caused many people to lament "the sickness of a society in which such a thing could happen." Do you agree that the tragedy implied anything about the general health of American society? Explain and justify your views.

(NOTE: Suggestions for topics requiring development by INDUCTION and DEDUCTION are on page 250, at the end of this section.)

THOMAS JEFFERSON (1743–1826) was born in Virginia, where he lived during his childhood and later attended William and Mary College. He became a lawyer, a member of the Virginia House of Burgesses and of the Continental Congress in 1775. His influence as a liberal democrat was always aided by his prolific and forceful writing. During the Revolutionary War he became Governor of Virginia. After the war he served the new government in various capacities, including those of special minister to France, Secretary of State under Washington, Vice-President, and, for two terms, the country's third President. He died on July 4, the fiftieth anniversary of the signing of the Declaration of Independence.

The Declaration of Independence

The Declaration of Independence, written and revised by Jefferson, was later further revised by the Continental Congress, meeting then in Philadelphia. In this way, as Jefferson later remarked, it drew its authority from "the harmonizing sentiments of the day"; it was, when signed on July 4, 1776, "an expression of the American mind." However, the document still retained much of the form and style of Jefferson's writing, and as literature it has long been admired for its lean and forthright prose. We can find no clearer example of the practical combination of deductive and inductive writing.

When in the course of human events, it becomes necessary for one 1
people to dissolve the political bands which have connected them with another, and to assume among the Powers of the earth, the separate and equal station to which the Laws of Nature and of Nature's God entitle them, a decent respect to the opinions of mankind requires that they should declare the causes which impel them to the separation.

We hold these truths to be self-evident, that all men are created   2
equal, that they are endowed by their Creator with certain unalien-
able Rights, that among these are Life, Liberty and the pursuit of
Happiness. That to secure these rights, Governments are instituted
among Men, deriving their just powers from the consent of the governed. That whenever any Form of Government becomes destructive of these ends, it is the Right of the People to alter or to abolish
it, and to institute new Government, laying its foundation on such
principles and organizing its powers in such form, as to them shall
seem most likely to effect their Safety and Happiness. Prudence, indeed, will dictate that Governments long established should not be
changed for light and transient causes; and accordingly all experience hath shown, that mankind are more disposed to suffer, while
evils are sufferable, than to right themselves by abolishing the
forms to which they are accustomed. But when a long train of
abuses and usurpations pursuing invariably the same Object evinces
a design to reduce them under absolute Despotism, it is their right,
it is their duty, to throw off such government, and to provide new
Guards for their future security. Such has been the patient sufferance of these Colonies; and such is now the necessity which
constrains them to alter their former Systems of Government. The
history of the present King of Great Britain is a history of repeated
injuries and usurpations, all having in direct object the establishment of an absolute Tyranny over these States. To prove this, let
Facts be submitted to a candid world.

He has refused his Assent to Laws, the most wholesome and   3
necessary for the public good.

He has forbidden his Governors to pass Laws of immediate and   4
pressing importance, unless suspended in their operation till his
Assent should be obtained; and when so suspended, he has utterly
neglected to attend to them.

He has refused to pass other Laws for the accommodation of   5
large districts of people, unless those people would relinquish the
right of Representation in the Legislature, a right inestimable to
them and formidable to tyrants only.

He has called together legislative bodies at places unusual, un-   6
comfortable, and distant from the depository of their Public Records,
for the sole purpose of fatiguing them into compliance with his
measures.

He has dissolved Representative Houses repeatedly, for opposing   7
with manly firmness his invasions on the rights of the people.

He has refused for a long time, after such dissolutions, to cause   8
others to be elected; whereby the Legislative Powers, incapable of
Annihilation, have returned to the People at large for their exercise;
the State remaining in the mean time exposed to all the dangers
of invasion from without, and convulsions within.

He has endeavoured to prevent the population of these States;   9
for that purpose obstructing the Laws for Naturalization of Foreigners; refusing to pass others to encourage their migration hither, and
raising the conditions of new Appropriations of Lands.

He has obstructed the Administration of Justice, by refusing his   10
Assent to Laws for establishing Judiciary Powers.

He has made Judges dependent on his Will alone, for the tenure   11
of their offices, and the amount and payment of their salaries.

He has erected a multitude of New Offices, and sent hither   12
swarms of Officers to harass our People, and eat out their substance.

He has kept among us, in time of peace, Standing Armies with-   13
out the Consent of our Legislature.

He has affected to render the Military independent of and su-   14
perior to the Civil Power.

He has combined with others to subject us to jurisdiction foreign   15
to our constitution, and unacknowledged by our laws; giving us
Assent to their acts of pretended Legislation:

For quartering large bodies of armed troops among us: 16

For protecting them, by a mock Trial, from Punishment for any   17
Murders which they should commit on the Inhabitants of these
States:

For cutting off our Trade with all parts of the world: 18

For imposing Taxes on us without our Consent: 19

For depriving us in many cases, of the benefits of Trial by Jury: 20

For transporting us beyond Seas to be tried for pretended offences: 21

For abolishing the free System of English Laws in a Neighbour-   22
ing Province, establishing therein an Arbitrary government, and en-
larging its boundaries so as to render it at once an example and
fit instrument for introducing the same absolute rule into these
Colonies:

For taking away our Charters, abolishing our most valuable   23
Laws, and altering fundamentally the Forms of our Governments:

For suspending our own Legislatures, and declaring themselves   24
invested with Power to legislate for us in all cases whatsoever.

He has abdicated Government here, by declaring us out of his   25
Protection and waging War against us.

He has plundered our seas, ravaged our Coasts, burnt our towns,   26
and destroyed the Lives of our people.

He is at this time transporting large Armies of foreign Mercen-   27
aries to compleat the works of death, desolation and tyranny, already begun with circumstances of Cruelty & perfidy scarcely
paralleled in the most barbarous ages, and totally unworthy the
Head of a civilized nation.

He has constrained our fellow Citizens taken Captive on the high   28
Seas to bear Arms against their Country, to become the execution-
ers of their friends and Brethren, or to fall themselves by their
Hands.

He has excited domestic insurrections amongst us, and has en-   29
deavoured to bring on the inhabitants of our frontiers, the merciless
Indian Savages, whose known rule of warfare, is an undistinguished
destruction of all ages, sexes and conditions.

In every stage of these Oppressions We have Petitioned for Re-   30
dress in the most humble terms: Our repeated petitions have been
answered only by repeated injury. A Prince, whose character is thus
marked by every act which may define a Tyrant, is unfit to be the
ruler of a free People.

Nor have We been wanting in attention to our British brethren.   31
We have warned them from time to time of attempts by their
legislature to extend an unwarrantable jurisdiction over us. We have
reminded them of the circumstances of our emigration and settlement here. We have appealed to their native justice and magnanimity and we have conjured them by the ties of our common kindred
to disavow these usurpations, which would inevitably interrupt our
connections and correspondence. They too have been deaf to the
voice of justice and of consanguinity. We must, therefore acquiesce
in the necessity, which denounces our Separation, and hold them, as
we hold the rest of mankind, Enemies in War, in Peace Friends.

We, therefore, the Representatives of the United States of Amer-   32
ica, in General Congress, Assembled, appealing to the Supreme
Judge of the world for the rectitude of our intentions, do, in the
Name, and by Authority of the good People of these Colonies,

solemnly publish and declare, That these United Colonies are, and of Right ought to be Free and Independent States; that they are Absolved from all Allegiance to the British Crown, and that all political connection between them and the State of Great Britain, is and ought to be totally dissolved; and that as Free and Independent States, they have full power to levy War, conclude Peace, contract Alliances, establish Commerce, and to do all other Acts and Things which Independent States may of right do. And for the support of this Declaration, with a firm reliance on the protection of Divine Providence, we mutually pledge to each other our lives, our Fortunes and our sacred Honor.

MEANINGS AND VALUES

1. For what practical reasons (other than the "decent respect to the opinions of mankind") did the Founding Fathers need to explain so carefully their reasons for declaring independence?

2. Many American colonials opposed the break with England and remained loyal to the Crown throughout the struggle for independence. What do you suppose could inspire such loyalty to a king whom most of them had never seen and who had shown little concern for their welfare?

3. If you have read "The Memory of a Nation" (preceding this selection), which of Kennedy's five reasons for studying history could the Declaration of Independence be used to exemplify? Briefly indicate how.

EXPOSITORY TECHNIQUES

1. The basis of the Declaration of Independence is deduction and can therefore be stated as a logical syllogism. The major premise, stated twice in the second paragraph, may be paraphrased as follows: When a government proves to be despotic, it is the people's right and duty to get rid of it.
   a. What, then, is the minor premise of the syllogism?
   b. Where is the syllogism's conclusion set forth? Restate it concisely in your own words.
   c. Write this resulting syllogism in standard form.

2. Twenty-eight pieces of inductive evidence are offered as support for one of the deductive premises.
   a. Which premise is thus supported?
   b. Demonstrate the meaning of "inductive leap" by use of materials from this selection. (Remember that the order of presentation in

inductive or deductive writing is merely an arrangement for *telling,* not necessarily that of the original reasoning.)

3a. Why, according to the document itself, is the other premise not supported by any inductive reasoning?

b. Would everyone agree with this premise? If not, why do you suppose the Founding Fathers did not present inductive evidence to support it?

4. What benefits are gained in the Declaration by the extensive use of parallel structures? (See Guide to Terms: *Parallel Structure.*)

5. Show as specifically as possible the effects that a "decent respect for the opinions of mankind" apparently had on the selection and use of materials in the Declaration of Independence.

DICTION AND VOCABULARY

1. Select five words or phrases from the Declaration of Independence to demonstrate the value of an awareness of connotation. (Guide: *Connotation/Denotation.*)

2. If not already familiar with the following words as they are used in this selection, consult your dictionary for their meanings: impel (par. 1); transient, usurpations, evinces, sufferance, constrains (2); inestimable (5); depository (6); dissolutions (8); mercenaries, perfidy (27); redress (30); magnanimity, conjured, consanguinity, acquiesce (31); rectitude, absolved (32).

SUGGESTIONS FOR WRITING AND DISCUSSION

1. George Santayana, an American writer and expatriate, called the Declaration of Independence "a salad of illusion." Develop this metaphor into a full-scale analogy to explain his meaning. Without arguing the matter, attempt to assess the truth of his allegation.

2. Select one important similarity or difference between the rebellion of the American colonials and that of some other country in recent history. Use comparison or contrast to develop a theme on this subject.

3. Compare or contrast any one of the Declaration signers with one of the leaders of some other country's more recent severance of ties with a colonial power.

4. Give evidence from your knowledge of history to support, or to negate, the following statement by Patrick Henry, one of the signers of the Declaration: "It is impossible that a nation of infidels or idolators should be a nation of freemen. It is when a people forget God, that tyrants forge their chains. A vitiated state of morals, a corrupted public conscience, is incompatible with freedom."

(NOTE: Suggestions for topics requiring development by INDUCTION and DEDUCTION are on page 250, at the end of this section.)

ROBERT ARDREY

ROBERT ARDREY, born in Chicago in 1908, was graduated from the University of Chicago, where he had begun his studies of the science of man. He was, however, a successful playwright for many years before he visited Africa and there decided henceforth to devote his time and energies exclusively to his former field. The result has been three important and extremely popular books: *African Genesis* (1963); *The Territorial Imperative* (1966); and *The Social Contract* (1970).

To Have and to Hold

"To Have and to Hold" is a portion of the chapter by that title in Ardrey's *The Territorial Imperative*. It exemplifies the distinctive qualities of Ardrey's style and approach to often controversial ideas. Although the inductive reasoning here is pervasive and clear, the selection also provides the best illustration we have had yet of the intertwining of various patterns of exposition to produce one completely integrated unit.

A riddle of our times — one far more agonizing to the Russians than to ourselves — has been the collapse of Soviet agriculture. That the world's second most powerful nation, one fully capable of exploring the moon, should be unable to feed itself is a truth finding testament in every grain market in the world. Why? We have answers by the dozen, but in all their collected urgency they cannot, in my opinion, explain the calamity that has come to the collective way. We and the Russians and the Chinese too will understand it, I maintain, only when we recognize that among the instruments of a successful modern farm — among the fertilizers, the insecticides, the proper seed, the proper machinery, the proper know-how — there stands an unseen tool. And that tool is the farmer's dedication to his work. No profit motive can command it, for there are easier ways to become a millionaire. No appeals to a sense of duty can summon it forth, for there are shorter roads to the patriot's pedestal. The dedication must spring from within the man.

If we think back, we shall recall that farm and farmer have been the central problem of civilization, even as they have been its central cause, ever since in neolithic times almost 10,000 years ago we began our domestication of plants and animals. Having gained control over an abundant food supply, we made possible populations of such number that the old hunting life could never again support us. We could not return. Like the beaver, we mastered a culture which in turn mastered us. Pasture and field, orchard and garden became like portions of our body, organs without which we could not exist. And like the beaver's dams and lodges and wooded acres, they commanded an intolerable lot of work.

Which of us from dawn to dark would bend in the rice paddies, cut hay in the fields?As the millennia progressed, we supplied many an ingenious answer. We tried at first to push the work off on our women, an answer favored in much of Africa even today. We tried human slavery, a solution respected throughout the civilized world until a century or so ago. We tried serfdom in many guises, chaining the worker to someone else's soil. But there was always a shortcoming: that the involuntary worker is inefficient.

Until the industrial revolution the inefficiency of our agriculture was of no alarming moment. So long as the slave in the field was pressed to feed only a handful of nobles and warriors and priests and artisans, involuntary labor was good enough. But with the rise of industry and the massive increase of a factory and office population, our old systems collapsed. Despite the most humane or brutal attentions of landlord and overseer, the involuntary worker in the field could not produce the surplus food which such populations required. Slavery and serfdom vanished. To whatever extent other forces, moral or political, may have caused the final dismissal of our ancient institutions, the first cause was that they no longer worked. And we turned, most of the world's peoples, to another old if less prevalent institution, the peasant family on its freehold.

It is an accident of history that in 1862 the American President, Abraham Lincoln, with his signature on the Homestead Act committed the American agricultural future to the principle of private ownership based on a one-family unit, and that two years later Karl Marx with his call for Communism's First International committed what would someday be the Soviet Union to public ownership and the collective way. A giant race, of which we are almost as unaware today as we were then, was set in motion. As in two enormous living laboratories, the two human populations that would someday dominate the world's affairs were placed on opposite courses to solve a common problem. And that problem, in an industrial age, became in time the problem of all peoples the world around.

How many workers can be released to the wheel by a single   6
man at a plow? As nations came to compete for power and prestige under the single racing flag of industrial worth, a stubborn equation of human mathematics came to limit their most splendid ambitions. What fraction of a people's numbers must remain in the field to free the remainder for the ultimate competition? And by what means may the energies of that farming fraction be so enhanced as to reduce its number to a minimum?

No argument exists — certainly not in Moscow's Central Statistical   7
Administration — concerning the current state of the competition. In the United States of America one worker on a farm produces food for himself and for almost twelve more in the city; 92 percent of all Americans are freed for industry by a rural 8 percent who not only feed them but produce a food surplus of politically embarrassing dimensions. In the Soviet Union one worker in the field, but only in good years, feeds one worker in the factory. A doubtful half of the Russian population is freed from the soil. And as if to confirm the Soviet calamity, its major partner in the collective way, China, pursuing more extreme communal policies, must combine the efforts of six in the field to free one man for the industrial adventure.

China's pretensions to power are young, enveloped in a cloak of   8
secrets, and cannot be inspected here. But the Soviet Union has been with us for almost half a century and makes no effort to hide or dismiss its failure. We know that many a blight besides proscription of private property has fallen on the Russian farm. Stalin's liquidation of the kulaks eliminated at an early date the ablest Russian farmers. The reign of Lysenko and his Lamarckian nostalgias all but annihilated Russia's science of plant genetics. Permafrost, that layer of permanently frozen earth underlying so much of the broad Russian plain, has been less than helpful. Drought,

combined with the blunder of putting to the plow so much virgin but marginal land, has enforced the disaster in recent years. And for decades there was the naive pressure to favor the factory over the field, to neglect fertilizers, farm machinery, irrigation.

Like Chekhov's man of two-and-twenty misfortunes, the Russian 9 farmer has had his full share. But does the total misfortune explain in full the catastrophe which has come to Russian hopes? There, of course, lies the argument. And I submit that were the ratio between American and Russian effectiveness, as measured by this final yardstick, a matter of two to one or three to one, or even of four or five to one, then American wealth, soil, science, and luck might account for the difference. But that the American farmer can feed twelve men besides himself, whereas the Russian can feed only one, is a little too much. I submit that a final multiplication of natural American assets arises from the biological value of the pair territory.[1]

The smallness of American farms is among the best-kept secrets 10 in the arsenal of American power. The Soviet Union's collective farms, in which workers shared until 1966 nothing but surplus earnings, average 15,000 acres, each with about 400 families. The state farm, hiring all workers at a fixed wage, averages 70,000 acres and employs 800 workers. Yet of America's two and one half million commercial farms, only one in ten is over 500 acres. The average number of workers, including the farmer and his sons if he has any, is five. Despite those advances in farm machinery which permit a worker to cultivate an acreage far greater than in Lincoln's day, still half of our farms are no larger now than then. The factory-in-the-field exists, but it is of minor significance. The American agricultural miracle has been produced by a man and his wife with a helper or two on a pair territory.

Many years ago I visited an enormous corporation cotton farm 11 in California's Central Valley. Water was drawn from wells 2000 feet deep, each costing $65,000. The resident manager shrugged off the entire giant enterprise. "It's all the cost of the wells," he said. "A normal water supply, and this place would be subdivided tomorrow. Nobody can compete with a farmer on his one hundred and sixty acres." I had never heard of territory in those days, and I did not believe him.

[1] This term, used throughout the book, applies to the system preferred by those species with an instinctive urge to live and work (with mate and offspring) on their own "territory." [Ed.]

Much more recently I visited a kibbutz in Israel. The kibbutz is   12
the only successful collective farm in the history of modern agriculture. I was skeptical: was it truly a success? Between Tel-Aviv and
Haifa there is one of the oldest and most respected of Israeli kib-
butzim, Gan Shmuel, the Garden of Samuel. Here 400 adults farm
1200 acres and in the year before my visit produced crops valued
at about $1.5 million. The special circumstance of Israeli vision and
dedication, and the special situation of their nation besieged, might
account for the success; but that Gan Shmuel is a success is unargu-
able. Then, however, I visited a private farm on comparable land
only a few miles away. Here a former Polish doctor and his son and
their wives worked thirty acres. Productivity per acre was about
the same as at the kibbutz, but I was struck by a difference. On
the collective farm it would have required nine adults to work
thirty acres; on the private farm it took only four. I inquired. The
former Polish doctor stretched: "Well, *they* work eight hours a day."

One recalls the beaver and his saplings, and a vigilance concern-   13
ing his dam that makes him so easily trapped. One recalls the parent
robins gathering a thousand caterpillars a day. One recalls the
platys and their duckweed, and the intruding cichlid fish who must
be twice as big to challenge a proprietor. One recalls the planarian
worm who will take twice as long to start feeding, despite all
hunger, if his plate is unfamiliar. Are we to believe that a biological
force, commanded by a sense of possession, which plays such a
measurable role in the affairs of animals plays no part in the measurable discrepancies of man?

In any final inspection of the Soviet-American experiment with   14
the territorial imperative[2] one might thumb through statistics as
dreary as they are endless to demonstrate the superior efficiency of
the man who owns over that of the man who shares or works for
wages. Some have their fascinations, such as that process called
stock raising, in which availability of fertilizer and machinery and
irrigation provide limited advantage. Yet to achieve a net gain of
one hundred pounds in a walking unit of beef, the American farmer
will expend three and one-half hours of labor, the wage worker on
a Soviet state farm twenty-one, the sharing worker on a collective
farm an impossible fifty-one. But it is a situation within the Soviet
farm economy that provides the last garish touch.

From the days of Stalin's enforced collectivization of the land,   15

---

[2] The basic, all-important urge for pair territory. [Ed.]

the peasant has been permitted to retain a tiny private plot for family cultivation. It is the last bedraggled remnant of the pair territory in the Soviet Union, and in times of political crisis and ideological pressure its size has been reduced. Today the private plot averages half an acre in size, but there is little likelihood of further reduction. Without it Russia would starve.

Private plots occupy about 3 percent of all Russian cultivated land, yet they produce almost half of all vegetables consumed, almost half of all milk and meat, three-quarters of all eggs, and two-thirds of that staff of Russian life, potatoes. After almost half a century the experiment with scientific socialism, despite all threats and despite all massacres, despite education and propaganda and appeals to patriotism, despite a police power and a political power ample, one would presume, to effect the total social conditioning of any being within its grasp, finds itself today at the mercy of an evolutionary fact of life: that man is a territorial animal. . . .   16

As we watch the farmer going out to his barn with the sun not risen above the wood lot's fringe, we witness the answer to civilization's central problem which none but our evolutionary nature could provide. Here is man, like any other territorial animal, acting against his own interest: in the city he would still be sleeping, and making more money too. What force other than territory's innate morality could so contain his dedications? But here also is the biological reward, that mysterious enhancement of energy and resolution — territory's prime law and prime enigma — which invests the proprietor on his own vested acres. We did not invent it. We cannot command it. Nor can we, not with all our policemen, permanently deny it.   17

He who has will probably hold. We do not know why; it is simply so. It is a law that rings harshly in the contemporary ear, but this is a defect of the ear, not the law. I believe . . . that, harsh though the law may be, in this territorial species of which you and I are members it has been the source of all freedom, the curse on the despot, and the last desperate roadblock in the path of aggression's might.   18

MEANINGS AND VALUES

1a. Explain briefly how this "truth" (par. 1) can find testament in grain markets.

b. Do you consider that testament completely reliable? Why, or why not?

2a. There is irony in the facts related early in paragraph 5. What kind is it? (See Guide to Terms: *Irony.*)
 b. Show precisely what makes it irony.

3. Do you see anything paradoxical in the statement (par. 11) that nobody can compete with a farmer on his 160 acres? (Guide: *Paradox.*) Explain.

4a. What logical weakness do you find, if any, in using overall American farm production figures as an indicator of pair territory production in America?
 b. In this respect do any of the author's other comparisons seem more valuable as evidence? If so, which ones? Why?

5. What other reasons, if any, can you find for a farmer's dedication to his work?

6a. What is the value, if any, in reading about this theory of farming?
 b. Does it have any special significance in the United States today? If so, explain.
 c. If you have read Kennedy's "The Memory of a Nation," show any relation you see between it and this selection.

EXPOSITORY TECHNIQUES

1a. What inductive evidence is offered to support the assertion that the Soviet Union is far behind the United States in agricultural production?
 b. Is it sufficient for the purpose, or is there still room for serious doubt?

2a. Which other theory of the author's does he think needs the greater inductive support?
 b. Do you agree? Why, or why not?
 c. How convincing is this induction?

3. Most of the inductive evidence is of a particularly effective type. In what ways is this true?

4a. What is gained, or lost, by placing the "private plots" statistics in last position (par. 16)?
 b. Do you consider this the best choice? Why, or why not?

5. Why does the author list the other difficulties of Soviet agriculture (par. 8), when they obviously tend to weaken his own thesis?

6a. What, in general, are the pattern and function of paragraphs 2–5?
 b. Do they contribute, as a tributary, to the central theme, therefore helping to maintain desirable unity? Explain. (Guide: *Unity.*)

7. Where, if at all, does the author use analogy?

8a. At least two of the other basic patterns of exposition are pervasive enough in this selection that it could have been used in those sections as well as in this one. What are they?
  b. Justify your answer, showing how each is basic to the overall structure as well as to more specific areas.
  c. Explain why it is, or is not, surprising that these three patterns should be so interwoven and important to each other.

DICTION AND VOCABULARY

1a. How can a food surplus be of "politically embarrassing dimensions" (par. 7)?
  b. What does the author mean by "Lamarckian nostalgias" (par. 8)?
  c. In what way can there be a "biological value" of the pair territory (par. 9)?
2. Statistics, as we all know, can make dry reading. Demonstrate with two or more well-chosen examples that an important and distinctive quality of Ardrey's style is his choice and arrangement of words to offset possible dryness.
3. Illustrate the stylistic contribution of figurative language to Ardrey's writing. (Guide: *Figures of Speech.*)
4. Use the dictionary as needed to understand the meanings of the following words: testament (par. 1); millennia, ingenious, guises (3); proscription, kulaks (8); garish (14); innate, invests (17); despot (18).

SUGGESTIONS FOR WRITING AND DISCUSSION

1. Why do you think people, even some Americans, would like to see large-scale collective agriculture throughout the world?
2. Of what relevance, if any, are Ardrey's theories to the smaller-scale hippie or religious communal farming enterprises that have gained popularity here during the past few years?
3. Provide a further, complete analysis of the satisfactions possible in the pair territory. If you prefer, concentrate on the hazards instead. Or present both, objectively.
4. Propose a practical plan for disposal of our food surpluses, bearing in mind that such a plan, to be completely successful, must somehow meet the approval of farmer, consumer, and taxpayer.
5. Prepare a comparative analysis of the advantages and disadvantages of raising a family on a limited income in the city or on a small, scrubby "freehold" in the country. Temper your romanticism, if any, with the practical, grim requirements of daily existence.

WRITING SUGGESTIONS FOR SECTION 8

Induction and Deduction

Choose one of the following unformed topics and then form your central theme concerning it. This could express whatever view you prefer or allow for opposing views. Develop your composition primarily by use of induction, alone or in combination with deduction. But unless otherwise directed by your instructor, be completely objective and limit yourself to exposition, rather than engaging in argumentation.

1. Little League Baseball (or the activities of 4-H clubs, Boy Scouts, Girl Scouts, etc.) as a molder of character.
2. Conformity as an expression of insecurity.
3. The display of *non*conformity as an expression of insecurity.
4. The status symbol as a motivator to success.
5. The hippie way of life as an effective "solution."
6. The liberal arts curriculum and its "relevance."
7. Student opinion as the guide to better educational institutions.
8. College education as a prerequisite for worldly success.
9. The values of education, beyond dollars and cents.
10. Knowledge and its relation to wisdom.
11. The right of the individual to select the laws he obeys.
12. The right of a group to its own use of public-owned property.
13. Television commercials as a molder of morals.
14. The unpronounced death of _____ Church.
15. The important new role of _____ Church.
16. The "other" side of one ecological problem.
17. Complete freedom from worry as a desirable goal.
18. Decreased effectiveness of the home as an influence in adolescent development.

9

Explaining with the Help of *Description*

Although usually classed as one of the four basic forms of prose, description is used nearly always as a supporting device of one of the other three. Exposition, as well as argument and narration, can be made more vivid, and hence more understandable, with this support. Most exposition does contain some elements of description, and at times description carries almost the entire burden of the explanation, becoming a basic pattern for the expository purpose.

Description is most useful in painting a word-picture of something concrete, such as a scene or a person. Its use is not restricted, however, to what we can perceive with our senses; we can also describe (or attempt to describe) an abstract concept, such as an emotion or quality or mood. But most attempts to describe fear, for instance, still resort to the physical — a "coldness around the heart," perhaps — and in such concrete ways communicate the abstract to the reader.

In its extreme forms, description is either *objective* or *impressionistic* (subjective), but most of its uses are somewhere between these extremes. Objective description is purely factual, uncolored by any feelings of the author; it is the type used for scientific papers and most business reports. But impressionistic description, as the term implies, at least tinges the purely factual with the author's personal impressions; instead of describing how something *is,* objectively, he describes how it *seems,* subjectively. Such a description might refer to the "blazing heat" of an August day. Somewhat less impressionistic would be "extreme heat." But the scientist would describe it precisely as "115 degrees Fahrenheit," and this would be purely objective reporting, unaffected by the impressions of the author. (No examples of the latter are included in this section, but many textbooks for other courses utilize the technique of pure objective description, as do encyclopedias. The Petrunkevitch essay in Section 5 provides some good examples of objective description, although not entirely unmixed with colorful impressionistic details.)

The first and most important job in any descriptive endeavor is the selection of details to be included. There are usually many from which to choose, and the writer must constantly keep in mind the kind of picture he wants to paint with words — for *his* purpose and *his* audience. Such a word-picture need not be entirely visual; in this respect the writer has more freedom than the artist, for he can use strokes that will add the dimensions of sound, smell, and even touch. Such "strokes," if made to seem natural enough, can help create a vivid and effective image in the reader's mind.

Most successful impressionistic description focuses on a single *dominant impression.* Of the many descriptive details ordinarily available for use, the author selects those which will help create a mood or atmosphere or emphasize a feature or quality. But more than the materials themselves are involved, for even diction can often assist in creating the desired dominant impression. Sometimes syntax is also an important factor, as in the use of short, hurried sentences to help convey a sense of urgency or excitement.

Actual structuring of passages is perhaps less troublesome in description than that in most of the other patterns. But some kind of orderliness is needed for the sake of both readability and a realistic effect. (Neither objective nor impressionistic description can afford not to be realistic, in one manner or another.) In visual description, orderliness is usually achieved by presenting details as the eye would find them — that is as arranged in space. We could describe a person from head to toe, or vice versa, or begin with his most noticeable feature and work from there. A scenic description might move from near to far or from far to near, from left to right or from right to left. It might also start with a broad, overall view, gradually narrowing to a focal point, probably the most significant feature of the scene. These are fairly standard kinds of description; but as the types and occasions for using description vary widely, so do the possibilities for interesting treatment. In many cases, the writer is limited only by his own ingenuity.

But ingenuity should not be allowed to produce *excessive* description, an amazingly certain path to reader boredom. A few well-chosen details are better than profusion. Economy of words is desirable in any writing, and description is no exception. Appropriate use of figurative language and careful choices of strong nouns and verbs will help prevent the need for strings of modifiers, which are wasteful and can seem amateurish.

To even the experienced writer, however, achieving good description remains a constant challenge; the beginner should not expect to attain this goal without working at it.

JOHN STEINBECK

JOHN STEINBECK (1902–1968), one of America's best-known novelists and short story writers, was a native of Salinas, California. In 1940 he was awarded the Pulitzer Prize in Fiction, and in 1962 the Nobel Prize for Literature. Among his many successful books are *Tortilla Flat* (1935), *Of Mice and Men* (1937), *The Grapes of Wrath* (1939), *The Moon Is Down* (1942), *Cannery Row* (1945), *East of Eden* (1952), and *Sweet Thursday* (1954).

The Giants

"The Giants" is the editor's title for this chapter from Steinbeck's book *Travels with Charley*, published in 1962. Though brief, it provides a good example of Steinbeck's descriptive style and demonstrates how even purely impressionistic description can be used effectively as a technique of exposition.

I stayed two days close to the bodies of the giants, and there were no trippers, no chattering troupes with cameras. There's a cathedral hush here. Perhaps the thick soft bark absorbs sound and creates a silence. The trees rise straight up to zenith; there is no horizon. The dawn comes early and remains dawn until the sun is high. Then the green fernlike foliage so far up strains the sunlight to a green gold and distributes it in shafts or rather in stripes of light and shade. After the sun passes zenith it is afternoon and quickly evening with a whispering dusk as long as was the morning.

Thus time and the ordinary divisions of the day are changed. To me dawn and dusk are quiet times, and here in the redwoods nearly the whole of daylight is a quiet time. Birds move in the dim light or flash like sparks through the stripes of sun, but they make little sound. Underfoot is a mattress of needles deposited for over two thousand years. No sound of footsteps can be heard on this thick blanket. To me there's a remote and cloistered feeling here. One holds back speech for fear of disturbing something — what? From my earliest childhood I've felt that something was going on in the groves, something of which I was not a part. And if I had forgotten the feeling. I soon got it back.

At night, the darkness is black — only straight up a patch of gray 3 and an occasional star. And there's a breathing in the black, for these huge things that control the day and inhabit the night are living things and have presence, and perhaps feeling, and, somewhere in deep-down perception, perhaps communication, I have had life-long association with these things. (Odd that the word "trees" does not apply.) I can accept them and their power and their age because I was early exposed to them. On the other hand, people lacking such experience begin to have a feeling of uneasiness here, of danger, of being shut in, enclosed and overwhelmed. It is not only the size of these redwoods but their strangeness that frightens them. And why not? For these are the last remaining members of a race that flourished over four continents as far back in geologic time as the upper Jurassic period. Fossils of these ancients have been found dating from the Cretaceous era while in the Eocene and Miocene they were spread over England and Europe and America. And then the glaciers moved down and wiped the Titans out beyond recovery. And only these few are left — a stunning memory of what the world was like once long ago. Can it be that we do not love to be reminded that we are very young and callow in a world that was old when we came into it? And could there be a strong resistance to the certainty that a living world will continue its stately way when we no longer inhabit it?

MEANINGS AND VALUES

1a. Clarify the concept that there might be a kind of communication even among ancient trees.

b. What do you consider the fundamental difficulty in our really believ- such a thing (at least, after we have passed early childhood, when we seemed to be able to communicate with nearly everything)?

2a. What do you think is the author's attitude toward his subject?
  b. How does the tone of his writing help you to determine his attitude? (See Guide to Terms: *Style/Tone.*)
  c. Show the relationship between dominant impression and tone.
 3. Evaluate this essay by using the three-point system. (Guide: *Evaluation.*)

EXPOSITORY TECHNIQUES

1a. List and support by illustration the various ways Steinbeck's dominant impression is created.
  b. How appropriate to the impressionistic description are the references to geologic periods?
 2. What is the justification, if any here, for closing with a pair of unanswered questions (ordinarily an unsatisfactory way of closing a composition)?

DICTION AND VOCABULARY

1. One distinctive quality of Steinbeck's style — primarily a matter of diction, but contributing at times to an almost poetic syntax — is his use of ordinary words in fresh and colorful combinations, such as "a whispering dusk" (par. 1).
  a. List or mark other examples of what seem to be original uses of simple words.
  b. How do these affect the tone? (Guide: *Style/Tone.*)
2a. Identify and show the time relationships among the four geologic periods mentioned in this selection.
  b. What famous animals would have shared the continents with redwoods during the Jurassic period?

SUGGESTIONS FOR WRITING AND DISCUSSION

1. If you have had occasion to learn about the continual controversy over California's redwoods, present an unbiased report that summarizes both sides of this difficult problem.
2. Show the practical values, if any, of keeping rare botanical and/or zoological species from becoming extinct. Use examples for illustration.
3. If there are reasons other than "practical" why we should protect rare species, explain them clearly.

4. A state governor was once quoted as saying, "When you've seen one redwood, you've seen them all" — an attitude perhaps common to many people. State your own philosophy regarding trees, limiting it in whatever way you see fit, and present your reasons for it.

5. Contrast some other serene natural wonder of America with a violent one. (Choose this project only if you are familiar with both.)

(NOTE: Suggestions for topics requiring development by use of DESCRIPTION are on page 282, at the end of this section.)

MICHAEL J. ARLEN

MICHAEL J. ARLEN, born in London in 1930, is a Harvard graduate. He has been a television critic for *The New Yorker* and is a contributing editor to *Harper's*. Arlen has traveled to Vietnam and produced a disturbing critique of the war coverage by the American press. His book *Exiles* was published in 1970.

Griefspeak

"Griefspeak" is from Arlen's book *Living-Room War* (1969). It provides a unique illustration of highly impressionistic description. All elements of style, tone, and organization seem intended, at least, to contribute to the dominant impression, to the subtle central theme itself. Although not the type of writing most people have occasion to emulate, it does offer clear evidence of how the careful writer can use the means at his disposal to create exactly the effect he desires.

When Robert Kennedy was shot, the reporters were already there — the cameras, the lights, the heralds of the people standing upon chairs and tabletops, trailing wire and tape recorders, the black tubelike microphones stretched out arclike into the room (that kitchen). He was shot, and it was real — a life, a death, the *event*, confusion, motion, people running, the man on the floor, young girls in straw hats crying, policemen, people pushing, yelling, the man on the floor, dying, dead, dying. It was all there for a moment, for a short while (it is perhaps this moment, stretching out forward and backward in our imaginations, that now remains), this event, this God knows what it was, and then the hands of people began to touch it. Inevitably, one will say. Inevitably. *Je suis touriste ici moi-*

même.[1] Soft hands, tired hands, sincere hands, oh those sincere hands touching it (and him), poking it, rubbing it, plumping it, patting it. The men in rumpled shirts, hastily buttoned coats, were on the tabletops (our witness-technicians), on sidewalks, in corridors, holding aloft their microphones and cameras. The other men, in better-fitting suits and serious expressions, were inside some room — it all seemed like the same room (some underground chamber), but it could not have been. They talked — to each other, out to us. "I suppose," said Charles Kuralt, "we ought to be giving some comfort to the country in times like this. . . ." Griefspeak. "I don't know about the rest of you," John Chancellor said, "but in the last few hours I seem to have lost part of my self-respect." Somebody handed a piece of paper to Edwin Newman. "I have some new information here," said Edwin Newman. "Sirhan has ordered two books." He looked at the piece of paper. "One is by Madame Blavatsky. The other is by C. W. Ledbetter. We don't know the meaning of this as yet. Or whether it has anything to do with the alleged, the — we want to remind you that all this is tentative, because in this country no man is guilty until judged by a court of law." They talked of irony awhile. It was a time for discovering ironies. It was ironic about "the family." It was ironic that he was shot at the time of his "greatest triumph." It was ironic that "he had spoken out so often against violence." It was ironic that only yesterday he had rescued one of his children from the surf at Malibu. "Excuse me, John," said Edwin Newman. "We just got this on Madame Blavatsky. She lived from 1830 to 1891 and was a Theosophist — although I want to say that we're not yet sure what relationship, if any, this has to the . . ." "I just thought of another irony," said Sander Vanocur. "In a speech just a few days ago Senator Kennedy said, 'We were killed in Oregon. I hope to be resurrected in Los Angeles.'" A psychiatrist appeared at some point to say he thought the violence in our country derived from showing films like *Bonnie and Clyde*. There were discussions across the nation about brain surgery. "I think each one of us is guilty," Mike Wallace said. Telephone calls from prominent people to the family were duly logged and reported. CBS announced telephone calls from President Johnson, Vice-President Humphrey, Governor Reagan, and Senator Mansfield. NBC announced tele-

[1] French, meaning "I am a tourist (or visitor) here myself." [Ed.]

phone calls from President Johnson, Governor Reagan, Robert McNamara, and Mayor Daley. The police chief of Los Angeles appeared before the press and spoke calmly and effectively. "I'll give you boys a moment to get your machines adjusted," he said before beginning. Prime Minister Harold Wilson was interviewed via satellite. The BBC announced "prayers for America." There were scenes of the coffin being placed into the plane in Los Angeles and being taken out of the plane in New York. There was an interview with Cardinal Cushing. Lord Harlech said that violence in America had become "an international scandal." There were interviews by satellite with former Prime Minister Macmillan and Romain Gary. There was an interview with an old gentleman seated in a chair upon a lawn, who had once been Robert Kennedy's grade-school principal. "I remember him very well," he said. "One day he brought one of these animals to school with him. A little pig, I think it was." They showed us the inside of the cathedral. Norman Mailer was standing at vigil around the coffin. "I think Nick Katzenbach is there," said an announcer. "There is George Plimpton. Ed, is that George Plimpton?" "No," said Edwin Newman. "But I think Mayor Lindsay is now coming down the aisle." They showed us Ethel Kennedy. Mrs. Robert Kennedy was seated in church beside a child, her head bent low over the child. The camera zoomed in. "How does one comfort a child at a time like that?" asked Edwin Newman. There was a Chevrolet ad. A man and a girl were seated on top of a convertible singing about "the big new savings on all regular Chevrolets." The song ended. "And on Chevelles too," the girl with a wink. CBS was running off a Western. A man and a very blond girl with frizzy hair were hiding behind some curtains. There were advance shots of the route to be taken by the funeral procession. There were shots of tree-lined streets in Washington. "He often enjoyed a brisk walk down streets such as these," a voice informed us. There were pictures of the White House. Leonard Bernstein, it was announced, would handle the musical arrangements. There were more scenes of Ethel Kennedy in church. There were scenes at Union Station. There were distant views of Hickory Hill. "He liked fresh air," said another voice. Jerome Wilson of WCBS had a number of people seated around him. "I realize it is hard for you to talk at a time like this," he said to a young man who had been a Citizen for Kennedy, "but what did you young people *especially* like about him?" The young man thought for a moment. "We especially liked him because he had leverage," he said. "I think I can say that business would have been happy with Robert Kennedy," said Roswell Gilpatric. They showed us the crowds lined up outside Saint Patrick's. "Young and old alike are joined in grief," an announcer said. They showed us the flags flying on the office buildings on Park Avenue. Some were flying at half-mast, some were not. "The flags fly at half-mast all across this mourning city," an announcer said. They showed us people filing by the coffin. They showed us the train on the way to Washington. They showed us the railroad stations. They showed us the train tracks. "What was it . . . what was the *mystique* that the Kennedy family had?" asked Johnny Carson. "Ethel Kennedy must now begin to build anew," Gabe Pressman said. The Red Cross, one learned, had already distributed four thousand cups of cold drink. They showed us the Lincoln Memorial. They showed us the Joint Chiefs of Staff. "As time goes on," said Louis Nizer, "the pain from his passing will diminish." They showed us John Kennedy's widow in church. I watched the television on and off those days, and the strangely disconnected people on the streets, in crowds, in the lines that rolled around Saint Patrick's down to Forty-fourth Street. "The people have come by to pay their last respects," the voices said. "The people file by . . . the people wait . . . the people touch . . . the people grieve. . . ." They showed us that throng of men and women waiting outside the station at Trenton — kids with American flags, parents in their shirtsleeves, the long train tracks, the crowded platform. "The question," the announcer said, "is how much the train has been slowed down en route from Newark." No. The question all along (we had known three days ago who had been killed) was who was dead.

MEANINGS AND VALUES

1. Briefly describe the dominant impression of this essay.
2a. What was the "it" that sincere hands began touching and patting?
 b. What symbolic function is served by the sincere hands? (See Guide to Terms: *Symbolism.*)
3. When Mike Wallace said that "each one of us is guilty," he was merely echoing a rather common lament during those days. Why would people believe that?

4. Consider the "ironies" discovered by the announcers. Explain briefly why each was ironic. (Guide: *Irony*.)

5a. What did the young Citizen for Kennedy mean when he said Robert Kennedy had "leverage"?
 b. How was this comment also ironic, given at that time and in reply to that question?

6. Explain more fully the author's meaning in his last sentence.

7a. To what extent, if at all, does this essay disparage the real horror and grief at the tragedy itself?
 b. Do you suppose that the author intended any such disparagement?
 c. On what do you base your answer?

8a. If you watched television during those days, were your reactions in any way similar to those expressed by Arlen?
 b. Are they similar now, in retrospect?
 c. If your answers to 8a and 8b are different, what do you think accounts for the difference?

EXPOSITORY TECHNIQUES

1. In highly impressionistic description such as this, the selection and placement of details (from the thousands available) are perhaps even more important than in most other types of writing. Comment briefly on each of the following details — i.e., the probable reason for its use and its effectiveness in helping to create the dominant impression.
 a. John Chancellor's self-respect.
 b. The various "ironies."
 c. The logging of telephone calls.
 d. The police chief's press appearance.
 e. The overseas comments.
 f. The Chevrolet commercial.
 g. The various scenes "they" showed us.
 h. The cold drinks dispensed by the Red Cross.

2a. Clichés need not always be mere phrases nor do they require years to form by overuse. Show, using examples, how Arlen has made use of these facts. (Guide: *Clichés*.)
 b. How has he *used* sentimentality to serve his own purposes? (Guide: *Sentimentality*.)

3a. Besides a rather loose chronological system, what other principle apparently helped determine the arrangement of details?
 b. Can you think of another kind of arrangement that would have been more beneficial to the dominant impression? If so, explain it.

4a. Coherence is ordinarily a highly desirable quality in any kind of composition. (Guide: *Coherence*.) Does this essay have it? Justify your answer.

b. Does your answer indicate a weakness, or a virtue, in this writing? Justify your answer.

5a. Undoubtedly the author decided not to paragraph. (It would not be likely to "just happen," would it?) Was this a sound decision? Why, or why not?

b. Would it have been a good decision in any college writing you have done? Why, or why not?

6. Summarize the means, subtle or otherwise, by which the author achieved emphasis. (Guide: *Emphasis*.)

7a. How successful do you consider the terse and rather abrupt ending? Explain your reasons.

b. Which of the standard methods of signaling the end has the author adapted to his use? (Guide: *Closings*.)

c. Do you see the last sentence as sarcasm? Why, or why not? (Guide: *Irony*.)

DICTION AND VOCABULARY

1a. Have you been able to determine the source of the coined word "Griefspeak"? If so, what is it?

b. Would we be correct to call it an allusion? (Guide: *Allusions*.)

c. What is its significance in this writing?

2. Explain why you think the author uses, or permits, so much repetition of sentence beginnings — e.g., "There were . . ." (Ten times); "They showed us . . ." (twelve times).

3a. What is the significance, here, of the French sentence "Je suis . . ."?

b. Was the author unwise to jeopardize rapport with his readers, many of whom do not read French? Why, or why not?

4a. What is a Theosophist?

b. What is meant by "mystique"? Why is it italicized?

5. There are few difficult words in this selection. Is that fact surprising? Why, or why not?

SUGGESTIONS FOR WRITING AND DISCUSSION

1. What effect does the showing of films such as *Bonnie and Clyde* have on violence, or on public attitudes toward violence?

2. Develop the theme that we are all to blame for crimes such as the assassinations of the two Kennedys and of Martin Luther King, Jr. (At the times these were popular self-accusations.) Or, if you prefer, show that it is a meaningless or purely emotional reaction.

3. Should photographers be permitted to film and to broadcast scenes such as those of grieving relatives in church? Show the significance of the problem, and, if you like, present both sides.

4. If you share Arlen's impressions of this sort of mass reaction, you may be able to find one or more examples of similar social phenomena (not necessarily pertaining to death). Explain — without trying to copy the author's style — the circumstances and the way they impress you.

5. Why do people willingly stand for long, hot hours for such purposes as watching a train go by?

(NOTE: Suggestions for topics requiring development by use of DESCRIPTION are on page 282, at the end of this section.)

MARTIN HOFFMAN

MARTIN HOFFMAN, born in 1935, is a staff psychiatrist at
the Center for Special Problems at the San Francisco
Health Department. He received a grant from the National
Institute of Mental Health for the study of male homosexuals in the San Francisco Bay area and has taught a
course on sexual deviance at both the undergraduate and
graduate levels at the University of California, Berkeley.
He is also experienced in psychoanalytic theory.

The Gay Bar

"The Gay Bar" is a portion of Hoffman's book *The Gay
World* (1968), the controversial report on his three-year
study of the homosexual scene in the San Francisco Bay
area. In it, according to *Publisher's Weekly*, Hoffman "does
for the homosexual subculture, its causes and patterns,
what Vance Packard has done in more conventional areas"
(see "New Directions of Marriage," Section 2). This selection provides us with a far different type of description
than have the preceding two.

The gay bar has almost become a social institution in America. 1
It is the central public place around which gay life revolves and is
to be found in all large and medium-sized cities across the country.
We would like to describe here the "typical gay bar," although, of
course, there is no such thing, any more than there is a "typical
straight bar." Perhaps, narrowing our focus a bit, what we want to
describe is what I call the "middle-class" gay bar, by which I mean
not that all its members are necessarily middle-class socioeconomi-
cally, but rather that middle-class proprieties are observed and
that there is nothing unique or specialized about the bar. We will

Excerpted from Chapter 3 of *The Gay World,* by Martin Hoffman, © 1968 by
Basic Books, Inc., Publishers, New York. Reprinted by permission.

not, for example, be concerned with the leather-jacket motorcycle bars, nor with the hustler bars so beautifully described by Rechy,[1] nor with those bars which provide entertainment such as drag shows and male go-go dancers.

Perhaps the most important fact about a gay bar is that it is a sexual marketplace. That is, men go there for the purpose of seeking sexual partners, and if this function were not served by the bar there would be no gay bars, for, although homosexuals also go there to drink and socialize, the search for sexual experience is in some sense the core of the interaction in the bar. It should, however, be obvious that there must be more going on in the bar than simply people meeting and leaving; otherwise the bar could not exist as a commercial enterprise. People have to come there for a time long enough to drink, in order to make it profitable to the management to run these bars. And gay bars are very profitable and have sprung up in large numbers. It is estimated that there are about 60 gay bars in Los Angeles and about 40 in San Francisco. A number of heterosexuals have converted their own taverns into gay bars simply because they have found it more profitable to run a gay bar, even though they are sometimes not particularly delighted with the clientele. The gay bar plays a central role in the life of very many homosexuals — one which is much more important than the role played by straight bars in the life of all but a few heterosexuals. This is connected intimately with the use of the gay bar as a sexual marketplace and, of course, with the fact that homosexuals, as homosexuals, have really no place else where they can congregate without disclosing to the straight world that they are homosexual.

What does a gay bar look like? In the first place, unlike most middle-class straight bars, it is almost exclusively populated by males. Sometimes non-homosexuals accidentally walk into a gay bar and it is usually this lack of women that makes them aware that they may have inadvertently walked into a homosexual setting. There are a few bars in which lesbians congregate along with male homosexuals, especially in cities which are not large enough to support a lesbian bar. But even in the larger cities, lesbian bars are not very common. They are never as large as the large metropolitan male gay bars. This is because female homosexuals are much less promiscuous than male homosexuals and really not able to support a sexual marketplace on the scale that males do.

[1] John Rechy, *City of Night* (1963).

Occasionally, "fruit flies," i.e., women who like to associate with   4
male homosexuals, are found in gay bars, although they are not a
very prominent part of any gay bar scene. Why a woman who is not
a lesbian would like to associate with male homosexuals is a question which cannot be altogether answered in general, except to say
that some of these women obviously find homosexual men a lot less
threatening than heterosexual men, since the former are not interested in them sexually. Since these women are not potential sexual
partners for the males, they are not potential sources of rejection for
them either, and thereby they find themselves the subject of much
attention by the male clientele. Consequently, they are the bene-
ficiaries of a great deal of sociability without being objects of seduction. Some women find this a very appealing position.

In the gay world there is a tremendous accent on youth and this   5
is reflected in the composition of the bar clientele. Youth is very
much at a premium and young men will go to the bars as soon as
they have passed the legal age limit. This varies from state to
state; it is 18 in New York and 21 in California. Along with the
younger men, there are somewhat older men who are trying to look
young. They attempt to accomplish this primarily by dress. The
typical bar costume is the same style of dress that an average college undergraduate might wear. It would consist of a sport shirt,
Levis, and loafers or sneakers. In this "typical" middle-class gay bar
which I am attempting to describe, extremely effeminate dress and
mannerisms are not well tolerated. Nevertheless, it would not be
correct to say that the scene in a gay bar looks like a fraternity stag
party. There is a tendency toward effeminacy in the overall impression one gets from observing the bar, although this may not necessarily be anything striking or flagrant. There is a certain softness
or absence of stereotypical masculine aggression present in the conversations and behavior of the bar patrons. Also, in spite of the fact
that the model bar costume is very much like that one would see
on a college campus, there is a good deal of special attention paid
by the bar patrons to their dress, so that they seem almost extraordinarily well groomed. There is thus a feeling of fastidiousness
about the appearance of the young men in the bar which, along
with their muted demeanor, rather clearly differentiates the overall
Gestalt of the gay bar from that which would be experienced upon
entering a gathering of young male heterosexuals. There are usually
a few clearly identifiable homosexuals, although the majority of
individuals in the bar are not identifiable and would not be thought

homosexual in another setting. It seems to be the general consensus of gay bar observers that fights are less likely to break out in a gay than in a straight bar. This is, I think, probably attributable to the psychological characteristics of the clientele rather than to anything about the structure of the bar itself. Male homosexuals would certainly rather make love than war.

One of the clearest differences between the gay and the straight 6 bar is that in the gay bar the attention of the patrons is focused directly on each other. In a gay bar, for example, the patrons who are sitting at the bar itself usually face away from the bar and look toward the other people in the room and toward the door. When a new patron walks in, he receives a good deal of scrutiny, and people engaged in conversation with each other just naturally assume that their interlocutors will turn away from them to watch each new entering patron. All this is, of course, part of the pervasive looking and cruising which goes on in the bar.

There is a great deal of milling about in the bar and individuals 7 tend to engage in short, superficial conversations with each other. They try to make the circuit around the bar to see everyone in it, perhaps stopping to chat with their friends but usually not for very long. In a way, the shortness and superficiality of the conversations in the bar mirror that same brevity and shallowness of interpersonal relations which characterize gay life as a whole.

Heterosexual observers and even homosexuals who are not ha- 8 bitués of the bar scene often express great perplexity about the bars — they cannot quite understand what's going on there. They seem to be bewildered by the sight of all these young men standing around and communicating so little with one another. The patrons stand along the walls, it seems, for hours, without speaking. They move around the room and talk at length with almost no one. One heterosexual observer said that he felt as if everyone in the room were standing around waiting for some important figure to come in, but of course he never comes. He likened the scene to a reception for a foreign ambassador, where everyone stands around simply marking time until the dignitary arrives. In a sense, this observer was correct, for the young men *are* waiting for some important person to arrive, one who will never arrive — but it is not a foreign ambassador. Each is waiting for a handsome young prince to come and carry him off in his arms. They're waiting for the ideal sexual object, and if they don't find him they may very well go home alone, in spite of the fact that there are sometimes hundreds of other attractive young men right there in the bar.

The gay bar, then, in a sense may be thought of as a stage on 9 which is played out a fantasy in which the hero never arrives. The reason why heterosexuals and even some homosexuals cannot understand what is going on is because they are not a party to this fantasy. They imagine that if you are going to a place to seek a sexual partner, you go in, look around a little bit, walk up to somebody that you like, engage in a conversation, and then go out together. And sometimes this is precisely what does occur in the gay bar. Very often, in fact, but the bewildering problem which confronts the uninitiated observer is why this does not happen more often: why, in fact, all these good-looking and well-dressed young men are standing around uncommunicative.

Sherri Cavan[2] has made the suggestion that in the homosexual 10 pickup bar it may happen that encounters are never begun because each party is waiting for the other to offer the first words of greeting. This is presumably due to the fact that when the situation involves two males, it is not clear who is expected to make the initial overture. One cannot deny the saliency of this observation. Nevertheless, I do not think it alone accounts fully for the strange situation in the gay bar, since one would expect the reverse to occur just as well, i.e., since both parties can make the initial overture, one would think that at least one of the members of the hypothetical pair could overcome his shyness. I think the sociological explanation fails to take into account the psychological factors involved. As many observers have noted, homosexuals are very much afraid of rejection, and hence, have an inordinate hesitancy about making an approach. I think this is due to the following reason: the only aspect of their self which male homosexuals are able to adequately present in a bar situation is their physical appearance. If they are rejected in making a conversational opening, this is interpreted (probably correctly) to mean a rejection of that crucial part of themselves, namely, their desirability as a sexual partner. Hence, their self-esteem is very much at stake and they have a great deal to lose by being rejected.

It must be remembered that in the gay world the only real 11 criterion of value is physical attractiveness; consequently, a re-

[2] Sherri Cavan, *Liquor License: An Ethnography of Bar Behavior* (1966), p. 192.

jection by a desired partner is a rejection of the only valued part of one's identity in that world. When we understand this, I think we understand why the fear of rejection is so prevalent among homosexual men.

The gay bar, is, then, a lot less licentious than people who are 12 not aware of what is going on there might be inclined to think. When heterosexual men enter a gay bar for the first time for the purpose of simply visiting it, they often seem afraid that somehow they will be rapidly approached, or perhaps even attacked, by the sexual deviants present inside the bar. This, of course, is about as far from reality as it is possible to imagine. It would not be unusual if none of the patrons would engage them in conversation during the entire course of the evening. If they are not young and handsome, they may well have great difficulty in communicating with anyone after even a great deal of effort on their part.

A word should be said, I suppose, about the function of the 13 gay bar as a source of group solidarity and as a place where one can meet one's friends and exchange gossip. I think, however, that this function is obvious and that it need not be elaborated upon. Many homosexuals frequent gay bars for reasons other than seeking sexual partners. If sex eventuates from the bar interaction, this is fine, but it is not the reason they went there in the first place. They went there for sociability. And yet this too must be qualified, for in the back of their minds is usually the thought that perhaps that special person will walk through the door tonight and they will meet him and go home with him.

The "cosmetic" quality of the gay bar is a result, in large part, 14 of the need for anonymity which pervades all the public places of the gay world. If one can only present the visible and non-identifying aspect of one's identity, one's physical appearance will be the central aspect that can be displayed to others. If homosexuals could meet *as homosexuals* in the kinds of social settings in which heterosexuals can (e.g., at school, at work) where the emphasis on finding sexual partners is not the controlling force behind all the social interaction which transpires, a great deal of the anonymous promiscuity which now characterizes homosexual encounters would be replaced by a more "normal" kind of meeting between two persons. Perhaps, then, the sexual relationships which develop would become more stable. Maybe the gay bar itself would not change — this can only be a matter for conjecture — but, at any rate, it would not be so central to gay life.

MEANINGS AND VALUES

1a. Where would you place this writing on an objective-subjective continuum? (See Guide to Terms: *Objective/Subjective.*)
 b. Is there a dominant impression? If so, what is it?
 c. If there is a dominant impression, is it sufficient to give the description desirable unity?

2a. Explain more fully the meaning of "stereotypical masculine aggression" (par. 5).
 b. If you have had some experience in a "typical straight bar," or in a similar setting, do you think one necessarily finds such "aggression" there? Explain.

3a. Clarify the author's meaning of the sentence beginning, "If homosexuals could meet . . ." (par. 14).
 b. Do you think that this is a valid observation? (Consider, for instance, whether even heterosexuals ordinarily meet *as* heterosexuals in "social settings" such as school and work.)

4. At the outset the author states that his purpose is to "describe" the gay bar (par. 1), but description was obviously not his only purpose, perhaps not even his primary one.
 a. What other do you think he had?
 b. How well did he succeed?
 c. Was it a worthwhile endeavor? Why, or why not? (Guide: *Evaluation.*)

EXPOSITORY TECHNIQUES

1. What useful functions are served by the introductory paragraph, other than simply providing a way to start the essay?

2a. A rhetorical question begins the actual physical description. What is it? (Guide: *Rhetorical Question.*)
 b. Why is it a rhetorical question?

3a. How effective do you think the author's choice of details is for his purposes?
 b. If you think other details would have improved his descriptive analysis, what are they? Why are they needed?
 c. Give several examples of details that might be desirable if the purpose had been to create a highly impressionistic description.

4a. What other patterns of exposition are used in this essay?
 b. Cite two examples of each.

5a. Some of the paragraphs here are somewhat longer than those in most modern writing. Are they too long? If so, what is the disadvantage?
 b. Select one of the longest, locate its topic sentence, and consider

whether or not all parts of the paragraph are related to it. What, if anything, does this tell you about its unity? (Guide: *Unity*.)

c. If unity is lacking, how might this weakness be overcome? Be specific.

DICTION AND VOCABULARY

1a. In the first paragraph Hoffman uses the editorial "we." Is this advantageous, or not? Why? (Guide: *Editorial "We."*)

b. Why do you think he did not continue its use throughout the essay?

2a. The seemingly excess wordiness of numerous passages in this essay might be criticized. Do any seem too wordy to you? (Guide: *Diction; Syntax*.)

b. If so, cite as many specific examples as you can.

c. Select one of these and rewrite it with the same exact meaning but with greater economy of language and therefore, perhaps, with greater clarity and more effective syntax.

3a. Hoffman uses several colloquial expressions, some so new that they cannot be found in some dictionaries. Cite five that you would classify as colloquial. (Guide: *Colloquial*.)

b. Why do they not alter the generally serious tone of the essay?

c. Would the writing be better, however, without them? Why, or why not?

4a. Why is *"Gestalt"* printed in italics (par. 5)?

b. What does it mean, as used here?

c. Is it really needed here, or would a more common word have done as well? If the latter, suggest one.

5. Study the author's uses of the following words, consulting the dictionary as needed: proprieties (par. 1); heterosexuals (2, and others); inadvertently, promiscuous (3); flagrant, fastidiousness, demeanor, consensus (5); interlocutors, pervasive (6); habitués (8); saliency, hypothetical, inordinate, crucial (10); criterion (11); licentious (12); eventuates (13); transpires, conjecture (14).

SUGGESTIONS FOR WRITING AND DISCUSSION

1. If, through observation or serious reading, you have noticed any changes of public attitude toward homosexuality, describe such changes and what you believe to be the reasons for them. If you like, project these trends into the future.

2. What do you think should be the function of law in attempting to regulate private morality — e.g., between "consenting adults"?

3. What possible cause/effect relationship, if any, do you see between "hard-core" pornography and sexual deviation?

4. If you have read or heard authoritative and recent discussions on the causes of homosexuality, explain one or more of these theories. If you like, compare two of them.

5. Some religions have traditionally taught that homosexuality is a "sin against nature." How would you interpret the meaning of this dictum?

(NOTE: Suggestions for topics requiring development by use of DESCRIPTION are on page 282, at the end of this section.)

ALBERT CAMUS (1913–1960) was born of French parents in Algeria, where he lived until 1939. From 1942 until the end of World War II, he served with the Resistance movement in France, writing for the underground newspaper *Combat*. A noted essayist, novelist and short story writer, playwright, and philosopher, Camus received the Nobel Prize for Literature in 1957. Among his books are the novels *The Stranger* (1942), *The Plague* (1947), and *The Fall* (1956), and the essay collections *The Rebel* (1951) *Resistance, Rebellion, and Death* (1961). His plays *Caligula* and *Cross Purpose* were published in English in 1948. Camus was killed in a car accident in France.

Return to Tipasa

"Return to Tipasa" is the major portion of Camus' essay by that title, which was written in 1952. It was translated from the original French into English by Justin O'Brien and published in 1955 in a collection of Camus' essays. This one is typical of Camus' writing in its descriptive and lyrical qualities and, to some extent, in the theme of personal disillusionment and "loss of innocence" during the hideous years of World War II and in the shambles of postwar Europe and northern Africa. Based on a sketchy narrative form, the essay's color and development and the significance of the theme itself are dependent on Camus' flair for highly impressionistic description.

For five days rain had been falling ceaselessly on Algiers and had 1 finally wet the sea itself. From an apparently inexhaustible sky, constant downpours, viscous in their density, streamed down upon the gulf. Gray and soft as a huge sponge, the sea rose slowly in the ill-defined bay. But the surface of the water seemed almost motionless under the steady rain. Only now and then a barely perceptible swelling motion would raise above the sea's surface a vague puff of smoke that would come to dock in the harbor, under an arc of wet boulevards. The city itself, all its white walls dripping, gave off a different steam that went out to meet the first steam. Whichever way you turned, you seemed to be breathing water, to be drinking the air.

In front of the soaked sea I walked and waited in that December 2 Algiers, which was for me the city of summers. I had fled Europe's night, the winter of faces. But the summer city herself had been emptied of her laughter and offered me only bent shining backs. In the evening, in the crudely lighted cafés where I took refuge, I read my age in faces I recognized without being able to name them. I merely knew that they had been young with me and that they were no longer so.

Yet I persisted without very well knowing what I was waiting 3 for, unless perhaps the moment to go back to Tipasa. To be sure, it is sheer madness, almost always punished, to return to the sites of one's youth and try to relive at forty what one loved or keenly enjoyed at twenty. But I was forewarned of that madness. Once already I had returned to Tipasa, soon after those war years that marked for me the end of youth. I hoped, I think, to recapture there a freedom I could not forget. In that spot, indeed, more than twenty years ago, I had spent whole mornings wandering among the ruins, breathing in the wormwood, warming myself against the stones, discovering little roses, soon plucked of their petals, which outlive the spring. Only at noon, at the hour when the cicadas themselves fell silent as if overcome, I would flee the greedy glare of an all-consuming light. Sometimes at night I would sleep open-eyed under a sky dripping with stars. I was alive then. Fifteen years later I found my ruins, a few feet from the first waves, I followed the streets of the forgotten walled city through fields covered with bitter trees, and on the slopes overlooking the bay I still caressed the bread-colored columns. But the ruins were now surrounded with barbed wire and could be entered only through certain openings. It was also forbidden, for reasons which it appears that morality approves, to walk there at night; by day one encountered an official guardian. It just happened, that morning, that it was raining over the whole extent of the ruins.

Disoriented, walking through the wet, solitary countryside, I 4 tried at least to recapture that strength, hitherto always at hand, that helps me to accept *what is* when once I have admitted that I cannot change it. And I could not, indeed, reverse the course of time and restore to the world the appearance I had loved which had disappeared in a day, long before. The second of September 1939, In fact, I had not gone to Greece, as I was to do. War, on the contrary, had come to us, then it had spread over Greece herself. That distance, those years separating the warm ruins from the barbed wire were to be found in me, too, that day as I stood before the sarcophaguses full of black water or under the sodden tamarisks. Originally brought up surrounded by beauty which was my only wealth, I had begun in plenty. Then had come the barbed wire — I mean tyrannies, war, police forces, the era of revolt. One had had to put oneself right with the authorities of night: the day's beauty was but a memory. And in this muddy Tipasa the memory itself was becoming dim. It was indeed a question of beauty, plenty, or youth! In the light from conflagrations the world had suddenly shown its wrinkles and its wounds, old and new. It had aged all at once, and we with it. I had come here looking for a certain "lift"; but I realized that it inspires only the man who is unaware that he is about to launch forward. No love without a little innocence. Where was the innocence? Empires were tumbling down; nations and men were tearing at one another's throats; our hands were soiled. Originally innocent without knowing it, we were now guilty without meaning to be: the mystery was increasing with our knowledge. This is why, O mockery, we were concerned with morality. Weak and disabled, I was dreaming of virtue? In the days of innocence I didn't even know that morality existed. I knew it now, and I was not capable of living up to its standard. On the promontory that I used to love, among the wet columns of the ruined temple, I seemed to be walking behind someone whose steps I could still hear on the stone slabs and mosaics but whom I should never again overtake. I went back to Paris and remained several years before returning home.

Yet I obscurely missed something during all those years. When one has once had the good luck to love intensely, life is spent in trying to recapture that ardor and that illumination. Forsaking beauty and the sensual happiness attached to it, exclusively serving misfortune, calls for a nobility I lack. But, after all, nothing is true that forces one to exclude. Isolated beauty ends up simpering;

solitary justice ends up oppressing. Whoever aims to serve one exclusive of the other serves no one, not even himself, and eventually serves injustice twice. A day comes when, thanks to rigidity, nothing causes wonder any more, everything is known, and life is spent in beginning over again. These are the days of exile, of desiccated life, of dead souls. To come alive again, one needs a special grace, self-forgetfulness, or a homeland. Certain mornings, on turning a corner, a delightful dew falls on the heart and then evaporates. But its coolness remains, and this is what the heart requires always. I had to set out again.

And in Algiers a second time, still walking under the same downpour which seemed not to have ceased since a departure I had thought definitive, amid the same vast melancholy smelling of rain and sea, despite this misty sky, these backs fleeing under the shower, these cafés whose sulphureous light distorted faces, I persisted in hoping. Didn't I know, besides, that Algiers rains, despite their appearance of never meaning to end, nonetheless stop in an instant, like those streams in my country which rise in two hours, lay waste acres of land, and suddenly dry up? One evening, in fact, the rain ceased. I waited one night more. A limpid morning rose, dazzling, over the pure sea. From the sky, fresh as a daisy, washed over and over again by the rains, reduced by these repeated washings to its finest and clearest texture, emanated a vibrant light that gave to each house and each tree a sharp outline, an astonished newness. In the world's morning the earth must have sprung forth in such a light. I again took the road for Tipasa.

For me there is not a single one of those sixty-nine kilometers that is not filled with memories and sensations. Turbulent childhood, adolescent daydreams in the drone of the bus's motor, mornings, unspoiled girls, beaches, young muscles always at the peak of their effort, evening's slight anxiety in a sixteen-year-old heart, lust for life, fame, and ever the same sky throughout the years, unfailing in strength and light, itself insatiable, consuming one by one over a period of months the victims stretched out in the form of crosses on the beach at the deathlike hour of noon. Always the same sea, too, almost impalpable in the morning light, which I again saw on the horizon as soon as the road, leaving the Sahel and its bronze-colored vineyards, sloped down toward the coast. But I did not stop to look at it. I wanted to see again the Chenoua, that solid, heavy mountain cut out of a single block of stone, which

borders the bay of Tipasa to the west before dropping down into
the sea itself. It is seen from a distance, long before arriving, a
light, blue haze still confused with the sky. But gradually it is
condensed, as you advance toward it, until it takes on the color
of the surrounding waters, a huge motionless wave whose amazing
leap upward has been brutally solidified above the sea calmed
all at once. Still nearer, almost at the gates of Tipasa, here is its
frowning bulk, brown and green, here is the old mossy god that
nothing will ever shake, a refuge and harbor for its sons, of whom
I am one.

While watching it I finally got through the barbed wire and   8
found myself among the ruins. And under the glorious December
light, as happens but once or twice in lives which ever after can
consider themselves favored to the full, I found exactly what I had
come seeking, what, despite the era and the world, was offered me,
truly to me alone, in that forsaken nature. From the forum strewn
with olives could be seen the village down below. No sound came
from it; wisps of smoke rose in the limpid air. The sea likewise
was silent as if smothered under the unbroken shower of dazzling,
cold light. From the Chenoua a distant cock's crow alone celebrated the day's fragile glory. In the direction of the ruins, as far
as the eye could see, there was nothing but pock-marked stones
and wormwood, trees and perfect columns in the transparence of
the crystalline air. It seemed as if the morning were stabilized, the
sun stopped for an incalculable moment. In this light and this
silence, years of wrath and night melted slowly away. I listened
to an almost forgotten sound within myself as if my heart, long
stopped, were calmly beginning to beat again. And awake now,
I recognized one by one the imperceptible sound of which the
silence was made up: the figured bass of the birds, the sea's faint,
brief sighs at the foot of the rocks, the vibration of the trees, the
blind singing of the columns, the rustling of the wormwood plants,
the furtive lizards. I heard that; I also listened to the happy tor-
rents rising within me. It seemed to me that I had at last come to
harbor, for a moment at least, and that henceforth that moment
would be endless. But soon after, the sun rose visibly a degree in
the sky. A magpie preluded briefly, and at once, from all directions,
birds' songs burst out with energy, jubilation, joyful discordance,
and infinite rapture. The day started up again. It was to carry
me to evening.

At noon on the half-sandy slopes covered with heliotropes like 9
a foam left by the furious waves of the last few days as they with-
drew, I watched the sea barely swelling at that hour with an exhausted motion, and I satisfied the two thirsts one cannot long
neglect without drying up — I mean loving and admiring. For there
is merely bad luck in not being loved; there is misfortune in not
loving. All of us, today, are dying of this misfortune. For violence
and hatred dry up the heart itself; the long fight for justice exhausts
the love that nevertheless gave birth to it. In the clamor in which
we live, love is impossible and justice does not suffice. This is why
Europe hates daylight and is only able to set injustice up against
injustice. But in order to keep justice from shriveling up like a
beautiful orange fruit containing nothing but a bitter, dry pulp, I
discovered once more at Tipasa that one must keep intact in oneself a freshness, a cool wellspring of joy, love the day that escapes
injustice, and return to combat having won that light. Here I
recaptured the former beauty, a young sky, and I measured my
luck, realizing at last that in the worst years of our madness the
memory of that sky had never left me. This was what in the end
had kept me from despairing. I had always known that the ruins
of Tipasa were younger than our new constructions or our bomb
damage. There the world began over again every day in an ever
new light. O light! This is the cry of all the characters of ancient
drama brought face to face with their fate. This last resort was
ours, too, and I knew it now. In the middle of winter I at last
discovered that there was in me an invincible summer.

MEANINGS AND VALUES

1a. How would you describe the author's point of view in "Return to
Tipasa"? (See Guide to Terms: *Point of View*.)
  b. How did the tone help determine your answer? (Guide: *Style/Tone*.)
2a. In paragraph 3 the author first says that he hoped to recapture a
freedom by going to Tipasa. What kind of freedom did he mean?
  b. What else does it seem he also hoped to recapture?
3. Camus says (par. 3) that walking among the ruins at night was
forbidden for reasons that "morality approves." What does he
mean?
4a. Considering that France had not been an aggressor, had been, in
fact, one of the countries devastated by aggression, why did Camus
feel that "our" hands were soiled (par. 4)?

b. He continues that "we were now guilty without meaning to be." Are the two statements identical in meaning? Explain.

5. Who was it, on his first return to Tipasa, that he "seemed to be walking behind" in the ruined temple (par. 4)?

6. What is the value, or potential value, of reading such a subjective account of the interior struggles of a stranger, one no longer even living?

EXPOSITORY TECHNIQUES

1a. Camus uses descriptive details that appeal to several of the five senses. Cite passages that illustrate this fact.

b. What, if anything, is the effect of this technique?

2a. This essay is, of course, the most highly impressionistic that we have studied (even though the framework itself is narrative). Rewrite any one of the paragraphs, condensing it into no more than one or two sentences of purely objective description.

b. Explain briefly how the use of either descriptive type would differ entirely from the use of the other.

c. Why do you think Camus chose almost purely impressionistic description to serve his purposes?

3. As you read this description-narration, you may gradually have become aware of the constant interweaving of references to contrasting elements — light and darkness or night, sun and rain, summer and winter.

a. Among the uses of this technique is, of course, the basic one of supplying some objective information. Why are such objective details provided in even impressionistic description?

b. Explain how these elements also help create desired atmosphere or mood. Is there a relation here with tone? (Guide: *Style/Tone.*)

4. Perhaps Camus uses these contrasting mood makers most subtly (and certainly intentionally) for their symbolic value. (Guide: *Symbolism.*) Explain this function for each of these contrasts:

a. Light and darkness or night.

b. Sun and rain.

c. Summer and winter.

DICTION AND VOCABULARY

1. What are the problems in gaining, from this reading, a valid critical impression of Camus' diction?

2a. There is a seemingly blatant cliché in the second half of paragraph 6. (Guide: *Clichés.*) What is it?

b. Why would it be unfair, however, to criticize the author for this usage?

3. Perhaps more than most modern writers, Camus regarded the essay as a form of art. Select five of Camus' sentences that especially appeal to you for their artistic power or charm.
a. What specific qualities, if any, do the five have in common?
b. What characteristics would set them apart from the work of less skilled and artistic writers?
c. How do you suppose a young writer can gain this artistic skill with verbal expression?

4. If any of the following words are unfamiliar to you, study their meanings in your dictionary: viscous (par. 1); wormwood (3); sarcophaguses, desiccated (5); definition, limpid, emanated (6); kilometers, impalpable (7); imperceptible, discordance (8); invincible (9).

SUGGESTIONS FOR WRITING AND DISCUSSION

1. Select one of the following quotations, qualify or negate it for your own purposes, and make a central theme of it for your oral or written composition.
a. ". . . it is sheer madness, almost always punished, to return to the sites of one's youth and try to relive . . . what one loved or keenly enjoyed . . ." (par. 3).
b. "When one has once had the good luck to love intensely, life is spent in trying to recapture that ardor and that illumination" (par. 5).
c. "Forsaking beauty and the sensual happiness attached to it, exclusively serving misfortune, calls for a nobility . . ." (par. 5).
d. ". . . nothing is true that forces one to exclude" (par. 5).
e. ". . . two thirsts one cannot long neglect without drying up . . . loving and admiring" (par. 9).
f. ". . . there is merely bad luck in not being loved; there is misfortune in not loving" (par. 9).
g. ". . . the long fight for justice exhausts the love that nevertheless gave birth to it" (par. 9).

Writing Suggestions for Section 9

Description

1. Primarily by way of impressionistic description that focuses on a single dominant impression, show and explain the mood, or atmosphere, of one of the following:

a. A county fair.	k. A party.
b. A ball game.	l. A family dinner.
c. A rodeo.	m. A traffic jam.
d. A wedding.	n. Reveille.
e. A funeral.	o. An airport (or bus depot).
f. A riot.	p. A drag race (or horse race).
g. A ghost town.	q. A home during one of its rush hours.
h. A cave.	r. The last night of Christmas shopping.
i. A mine.	s. A natural scene at a certain time of day.
j. An antique shop.	t. The campus at examination time.

u. A certain person at a time of great emotion — e.g., joy, anger, grief.

2. Using objective description as your basic pattern, explain the functional qualities or the significance of one of the following:

a. A passenger train.	g. An ideal workshop (or hobby room).
b. A freeway system.	h. An ideal garage.
c. A state park.	i. A hippie-type commune.
d. A house for sale.	j. The layout of a town (or airport).
e. A public building.	k. The layout of a farm.
f. A dairy barn.	l. A certain type of boat.

10

Using *Narration* as an Expository Technique

Attempts to classify the functions of narration seem certain to develop difficulties and end in arbitrary and sometimes fuzzy distinctions. These need not distress us, however, if we remember that narration remains narration — a factual or fictional report of a sequence of events — and that our only reason for trying to divide it into categories is to find some means of studying its uses.

ration assumes importance in its own right as one of the four basic by process analysis makes one important, if rather narrow, use of narration, since it explains in sequence how specific steps lead to completion of some process. But at the other extreme is narration that has very little to do with exposition: the story itself is the important thing, and instead of a series of steps leading obviously to a completed act, events *develop* out of each other and build suspense, however mild, through some kind of conflict. Here nar-

In a sense, as we have already seen in Section 5, exposition forms of prose, and it includes the novel and short story, as well as some news and sports reporting. Because we are studying exposition, however, we must avoid getting too involved with these uses of narration; they require special techniques, the study of which would require a whole course or, in fact, several courses.

Between the extremes of a very usable analysis of process and a very intriguing narration for the story's sake — and often seeming to blur into one or the other — is narration for *explanation's* sake, to explain a concept that is more than process and that might have been explained by one of the other patterns of exposition. Here only the form is narrative; the function is expository.

283

Fortunately, the average student seldom needs to use narration for major explanatory purposes, as it has been used in each of the following selections. But to learn the handling of even minor or localized narration, the best procedure (short of taking several college courses, or at least one that concentrates on the narrative form) is simply to observe how successful writers use it to perform an aid in developing any of the other major patterns of exposition. various functions. Localized narration can sometimes be helpful as The most common problems can be summarized as follows:

1. *Selection of details.* As in writing description, the user of narration always has far more details available than he can or should use. Good unity demands that he select only those which are most relevant to his purpose and the effect he wants to create.

2. *Time order.* The writer can use straight chronology, relating events as they happen (the usual method in minor uses of narration); or he can use the flashback method, leaving the sequence temporarily in order to go back and relate some now-significant happening of a time prior to the main action. If flashback is used, it should be deliberate and for a valid reason — not merely because the episode was neglected at the beginning.

3. *Transitions.* The lazy writer of narration is apt to resort to the transitional style of a three-year-old: ". . . and then we . . . and then she . . . and then we. . . ." Avoiding this style may tax his ingenuity, but invariably the result is worth the extra investment of time and thought.

4. *Point of view.* This is a large and complex subject if dealt with fully, as a course in narration would do. Briefly, however, the writer should decide at the beginning whether the reader is to experience the action through a character's eyes (and ears and brain), or from an overall, objective view. This decision makes a difference in how much can be told, whose thoughts or secret actions can be included. The writer must be consistent throughout the narrative and include only information that could logically be known through the adopted point of view.

5. *Dialogue.* Presumably the writer already knows the mechanics of using quotations. Beyond these, his problems are to make conversation as natural-sounding as possible and yet to keep it from rambling through many useless details — to keep the narrative moving forward by *means* of dialogue.

As in most patterns of writing, the use of expository narration is most likely to be successful if the writer constantly keeps his purpose and his audience in mind, remembering that the only reason for using the method in the first place — for doing *any* writing — is to communicate ideas. Soundness, clarity, and interest are the best means of attaining this goal.

ARTHUR HOPPE, born in Honolulu in 1925, is a Harvard graduate and Navy veteran. Since 1949 he has been a staff member of the *San Francisco Chronicle,* for which since 1960 he has written his own column, now syndicated in more than a hundred other newspapers. In addition to his three books, *Dreamboat* and *The Love Everybody Crusade* (1962) and *The Perfect Solution to Absolutely Everything* (1968), his writing has appeared in *The New Yorker, Harper's,* and numerous other magazines.

The Greatest Generation

"The Greatest Generation" was Hoppe's column of February 1, 1970. It is apparently based on "Abou Ben Adhem," a familiar poem by James Henry Leigh Hunt (1784–1859). Hoppe has adapted the narrative pattern of Hunt's poem to his usual humorous, if biting, style. The result is a good illustration of the narrative pattern in its simplest form.

Once upon a time there was a man named Ben Adam, who, like   1
most members of The Older Generation, had little hair and overwhelming guilt feelings.

He also had a son named Irwin, who, like most members of The   2
Younger Generation, had lots of hair and an overwhelming contempt for anybody over 30.

"Man, what a mess your generation made of things," Irwin was   3
fond of saying, several times daily. "Because of your bumbling, we face a society that's racist, militaristic, polluted, overpopulated and terrorized by the hydrogen bomb. Thanks a lot."

"I guess we're about the worst generation that ever lived," Ben   4

Adam would say, nodding guiltily. "I'm sorry, Irwin." And Irwin would shrug and go off with his friends to smoke pot.

Ben Adam couldn't help feeling that he was in for a bit of divine 5 wrath in return for his sins. And he was therefore somewhat shaken on awakening one night to find an Angel at the foot of his bed writing in a Golden Book.

"I have come, Ben Adam," said the Angel, "to grant you one wish." 6

"Me?" said Ben Adam with surprise. "Why me?" 7

"You have been selected by the Heavenly Computer as typical 8 of your generation," said the Angel "And your generation is to be rewarded for its magnificence."

"There must be some mistake," said Ben Adam with a frown. 9 "We've been awful. We created a racist society . . ."

"Mankind has always been racist," said the Angel gently. "You 10 were the first to admit it and attempt a remedy."

"And we militarized our democracy. Why, when I was a boy, 11 we only had an Army of 134,000 men."

"You built an Army of four million men in hopes of bringing 12 freedom and democracy to all the world," said the Angel. "Truly, a noble goal,"

"Well, maybe," said Ben Adam. "But you can't deny that we 13 polluted the water and the air and scattered garbage far and wide."

"That is so," said the Angel. "But the environment is polluted 14 solely because you constructed the most affluent society the world has ever seen."

"I guess that's right," said Ben Adam. "Yet look at the Population 15 Explosion. Famine and pestilence threaten mankind."

"Only because your generation cured diseases, increased the food 16 supply and thereby lengthened man's life span," said the Angel. "A tremendous achievement."

"And we live in the terror of the hydrogen bomb," said Ben 17 Adam gloomily. "What a legacy."

"Only because your generation unlocked the secrets of the atom 18 in its search for wisdom," said the Angel. "What a glorious triumph."

"You really think so?" said Ben Adam, sitting straighter and smil- 19 ing tentatively.

"Your motives were excellent, your goals ideal, your energies 20 boundless and your achievements tremendous," said the Angel, reading from the Golden Book. "In the eons of mankind, the names of your generation, Ben Adam, lead all the rest. And therefore, by the authority vested in me, I am empowered to grant you one wish. What shall it be?"

"I wish," said Ben Adam, the heavenly-chosen representative of   21
The Older Generation, with a sigh, "that you'd have a little talk with Irwin."

MEANINGS AND VALUES

1a. The author characterizes father and son with only a few details, mostly indirect. What personality traits do we know about them by the end of the selection? How?
 b. Are the characterizations sufficient for their purpose? Explain.
 c. To what extent do you agree that they are "like most members" of their generations?

2a. There is a subtle touch of irony in paragraph 4. What is it? (See Guide to Terms: *Irony.*)
 b. What irony, if any, does the central theme of the story itself demonstrate?
 c. Some people may see paradox in paragraph 8. Do you? If so, explain. (Guide: *Paradox.*)

3a. Do you suppose the author is really saying that the older generation is the greatest of all times?
 b. If not, what is he saying about it?

4a. The closing paragraph may seem offhand to be merely a bit of humor. Does it seem so to you?
 b. If not, what broader significance does it have?

5. If you have read Arlen's "Griefspeak" in the preceding section, what relation, if any, do you see between Ben Adam's guilt feelings and the comments of any of the announcers? Show the significance, if any.

EXPOSITORY TECHNIQUES

1a. How could paragraphs 1 and 2 be used to illustrate parallel structure? (Guide: *Parallel Structure.*)
 b. What is gained, or lost, by the use of such conspicuous parallels at the very beginning of the selection?

2a. What organizational function is accomplished by use of Irwin's quotation in paragraph 3?
 b. The four-paragraph introduction also provides other important services, besides merely starting the narration. What are they? (Guide: *Introductions.*)

3. How successful do you consider the author's development of dialogue? (Refer as necessary to the introductory remarks on dialogue.)

4a. Suggest other patterns of exposition that the author might have chosen to develop the same central theme.
  b. Select the one that seems to you the most feasible and explain how you would have used it.
  c. Would this method have been more, or less, effective? Explain.

DICTION AND VOCABULARY

1a. What is gained, or lost, by using a cliché to start this selection? (Guide: *Clichés*.)
  b. To what extent, if at all, do you think Irwin's indictments (par. 3) are clichés? Why?

2. The quotation in paragraph 3 includes an example of sarcasm. What is it? Why? (Guide: *Irony*.)

3. Does the simple diction and syntax of this selection indicate anything about the expected reader-audience — or are there other reasons for its use? Explain.

SUGGESTIONS FOR WRITING AND DISCUSSION

1. Select any one of Ben Adam's self-accusations and objectively present *both* sides of the question.

2. What contemporary evidence do you find of any widespread "guilt feelings" in the older generation? Show the nature of your observations and explain your interpretation of them.

3. Explain, if you are in a position to do so objectively, why some people choose pot in preference to more active confrontation with the "mess" of society.

4. Compare and/or contrast what you consider to be an effective kind of group protest with one that is less effective. Use examples as needed in your explanation.

(NOTE: Suggestions for topics requiring development by NARRATION are on page 314, at the end of this section.)

MARTIN GANSBERG, born in Brooklyn, N.Y., in 1920, received a Bachelor of Social Sciences degree from St.
John's University. He has been an editor and reporter on
the *New York Times* since 1942, including a three-year
period as editor of its international edition in Paris. He
also served on the faculty of Fairleigh Dickinson University for fifteen years. Gansberg has written for many magazines, including *Diplomat, Catholic Digest, Facts,* and
U.S. Lady.

38 Who Saw Murder Didn't Call the Police

"38 Who Saw Murder . . ." was written for the *New York
Times* in 1964, and for obvious reasons it has been anthologized frequently since then. Cast in a deceptively simple
news style, it still provides material for serious thought, as
well as a means of studying another use and technique of
narration.

For more than half an hour 38 respectable, law-abiding citizens in   1
Queens watched a killer stalk and stab a woman in three separate
attacks in Kew Gardens.

Twice their chatter and the sudden glow of their bedroom lights   2
interrupted him and frightened him off. Each time he returned,
sought her out, and stabbed her again. Not one person telephoned
the police during the assault; one witness called after the woman
was dead.

That was two weeks ago today.   3

Still shocked is Assistant Chief Inspector Frederick M. Lussen, in   4
charge of the borough's detectives and a veteran of 25 years of homicide investigations. He can give a matter-of-fact recitation on many
murders. But the Kew Gardens slaying baffles him — not because it is
a murder, but because the "good people" failed to call the police.

"As we have reconstructed the crime," he said, "the assailant had   5
three chances to kill this woman during a 35-minute period. He returned twice to complete the job. If we had been called when he
first attacked, the woman might not be dead now."

This is what the police say happened beginning at 3:20 A.M. in   6
the staid, middle-class, tree-lined Austin Street area:

Twenty-eight-year-old Catherine Genovese, who was called Kitty   7
by almost everyone in the neighborhood, was returning home from
her job as manager of a bar in Hollis. She parked her red Fiat in a
lot adjacent to the Kew Gardens Long Island Rail Road Station, fac-
ing Mowbray Place. Like many residents of the neighborhood, she
had parked there day after day since her arrival from Connecticut
a year ago, although the railroad frowns on the practice.

She turned off the lights of her car, locked the door, and started to   8
walk the 100 feet to the entrance of her apartment at 82-70 Austin
Street, which is in a Tudor building, with stores in the first floor
and apartments on the second.

The entrance to the apartment is in the rear of the building be-   9
cause the front is rented to retail stores. At night the quiet neighborhood is shrouded in the slumbering darkness that marks most resi-
dential areas.

Miss Genovese noticed a man at the far end of the lot, near a   10
seven-story apartment house at 82-40 Austin Street. She halted.
Then, nervously, she headed up Austin Street toward Lefferts Boulevard, where there is a call box to the 102nd Police Precinct in nearby
Richmond Hill.

She got as far as a street light in front of a bookstore before the   11
man grabbed her. She screamed. Lights went on in the 10-story
apartment house at 82-67 Austin Street, which faces the bookstore.
Windows slid open and voices punctuated the early-morning stillness.

Miss Genovese screamed: "Oh, my God, he stabbed me! Please   12
help me! Please help me!"

From one of the upper windows in the apartment house, a man   13
called down: "Let that girl alone!"

The assailant looked up at him, shrugged, and walked down Aus-   14
tin Street toward a white sedan parked a short distance away. Miss
Genovese struggled to her feet.

Lights went out. The killer returned to Miss Genovese, now try-   15 ing to make her way around the side of the building by the parking lot to get to her apartment. The assailant stabbed her again.

"I'm dying!" she shrieked. "I'm dying!"   16

Windows were opened again, and lights went on in many apart-   17 ments. The assailant got into his car and drove away. Miss Genovese staggered to her feet. A city bus, O-10, the Lefferts Boulevard line to Kennedy International Airport, passed. It was 3:35 A.M.

The assailant returned. By then, Miss Genovese had crawled to   18 the back of the building, where the freshly painted brown doors to the apartment house held out hope for safety. The killer tried the first door; she wasn't there. At the second door, 82-62 Austin Street, he saw her slumped on the floor at the foot of the stairs. He stabbed her a third time — fatally.

It was 3:50 by the time the police received their first call, from a   19 man who was a neighbor of Miss Genovese. In two minutes they were at the scene. The neighbor, a 70-year-old woman, and another woman were the only persons on the street. Nobody else came forward.

The man explained that he had called the police after much de-   20 liberation. He had phoned a friend in Nassau County for advice and then he had crossed the roof of the building to the apartment of the elderly woman to get her to make the call.

"I didn't want to get involved," he sheepishly told the police.   21

Six days later, the police arrested Winston Moseley, a 29-year-old   22 business-machine operator, and charged him with homicide. Moseley had no previous record. He is married, has two children and owns a home at 133-19 Sutter Avenue, South Ozone Park, Queens. On Wednesday, a court committed him to Kings County Hospital for psychiatric observation.

When questioned by the police, Moseley also said that he had   23 slain Mrs. Annie May Johnson, 24, of 146-12 133d Avenue, Jamaica, on Feb. 29 and Barbara Kralik, 15, of 174-17 140th Avenue, Spring-field Gardens, last July. In the Kralik case, the police are holding Al-vin L. Mitchell, who is said to have confessed that slaying.

The police stressed how simple it would have been to have got-   24 ten in touch with them. "A phone call," said one of the detectives, "would have done it." The police may be reached by dialing "O" for operator or SPring 7-3100.

Today witnesses from the neighborhood, which is made up of one-   25 family homes in the $35,000 to $60,000 range with the exception of the two apartment houses near the railroad station, find it difficult to explain why they didn't call the police.

A housewife, knowingly if quite casual, said, "We thought it was   26
a lover's quarrel." A husband and wife both said, "Frankly, we were afraid." They seemed aware of the fact that events might have been different. A distraught woman, wiping her hands in her apron, said, "I didn't want my husband to get involved."

One couple, now willing to talk about that night, said they heard   27
the first screams. The husband looked thoughtfully at the bookstore where the killer first grabbed Miss Genovese.

"We went to the window to see what was happening," he said,   28
"but the light from our bedroom made it difficult to see the street." The wife, still apprehensive, added: "I put out the light and we were able to see better."

Asked why they hadn't called the police, she shrugged and re-   29
plied: "I don't know."

A man peeked out from a slight opening in the doorway to his   30
apartment and rattled off an account of the killer's second attack. Why hadn't he called the police at the time? "I was tired," he said without emotion. "I went back to bed."

It was 4:25 A.M. when the ambulance arrived to take the body   31
of Miss Genovese. It drove off. "Then," a solemn police detective said, "the people came out."

MEANINGS AND VALUES

1. Why has this narrative account of old news (the murder provided its only headlines in 1964) retained its significance to this day?

2. Are you able to see in this event a sort of microcosm of any larger condition or situation? If so, explain, using examples as needed to illustrate your ideas.

3a. If one of the author's chief purposes was to propound such a central theme (as indicated in your answers to questions 1 and 2), how might he have done so without using narration at all? Specify what patterns of exposition he could have used instead.

  b. Would any of them have been as effective as narration *for the purpose?* Why, or why not?

4. Show how this selection could be used as an illustration in an explanatory discussion of abstract and concrete writing. (See Guide to Terms: *Concrete/Abstract.*)

294

5. If you have read "On Courage . . ." in Section 7, relate the Genovese murder, however you can, to any *specific* portion of the earlier
essay.

EXPOSITORY TECHNIQUES

1a. What standard introductory technique is exemplified in paragraph 1?
(Guide: *Introductions.*)
 b. How effective do you consider it?
 c. If you see anything ironic in the fact stated there, explain what the
irony is. (Guide: *Irony.*)
2a. Where does the main narration begin?
 b. What, then, is the function of the preceding paragraphs?
3a. Study several of the paragraph transitions within the narration itself
to determine Gansberg's method of advancing the time sequence (to
avoid overuse of "and then"). What is the technique?
 b. Is another needed? Why, or why not?
4a. What possible reasons do you see for the predominant use of short
paragraphs in this piece?
 b. Does this selection lose any effectiveness because of the short paragraphs?
5. Undoubtedly, the author carefully selected the few quotations from
witnesses that he uses. What principle, or principles, do you think
applied to his selection?
6. Explain why you think the quotation from the "solemn police detective" was, or was not, deliberately and carefully chosen to conclude
the piece. (Guide: *Closings.*)
7a. Briefly identify the point of view of the writing. (Guide: *Point of
View.*)
 b. Is it consistent throughout?
 c. Show the relation, as you see it, between this point of view and the
author's apparent attitude toward his subject matter.
8a. Does he permit himself any sentimentality? If so, where? (Guide:
Sentimentality.)
 b. If not, specifically what could he have permitted that would have
slipped into melodrama or sentimentality?

DICTION AND VOCABULARY

1a. Why do you think the author used no difficult words in this narration?
 b. Do you find the writing at all belittling to college people because of
this fact? Why, or why not?

SUGGESTIONS FOR WRITING AND DISCUSSION

1. Use both developed and undeveloped examples to show the prevalence, among individuals, of an anti-involvement attitude today. Or, if you prefer, show that this accusation is unjustified.

2. If this narration can be regarded as a sort of microcosm (see question 2 of "Meanings and Values"), select one example from the larger subject and develop it on whatever theme you choose. Your example could be from the international level, if you like (and if you don't mind becoming the center of a controversy) — e.g., the recent cries of "murder!" from numerous small countries. If you prefer, go into more distant (and therefore less controversial) history for your example.

3. If such a crime as the Genovese murder were happening in an area or a situation where police were not so instantly available, what do you think an observer should do about it? What would *you* do? Justify your stand on all possible grounds.

(NOTE: Suggestions for topics requiring development by NARRATION are on page 314, at the end of this section.)

GEORGE ORWELL (1903–1950), whose real name was Eric
Blair, was a British novelist and essayist, one of the best-
known satirists of the twentieth century. He was born in
India, educated at Eton in England, and then served for
five years with the Imperial Police in Burma. During the
1930's, Orwell spent several years writing in Paris and
one year fighting in the Spanish Civil War, during which
he was wounded. He finally settled in England, where he
wrote his best-known books, *Animal Farm* (1945), a satire
on Soviet history, and *1984* (1949), a vivid picture of life
in a projected totalitarian society. He was sharply aware
of injustices in democratic societies and was consistently
socialistic in his views. Many of Orwell's best essays are
collected in *Critical Essays* (1946), *Shooting an Elephant*
(1950), and *Such, Such Were the Joys* (1953).

A Hanging

"A Hanging" is typical of Orwell's essays in its setting —
Burma — and in its subtle but biting commentary on
colonialism, on capital punishment, even on one aspect of
human nature itself. Although he is ostensibly giving a
straightforward account of an execution, the author mas-
terfully uses descriptive details and dialogue to create
atmosphere and sharply drawn characterizations. The
essay gives concrete form to a social message that is often
delivered much less effectively in abstract generalities.

It was in Burma, a sodden morning of the rains. A sickly light, like   1
yellow tinfoil, was slanting over the high walls into the jail yard.
We were waiting outside the condemned cells, a row of sheds
fronted with double bars, like small animal cages. Each cell meas-

From *Shooting an Elephant and Other Essays*, by George Orwell. Copyright
1945, 1946, 1949, 1950, by Sonia Brownell Orwell. Reprinted by permission of
Harcourt Brace Jovanovich, Inc., Miss Sonia Brownell, and Martin Secker &
Warburg Ltd.

ured about ten feet by ten and was quite bare within except for a
plank bed and a pot for drinking water. In some of them brown,
silent men were squatting at the inner bars, with their blankets
draped round them. These were the condemned men, due to be
hanged within the next week or two.

One prisoner had been brought out of his cell. He was a Hindu, a 2
puny wisp of a man, with a shaven head and vague liquid eyes. He
had a thick, sprouting moustache, absurdly too big for his body,
rather like the moustache of a comic man on the films. Six tall
Indian warders were guarding him and getting him ready for the
gallows. Two of them stood by with rifles and fixed bayonets, while
the others handcuffed him, passed a chain through his handcuffs
and fixed it to their belts, and lashed his arms tight to his sides.
They crowded very close about him, with their hands always on
him in a careful, caressing grip, as though all the while feeling him
to make sure he was there. It was like men handling a fish which
is still alive and may jump back into the water. But he stood quite
unresisting, yielding his arms limply to the ropes, as though he
hardly noticed what was happening.

Eight o'clock struck and a bugle call, desolately thin in the wet 3
air, floated from the distant barracks. The superintendent of the
jail, who was standing apart from the rest of us, moodily prodding
the gravel with his stick, raised his head at the sound. He was an
army doctor, with a grey toothbrush moustache and a gruff voice.
"For God's sake hurry up, Francis," he said irritably. "The man
ought to have been dead by this time. Aren't you ready yet?"

Francis, the head jailer, a fat Dravidian in a white drill suit and 4
gold spectacles, waved his black hand. "Yes sir, yes sir," he bubbled.
"All iss satisfactorily prepared. The hangman iss waiting. We shall
proceed."

"Well, quick march, then. The prisoners can't get their breakfast 5
till this job's over."

We set out for the gallows. Two warders marched on either side 6
of the prisoner, with their rifles at the slope; two others marched
close against him, gripping him by arm and shoulder, as though at
once pushing and supporting him. The rest of us, magistrates and
the like, followed behind. Suddenly, when we had gone ten yards,
the procession stopped short without any order or warning. A dreadful thing had happened — a dog, come goodness knows whence,
had appeared in the yard. It came bounding among us with a loud
volley of barks and leapt round us wagging its whole body, wild

with glee at finding so many human beings together. It was a large woolly dog, half Airedale, half pariah. For a moment it pranced round us, and then, before anyone could stop it, it had made a dash for the prisoner, and jumping up tried to lick his face. Everybody stood aghast, too taken aback even to grab the dog.

"Who let that bloody brute in here?" said the superintendent   7 angrily. "Catch it, someone!"

A warder detached from the escort, charged clumsily after the   8 dog, but it danced and gambolled just out of his reach, taking everything as part of the game. A young Eurasian jailer picked up a handful of gravel and tried to stone the dog away, but it dodged the stones and came after us again. Its yaps echoed from the jail walls. The prisoner, in the grasp of the two warders, looked on incuriously, as though this was another formality of the hanging. It was several minutes before someone managed to catch the dog. Then we put my handkerchief through its collar and moved off once more, with the dog still straining and whimpering.

It was about forty yards to the gallows. I watched the bare brown   9 back of the prisoner marching in front of me. He walked clumsily with his bound arms, but quite steadily, with that bobbing gait of the Indian who never straightens his knees. At each step his muscles slid neatly into place, the lock of hair on his scalp danced up and down, his feet printed themselves on the wet gravel. And once, in spite of the men who gripped him by each shoulder, he stepped lightly aside to avoid a puddle on the path.

It is curious; but till that moment I had never realized what it   10 means to destroy a healthy, conscious man. When I saw the prisoner step aside to avoid the puddle I saw the mystery, the unspeakable wrongness, of cutting a life short when it is in full tide. This man was not dying, he was alive just as we are alive. All the organs of his body were working — bowels digesting food, skin renewing itself, nails growing, tissues forming — all toiling away in solemn foolery. His nails would still be growing when he stood on the drop, when he was falling through the air with a tenth-of-a-second to live. His eyes saw the yellow gravel and the grey walls, and his brain still remembered, foresaw, reasoned — even about puddles. He and we were a party of men walking together, seeing, hearing, feeling, understanding the same world; and in two minutes, with a sudden snap, one of us would be gone — one mind less, one world less.

The gallows stood in a small yard, separate from the main grounds   11
of the prison, and overgrown with tall prickly weeds. It was a brick
erection like three sides of a shed, with planking on top, and above
that two beams and a crossbar with the rope dangling. The hangman, a greyhaired convict in the white uniform of the prison, was
waiting beside his machine. He greeted us with a servile crouch as
we entered. At a word from Francis the two warders, gripping the
prisoner more closely than ever, half led, half pushed him to the
gallows and helped him clumsily up the ladder. Then the hangman
climbed up and fixed the rope round the prisoner's neck.

We stood waiting, five yards away. The warders had formed in a   12
rough circle round the gallows. And then, when the noose was
fixed, the prisoner began crying out to his god. It was a high, re-
iterated cry of "Ram! Ram! Ram! Ram!" not urgent and fearful like
a prayer or cry for help, but steady, rhythmical, almost like the toll-
ing of a bell. The dog answered the sound with a whine. The hangman, still standing on the gallows, produced a small cotton bag
like a flour bag and drew it down over the prisoner's face. But the
sound, muffled by the cloth, still persisted, over and over again:
"Ram! Ram! Ram! Ram! Ram!"

The hangman climbed down and stood ready, holding the lever.   13
Minutes seemed to pass. The steady, muffled crying from the prisoner went on and on, "Ram! Ram! Ram!" never faltering for an
instant. The superintendent, his head on his chest, was slowly poking the ground with his stick; perhaps he was counting the cries,
allowing the prisoner a fixed number — fifty, perhaps, or a hundred.
Everyone had changed colour. The Indians had gone grey like bad
coffee, and one or two of the bayonets were wavering. We looked
at the lashed, hooded man on the drop, and listened to his cries —
each cry another second of life; the same thought was in all our
minds; oh, kill him quickly, get it over, stop that abominable noise!

Suddenly the superintendent made up his mind. Throwing up his   14
head he made a swift motion with his stick. "Chalo!" he shouted
almost fiercely.

There was a clanking noise, and then dead silence. The prisoner   15
had vanished, and the rope was twisting on itself. I let go of the
dog, and it galloped immediately to the back of the gallows; but
when it got there it stopped short, barked, and then retreated into
a corner of the yard, where it stood among the weeds, looking
timorously out at us. We went round the gallows to inspect the

prisoner's body. He was dangling with his toes pointed straight downwards, very slowly revolving, as dead as a stone.

The superintendent reached out with his stick and poked the bare brown body; it oscillated slightly. *"He's* all right," said the superintendent. He backed out from under the gallows, and blew out a deep breath. The moody look had gone out of his face quite suddenly. He glanced at his wrist-watch. "Eight minutes past eight. Well, that's all for this morning, thank God." 16

The warders unfixed bayonets and marched away. The dog, sobered and conscious of having misbehaved itself, slipped after them. We walked out of the gallows yard, past the condemned cells with their waiting prisoners, into the big central yard of the prison. The convicts, under the command of warders armed with lathis, were already receiving their breakfast. They squatted in long rows, each man holding a tin pannikin, while two warders with buckets marched round ladling out rice; it seemed quite a homely, jolly scene, after the hanging. An enormous relief had come upon us now that the job was done. One felt an impulse to sing, to break into a run, to snigger. All at once everyone began chattering gaily. 17

The Eurasian boy walking beside me nodded towards the way we had come, with a knowing smile: "Do you know, sir, our friend (he meant the dead man) when he heard his appeal had been dismissed, he pissed on the floor of his cell. From fright. Kindly take one of my cigarettes, sir. Do you not admire my new silver case, sir? From the boxwallah, two rupees eight annas. Classy European style." 18

Several people laughed — at what, nobody seemed certain. 19

Francis was walking by the superintendent, talking garrulously: "Well, sir, all hass passed off with the utmost satisfactoriness. It was all finished — flick! Like that. It iss not always so — oah, no! I have known cases where the doctor wass obliged to go beneath the gallows and pull the prissoner's legs to ensure decease. Most disagreeable!" 20

"Wriggling about, eh? That's bad," said the superintendent. 21

"Arch, sir, it iss worse when they become refractory! One man, I recall, clung to the bars of hiss cage when we went to take him out. You will scarcely credit, sir, that it took six warders to dislodge him, three pulling at each leg. We reasoned with him, 'My dear fellow,' we said, 'think of all the pain and trouble you are causing to us!' But no, he would not listen! Ach, he wass very troublesome!" 22

I found that I was laughing quite loudly. Everyone was laughing. 23
Even the superintendent grinned in a tolerant way. "You'd better
all come out and have a drink," he said quite genially. "I've got a
bottle of whisky in the car. We could do with it."

We went through the big double gates of the prison into the 24
road. "Pulling at his legs!" exclaimed a Burmese magistrate suddenly, and burst into a loud chuckling. We all began laughing
again. At that moment Francis' anecdote seemed extraordinarily
funny. We all had a drink together, native and European alike,
quite amicably. The dead man was a hundred yards away.

MEANINGS AND VALUES

1. What was the real reason for the superintendent's impatience?
2. On first impression it may have seemed that the author gave undue
   attention to the dog's role in this narrative.
   a. Why was the episode such a "dreadful thing" (par. 6)?
   b. Why did the author think it worth noting that the dog was excited at
      "finding so many human beings together"?
   c. Of what significance was the dog's trying to lick the prisoner's face?
3. Explain how the prisoner's stepping around a puddle could have
   given the author a new insight into what was about to happen
   (par. 10)?
4. Why was there so much talking and laughing after the hanging was
   finished?
5. What is the broadest meaning of Orwell's last sentence?

EXPOSITORY TECHNIQUES

1. Cite examples of both objective and impressionistic description in
   the first paragraph.
2a. What time order is used primarily in this narrative?
 b. If there are any exceptions, state where.
3. Considering the relatively few words devoted to them, several of the
   characterizations in this essay are remarkably vivid — a result, obviously, of highly discriminating selection of details from the multitude
   of those that must have been available to the author. For each of the
   following people, list the character traits that we can observe, and
   state whether these impressions come to us through details of description, action, and/or dialogue.
   a. The prisoner.

b. The superintendent.
c. Francis.
d. The Eurasian boy.
4a. Why do you think the author included so many details of the preparation of the prisoner (par. 2)?
b. Why did he include so many details about the dog and his actions?
c. What is gained by the assortment of details in paragraph 10?
5. The tone of a writing such as this can easily slip into sentimentality or even melodrama without the author's realizing what is happening. (See Guide to Terms: *Sentimentality.*) Select three places in this narrative where a less-skilled writer might have had such trouble, and note by what restraints Orwell prevented sentimentality.

DICTION AND VOCABULARY

1. A noteworthy element of Orwell's style is his occasional use of figurative language. Cite six metaphors and similes, and comment on their choice and effectiveness.

2. Orwell was always concerned with the precise effects that words could give to meaning and style.
   a. Cite at least six nonfigurative words that seem to you particularly well chosen for their purpose.
   b. Show what their careful selection contributes to the description of atmosphere or to the subtle meanings of the author.
   c. How is this attention to diction a matter of style? (Guide: *Style/Tone.*)

SUGGESTIONS FOR WRITING AND DISCUSSION

1. Select *one* of the points of controversy over capital punishment and present both sides with equal objectivity.
2. Consider the dilemma of a person whose "duty" seems to require one course of action and "conscience" just the opposite course. Use concrete illustrations to show how serious such dilemmas can be.
3. Examine the moral right, or lack of it, of the people of one country to impose their laws on the people of another country.
4. Discuss one benefit of colonialism to the people colonized. Use specific illustrations.
5. Explain how, in your own experience, a seemingly minor incident led to much deeper insight into a matter not fully understood before.

(NOTE: Suggestions for topics requiring development by NARRATION are on page 314, at the end of this section.)

ANTOINE DE SAINT-EXUPÉRY

ANTOINE DE SAINT-EXUPÉRY (1900–1944) was a French author, airline pilot, and wartime reconnaissance pilot. Much of his finest writing, in fact, is about flying. Not long before the end of World War II, Saint-Exupéry and his plane were lost during a reconnaissance mission over enemy territory in Europe. He was a prolific writer; his books that have been translated into English include *Wind, Sand and Stars, Wisdom of the Sands, A Sense of Life,* and *The Little Prince,* a children's book.

Enemy Voices in the Night Speak Across No Man's Land

"Enemy Voices . . ." is from *A Sense of Life* and *Wind, Sand and Stars.* It is concerned with what many people are coming to regard as the most tragic flaw in the human race: the inability to really communicate about matters of deepest importance. Saint-Exupéry's rich figurative style and his thoughtful insights into the human condition — qualities that are rapidly enhancing his reputation in America as they did years ago in Europe — are fully demonstrated in this narrative essay.

On the Guadalajara front I sat at night in a dugout with a Republican squad made up of a lieutenant, a sergeant, and three men. They were about to go out on patrol duty. One of them (the night was cold) stood half in shadow with his head not quite through the neck of a sweater he was pulling on, his arms caught in the sleeves and waving slowly and awkwardly in the air like the short arms of   1

a bear. Smothered curses, stubbles of beard, distant muffled explo-
sions — the atmosphere was a strange compound of sleep, waking,
and death. I thought of tramps on the road bestirring themselves,
raising themselves up off the ground on heavy sticks. Caught in the
earth, painted by the earth, their hands grubby with their garden-
less gardening, these men were raising themselves painfully out of
the mud in order to emerge under the stars. In these blocks of
caked clay I could sense the awakening of consciousness, and as I
looked at them I said to myself that across the way, at this very
moment, the enemy was getting into his harness, was thickening his
body with woolen sweaters; earth-crusted, he was breaking out of
his mold of hardened mud. Across the way the same clay shaping
the same beings was wakening in the same way into consciousness.

Across the way, Lieutenant, slowly struggling to his feet is a man   2
who is your double, and who presently will die by your hand. He
also has renounced everything to serve the cause he believes in.
But what he believes in you believe in, too, for who would consent
to risk death except for truth, justice, and love of his fellow men?

"They've been misled — I mean, the men opposite have been mis-   3
led," you'll tell me. But I have no use for politicians, profiteers, and
armchair experts, no matter which side they belong to. They are
the men who pull the strings, use the big words, and fancy themselves leaders of men. The rest of us they consider simpletons. But
if their big words do take root, it is because, like seeds borne by
the winds to some distant land, they fall upon a rich soil prepared
to bear the burden of the harvest.

The patrol moved forward across fields through crackling stubble,   4
knocking its toe against unseen rocks in the dark. We were making
our way down into a narrow valley on the other side of which the
enemy was entrenched. Caught in the crossfire of artillery, the peasants had evacuated this valley, and their deserted village lay here
drowned in the waters of war. Only their dogs remained, ghostly
creatures that hunted their pitiful prey in the day and howled in
the night. At four in the morning, when the moon rose white as a
picked bone, a whole village bayed at the dead divinity.

"Go down and find out if the enemy is hiding in that village," the   5
commanding officer had ordered. Very likely on the other side the
same order had been given.

We were accompanied by a sort of political agent, a civilian.   6

"You'll hear them," he told me. "When we get nearer, we'll call out to the enemy. They're just across the valley, on that hill. Sometimes they answer."

I have forgotten his name, though not what he looked like. It seems to me that he must have been rheumatic, and I remember that he leaned heavily on a knotted stick as we tramped forward in the night. His face was the face of a conscientious and elderly workman. I would have sworn that he was above politics and parties, above ideological rivalries. "Pity it is," he would say, "that as things are we cannot explain our point of view to the other fellow." He walked weighed down by his doctrine, like an evangelist. Across the way, meanwhile, was the other evangelist, a believer just as enlightened as this one, his boots just as muddy, his duty taking him on exactly the same errand.

7

We were moving steadily forward toward the lip of land that dominated the valley, toward that farthermost promontory, that ultimate terrace, toward the question we would call out to the enemy, as if we were questioning ourselves.

8

The night arched above us like a cathedral. No rifle shattered the silence. A truce? No, no, not that. It was more the feeling of a presence. One was listening for the two adversaries to speak forth in a single voice. Fraternization? Definitely not, if this means the weariness that fragments a front line into individuals and moves men to share their cigarettes and mingle with each other out of their sense of a common loss of human status.

9

Try making a gesture toward the enemy. It will lead to a kind of fraternization, perhaps, but at a level that engages an inarticulate segment of the mind and will not save us here below from carnage. For still we do not command the language to express what it is that unites us.

10

I felt I understood this agent who was accompanying us. Where did he come from, this man who kept his face set so steadily ahead? First, he and the peasants he grew up with had watched the land and learned how it lives. Surely he had walked long years behind a plow. Then he left village for factory, and he watched how men live. "Metallurgist . . . been a metallurgist for twenty years."

11

I have never heard a man speak about himself with such noble freedom and directness. "No schooling for me, though. . . . And teaching myself was hard, hard. . . . Tools you see, I knew about. I knew how to use them, talk about them. I understood tools. . . .

12

But when I wanted to think about things, about ideas and life, or if I wanted to talk to someone about such things. . . . You people, you see, are used to thinking abstractly. From the time you're children, they teach you how to find your way through those mazes of words that are all so full of contradictions. You don't remember, you can't even imagine any more how hard it is to reason. . . . But I worked at it, I kept at it. And little by little I began to limber up. I could feel it. Oh, don't think I don't know my limitations. . . . I'm a bumpkin still. I haven't ever learned about courtesy, for example, and manners bespeak the man, you know. . . ."

As I was listening to him, I remembered an impromptu school 13 I'd come across one day, quite near the front. It had been set up in the shelter of a few rocks. A corporal was giving a lesson in botany. He was separating the petals of a wild poppy, initiating his pupils into one of the more gentle mysteries of nature. Old and hardened by life as they were, the men were almost childishly anxious as they struggled to understand. They had been told: "You're like brutes who've scarcely crawled out of your caves. You've got to join the civilized race." And they were hastening on, in their heavy, clumsy boots, to catch up.

What I had witnessed that day was the mind's awakening, and it 14 was very like the rising of sap. Born out of clay, in the shadows of prehistory, the mind has ascended step by step to the peaks of a Descartes, Bach, or Pascal. And I was moved now as I listened to this man talk about the effort of thinking, or the impulse to grow. This is the way a tree grows. The mystery of life lies here. Life alone draws its stocks from the soil and against the drag of gravity raises them skyward.

How well I remember that cathedral night. The spirit of man 15 sallying forth with bow and arrow. . . . The enemy to whom presently we would be calling. . . . And we ourselves, a caravan of pilgrims plodding over a black, crackling earth seeded with stars.

We do not know it, but we are in search of a gospel that will 16 embrace all our provisional gospels. They spill too much human blood. We are marching toward a stormy Sinai.

And we have arrived. We stumble over a dazed sentinel, half 17 asleep in the shelter of a low stone wall.

"Yes, here they sometimes answer. . . . Other times they call to 18 us. . . . But sometimes they don't answer. It depends on how they feel."

Just like the gods.   19

The winding front-line trenches lie about a hundred yards behind   20
us. Here the low breastworks shield a man only up to his chest;
they serve as lookouts at night and during the day are abandoned.
They face directly out over the abyss. We feel as if we are prop-
ping our elbows on a railing or parapet that has been flung out
above the unknown, above the void.

I strike a match, intending to light a cigarette, and two power-   21
ful hands duck my head. Everybody has ducked, and I hear the
whistle of bullets in the air. Then silence. The shots were fired high
and the volley was not repeated, a mere reminder from the enemy
of what constitutes decorum here. One does not light a cigarette in
the face of the enemy.

We are joined by three or four men, wrapped in blankets, who   22
had been posted behind neighboring walls.

"Looks as if the lads across the way were awake," one of them   23
remarks.

"Do you think they'll talk tonight? We'd like to talk to them."   24

"One of them, Antonio, he talks sometimes."   25

"Call him."   26

The man in the blanket straightens up, cups his hands round his   27
mouth, takes a deep breath, and calls out slowly and loudly:
"An . . . to . . . ni . . . o!"

The call swells, unfurls, floats across the valley and echoes back.   28

"Better duck," my neighbor advises. "Sometimes when you call   29
them, they let fly."

Crouched behind the stone wall, we listen. No sound of a shot.   30
Yet we cannot say we have heard nothing at all, for the whole
night is singing like a seashell.

"Hi! Antonio . . . o! Are you . . . ?"   31

The man in the blanket draws another deep breath and goes on: 32
"Are you asleep?"   33

"Asleep?" says the echo. "Asleep?" the valley asks. "Asleep?" the   34
whole night wants to know. The sound fills all space. We scramble
to our feet and stand erect in perfect confidence. They have not
touched their guns.

I stand imagining them on their side of the valley as they listen,   35
hear, receive this human voice, this voice that obviously has not
stirred them to anger since no finger has pressed a trigger. True,
they do not answer, they are silent; but how attentive must be
that silent audience from which, a moment ago, a match had sufficed

to draw a volley. Borne on the breeze of a human voice, invisible
seeds are fertilizing that black earth across the valley. Those men
thirst for our words as we for theirs. But their fingers, meanwhile,
are on their triggers. They put me in mind of those wild things we
would try in the desert to tame and that would stare at us, eat the
food and drink the water we set out for them, and would spring
at our throats when we made a move to stroke them.

We squatted well down behind the wall and held up a lighted   36
match above it. Three bullets passed overhead. To the match they
said, "You are forgetting that we are at war." To us, "We are listening, nevertheless. We can still love, though we stick to our rules."

Another giant peasant rested his gun against the wall, stood up,   37
drew a deep breath, and let go:

"Antonio . . . o! It's me! Leo!"   38

The sound moved across the valley like a ship new-launched.   39
Eight hundred yards to the far shore, eight hundred back — sixteen
hundred yards. If they answered, there would be five seconds of
time between our questions and their replies. Five seconds of
silence, in which all war would be suspended, would go between
each question and each answer. Like an embassy on a journey, each
time. What this meant was that even if they answered, we should
still feel ourselves separated from them. Between them and us the
inertia of an invisible world would still be there to be stirred into
action. For the considerable space of five seconds we should be like
men shipwrecked and fearful lest the rescue party had not heard
their cries.

". . . ooo!"   40

A distant voice like a feeble wave has curled up to die on our   41
shore. The phrase, the word, was lost on the way and the result is
an undecipherable message. Yet it strikes me like a blow. In this
impenetrable darkness a sudden flash of light has gleamed. All of us
are shaken by a ridiculous hope. Something has made known to us
its existence. We can be sure now that there are men across the
way. It is as if in invisibility a crack had opened, as if. . . .
Imagine a house at night, dark and its doors all locked. You, sitting
in its darkness, feel a breath of cold air on your face. A single
breath. What a presence!

Have you ever leaned over an abyss? I remember the fault at   42
Chézery: it was a black fissure lost in the woods, perhaps four or
five feet wide and ninety feet long. Not amounting to much, that is.

I used to lie flat on my belly on the pine needles and let a stone slip from my hand down the smooth side of the crevice. No reply. One, two, three seconds passed and after that eternity I would finally hear a faint rumble, all the more stirring to me for its being so slow and so slight. Then the abyss seemed to me bottomless. And so it was that now a delayed echo created a whole world. The enemy, we, life, death, the war — all were contained and expressed in a few seconds of silence.

Again our signal is released, our ship sent forth, our caravan despatched into the desert, and we wait. They no doubt are preparing to receive that voice which strikes like a bullet to the heart. 43

There it comes again! ". . . time . . . sleep!" 44

Torn, mutilated as a truly urgent message must be, washed by the waves and soaked in brine, here is our message. The men who fired at our cigarettes have blown up their chests with air in order to send us this motherly bit of advice: 45

"Quiet! Go to bed! Time to sleep!" 46

It excites us. You who read this will perhaps think that these men were merely playing a game. In a sense they were. I am sure that, being simple men, if you had caught them at their sport they would have denied that it was serious. But games cover something deep and intense, else there would be no excitement in them, no pleasure, no power to stir us. 47

The game we perhaps thought we were only playing was too well attuned to the vaulted night, the march toward Sinai; it made our hearts beat too wildly for it not to be the answer to some real if undefined need within us. We exulted because communication had been re-established. Thus the scientist's hand trembles as the crucial experiment proceeds and he prepares to weigh the molecule. He will be noting one constant among a hundred thousand variables, and it might seem as if he were merely adding one grain of sand to the towers of science. Yet his heart pounds, for it is not a matter of a grain of sand. He holds a thread. He holds in his hand the thread by which knowledge of the universe is gathered in, for all things are interconnected. The rescue team trembles in the same way when they have cast their rope once, twice, twenty times, and feel at last the almost imperceptible tug telling them that the shipwrecked crew has grasped it. A tiny huddle of men had been lost among the fog-shrouded reefs, cut off from the world. And now the magic of a 48 thread of cable links them to the men and women safely in port everywhere. Here we threw a fragile bridge out into the night, toward the unknown, and now it links the two sides of the world. It was as if we were marrying our enemy before dying by his hand.

But so slight, so fragile was the pontoon flung between our two   49
shores that a question too awkward, a phrase too clumsy, would certainly upset it. Words lose themselves: only essential words, only the truth of truths would leave this frail bridge whole. And I can see him now, that peasant who stirred Antonio to speech and thus made himself our pilot, our ambassador; I can see him as he stood erect, as he rested his strong hands on the low stone wall and sent forth from his great chest that question of questions:

"Antonio! What are you fighting for?"   50

Let me say again that he and Antonio would be ashamed to think   51
that you took them seriously. They would insist that it was all in fun. Later they would actually believe this, when they groped for words to describe what had moved them to do this thing and did not find them because in our meager language such words do not exist. Yet they had acted on the impulse of a being that lives within all of us and that someday with a mighty effort we will deliver. But I was there as that soldier stood waiting, and I knew that his whole soul gaped wide to receive the answer. Here is the truncated message, the secret mutilated by five seconds of travel across the valley as an inscription in stone is defaced by the passing of the centuries:

". . . Spain!"   52

And then I heard: 53

". . . You?"   54

He got his answer. I heard the great reply as it was flung forth   55
into space:

"The bread of our brothers."   56

And then the amazing: 57

"Good night, friend!"   58

And the response from the other side of the world: 59

"Good night, friend!"   60

And silence.   61

Probably they on the other side had, like us, snatched only a few   62
ragged words. Such was the fruit of an hour's hard and dangerous march. These few words, echoes oscillating from hill to hill under the silent stars: "Spain" . . . "bread of our brothers."

And then, the hour having come, our patrol resumed its march. 63
We began the descent toward the village that had been appointed
for our rendezvous. On the other side, the same patrol, governed by
the same necessities, was plunging into the same abyss. Under the
guise of different words, both had proclaimed the same truths, yet
this was not to preclude their dying together.

MEANINGS AND VALUES

1a. The significance of this essay has its basis in irony, always at least
implicit, sometimes explicit. What is the irony? (See Guide to Terms:
Irony.)

 b. What kind of irony is it? Explain why.

 c. Identify two places where the author makes it explicit.

 d. Although it is not quite his central theme, there is a close relationship. What is it?

2a. Show the significance of this writing by explaining how the event
narrated in this selection can be regarded as a microcosm of war in
general.

 b. In what areas other than war can the same theme apply? Use examples to illustrate.

3. Subtle uses of symbolism contribute valuably to the theme and to
the quality of tone. (Guide: *Symbol*.)

 a. In the first paragraph, what is symbolized by the mud and by the
stars?

 b. What is later symbolized by the dark valley?

 c. Identify whatever other symbolic details you can find and explain
their larger significance.

4. What is really meant by "the two sides of the world" (par. 48)?

5a. How would you describe the tone of this writing? (Guide: *Style/
Tone*.)

 b. Can we assume that this tone reflects the author's real attitude?
Explain.

6. If you have read "War's Place in Human Progress" in Section 6,
how do you think Emerson would have reacted to Saint-Exupéry's
narrative account?

EXPOSITORY TECHNIQUES

1. The function of this narration is to make concrete an abstract theme
that also could have been developed by use of other basic patterns.
Use this essay to illustrate precisely the meaning of "concrete."
(Guide: *Concrete/Abstract*.)

2a. During the suspenseful portion of the essay, the author repeatedly interrupts the narration. In which paragraphs are these delaying tactics used?

b. Which of these interruptions exemplify the "flashback" method?

c. At least four benefits are gained by the interruptions. What are they?

3. Paragraph 48 is built on what basic pattern of exposition?

4. Locate at least three uses of impressionistic description and identify the dominant impression of each. (See Section 9.)

5. Cite at least three sentences that you consider examples of particularly effective syntax, and identify the reasons for their success. (Guide: *Syntax.*)

6a. Sentimentality and melodrama are not easy to avoid when writing of an emotional or dramatic situation. (Guide: *Sentimentality.*) How successfully does Saint-Exupéry avoid them?

b. Explain the importance of paragraphs 47 and 51 in this respect.

c. How does the type and consistency of viewpoint help in avoiding these hazards? (Guide: *Point of View.*)

DICTION AND VOCABULARY

1a. List or mark what you consider the most effective metaphor or simile in ten different paragraphs and indicate which of the two it is. (Guide: *Figures of Speech.*)

b. Show what effect, if any, these have on the tone. (Guide: *Style/ Tone.*)

2. Explain the source of the allusion to Sinai in paragraphs 16 and 48, as well as its significance in context.

3. Of what importance to the author's theme is the personification in paragraph 51? Explain fully.

4. Consider each of the following words, using your dictionary as necessary to be sure of their meanings: renounced (par. 2); inarticulate, carnage (10); abyss (20); constitutes, decorum (21); fissure (42); truncated (51); oscillating (62); guise, preclude (63).

SUGGESTIONS FOR WRITING AND DISCUSSION

1. As the civilian said, "Pity it is that as things are we cannot explain our point of view to the other fellow" (par. 7). Apply this observation to some other "dark valley" between people who need to communicate. Use examples, comparison, and perhaps process or cause-and-effect analysis to thoroughly develop your theme.

2. Does it seem possible that a better ability to explain points of view "to the other fellow" might have spared the United States its own Civil War? If so, explain.

3. What might be the nature of the "mighty effort" mentioned in the personification of paragraph 51? By process or cause-and-effect analysis, show how this could come about and what the results might be.

4. If you have had the same difficulty with abstract reasoning that the civilian had (par. 12), explain what caused the trouble and how you overcame it (or have managed without overcoming it).

5. Use the last sentence of paragraph 47 as your own central theme. Develop your discussion or composition primarily by means of examples.

6. When Saint-Exupéry says that "all things are interconnected" (par. 48), he is briefly summarizing one aspect of existentialism — the far-reaching importance of each person's choices, however small. (This does not necessarily make Saint-Exupéry an existentialist, however.) By using cause-and-effect analysis, show how an unexpected chain reaction did result (or may have resulted) when some apparently minor decision of yours eventually affected many people.

WRITING SUGGESTIONS FOR SECTION 10

Narration

Use narration as at least a partial pattern (e.g., in developed examples or in comparison) for one of the following expository themes or another suggested by them. You should avoid the isolated personal account that has little broader significance. Remember, too, that the essay's development itself should make your point, without excessive moralizing.

1. People can still succeed without a college education.

2. The frontiers are not all gone.

3. When people succeed in communicating, they can learn to get along with each other.

4. Innocent people can be executed by even "careful" use of capital punishment.

5. Judging by appearance and mannerisms is a poor way to recognize a homosexual as such.

6. True courage is different from boldness in time of sudden danger.

7. Prior conditioning to the realities of his job is as important to the policeman as training in the techniques of his profession.

8. It is possible for the employee himself to determine when he has reached his highest level of competence.

9. Wartime massacres are not a new development.

10. The issue of hair length still is not dead.

11. Worn-out land can be restored, without chemicals, to its original productivity.

12. Back-to-the-earth, "family" style communes can be made to work.

13. Such communes (as in 12 above) are a good (or poor) place to raise children.

14. Both heredity and environment shape the personality.

ESSAYS FOR FURTHER READING
AND ANALYSIS

CHARLES A. REICH, born in New York City in 1928, received his B.A. degree from Oberlin College and his LL.B. degree from Yale University in 1952. Soon afterward he was admitted to both the New York and the District of Columbia bars. He practiced law until 1960, during which time he served two years as law clerk to Supreme Court Justice Hugo Black. In 1960 he joined the faculty at Yale, and he has been a professor of law since 1964. The following selection, a *New York Times* article in March 1971, is a defense of Reich's controversial book, *The Greening of America* (1970).

Beyond Consciousness

Those who look with skepticism upon the possibilities of revolution   1
by consciousness (and they include the young as well as the old)
quite understandably ask: Where do we go from here?

Around them they see only numbness, apathy and despair, a war   2
machine increasingly out of control, and evidence of the domestic
repression everywhere. The signs of new consciousness look trivial,
self-indulgent and faddish. The chances of a new society, apparently
to be based on dancing in the streets or retreat to the woods, seem
just plain silly, and optimism under the circumstances sounds delu-
sive and criminally insensitive.

Revolution by consciousness is in no sense equivalent to the   3
present youth culture. It is a philosophic concept, based on an interpretation of American history, and of the nature of work and institutions in contemporary America. Beads and bell bottoms are indeed
passing fads, like the hula hoop. But in their moment on the stage,
they are metaphors for something far deeper, a growth of awareness,
a change of values, a renewal of knowledge and a step toward

liberation. Attention is focused on youth because that is where awareness is now most apparent, but the philosophic change is taking place in all of us.

This process of liberation must be conceived as only Part One in a process of social change. Of course there must be structural change as well; the debate is mostly about what comes first — structural reform, radical struggle, or change of consciousness. If we assume *arguendo* that the latter must come first, then the full process might be like this: (1) change of consciousness; (2) development of an actual way of life and a culture based on the new consciousness; (3) the rediscovery of nonalienated work; (4) the restructuring of economic, political and legal institutions to reflect the new values. Sooner or later, liberals, radicals and those who believe in new consciousness must have answers to the same existing societal evils.

The reason consciousness must initiate change derives from an explanation of our present corporate state. Its essence is the supremacy of purely materialistic and technological values over all others, and its use of false consciousness to prevent those values from being revived. Institutional change, without a new source of values, would thus be an empty exercise. The "reformed" structures would be worse than the old. Real change can take place only after new values are introduced, and the only possible source of such values is man, and a new awareness and culture created by him.

Those radicals who currently emphasize culture, and seem to ignore politics and economics, do so because today's "politics" deals only with the trivial antiephemeral, and it is only culture which puts in issue the true political questions that confront us. Today almost all public discussion, especially by politicians, is both puerile and factitious. . . . There is an urgent need for a genuine politics, a politics where real and not illusory choices are debated.

The scope and dimensions of that politics may be seen in the developing new culture, provided only that one is able to ignore particulars and think in terms of symbols. Long hair and bare feet and unhomogenized peanut butter are not ultimate statements about society; they are, it must be repeated, metaphors. They stand for values now neglected or abused, such as personal autonomy and rediscovery of the natural. A new social structure would write into social terms what the metaphors are now saying. Any future society will be based on technology and organization, as the new culture itself is. When we want to, we will bake our own bread or live on the land, but man cannot reject his own development. Society will build and operate machines, but it will use them for human ends.

To achieve these goals, the community will need a structure better 8 adapted than our present government and law. The object of such a structure must be to translate the values now symbolized by the transitory youth culture into terms that will give them lasting effect in the post-industrial society. We cannot retreat from organized society, but we can begin searching for ways to make certain that organizations reflect both the requirements of technology and what we are learning about from our youth — the needs of nature and man.

GLORIA STEINEM, born in Ohio in 1936, was graduated
from Smith College and did graduate work on fellowships
at the universities of Calcutta and Delphi. She has been
director of educational foundations and research services
and has worked as a script writer for television (including
"That Was the Week That Was," 1964–1965). Steinem is
a versatile and prolific writer who has contributed to
*Esquire, Life, Harper's, Vogue, Glamour, New York Times
Magazine, McCall's, Ladies' Home Journal, New York,
Look*, and others. At present she is also editorial consultant
for Curtis Publishing Company and a member of various
authors' guilds. Her books are *The Thousand Indias* (1957)
and *The Beach Book* (1963). The following selection was
first published as a *Time* magazine essay in August 1970.

What It Would Be Like if Women Win

Any change is fearful, especially one affecting both politics and sex   1
roles, so let me begin these utopian speculations with a fact. To
break the ice.

Women don't want to exchange places with men. Male chauvin-   2
ists, science-fiction writers and comedians may favor that idea for
its shock value, but psychologists say it is a fantasy based on ruling-
class ego and guilt. Men assume that women want to imitate them,
which is just what white people assumed about blacks. An assumption so strong that it may convince the second-class group of the
need to imitate, but for both women and blacks that stage has
passed. Guilt produces the question: What if they could treat us as
we have treated them?

That is not our goal. But we do want to change the economic   3
system to one more based on merit. In Women's Lib Utopia, there
will be free access to good jobs — and decent pay for the bad ones

women have been performing all along, including housework. Increased skilled labor might lead to a four-hour workday, and higher wages would encourage further mechanization of repetitive jobs now kept alive by cheap labor.

With women as half the country's elected representatives, and a   **4** woman President once in a while, the country's *machismo* problems would be greatly reduced. The old-fashioned idea that manhood depends on violence and victory is, after all, an important part of our troubles in the streets, and in Viet Nam. I'm not saying that women leaders would eliminate violence. We are not more moral than men; we are only uncorrupted by power so far. When we do acquire power, we might turn out to have an equal impulse toward aggression. Even now, Margaret Mead believes that women fight less often but more fiercely than men, because women are not taught the rules of the war game and fight only when cornered. But for the next 50 years or so, women in politics will be very valuable by tempering the idea of manhood into something less aggressive and better suited to this crowded, post-atomic planet. Consumer protection and children's rights, for instance, might get more legislative attention.

Men will have to give up ruling-class privileges, but in return   **5** they will no longer be the only ones to support the family, get drafted, bear the strain of power and responsibility. Freud to the contrary, anatomy is not destiny, at least not for more than nine months at a time. In Israel, women are drafted, and some have gone to war. In England, more men type and run switchboards. In India and Israel, a woman rules. In Sweden, both parents take care of the children. In this country, come Utopia, men and women won't reverse roles; they will be free to choose according to individual talents and preferences.

If role reform sounds sexually unsettling, think how it will change   **6** the sexual hypocrisy we have now. No more sex arranged on the barter system, with women pretending interest, and men never sure whether they are loved for themselves or for the security few women can get any other way. (Married or not, for sexual reasons or social ones, most women still find it second nature to Uncle-Tom.) No more men who are encouraged to spend a lifetime living with inferiors; with housekeepers, or dependent creatures who are still children. No more domineering wives, emasculating women, and

"Jewish mothers," all of whom are simply human beings with all their normal ambition and drive confined to the home. No more unequal partnerships that eventually doom love and sex.

In order to produce that kind of confidence and individuality, child rearing will train according to talent. Little girls will no longer be surrounded by air-tight, self-fulfilling prophecies of natural passivity, lack of ambition and objectivity, inability to exercise power, and dexterity (so long as special aptitude for jobs requiring patience and dexterity is confined to poorly paid jobs; brain surgery is for males). 7

Schools and universities will help to break down traditional sex roles, even when parents will not. Half the teachers will be men, a rarity now at preschool and elementary levels; girls will not necessarily serve cookies or boys hoist up the flag. Athletic teams will be picked only by strength and skill. Sexually segregated courses like auto mechanics and home economics will be taken by boys and girls together. New courses in sexual politics will explore female subjugation as the model for political oppression, and women's history will be an academic staple, along with black history, at least until the white-male-oriented textbooks are integrated and rewritten. 8

As for the American child's classic problem — too much mother, too little father — that would be cured by an equalization of parental responsibility. Free nurseries, school lunches, family cafeterias built into every housing complex, service companies that will do household cleaning chores in a regular, businesslike way, and more responsibility by the entire community for the children: all these will make it possible for both mother and father to work, and to have equal leisure time with the children at home. For parents of very young children, however, a special job category, created by Government and unions, would allow such parents a shorter work day. 9

The revolution would not take away the option of being a house-wife. A woman who prefers to be her husband's housekeeper and/or hostess would receive a percentage of his pay determined by the domestic relations courts. If divorced, she might be eligible for a pension fund, and for a job-training allowance. Or a divorce could be treated the same way that the dissolution of a business partner-ship is now. 10

If these proposals seem farfetched, consider Sweden, where most 11 of them are already in effect. Sweden is not yet a working Women's Lib model; most of the role-reform programs began less than a decade ago, and are just beginning to take hold. But that country is so far ahead of us in recognizing the problem that Swedish statements on sex and equality sound like bulletins from the moon.

Our marriage laws, for instance, are so reactionary that Women's   12
Lib groups want couples to take a compulsory written exam on the law, as for a driver's license, before going through with the wedding. A man has alimony and wifely debts to worry about, but a woman may lose so many of her civil rights that in the U.S. now, in important legal ways, she becomes a child again. In some states, she cannot sign credit agreements, use her maiden name, incorporate a business, or establish a legal residence of her own. Being a wife, according to most social and legal definitions, is still a 19th century thing.

Assuming, however, that these blatantly sexist laws are abolished   13
or reformed, that job discrimination is forbidden, that parents share financial responsibility for each other and the children, and that sexual relationships become partnerships of equal adults (some pretty big assumptions), then marriage will probably go right on. Men and women are, after all, physically complementary. When society stops encouraging men to be exploiters and women to be parasites, they may turn out to be more complementary in emotion as well. Women's Lib is not trying to destroy the American family. A look at the statistics on divorce — plus the way in which old people are farmed out with strangers and young people flee the home — shows the destruction that has already been done. Liberated women are just trying to point out the disaster, and build compassionate and practical alternatives from the ruins.

What will exist is a variety of alternative life-styles. Since the   14
population explosion dictates that childbearing be kept to a minimum, parents-and-children will be only one of many "families": couples, age groups, working groups, mixed communes, blood-related clans, class groups, creative groups. Single women will have the right to stay single without ridicule, without the attitudes now betrayed by "spinster" and "bachelor." Lesbians or homosexuals will no longer be denied legally binding marriages, complete with mutual-support agreements and inheritance rights. Paradoxically, the number of homosexuals may get smaller. With fewer overpossessive

mothers and fewer fathers who hold up an impossibly cruel or per-
fectionist idea of manhood, boys will be less likely to be denied or
reject their identity as males.

Changes that now seem small may get bigger: 15

Men's Lib. Men now suffer from more diseases due to stress,   16
heart attacks, ulcers, a higher suicide rate, greater difficulty living
alone, less adaptability to change and, in general, a shorter life span
than women. There is some scientific evidence that what produces
physical problems is not work itself, but the inability to choose
which work, and how much. With women bearing half the financial
responsibility, and with the idea of "masculine" jobs gone, men
might well feel freer and live longer.

Religion. Protestant women are already becoming ordained minis-   17
ters; radical nuns are carrying out liturgical functions that were
once the exclusive property of priests; Jewish women are rewriting
prayers — particularly those that Orthodox Jews recite every morning thanking God they are not female. In the future, the church will
become an area of equal participation by women. This means, of
course, that organized religion will have to give up one of its great
historical weapons: sexual repression. In most structured faiths,
from Hinduism through Roman Catholicism, the status of women
went down as the position of priests ascended. Male clergy implied,
if they did not teach, that women were unclean, unworthy and
sources of ungodly temptation, in order to remove them as rivals for
the emotional forces of men. Full participation of women in ecclesiastical life might involve certain changes in theology, such as, for
instance, a radical redefinition of sin.

Literary Problems. Revised sex roles will outdate more children's   18
books than civil rights ever did. Only a few children had the problem of a *Little Black Sambo,* but most have the male-female stereotypes of "Dick and Jane." A boomlet of children's books about
mothers who work has already begun, and liberated parents and
editors are beginning to pressure for change in the textbook industry. Fiction writing will change more gradually, but romantic
novels with wilting heroines and swashbuckling heroes will be
reduced to historical value. Or perhaps to the sado-masochist trade.
(*Marjorie Morningstar*, a romantic novel that took the '50s by storm,

has already begun to seem as unreal as its '20s predecessor, *The Sheik*.) As for the literary plots that turn on forced marriages or horrific abortions, they will seem as dated as Prohibition stories. Free legal abortions and free birth control will force writers to give up pregnancy as the *deus ex machina*.

Manners and Fashion. Dress will be more androgynous, with class   19
symbols becoming more important than sexual ones. Pro- or anti-Establishment styles may already be more vital than who is wearing them. Hardhats are just as likely to rough up antiwar girls as anti-war men in the street, and police understand that women are just as likely to be pushers or bombers. Dances haven't required that one partner lead the other for years, anyway. Chivalry will transfer itself to those who need it, or deserve respect: old people, admired people, anyone with an armload of packages. Women with normal work identities will be less likely to attach their whole sense of self to youth and appearance; thus there will be fewer nervous breakdowns when the first wrinkles appear. Lighting cigarettes and other treasured niceties will become gestures of mutual affection. "I like to be helped on with my coat," says one Women's Lib worker, "but not if it costs me $2,000 a year in salary."

For those with nostalgia for a simpler past, here is a word of   20
comfort. Anthropologist Geoffrey Gorer studied the few peaceful human tribes and discovered one common characteristic: sex roles were not polarized. Differences of dress and occupation were at a minimum. Society, in other words, was not using sexual blackmail as a way of getting women to do cheap labor, or men to be aggressive.

Thus Women's Lib may achieve a more peaceful society on the   21
way toward its other goals. That is why the Swedish government considers reform to bring about greater equality in the sex roles one of its most important concerns. As Prime Minister Olof Palme explained in a widely ignored speech delivered in Washington this spring: "It is *human beings* we shall emancipate. In Sweden today, if a politician should declare that the woman ought to have a different role from man's, he would be regarded as something from the Stone Age." In other words, the most radical goal of the movement is egalitarianism.

If Women's Lib wins, perhaps we all do.   22

JOHN FISCHER was born in Oklahoma in 1910. He attended the University of Oklahoma and Oxford University and holds several honorary degrees. He has been a reporter for various newspapers in Oklahoma, Texas, and New Mexico, for United Press International in England and Germany, and for Associated Press in Washington, D.C. Between 1937 and 1944 he served in numerous capacities with the United States government, including that of director of economic intelligence and lend-lease with the Foreign Economics Administration in Washington. Fischer was associate editor of *Harper's* magazine from 1944 to 1947 and editor-in-chief from 1953 to 1967, after which he became contributing editor of that magazine. More recently he has served as acting editor-in-chief. His books are *Why They Behave Like Russians* (1947), *Master Plan, U.S.A.* (1951), and *The Stupidity Problem* (1964). The following essay appeared in *Harper's* in September 1969.

Survival U: Prospectus for a Really Relevant University

It gets pretty depressing to watch what is going on in the world and realize that your education is not equipping you to do anything about it.

> — *From a letter by a University of California senior*

She is not a radical, and has never taken part in any demonstration. She will graduate with honors, and profound disillusionment. From listening to her — and a good many like-minded students at California and East Coast campuses — I think I am beginning to understand what they mean when they say that a liberal-arts education isn't relevant.

They mean it is incoherent. It doesn't cohere. It consists of bits   2
and pieces which don't stick together, and have no common purpose.
One of our leading Negro educators, Arthur Lewis of Princeton,
recently summed it up better than I can. America is the only country, he said, where youngsters are required "to fritter away their
precious years in meaningless peregrination from subject to subject
. . . spending twelve weeks getting some tidbits of religion, twelve
weeks learning French, twelve weeks seeing whether the history
professor is stimulating, twelve weeks seeking entertainment from
the economics professor, twelve weeks confirming that one is not
going to be able to master calculus."

These fragments are meaningless because they are not organized   3
around any central purpose, or vision of the world. The typical
liberal-arts college has no clearly defined goals. It merely offers a
smorgasbord of courses, in hopes that if a student nibbles at a few
dishes from the humanities table, plus a snack of science, and a
garnish of art or anthropology, he may emerge as "a cultivated
man" — whatever that means. Except for a few surviving church
schools, no university even pretends to have a unifying philosophy.
Individual teachers may have personal ideologies — but since they
are likely to range, on any given campus, from Marxism to worship
of the scientific method to exaltation of the irrational (à la Norman
O. Brown), they don't cohere either. They often leave a student
convinced at the end of four years that any given idea is probably
about as valid as any other — and that none of them has much relationship to the others, or to the decisions he is going to have to make
the day after graduation.

Education was not always like that. The earliest European uni-   4
versities had a precise purpose: to train an elite for the service of
the Church. Everything they taught was focused to that end.
Thomas Aquinas had spelled it all out: what subjects had to be
mastered, how each connected with every other, and what meaning
they had for man and God.

Later, for a span of several centuries, Oxford and Cambridge had   5
an equally clear function: to train administrators to run an empire.
So too did Harvard and Yale at the time they were founded; their
job was to produce the clergymen, lawyers, and doctors that a new
country needed. In each case, the curriculum was rigidly prescribed.
A student learned what he needed, to prepare himself to be a com-

petent priest, district officer, or surgeon. He had no doubts about the relevance of his courses — and no time to fret about expanding his consciousness or currying his sensual awareness.

This is still true of our professional schools. I have yet to hear an   6
engineering or medical student complain that his education is meaningless. Only in the liberal-arts colleges — which boast that "we are not trade schools" — do the youngsters get that feeling that they are drowning in a cloud of feathers.

For a long while some of our less complacent academics have   7
been trying to restore coherence to American education. When Robert Hutchins was at Chicago, he tried to use the Great Books to build a comprehensible framework for the main ideas of civilized man. His experiment is still being carried on, with some modifications, at St. John's — but it has not proved irresistibly contagious. Sure, the thoughts of Plato and Machiavelli are still pertinent, so far as they go — but somehow they don't seem quite enough armor for a world beset with splitting atoms, urban guerrillas, nineteen varieties of psychotherapists, amplified guitars, napalm, computers, astronauts, and an atmosphere polluted simultaneously with auto exhaust and TV commercials.

Another strategy for linking together the bits-and-pieces has been   8
attempted at Harvard and at a number of other universities. They require their students to take at least two years of survey courses, known variously as core studies, general education, or world civilization. These too have been something less than triumphantly successful. Most faculty members don't like to teach them, regarding them as superficial and synthetic. (And right they are, since no survey course that I know of has a strong unifying concept to give it focus.) Moreover, the senior professors shun such courses in favor of their own narrow specialities. Consequently, the core studies which are meant to place all human experience — well, at least the brightest nuggets — into One Big Picture usually end up in the perfunctory hands of resentful junior teachers. Naturally the undergraduates don't take them seriously either.

Any successful reform of American education, I am now con-   9
vinced, will have to be far more revolutionary than anything yet attempted. At a minimum, it should be:

1. Founded on a single guiding concept — an idea capable of   10

knotting together all strands of study, thus giving them both coherence and visible purpose.

2. Capable of equipping young people to do something about 11 "what is going on in the world" — notably the things which bother them most, including war, injustice, racial conflict, and the quality of life.

Maybe it isn't possible. Perhaps knowledge is proliferating so fast, 12 and in so many directions, that it can never again be ordered into a coherent whole, so that molecular biology, Robert Lowell's poetry, and highway engineering will seem relevant to each other and to the lives of ordinary people. Quite possibly the knowledge explosion, as Peter F. Drucker has called it, dooms us to scholarship which grows steadily more specialized, fragmented, and incomprehensible.

The Soviet experience is hardly encouraging. Russian education 13 is built on what is meant to be a unifying ideology: Marxism-Leninism. In theory, it provides an organizing principle for all scholarly activity — whether history, literature, genetics, or military science. Its purpose is explicit: to train a Communist elite for the greater power and glory of the Soviet state, just as the medieval universities trained a priesthood to serve the Church.

Yet according to all accounts that I have seen, it doesn't work 14 very well. Soviet intellectuals apparently are almost as restless and unhappy as our own. Increasing numbers of them are finding Marxism-Leninism too simplistic, too narrowly doctrinaire, too oppressive; the bravest are risking prison in order to pursue their own heretical visions of reality.

Is it conceivable, then, that we might hit upon another idea which 15 could serve as the organizing principle for many fields of scholarly inquiry; which is relevant to the urgent needs of our time; and which would not, on the other hand, impose an ideological strait jacket, as both ecclesiastical and Marxist education attempted to do?

Just possibly it could be done. For the last two or three years I 16 have been probing around among professors, college administrators, and students — and so far I have come up with only one idea which might fit the specifications. It is simply the idea of survival.

For the first time in history, the future of the human race is now 17 in serious question. This fact is hard to believe, or even think about

— yet it is the message which a growing number of scientists are trying, almost frantically, to get across to us. Listen, for example, to Professor Richard A. Falk of Princeton and of the Center for Advanced Study in the Behavioral Sciences:

> The planet and mankind are in grave danger of irreversible catas- 18
> trophe. . . . Man may be skeptical about following the flight of the
> dodo into extinction, but the evidence points increasingly to just
> such a pursuit. . . . There are four interconnected threats to the
> planet — wars of mass destruction, overpopulation, pollution, and
> the depletion of resources. They have a cumulative effect. A prob-
> lem in one area renders it more difficult to solve the problems in
> any other area. . . . The basis of all four problems is the inade-
> quacy of the sovereign states to manage the affairs of mankind in
> the twentieth century.

Similar warnings could be quoted from a long list of other social 19
scientists, biologists, and physicists, among them such distinguished thinkers as Rene Dubos, Buckminster Fuller, Loren Eiseley, George Wald, and Barry Commoner. They are not hopeless. Most of them believe that we still have a chance to bring our weapons, our population growth, and the destruction of our environment under control before it is too late. But the time is short, and so far there is no evidence that enough people are taking them seriously.

That would be the prime aim of the experimental university I'm 20
suggesting here: to look seriously at the interlinking threats to human existence, and to learn what we can do to fight them off.

Let's call it Survival U. It will not be a multiversity, offering 21
courses in every conceivable field. Its motto — emblazoned on a life jacket rampant — will be: "What must we do to be saved?" If a course does not help to answer that question, it will not be taught here. Students interested in musicology, junk sculpture, the Theater of the Absurd, and the literary *dicta* of Leslie Fiedler can go somewhere else.

Neither will our professors be detached, dispassionate scholars. 22
To get hired, each will have to demonstrate an emotional commitment to our cause. Moreover, he will be expected to be a moralist; for this generation of students, like no other in my lifetime, is hungering and thirsting after righteousness. What it wants is a moral system it can believe in — and that is what our university will try to provide. In every class it will preach the primordial ethic of survival.

The biology department, for example, will point out that it is   23
sinful for anybody to have more than two children. It has long since
become glaringly evident that unless the earth's cancerous growth
of population can be halted, all other problems — poverty, war,
racial strife, uninhabitable cities, and the rest — are beyond solution.
So the department naturally will teach all known methods of birth
control, and much of its research will be aimed at perfecting cheap-
er and better ones.

Its second lesson in biological morality will be: "Nobody has a   24
right to poison the environment we live in." This maxim will be
illustrated by a list of public enemies. At the top will stand the
politicians, scientists, and military men — of whatever country —
who make and deploy atomic weapons; for if these are ever used,
even in so-called defensive systems like the ABM, the atmosphere
will be so contaminated with strontium 90 and other radioactive
isotopes that human survival seems most unlikely. Also on the list
will be anybody who makes or tests chemical and biological weapons
— or who even attempts to get rid of obsolete nerve gas, as our
Army recently proposed, by dumping the stuff in the sea.

Only slightly less wicked, our biology profs will indicate, is the   25
farmer who drenches his land with DDT. Such insecticides remain
virulent indefinitely, and as they wash into the streams and oceans
they poison fish, water fowl, and eventually the people who eat
them. Worse yet — as John Hay noted in his recently published
In Defense of Nature — "The original small, diluted concentrations
of these chemicals tend to build up in a food chain so as to end in
a concentration that may be thousands of times as strong." It is
rapidly spreading throughout the globe. DDT already has been
found in the tissues of Eskimos and of Antarctic penguins, so it
seems probable that similar deposits are gradually building up in
your body and mine. The minimum fatal dosage is still unknown.

Before he finishes this course, a student may begin to feel twinges   26
of conscience himself. Is his motorcycle exhaust adding carbon
monoxide to the smog we breathe? Is his sewage polluting the
nearest river? If so, he will be reminded of two proverbs. From
Jesus: "Let him who is without sin among you cast the first stone."
From Pogo: "We have met the enemy and he is us."

In like fashion, our engineering students will learn not only how   27
to build dams and highways, but where *not* to build them. Unless

they understand that it is immoral to flood the Grand Canyon or destroy the Everglades with a jetport, they will never pass the final exam. Indeed, our engineering graduates will be trained to ask a key question about every contract offered them: "What will be its effect on human life?" That obviously will lead to other questions which every engineer ought to comprehend as thoroughly as his slide rule. Is this new highway really necessary? Would it be wiser to use the money for mass transit — or to decongest traffic by building a new city somewhere else? Is an offshore oil well really a good idea, in view of what happened to Santa Barbara?

Our engineering faculty also will specialize in training men for a new growth industry: garbage disposal. Americans already are spending $4.5 billion a year to collect and get rid of the garbage which we produce more profusely than any other people (more than five pounds a day for each of us). But unless we are resigned to stifling in our own trash, we are going to have to come up with at least an additional $835 million a year.[1] Any industry with a growth rate of 18 per cent offers obvious attractions to a bright young man — and if he can figure out a new way to get rid of our offal, his fortune will be unlimited.

Because the old ways no longer work. Every big city in the United States is running out of dumping grounds. Burning won't do either, since the air is dangerously polluted already — and in any case, 75 per cent of the incinerators in use are inadequate. For some 150 years Californians happily piled their garbage into San Francisco Bay, but they can't much longer. Dump-and-fill operations already have reduced it to half its original size, and in a few more decades it would be possible to walk dry-shod from Oakland to the Embarcadero. Consequently San Francisco is now planning to ship garbage 375 miles to the yet-uncluttered deserts of Lassen County by special train — known locally as "The Twentieth Stenchery Limited" and "The Excess Express." The city may actually get away with this scheme, since hardly anybody lives in Lassen County except Indians, and who cares about them? But what is the answer for the metropolis that doesn't have an unspoiled desert handy?

A few ingenious notions are cropping up here and there. The Japanese are experimenting with a machine which compacts gar-

28

29

30

[1] According to Richard D. Vaughn, chief of the Solid Wastes Program of HEW, in his recent horror story entitled "1968 Survey of Community Solid Waste Practices."

bage, under great heat and pressure, into building blocks. A New York businessman is thinking of building a garbage mountain somewhere upstate, and equipping it with ski runs to amortize the cost. An aluminum company plans to collect and reprocess used aluminum cans — which, unlike the old-fashioned tin can, will not rust away. Our engineering department will try to Think Big along these lines. That way lies not only new careers, but salvation.

Survival U's Department of Earth Sciences will be headed — if   31 we are lucky — by Dr. Charles F. Park, Jr., now professor of geology and mineral engineering at Stanford. He knows as well as anybody how fast mankind is using up the world's supply of raw materials. In a paper written for the American Geographical Society he punctured one of America's most engaging (and pernicious) myths: our belief that an ever-expanding economy can keep living standards rising indefinitely.

It won't happen; because, as Dr. Park demonstrates, the tonnage   32 of metal in the earth's crust won't last indefinitely. Already we are running short of silver, mercury, tin, and cobalt — all in growing demand by the high-technology industries. Even the commoner metals may soon be in short supply. The United States alone is consuming one ton of iron and eighteen pounds of copper every year, for each of its inhabitants. Poorer countries, struggling to industrialize, hope to raise their consumption of these two key materials to something like that level. If they should succeed — and if the globe's population doubles in the next forty years, as it will at present growth rates — then the world will have to produce, somehow, *twelve times* as much iron and copper every year as it does now. Dr. Parks sees little hope that such production levels can ever be reached, much less sustained indefinitely. The same thing, of course — doubled in spades — goes for other raw materials: timber, oil, natural gas, and water, to note only a few.

Survival U, therefore, will prepare its students to consume less.   33 This does not necessarily mean an immediate drop in living standards — perhaps only a change in the yardstick by which we measure them. Conceivably Americans might be happier with fewer automobiles, neon signs, beer cans, supersonic jets, barbecue grills, and similar metallic fluff. But happy or not, our students had better learn how to live The Simpler Life, because that is what most of them are likely to have before they reach middle age.

To help them understand how very precious resources really are, 34
our mathematics department will teach a new kind of bookkeeping:
social accounting. It will train people to analyze budgets — both
government and corporate — with an eye not merely to immediate
dollar costs, but to the long-range costs to society.

By conventional bookkeeping methods, for example, the coal 35
companies strip-mining away the hillsides of Kentucky and West
Virginia show a handsome profit. Their ledgers, however, show
only a fraction of the true cost of their operations. They take no account of destroyed land which can never bear another crop; of
rivers poisoned by mud and seeping acid from the spoil banks; of
floods which sweep over farms and towns downstream, because the
ravaged slopes can no longer hold the rainfall. Although these costs
are not borne by the mining firms, they are neverthless real. They
fall mostly on the taxpayers, who have to pay for disaster relief,
flood-control levees, and the resettlement of Appalachian farm families forced off the land. As soon as our students (the taxpayers
of tomorrow) learn to read a social balance sheet, they obviously
will throw the strip miners into bankruptcy.

Another case study will analyze the proposal of the Inhuman 36
Real Estate Corporation to build a fifty-story skyscraper in the most
congested area of midtown Manhattan. If 90 per cent of the office
space can be rented at $12 per square foot, it looks like a sound
investment, according to antique accounting methods. To uncover
the true facts, however, our students will investigate the cost of
moving 12,000 additional workers in and out of midtown during
rush hours. The first (and least) item is $8 million worth of new
city buses. When they are crammed into the already clogged avenues, the daily loss of man-hours in traffic jams may run to a couple
of million more. The fumes from their diesel engines will cause
an estimated 9 per cent increase in New York's incidence of em-
physema and lung cancer; this requires the construction of three
new hospitals. To supply them, plus the new building, with water
— already perilously short in the city — a new reservoir has to be
built on the headwaters of the Delaware River, 140 miles away.
Some of the dairy farmers pushed out of the drowned valley will
move promptly into the Bronx and go on relief. The subtraction of
their output from the city's supply leads to a price increase of two
cents a quart. For a Harlem mother with seven hungry children,
that is the last straw. She summons her neighbors to join her in

riot, seven blocks go up in flames, and the Mayor demands higher taxes to hire more police. . . .

Instead of a sound investment, Inhuman Towers now looks like   37 criminal folly, which would be forbidden by any sensible government. Our students will keep that in mind when they walk across campus to their government class.

Its main goal will be to discover why our institutions have done   38 so badly in their efforts (as Dr. Falk put it) "to manage the affairs of mankind in the twentieth century." This will be a compulsory course for all freshmen, taught by professors who are capable of looking critically at every political artifact, from the Constitution to the local county council. They will start by pointing out that we are living in a state of near-anarchy, because we have no government capable of dealing effectively with public problems.

Instead we have a hodgepodge of 80,000 local governments —   39 villages, townships, counties, cities, port authorities, sewer districts, and special purpose agencies. Their authority is so limited, and their jurisdictions so confused and overlapping, that most of them are virtually impotent. The states, which in theory could put this mess into some sort of order, usually have shown little interest and less competence. When Washington is called to help out — as it increasingly has been for the last thirty-five years — it often has proved hamhanded and entangled in its own archaic bureaucracy. The end result is that nobody in authority has been able to take care of the country's mounting needs. Our welfare rolls keep growing, our air and water get dirtier, housing gets scarcer, airports jam up, road traffic clots, railways fall apart, prices rise, ghettos burn, schools turn out more illiterates every year, and a war nobody wants drags on and on. Small wonder that so many young people are losing confidence in American institutions. In their present state, they don't deserve much confidence.

The advanced students of government at Survival U will try to   40 find out whether these institutions can be renewed and rebuilt. They will take a hard look at the few places — Jacksonville, Minnesota, Nashville, Appalachia — which are creating new forms of government. Will these work any better, and if so, how can they be duplicated elsewhere? Can the states be brought to life, or should we start thinking about an entirely different kind of arrangement? Ten regional prefectures, perhaps, to replace the fifty states? Or should we take seriously Norman Mailer's suggestion for a new kind of city-state to govern our great metropolises? (He merely called for New York City to secede from its state; but that isn't radical enough. To be truly governable, the new Republic of New York City ought to include chunks of New Jersey and Connecticut as well.) Alternatively, can we find some way to break up Megalopolis, and spread our population into smaller and more livable communities throughout the continent? Why should we keep 70 per cent of our people crowded into less than 2 per cent of our land area, anyway?

Looking beyond our borders, our students will be encouraged to   41
ask even harder questions. Are nation-states actually feasible, now that they have power to destroy each other in a single afternoon? Can we agree on something else to take their place, before the balance of terror becomes unstable? What price would most people be willing to pay for a more durable kind of human organization — more taxes, giving up national flags, perhaps the sacrifice of some of our hard-won liberties?

All these courses (and everything else taught at Survival U) are   42
really branches of a single science. Human ecology is one of the youngest disciplines, and probably the most important. It is the study of the relationship between man and his environment, both natural and technological. It teaches us to understand the consequences of our actions — how sulfur-laden fuel oil burned in England produces an acid rain that damages the forests of Scandinavia, why a well-meant farm subsidy can force millions of Negro tenants off the land and lead to Watts and Hough. A graduate who comprehends ecology will know how to look at "what is going on in the world," and he will be equipped to do something about it. Whether he ends up as a city planner, a politician, an enlightened engineer, a teacher, or a reporter, he will have had a relevant education. All of its parts will hang together in a coherent whole.

And if we can get enough such graduates, man and his environ-   43
ment may survive a while longer, against all the odds.

JOHN W. GARDNER, born in California in 1912, is a graduate of Stanford and holds advanced degrees from the University of California, as well as various honorary degrees from other universities. He served as a Marine officer in World War II. Gardner has been active on numerous public service commissions, boards, and foundations, and was president of the Carnegie Foundation for the Advancement of Teaching from 1955 to 1965. During the next three years he was a member of the President's Cabinet as Secretary of Health, Education and Welfare, resigning in 1968 to become chairman of the Urban Coalition, a private organization that works to help cities solve their problems. While still serving in that capacity, he is also a visiting professor at Massachusetts Institute of Technology and a fellow at Harvard's Kennedy Institute of Politics. His books include *To Turn the Tide* (as editor, 1962), *Excellence, Self-Renewal,* and *No Easy Victories* (1968), and *The Recovery of Confidence* (1969), from which the following essay was his adaptation for the September 1969 *Reader's Digest.*

What Kind of Society Do We Want?

There are many ways in which a nation can die. It can die from   1
internal strife, tearing itself apart. It can die of indifference, of an
unwillingness to face its problems, an incapacity to respond to the
suffering of its people. It can die of old age — a waning of energy
and an inability to learn new ways which, little by little, cause a
society to lose a commanding grip on its future.

In all of history, no people has seriously attempted to take into   2
account the *aging* of institutions and to provide for their continuous renewal. Why shouldn't we of the United States be the first to
do so?

As a nation, we have done quite a lot of social inventing and   3
innovating. Among the consequences: the Bill of Rights, the land-
grant college, the county agent, the Federal Reserve and Social
Security systems. But we do not have to look far today to identify
signs of age and rigidity in our institutions. The departments of
the federal government are in grave need of renewal; state government is in most places a 19th-century relic; most municipal government is a waxwork of stiffly preserved anachronisms; the system
of taxation is a tangle of dysfunctional measures. The unions, the
professions, the universities, the corporations — each has spun its
own impenetrable web of vested interests. And we seem to have
steadily mounting difficulty in getting at all of our problems. Why?

One of the reasons is that people interested in improving our   4
society never quite come to grips with the complex and technical
processes by which it functions. They are preoccupied with specific
evils that must be corrected. I don't blame them. So am I. But
the result is that each reformer comes to his task with a little
bundle of desired changes. The implication is that if his reforms are
carried through, the society will be wholly satisfactory.

That is a primitive way of viewing social change. The true task   5
is to design a society (and institutions) capable of continuous
change, continuous renewal, continuous responsiveness.

BEEHIVE OR PLURALISM?

What would be the attributes of a society capable of such con-   6
tinuous renewal? First of all, it would be characterized by pluralism
— by variety, alternatives, choices, and multiple foci of power and
initiative. We have just such pluralism in our society today. But
it would be folly to ignore that the logic of modern, large-scale
organization tends to squeeze out pluralism, and to move us toward
one comprehensively articulated system of power.

In the private sphere, corporations merge, newspapers merge,   7
and small colleges and small businesses find survival increasingly
difficult. As I contemplate this, I find myself treasuring every remaining bit of pluralism, everything that stands between us and the one
all-embracing System. So, when I hear young people recommend-
ing the abolition of private enterprise, I am inclined to question
whether they have weighed the consequences. It may not have oc-
cured to them that socialism, or any other alternative to private

enterprise, would inevitably mean a vast expansion of the federal government. General Motors would not disappear; it would simply be lumped with Ford, Chrysler, Boeing, Pan American and so on in a vast Ministry of Transportation. And bureaucracy would conquer all.

No society that cares about its own vitality will permit that to   8
happen. A society that deadens the individual cuts off its own sources of renewal and cements over the seedbed of its future growth. But, unfortunately, the end toward which all modern societies, whatever their ideology, seem to be moving is the beehive model, in which the system perfects itself as the individual is steadily dwarfed. Our ideology tells us that every person is important, that organizations and institutions exist for individuals. But the trend I have described transforms individuals into specialist-links in larger systems, increasingly incapable of autonomous functioning.

Even the alert, informed, exceptional American is farther down   9
the path toward the beehive model, more securely "locked in" to a specialist role in the society, than he realizes. He is more cowed by the over-arching systems that govern our lives than he would be willing to admit. The whole style of modern social organization tells him in a thousand ways, "You aren't important. What you do won't make a difference." So he works within the lines of his own specialty, plays his own highly defined role and hopes that somehow everything will come out all right. Everyone has noted the passivity that results. Carried to its logical end, it could be the death of this "self-governing" society.

NEW KINDS OF LOCAL LEADERSHIP

The society capable of continuous renewal will be one that   10
develops to the fullest its human resources, that removes obstacles to individual fulfillment, that emphasizes education, lifelong learning and self-discovery. We shall have to work simultaneously along two parallel lines: we must ask the individual to accept certain kinds of responsibility, and we must create the institutional framework in which individual responsibility and participation are feasible.

It is not essential that *everyone* participate. As a matter of fact,   11
if everyone suddenly did, the society would fly apart! But the fact that opportunities exist and that a good many people are taking ad-

vantage of them will affect the attitude of those who don't participate. The essence of it is that participation should be an available option.

The possibility of participation is closely linked to the revival of   12
local government and local leadership. It is hard to feel individually
responsible with respect to the invisible processes of a huge and
distant government. Responsibility comes most readily when one
can see the consequences of one's actions. That implies participation
in a vital local community.

Now comes a tough and decisive question: Can action on the   13
part of the individual at the grass roots ever really be effective?

It all depends on how we design our society. Local leadership in   14
the old-fashioned sense — wise in the lore of the locality, but intensely parochial in its perspective — is dead. We must create a
wholly new form and style of local leadership, skillful in relating
its own efforts and programs to larger systems. Local leaders must
understand how the economy of their area relates to larger economic
trends, patterns and programs. They must understand that the significant gains in the years ahead will come through a creative interplay of federal, state and local levels.

THE NEED TO BE NEEDED

We must identify those features of modern organization that   15
strengthen the individual and those that diminish him. Given such
analysis, we can design institutions responsive to human need,
institutions that will strengthen and nourish each person, that will
permit each individual the fulfillment that comes with the exercise
of his talents. In short, we can build a society to man's measure
— if we have the will.

The struggle begins with preservation of the natural resources   16
and natural beauty of the land, and with control of environmental
pollution. It must extend to considerations of population control,
to the use of leisure, to the pace and space of life.

One of the least recognized of human motives is the need to be   17
needed. The experience of recent years suggests that the *service*
idea, as exemplified in the Peace Corps and VISTA, taps a rich vein
of motivation in the American people. When people are serving,
life is no longer meaningless. They no longer feel rootless or unconnected; they feel responsible. As we enable the individual to

enjoy greater freedom, we must at the same time provide him with opportunities for allegiance and commitment to goals larger than himself. Otherwise, individual freedom degenerates into a sterile self-preoccupation.

FAITH IN OUR IDEALS

We can make great progress in improving the functioning of our 18 society and still not have anything that will live or last unless we concern ourselves with the *values* that underlie the enterprise. If a society believes in nothing, if it does not generate in its members a sense of moral purpose, there is no possibility that it can develop the high level of motivation essential to renewal.

We have in the tradition of this nation a well-tested framework 19 of values: justice, liberty, equality of opportunity, the worth and dignity of the individual, brotherhood, individual responsibility — all supremely compatible with social renewal. Our problem is not to find better values but to be faithful to those we profess — and to make them live in our institutions.

We cannot speak of our values apart from the down-to-earth pro- 20 grams that are necessary to put them into effect. For example: if we believe in individual dignity and responsibility, then we must do the necessary, sometimes expensive, often complicated things that will make it possible for each person to have a decent job if he wants one. We must provide the kind of education that will enable him to hold a job, the kinds of work training necessary to prepare him for specific lines of work. If he has reached adulthood without learning to read and write, we must offer him basic literacy education. If he has a physical impairment, we must see that he gets medical treatment or rehabilitation services. And we must take any and all of the measures necessary to ensure that there is a job available when he is ready for it.

CALL TO ACTION

To redesign our society, there is heavy work ahead — work for 21 able and courageous men and women who are willing to tackle the evils of the day in a problem-solving mood. We have plenty of debaters, plenty of blamers, plenty of provocateurs, plenty of people who treat public affairs as an opportunity for personal catharsis or glorification. We *don't* have plenty of problem-solvers.

A relevant call to action would address itself first to that compla- 22
cent lump of self-satisfied Americans who fatten on the yield of this
society but never bestir themselves to solve its problems. It would
address itself to the powerful men who rest complacently with out-
worn institutions when they have it in their power to redesign those
institutions. It would address itself to those Americans who are still
uncommitted to the values we profess to cherish as a people.

As a people, we still have a choice. If we want a society on the 23
beehive model, all we need do is relax — we'll drift into it. If we
want a society built around the creative possibilities of the self-
directing individual, then we have tasks to perform.

I am not proposing new duties; I am recalling old duties. Re- 24
member the Preamble to the Constitution? "We the people of the
United States, in order to form a more perfect union, establish
justice, insure domestic tranquility, provide for the common defense, promote the general welfare, and secure the blessings of
liberty to ourselves and our posterity. . . ." Great phrases, and the
greatest of all is "We the people of the United States." Not we the
public officials of the United States. Not we the certified experts
on public administration. Not we who happen to have time to think
about these things when we're not busy running our businesses or
practicing our profession. Just we the people.

We, acting in our communities across the nation, can pull this 25
fragmented society together again. We can re-create an America in
which men speak to one another in trust and mutual respect, sharing
common objectives, working toward common goals. We can return
this nation to a path of confidence and well-being. We can design
a society capable of continuous renewal.

We can do these things. No one can do them for us.   26

A GUIDE TO TERMS

Abstract   (See *Concrete/Abstract.*)
Allusion   (See *Figures of Speech.*)
Analogy   (See *Section 4.*)
Argument is one of the four basic forms of prose. It usually employs one or all of the other forms — exposition, narration, description — sometimes becoming difficult to distinguish from them. The difference is in its basic motivation: argument assumes that there are two sides to the matter under discussion, but it aims to resolve the conflict by influencing the reader to favor one side.

A distinction is ordinarily made between *logical argument* (usually called simply "argument") and *persuasive argument* (usually termed "persuasion").   Whereas logical argument appeals to reason, persuasion appeals to the emotions. The aim of both is to convince, however, and they are nearly always blended into whatever mixture seems most likely to do the convincing. After all, reason and emotion are both important human elements — and we may have to persuade someone even to listen to our logic. The emphasis on one or the other, of course, should depend on the subject and the audience.

Some authorities make a somewhat different distinction: we argue merely to get someone to change his mind; we use persuasion to get him to *do* something about it — e.g., to vote a Republican ticket, not just agree with the party platform. But this view is not entirely inconsistent with the other. We can hardly expect to change a *mind* by emotional appeal, but we can hope to get someone to *act* because of it, whether or not his mind has been changed.

Cause   (See *Section 6.*)
Central Theme   (See *Unity.*)
Classification   (*See Section 2.*)
Clichés are tired expressions, perhaps once fresh and colorful, that have been overused until they have lost most of their effectiveness and become trite or hackneyed. (The term is also applied, less often, to trite ideas or attitudes.)

We may need to use clichés in conversation, of course, where the quick and economical phrase is an important and useful tool of expression — and where no one expects us to be constantly original. We are fortunate, in a way, to have a large accumulation of clichés from which to draw. To describe someone, without straining our originality very much, we can always declare that he is *as innocent as a lamb, as thin as a rail,* or *as fat as a pig;* that he is *as dumb as an ox, as sly as a fox,* or *as wise as an owl;* that he is *financially embarrassed* or *has a fly in the ointment* or *his ship has come in;* or that, *last but not least, in this day and age,* the *Grim Reaper* has taken him to *his eternal reward.* There is indeed a *large stockpile* from which we can draw for ordinary conversation.

But the trite expression, written down on paper, is a permanent reminder that the writer is either lazy or not aware of the dullness of stereotypes — or, even more damaging, it is a clue that his ideas themselves may be threadbare, therefore requiring threadbare language to express them.

Occasionally, of course, a writer can use obvious clichés deliberately, for his own purposes. (See Casler, paragraph 4; Arlen; Hoppe, 1.) But usually to be fully effective, writing must be fresh and should seem to have been written specifically for the occasion. Clichés, however fresh and appropriate at one time, have lost these qualities.

Closings are almost as much of a problem as introductions, and they are fully as important. The function of a closing is simply "to close," of course; but this implies somehow tying the entire writing into a neat package, giving the final sense of unity to the whole endeavor, and thus leaving the reader with a sense of satisfaction instead of an uneasy feeling that he ought to be looking around for another page.

There is no standard length for closings. A short composition may be effectively ended with one sentence — or even without any real closing at all, if the last point discussed is a strong or climactic one. A longer piece of writing, however, may be more slowly finished, perhaps through several paragraphs.

A few types of weak endings are so common that warnings are in order here. The careful writer will avoid these faults: (1) giving the effect of having suddenly become tired and quit; (2) ending on a minor detail or an apparent afterthought; (3) bringing up a new point in the closing; (4) using any new qualifying remark in the closing (if he wants his opinions to seem less dogmatic or generalized, he should go back and do his qualifying where the damage was done); (5) ending with an apology of any kind (if the author is not interested enough to become at least a minor expert in his subject, he should not be wasting the reader's time).

Of the several acceptable ways of giving the sense of finality to a paper, the easiest is the *summary,* but it is also the least desirable for most short papers. If the reader has read and understood something only a page or two before, he probably does not need to have it reviewed for him now. It is apt to seem merely repetitious. Longer writings, of course, such as research or term papers, may require thorough summaries.

Several other closing techniques are available to the writer. The following, which do not represent all the possibilities, may be usable at one time or another, and they are frequently employed in combinations with each other:

1. *Using word signals* — e.g., *finally, at last, thus, and so, in conclusion,* as well as more original devices suggested by the subject itself. (See Thurber, Casler.)

2. *Changing the tempo* — usually a matter of sentence length or pace. This is a very subtle indication of finality, and it is difficult to achieve. (For examples of modified use, see *Time,* Arlen.)

3. *Restating the central idea* of the writing — sometimes a "statement" so fully developed that it practically becomes a summary itself. (See Catton.)

4. *Using climax to end the writing* — a natural culmination of preceding points or, in some cases, the last major point itself. This is suitable, however, only if the materials have been so arranged that the last point is noticeably outstanding. (See Catton, Nader, Kennedy.)

5. *Making suggestions,* perhaps mentioning a possible solution to the problem being discussed — a useful technique for exposition as well as for argument, and a natural signal of the end. (See Peter/Hull, Gregory, White, Casler.)

6. *Showing the topic's significance,* its effects, or the universality of its meaning — a commonly used technique that if carefully handled, is an excellent indication of closing. (At least ten of our selections are closed by this method; see, e.g., Krutch, Gregory, Baker, Hoffman.)

7. *Echoing the introduction* — a technique that has the decided virtue of improving the effect of unity since it brings the develop-

ment around full circle, so to speak. The echo may be a reference to a problem posed or a significant expression, quotation, analogy, or symbol used in the introduction. (See Thurber, Franklin.)

8. *Using some rhetorical device* — a sort of catchall category, but a good supply source because it includes several very effective techniques: pertinent quotations, anecdotes and brief dialogues, metaphors, allusions, ironic comments, and various kinds of witty or memorable remarks. All run the risk of seeming "forced," and hence amateurish; but properly handled they can do an effective job of closing. (See Gregory, Auden, Baker, Leopold, Kennedy, Steinbeck.)

Coherence is the quality of good writing that results from the presentation of all parts in logical and clear relations.

Coherence and unity are usually studied together and, indeed, are almost inseparable. But whereas unity refers to the relation of parts to the central theme (see *Unity*), coherence refers to their relations with each other. In a coherent writing, each sentence, each paragraph, each major division seems to grow out of those preceding it.

Several transitional devices (see *Transition*) help to make these relations clear, but far more fundamental to coherence is the sound organization of materials. From the moment he first begins to visualize his subject materials in patterns, the writer's goal must be clear and logical development. If it is, coherence is almost assured.

Colloquial expressions are characteristic of conversation and informal writing, and they are normally perfectly appropriate for those media. However, most writing done for college, business, or professional purposes is considered "formal" writing; and for such usage colloquialisms are too informal, too *folksy* (a word itself which most dictionaries label "colloq.").

Some of the expressions appropriate only for informal usage are *kid* (for child), *boss* (for employer), *flunk, buddy, snooze, gym, a lot of, phone, skin flicks, porno*. In addition, contractions such as *can't* and *I'd* are usually regarded as colloquialisms and are never permissible in, for instance, a research or term paper.

Slang is defined as a low level of colloquialism, but it is sometimes placed "below" colloquialism in respectability; even standard dictionaries differ as to just what the distinction is. (Some of the examples in the preceding paragraph, if included in dictionaries at all, are identified both ways.) At any rate, slang generally comprises words either coined or given novel meanings in an attempt at colorful or humorous expression. Slang soon becomes limp with overuse, however, losing whatever vigor it had to start with. In widely varying lengths of time, slang expressions either disappear completely or graduate to more acceptable colloquial status and thence, possibly, into standard usage. (That is one way in which our language is constantly changing.) But until their "graduations," all forms of slang and colloquialism have an appropriate function in formal writing only if used sparingly and for special effect. Because dictionaries frequently differ in matters of usage, the student should be sure he is using a standard edition approved by his instructor.

(For further examples, see Gregory, Brown, Hoffman, Hoppe.)

Comparison   (See *Section 3.*)

Conclusions   (See *Closings.*)

Concrete and **Abstract** words are both indispensable to the language, but a good rule in most writing is to use the concrete whenever possible. This policy also applies, of course, to sentences that express only abstract ideas, which can often be made clearer, more effective, by use of concrete examples. Many expository paragraphs are constructed with an abstract topic sentence and its concrete support. (See *Unity.*)

A concrete word names something that exists as an entity in itself, something that can be perceived by the human senses. We can see, touch, hear, and smell a horse — hence *horse* is a concrete word. But a horse's *strength* is not. We have no reason to doubt that strength exists, but it does not have an independent existence: something else must *be* strong or there is no strength. Hence, *strength* is an abstract word.

Purely abstract reading is difficult for the average reader; with no concrete images provided for him, he is constantly forced to make his own. Concrete writing helps the reader to visualize and is therefore easier and faster to read.

(See *Specific/General* for further discussion.)

Connotation and **Denotation** both refer to the meanings of words. Denotation is the direct, literal meaning as it would be found in a dictionary, whereas connotation refers to the response a word *really* arouses in the reader or listener.

There are two types of connotation: personal and general. Personal connotations vary widely, depending on the experiences and moods that an individual associates with the word. (This corresponds with personal symbolism; see *Symbolism.*) *Waterfall* is not apt to have the same meaning for the happy young honeymooner at Yosemite as it has for the grieving mother whose child has just drowned in a waterfall. But general connotations are those shared by many people. *Fireside,* far beyond its obvious dictionary definition, generally connotes warmth and security and good companionship. *Mother,* which denotatively means simply "female parent," means much more connotatively.

A word or phrase considered less distasteful or offensive than a more direct expression is called a *euphemism,* and this is also a matter of connotation. (See Mitford.) The various expressions used instead of the more direct "four-letter words" are examples of euphemisms. *Remains* is often used instead of *corpse,* and a few newspapers still have people *passing away* and being *laid to rest,* rather than *dying* and being *buried.*

But a serious respect for the importance of connotations goes far beyond euphemistic practices. The young writer can hardly expect to know all the different meanings of words for all his potential readers, but he can at least be aware that they do *have* different meanings. Of course, this is most important in persuasive writing — in political speeches, in advertising copywriting, and in any endeavor where some sort of public image is being created. When President Franklin Roosevelt began his series of informal radio talks, he called them "fireside chats," thus putting connotation to work. An advertising copywriter trying to evoke the feeling of love and tenderness associated with motherhood is not seriously tempted to use *female parent* instead of *mother.*

In exposition, however, where the primary purpose is to explain, the writer ordinarily tries to avoid words that may have emotional overtones, unless these can somehow be used to increase understanding.

(For further connotative examples, see Gregory, Mitford, White, Brown.)

Contrast   (See *Section 3.*)

Denotation   (See *Connotation/Denotation.*)

Description   (See *Section 9.*)

Diction refers simply to "choice of words," but, not so simply, it involves many problems of usage, some of which are explained under several other headings in this guide, e.g., *Clichés, Colloquial, Connotation/Denotation, Concrete/Abstract* — anything, in fact, which pertains primarily to word choices. But the characteristics of good diction may be more generally classified as follows:

1. *Accuracy* — the choice of words that mean exactly what the author intends.

2. *Economy* — the choice of the simplest and fewest words that will convey the exact shade of meaning intended.

3. *Emphasis* — the choice of fresh, strong words, avoiding clichés and unnecessarily vague or general terms.

4. *Appropriateness* — the choice of words that are appropriate to the subject matter, to the prospective reader-audience, and to the purpose of the writing.

(For contrasts of diction, see Thurber, Gregory, Auden, Baker, Catton, Eiseley, Mailer, Brown, Kennedy.)

Deduction   (See *Section 8.*)

Division   (See *Section 2.*)

Editorial "We" is still used, although not as much as it used to be, by some editorial and column writers of newspapers and by the authors of some magazine departments, such as "The Talk of the Town" in *The New Yorker*. It has the advantage of avoiding the narrow, one-man implications of *I* or *me*, but it sometimes leads to the strange form *ourself* in avoiding the actual plural effect that *ourselves* would give.

(For examples of a somewhat modified usage, see Packard, Hoffman, and Casler.)

Effect   (See *Section 6.*)

Emphasis is almost certain to fall *somewhere*, and the author should be the one to decide where. He should make certain that a major point, not some minor detail, is emphasized.

Following are the most common ways of achieving emphasis. Most of them apply to the sentence, the paragraph, or the overall writing — all of which can be seriously weakened by emphasis in the wrong places.

1. By *position*. The most emphatic position is usually at the end, the second most emphatic at the beginning. (There are a few exceptions, including news stories and certain kinds of scientific reports.) The middle, therefore, should be used for materials that do not deserve special emphasis. (See Auden's positioning of the American

attitude toward money; Peter/Hull, for the order of examples; Nowlis; Catton, paragraph 16; *Time,* for using positives last; Franklin; Ardrey, for positioning of his last inductive evidence.)

A sentence in which the main point is held until the last is called a *periodic sentence;* in a *loose sentence,* the main point is disposed of earlier and followed by dependencies, e.g., "The barn burned in the middle of the night." (For examples of both loose and periodic sentences, see Deloria, paragraphs 1–3.)

2. By *proportion.* Ordinarily, but not necessarily, important elements are given the most attention and automatically achieve a certain emphasis because of this. (See Krutch's and Gregory's developed examples, and Auden's proportionate attention to the American attitude.)

3. By *repetition.* Words and ideas may sometimes be given emphasis by re-use, usually in a different manner. If not cautiously handled, however, this method can seem merely repetitious, not emphatic. (See Thurber, Peter/Hull, Gregory, Arlen.)

4. By *flat statement.* Although an obvious way to achieve emphasis is simply to *tell* the reader what is most important, it is often least effective, at least when used as the only method. Readers have a way of ignoring such pointers as "most important of all" and "especially true." (See Gregory; Catton, paragraph 16; Schweitzer; Kennedy, 8.)

5. By *mechanical devices.* Emphasis can be achieved by the use of italics (underlining), capital letters, or exclamation points. But too often these devices are used, however unintentionally, as a cover-up for deficiencies of content or style. Their employment can quickly be overdone and their impact lost. (See Franklin. Notice that Mitford, with more emphatic style than most, uses none of these devices.)

6. By *distinctiveness of style.* The author can emphasize subtly with fresh and concrete words or figures of speech, crisp or unusual structures, and careful control of paragraphs or sentence lengths. (These methods are used in many of the essays in this book. See Catton, paragraphs 3, 4; White; Arlen; Hoppe.) *Verbal irony* (See *Irony*), including *sarcasm* and the rather specialized form known as *understatement,* if handled judiciously, is another valuable means of achieving distinctiveness of style and increasing emphasis.

Essay refers to a brief prose composition on a single topic, usually, but not always, communicating the author's personal ideas and impressions. Beyond this, because of the wide and loose application of the term, no really satisfactory definition has been arrived at.

Classifications of essay types have also been widely varied and sometimes not very meaningful. One basic and useful distinction, however, is between *formal* and *informal* essays, although many defy classification even in such broad categories as these. It is best to regard the two types as opposite ends of a continuum, along which most essays may be placed.

The formal essay usually develops an important theme through a logical progression of ideas, with full attention to unity and coherence, and in a serious tone. Although the style is seldom completely impersonal, it is literary rather than colloquial. (For examples of essays that are somewhere near the "formal" end of the continuum, see Nowlis, Packard, Catton, Hoyle, Smith, Leopold, Casler, or Kennedy. The Declaration of Independence, a completely formal document, is not classifiable as an "essay" at all.)

The informal, or personal, essay is less elaborately organized and more chatty in style. First-person pronouns, contractions, and other colloquial or even slang expressions are usually freely used. Informal essays are less serious in apparent purpose than formal essays. Although most do contain a worthwhile message or observation of some kind, an important purpose of many is to entertain.

The more personal and intimate infomal essays may be classifiable as *familiar* essays, although, again, there is no well-established boundary. Familiar essays pertain to the author's own experiences, ideas, or prejudices, frequently in a light and humorous style.

(For examples of informal essays, see Thurber, Gregory, Michener, Brown, Steinbeck, Arlen.)

Evaluation of a literary piece, like that of any other creative endeavor, is meaningful only when based somehow on the answers to three questions: (1) What was the author's purpose? (2) How successfully does he fulfill it? (3) How worthwhile was it?

An architect could hardly be blamed for designing a poor gymnasium if his commission had been to design a library. Similarly, if an author is trying to explain the interdependence of all living things (as is Leopold), he cannot be faulted for failing to make the reader laugh. However, if his purpose is simply to amuse (a worthy enough goal, by the way), he should not be condemned for teaching little about land pyramids. (Nothing prevents his trying to explain an ecological problem through the use of humor, or trying to amuse by telling about ecology; but in these situations his purpose has changed — and grown almost unbearably harder to achieve.)

If the architect was commissioned to design a gymnasium, however, he could be justifiably criticized on whether the building is successful and attractive *as a gymnasium.* If an author is trying to explain why American men are concerned about their masculinity (as is Schlesinger), the reader has a right to expect sound reasoning and clear expository prose.

Many things are written and published that succeed very well in carrying out the author's intent — but simply are not worthwhile. Although this is certainly justifiable ground for unfavorable criticism, the reader should first make full allowance for his own limitations and perhaps his narrow range of interests, evaluating the work as nearly as possible from the standpoint of the average reader for whom the writing was intended.

Figures of Speech are short, vivid comparisons, either stated or implied; but they are not literal comparisons (e.g., "Your car is like my car," which is presumably a plain statement of fact). Figures of speech are more imaginative. They imply analogy but, unlike analogy, are used less to inform than to make quick and forceful impressions. All figurative language is a comparison of unlikes, but the unlikes do have some interesting point of likeness, perhaps one never noticed before.

A *metaphor* merely suggests the comparison and is worded as if the two unlikes were the same thing — e.g., the "strangling rope of Puritanism" (Michener, paragraph 6) and "a great chapter in American life" (Catton, 1). (For some of the many other examples in this book, see Mitford; Schlesinger, 1, 2; Schweitzer; *Time;* Kennedy; Ardrey; Camus; Saint-Exupéry.)

A *simile* (which is sometimes classified as a special kind of metaphor) expresses a similarity directly, usually with the word *like* or *as* — e.g., "can stretch like a life line across the scary present" (Kennedy, paragraph 7). (For further illustrations, see Eiseley, 6; Franklin, 1; Orwell, 1, 2; Saint-Exupéry.)

A *personification,* which is actually a special type of either metaphor or simile, is usually classified as a "figure" in its own right. In personification, inanimate things are given the qualities or powers of a person in order to describe their function or appearance — e.g., "that big, beautiful, bountiful black bitch," with which the Brown essay is finished. Some people would also label as personification any characterization of inanimate objects as animals or of animals as humans — e.g., the many descriptions and "love displays" of the Thurber piece.

An *allusion* is literally any casual reference, any alluding, to something; but rhetorically it is limited to a figurative reference to a famous or literary person or event, and it should be distinguished from the casual reference that has a literal function in the subject matter. Hence, casual mention of Judas Iscariot's betrayal of Jesus is merely a reference, but calling a modern traitor a "Judas" is an allusion. A rooster might be referred to as "the Hitler of the barnyard," or a lover as a "Romeo." Many allusions refer to mythological or biblical persons or places — e.g., "marching toward a stormy Sinai" (Saint-Exupéry, paragraphs 16, 48). (See also Auden, 5; Petrunkevitch, 9; Emerson, 3.)

Irony and paradox (both discussed under their own headings) and analogy (Section 4) are also frequently classed as figures of speech, and there are several other, less common types that are really subclassifications of those already discussed.

General (See *Specific/General.*)

Illustration (See *Section 1.*)

Impressionistic Description   (See *Section 9.*)

Induction   (*See Section 8.*)

Introductions give readers their first impressions, and these often turn out to be lasting ones. In fact, unless an introduction succeeds in somehow attracting a reader's interest, he probably will go no further. Its importance is one reason that its writing is nearly always difficult.

Sometimes, when the writer remains at a loss to know how to begin, he should forget about the introduction for a while and go ahead with the main body of his writing. Later he may find that a suitable introduction has suggested itself or even that the way he did start is actually introduction enough.

Introductions may vary in length from one sentence in a short composition to several paragraphs or even several pages in longer and more complex expositions, such as research papers and reports of various kinds.

Good introductions to expository writings have at least three and sometimes four functions:

1. *To identify the subject and set its limitations,* thus building a solid foundation for unity. This function usually includes some indication of the central theme, letting the reader know what point is to be made about the subject. Unlike the other forms of prose, which can often benefit by some degree of mystery, exposition has the primary purpose of explaining, so the reader has a right to know from the beginning just *what* is being explained.

2. *To interest the reader,* and thus ensure his attention. To be sure of doing this, the writer must analyze his prospective readers and their interest in his subject. The account of a new X-ray technique would need an entirely different kind of introduction if written for doctors than if written for the campus newspaper.

3. *To set the tone* of the rest of the writing. (See *Style/Tone.*) Tones vary greatly in writing, just as the tones of a person's voice vary with his attitudes. One function of the introduction is to let the reader know the author's attitude since it may have a subtle but important bearing on the communication he is about to receive.

4. *Frequently,* but not always, *to indicate the plan of organization.* Although seldom important in short, relatively simple compositions and essay examinations, this function of introductions can be especially valuable in more complex papers.

Besides failure to perform these necessary functions, introductions are subject to several common weaknesses that can be easily overcome: (1) Avoid referring to the title, or even assuming that the reader has seen it. Make the introduction do all the introducing. (2) Avoid crude and uninteresting beginnings, such as "This paper is about. . . ." (3) Avoid going too abruptly into the main body — smooth transition is at least as important here as anywhere else. (4) Avoid overdoing the introduction, either in length or in extremes of style.

Fortunately, however, there are many good ways to introduce expository writing, and several of the most useful may be illustrated by the selections in this book. Many writings, of course, combine two or more of the techniques into interesting introductions.

1. *Stating the central theme,* which is sometimes fully enough explained in the introduction to become almost a preview-

summary of the exposition to come. (See Thurber, Deloria, Eiseley, Smith, White, Kennedy.)

2. *Showing the significance of the subject,* or stressing its importance. (See Nowlis, Packard, Catton, White, Casler, Kennedy, Hoffman.)

3. *Giving the background of the subject,* usually in brief form, in order to bring the reader up to date as early as possible for a better understanding of the current matter. (See Peter/Hull, Packard, White, Casler, Schlesinger, Arlen.)

4. *"Focusing down"* to one aspect of the subject, a technique similar to that used in some movies, showing first a broad scope (of subject area, as of landscape) and then progressively narrowing views until the focus is on one specific thing (perhaps the name "O'Flinnigan Jones" on a mailbox by a gate or the specific "attitudes towards money" to be discussed in the exposition, as in the selection by Auden). (See also Krutch, Emerson, *Time,* Arlen.)

5. *Using a pertinent rhetorical device* that will attract interest as it leads into the main exposition – e.g., the use of an anecdote, analogy, allusion, quotation, or paradox. (See King, Casler, Schlesinger, *Time.*)

6. *Using a short but vivid comparison or contrast* to emphasize the central idea. (See Thurber, Petrunkevitch.)

7. *Posing a challenging question,* the answering of which the reader will assume to be the purpose of the writing. (See Gardner.)

8. *Referring to the writer's experience* with the subject, perhaps even giving a detailed account of that experience. (Some writings, of course, especially descriptive or narrative essays, are simply continuations of experience so introduced, perhaps with the expository purpose of the telling made entirely evident only at the end or slowly unfolding as the account progresses. For examples see Krutch, Peter/Hull, Steinbeck, Orwell, Saint-Exupéry.)

9. *Presenting a startling statistic or other fact* that will indicate the nature of the subject to be discussed. (See Thurber, Deloria.)

10. *Making an unusual statement* that can intrigue as well as introduce. (See Berne, Eiseley, Hemingway, Brown, Hoppe, Gansberg.)

11. *Making a commonplace remark* that can draw interest because of its very commonness in sound or meaning. (See King.)

Irony, in its verbal form sometimes classed as a figure of speech, is saying one thing on the surface but meaning exactly (or nearly) the opposite — e.g., "this swanky neighborhood we live in" may really mean it is slated for urban renewal. (For other illustrations, see Thurber, Mitford, Baker.)

Verbal irony has a wide range of tones, from the gentle, gay, or affectionate to the sharpness of outright *sarcasm,* which is always intended to cut. It may consist of only a word or phrase, it may be a simple *understatement* (see Mitford), or it may be sustained as one of the major components of satire.

Irony can be an effective tool of exposition if its tone is consistent with the overall tone and if the writer is sure that his audience is bright enough to recognize it as irony. In speech, a person usually indicates by voice or eye-expression that he is not to be taken literally; in writing, the words on the page have to speak for themselves.

In addition to verbal irony, there is also an *irony of situation,* in which there is a sharp contradiction between what is logically expected to happen and what does happen — e.g., a man sets a trap for an obnoxious neighbor and then gets caught in it himself. Or the ironic situation may simply be some discrepancy that the observer can see but that those involved can not. (Much of the Arlen essay has this kind of irony, as does the principle itself in "The Peter Principle." For other examples of irony of situation, see Krutch, paragraphs 1, 2; Thurber; Gregory, 12; Nowlis; Baker; Deloria; White; Ardrey; Hoppe.)

Logical Argument   (See *Agrument.*)
Loose Sentences   (See *Emphasis.*)
Metaphor   (See *Figures of Speech.*)
Narration   (See *Section 10.*)
Objective writing and **Subjective** writing are distinguishable from each other by the extent to which the author's personal attitudes or emotions enter into them. The difference is usually one of degree, as few writing endeavors can be completely objective or subjective.

Objective writing, seldom used in its purest form except in business or scientific reports, is impersonal and concerned almost entirely with straight narration, with logical analysis, or with the description of external appearances. (For somewhat objective writing, see Deloria, Smith.)

Subjective writing (in description usually called "impressionistic" — see *Section 9*) is more personalized, more expressive of the beliefs, ideals, or impressions of the author. Whereas in objective writing the emphasis is on the object being written about, in subjective writing the emphasis is on how the object is seen and interpreted by the author. (For a few of the many examples in this book, see Gregory, Michener, Eiseley, King, Mitford, Mailer, Schweitzer, Brown, Arlen, Hoffman, Camus.)

Paradox is a statement or remark that, although seeming to be contradictory or absurd, may actually contain some truth. Smith's assertion that law actually makes us free undoubtedly seems paradoxical to many people, as does Michener's assertion that Mickey Mouse was "one of the most disastrous cultural influences ever to hit America."

Paragraph Unity (See *Unity.*)

Parallel Structure refers in principle to the same kind of "parallelism" that is studied in grammar: the principle that coordinate elements shuld have coordinate presentation, as in a pair or a series of verbs, prepositional phrases, gerunds. It is as much a matter of "balance" as it is of parallelism.

But the principle of parallel structure, far from being just a negative "don't mix" set of rules, is also a positive rhetorical device. Many writers use it as an effective means of emphasizing parallel ideas in sentence parts, in two or more sentences, or even in two or more paragraphs. At times it can also be useful stylistically, to give a subtle poetic quality to the prose.

(For illustrations of parallel structure of parts within a sentence, see Berne, paragraph 5; King, 1; Schweitzer, 6–8. Of sentences themselves: Peter/Hull; Nowlis; Berne, 4; Catton, 14; Schlesinger, 4, 5, 8; Franklin; Jefferson; Arlen. Of both parts and sentences: King, 4, 5, 12; Kennedy, 4–8; Arlen, 1, 3; Hoppe, 1, 2. Of paragraphs: Kennedy, Jefferson, Hoppe.)

Periodic Sentence   (See *Emphasis.*)

Personification   (See *Figures of Speech.*)

Point of View is simply the position of the author in relation to his subject matter. Rhetorical point of view, our only concern here, has little in common with the grammatical sort and differs somewhat from that important to fiction.

A ranch in a mountain valley is seen differently by the practical stockman working at the corral, by his wife deciding where to plant her petunias, by the artist or poet viewing the ranch from the mountainside, and by the careful geographer in a plane above, map-sketching the valley in relation to the entire range. It is the same ranch, but the positions and attitudes of the viewers are varied.

So it is with expository prose. The position and attitude of the author are the important lens through which the reader also sees the subject. Consistency is important, because if the lens is changed without sufficient cause and explanation, the reader will become disconcerted, if not annoyed.

Obviously, since the point of view is partially a matter of attitude, the tone and often the style of writing are closely linked to it. (See *Style/Tone.*)

The selections in this book provide examples of numerous points of view. Thurber is the cynical but amused observer, Eiseley is the pensive philosopher, Mitford is the debunking prober, King is the passionately caring explainer. In each of these (and the list could be extended to include all the selections in the book), the subject would seem vastly different if seen from some other point of view.

Process Analysis   (See *Section 5.*)

Purpose that is clearly understood by the author before he starts to write is essential to both unity and coherence. A worthwhile practice, certainly in the training stages, is to write down the controlling purpose before even beginning the outline. Some instructors require both a statement of purpose and a statement of central theme. (See *Unity.*)

The most basic element of a statement of purpose is the commitment to "explain," or perhaps for some assignments to "convince" (argument), to "relate" (narration), or to "describe." But the statement of purpose, whether written or only decided upon, goes further — e.g., "to explain that most employees are promoted until they are on their level of incompetence, where they remain" (Peter/Hull) or "to explain that love is a learned emotion" (Casler).

Qualification is the tempering of broad statements to make them more valid and acceptable, the author himself admitting the probability of exceptions. This qualifying can be done inconspicuously, to whatever degree needed, by the use of *possibly, nearly always* or *most often, usually* or *frequently, sometimes* or *occasionally.* Instead of saying that "freshman composition is the most valuable course in college," it may be more accurate and defensible to say that it is for *some people* or that *it can be* the most valuable.

Eiseley uses many such qualifiers; Peter and Hull's principle states that "every employee *tends* to rise to his level of incompetence." (You may decide that some of the other authors should have made greater use of qualification than they did.)

Rhetorical Question is one posed with no expectation of receiving an answer; it is used solely as a structural device to launch or to further a discussion. Questions that are formulated as an integral part of the subject itself (such as the series in the Nowlis piece on campus drugs) would *not* be considered rhetorical questions. (See Berne's title; Smith, paragraph 2; Leopold, 25; Casler, 15; Schlesinger, 1, 7, 11; Hoffman, 3; Nader.)

Sarcasm   (See *Irony.*)

Sentimentality, also called *sentimentalism,* is an exaggerated show of emotion, whether intentional or caused by lack of restraint. An author can oversentimentalize almost any situation, but the trap is most dangerous when he writes of time-worn emotional symbols or scenes — e.g., a broken heart, mother love, a lonely death, the conversion of a sinner. However sincere the author may be, if his reader is not fully oriented to the worth and uniqueness of the situation described, he may be either resentful or amused at any attempt to play on his emotions. Sentimentality is, of course, one of the chief characteristics of melodrama. (For examples of writing that, less adeptly handled, could easily have slipped into sentimentality, see Gregory, Catton, King, Leopold, Brown, Steinbeck, Gansberg, Orwell, Saint-Exupéry. In "Griefspeak" Arlen *uses* sentimentality to accomplish his own purposes.)

Simile   (See *Figures of Speech.*)

Slang   (See *Colloquial.*)

Specific and **General** terms, and the distinctions between the two, are similar to concrete and abstract terms (as discussed under their own heading), and for our purpose there is no real need to keep the two sets of categories separated. Whether *corporation* is thought of as "abstract" and *Ajax Motor Company* as "concrete," or whether they are assigned to "general" and "specific" categories, the principle is the same: in most writing, *Ajax Motor Company* is better.

But "specific" and "general" are relative terms. For instance, the word *apple* is more specific than *fruit* but less so than *Winesap.* And *fruit,* as general as it certainly is in one respect, is still more specific than *food.* Such relationships are shown more clearly in a series, progressing from general to specific: *food, fruit, apple,*

Winesap; or *vehicle, automobile, Ford, Mustang.* Modifiers and verbs can also have degrees of specificity: *bright, red, scarlet;* or *moved, sped, careened.* It is not difficult to see the advantages to the reader — and, of course, to the writer who needs to communicate an idea clearly — in "the scarlet Mustang careened through the pass," instead of "the bright-colored vehicle moved through the pass."

Obviously, however, there are times when the general or the abstract term or statement is essential — e.g., "a balanced diet includes some fruit," or "there was no vehicle in sight." But the use of specific language whenever possible is one of the best ways to improve diction and thus gain clarity and forcefulness in writing.

(Another important way of strengthening general, abstract writing is, of course, to use examples or other illustrations. See *Section 1.*)

Style and **Tone** are so closely linked to each other, so often even elements of each other, that it is best to consider them together.

But there is a difference between them. Think of two young men, each with his girl friend on separate moonlight dates, whispering in nearly identical, tender and loving tones of voice. One young man says, "Your eyes, dearest, reflect a thousand sparkling candles of heaven," and the other says, "Them eyes of yours — in this light — they really bug me." Their *tones* were the same; their *styles* considerably different.

The same distinction exists in writing. But naturally, with more complex subjects than the effect of moonlight on a maiden's eyes, there are more complications in separating the two qualities, even for the purpose of study.

The tone is determined by the *attitude* of the writer toward his subject and toward his audience. He, too, may be tender and loving, but he may be indignant, solemn, playful, enthusiastic, belligerent, contemptuous — the list could be as long as a list of the many "tones of voice." (In fact, wide ranges of tone may be illustrated by essays of this book. Compare, e.g., those of Eiseley and Mitford or Gregory and Brown.)

Style, on the other hand, expresses the author's individuality through his choices of words (see *Diction*), his sentence patterns (see *Syntax*), and his selection and arrangement of his basic materials. (All these elements of style are illustrated in the contrasting statements of the moonstruck lads.) These matters of style are partially prescribed, of course, by the adopted tone, but they are still bound to reflect the writer's personality and mood, his education and general background.

(Some of the many widely varying styles — partially affected by and affecting the tones — represented by essays in this book are those of Thurber, Gregory, Auden, Eiseley, Hemingway, Mitford, Mailer, Arlen, Hoffman, Ardrey, Camus, Saint-Exupéry.)

Subjective Writing (See *Objective/Subjective.*)

Symbol refers to anything that, although real itself, also suggests something broader or more significant — not just in greater numbers, however, as a man would not symbolize a group or even mankind itself, although he might be typical or representative in one or more abstract qualities. On the most elementary level, even words are symbols — e.g., *bear* brings to mind the furry beast itself. But more important is that things, persons, or even acts may also be symbolic, if they invoke abstract concepts, values, or qualities apart from themselves or their own kind. Such symbols, in everyday life as well as in literature and the other arts, are generally classifiable according to three types, which, although terminology differs, we may label *natural, personal,* and *conventional.*

In a natural symbol, the symbolic meaning is inherent in the thing itself. The sunrise naturally suggests new beginnings to most people, an island is almost synonymous with isolation, a cannon automatically suggests war; hence these are natural symbols. It does not matter that some things, by their nature, can suggest more than one concept: Although a valley may symbolize security to one person and captivity to another, both meanings, contradictory as they might seem, are inherent, and in both respects the valley is a natural symbol. (Saint-Exupéry uses a valley in still another symbolic way, but it may be questionable whether his is a natural symbol or a personal one that he shares with his reader.)

The personal symbol, depending as it does on private experience or perception, is meaningless to others unless they are told about it or allowed to see its significance in context, as in literature. Although the color green may symbolize the outdoor life to the farm boy trapped in the gray city (in this respect perhaps a natural symbol), it can also symbolize romance to the girl proposed to while wearing her green blouse, or dismal poverty to the woman who grew up in a weathered green shanty; neither of these meanings is suggested by something *inherent* in the color green, so they are personal symbols. Anything at all could take on private symbolic meaning, even the odor of marigolds or the sound of a lawnmower. The sunrise itself could mean utter despair, instead of fresh opportunities, to the man who has long despised his daily job and cannot find another.

Conventional symbols usually started as personal symbols, but continued usage in life or art permits them to be generally recognized for their broader meanings, which depend on custom rather than any inherent quality — e.g., the olive branch for peace, the flag for love of country, the cross for Christianity, the jack-o'-lantern for Hallowe'en fun.

Symbols are used less in expository writing than in fiction and poetry, but several of the authors represented in this book have made beautiful and effective use of symbolism to help convey their ideas, or at least to give them added significance. (See Saint-Exupéry, paragraph 1, and his repeated use of the dark valley; and although less exemplary, the selections by Baker, Mailer, Hemingway, White, Arlen, Camus.)

Syntax is a very broad term — too broad, perhaps, to be very useful — referring to the arrangement of words in a sentence. Good syntax implies the use not only of correct grammar but also of effective patterns. These patterns depend on sentences with good unity, coherence, and emphasis, on the use of subordination and parallel construction as appropriate, on economy, and on a consistent and interesting point of view. A pleasing variety of sentence patterns is also important in achieving effective syntax.

Theme   (See *Unity*.)

Thesis   (See *Unity*.)

Tone   (See *Style/Tone*.)

Transition is the relating of one topic to the next, and smooth transition is an important aid to the coherence of a sentence, a paragraph, or an entire writing. (See *Coherence*.)

The most effective coherence, of course, comes about naturally with sound development of ideas, one growing logically into the next — and that virtue depends on sound organization. But sometimes beneficial even in this situation, particularly in going from one paragraph to the next, is the use of appropriate transitional devices.

Readers are apt to be sensitive creatures, easy to lose. (And, of course, the writer is literally the loser since he is the one who presumably has something to communicate.) If the reader gets into a new paragraph and the territory seems familiar, chances are that he will continue. But if there are no identifying landmarks, he will often begin to feel uneasy and will either start worrying about his slow comprehension or take a dislike to the author and subject matter. Either way, a communication block arises, and very likely the author will soon have one less reader.

A good policy, then, unless the progression of ideas is exceptionally smooth and obvious, is to provide some kind of familiar identification early in the new paragraph, to keep the reader feeling at ease with the different ideas. The effect is subtle but important. These familiar landmarks or transitional devices are sometimes applied deliberately but more often come naturally, especially when the prospective reader is kept constantly in mind at the time of writing.

An equally important reason for using some kinds of transitional devices, however, is a logical one: while functioning as bridges between ideas, they also assist the basic organization by pointing out the *relationship* of the ideas — and thus contributing still further to readability.

Transitional devices useful for bridging paragraph changes (and, some of them, to improve transitional flow within paragraphs) may be roughly classified as follows:

1. *Providing an "echo"* from the preceding paragraph. This may be the repetition of a key phrase or word, or a pronoun referring back to such a word, or a casual reference to an idea. (See Thurber; Mitford; Saint-Exupéry's use of "across the way," paragraphs 1, 2.) Such an echo cannot be superimposed on new ideas, but, by careful planning, must be an organic part of them.

2. *Devising a whole sentence* to bridge between paragraphs or major divisions. (See Peter/Hull, paragraph 30; Gregory, 4; Brown 6.)

3. *Using parallel structure* between an important sentence of one paragraph and the first sentence of the next. This is a subtle means of making the reader feel at ease in the new surroundings, but it is seldom used because it is much more limited in its potential than the other methods of transition.

4. *Using standard transitional expressions,* most of which have the additional advantage of indicating relationship of ideas. Only a few of those available are classified below, but nearly all the

reading selections of this book can amply illustrate such transitional expressions:

Time — soon, immediately, afterward, later, meanwhile, after a while.

Place — nearby, here, beyond, opposite to.

Result — as a result, therefore, thus, consequently, hence.

Comparison — likewise, similarly, in such a manner.

Contrast — however, nevertheless, still, but, yet, on the other hand, after all, otherwise.

Addition — also, too, and, and then, furthermore, moreover, finally, first, third, etc.

Miscellaneous — for example, for instance, in fact, indeed, on the whole, in other words.

Trite   (See *Clichés.*)

Unity in writing is the same as unity in anything else — in a picture, a musical arrangement, a campus organization — and that is a *one*ness, in which all parts contribute to an overall effect.

Many elements of good writing contribute in varying degrees to the effect of unity. Some of these are properly designed introduction and closing; consistency of point of view, tone, and style; sometimes the recurring use of an analogy or thread of symbolism; occasionally the natural time boundaries of an experience or event, as in the Mitford and Saint-Exupéry selections.

But in most expository writing the only dependable unifying force is the *central theme,* which every sentence, every word, must somehow help to support. (The central theme is also called the *central idea* or the *thesis* when pertaining to the entire writing. In an expository paragraph it is the same as the *topic sentence,* which may be implied or, if stated, may be located anywhere in the paragraph, but is usually placed first.) As soon as anything appears which is not related to the central idea, then there are *two* units instead of one. Hence, unity is basic to all other virtues of good writing, even to coherence and emphasis, the other two organic essentials. (See *Coherence; Emphasis.*)

An example of unity may be found in a single river system (for a practical use of analogy), with all its tributaries, big or little, meandering or straight, flowing into the main stream and making it bigger — or at least flowing into another tributary that finds its way to the main stream. This is *one* river system, an example of unity. But now also picture another, nearby stream that does not empty into the river but goes off in some other direction. There are now two systems, not one, and there is no longer unity.

It is the same way with writing. The central theme is the main river, flowing along from the first capital letter to the very last period. Every drop of information must find its way into this theme-river, or it is not a part of the system at all. It matters not even slightly if the water is good, the idea-stream perhaps deeper and finer than any of the others: if it is not a tributary, it has no business pretending to be relevant to *this* theme of writing.

And that is why most students are required to state their central idea, usually in solid sentence form, before even starting to organize their ideas. If the writer can use only tributaries, it is very important to know from the start just what the river is.

- from some kind of reaction w. it.
- Paraphrase it. (restate in own words)
- something you've read on same topic
- questions on things you don't understand
- try to answer questions)

- Evaluate

- Place it on other things you've read on topic.